Comics in Translation

Edited by

Federico Zanettin

Dipartimento di Lingue e Letterature Antiche, Moderne e Comparate

Università degli Studi di Perugia, Italy

Routledge
Taylor & Francis Group

LONDON AND NEW YORK

First published 2008 by St. Jerome Publishing

Published 2014 by Routledge
2 Park Square, Milton Park, Abingdon, Oxfordshire OX14 4RN
711 Third Avenue, New York, NY 10017

Routledge is an imprint of the Taylor and Francis Group, an informa business

First issued in hardback 2015

Notices
Knowledge and best practice in this field are constantly changing. As new research and experience broaden our understanding, changes in research methods, professional practices, or medical treatment may become necessary.

Practitioners and researchers must always rely on their own experience and knowledge in evaluating and using any information, methods, compounds, or experiments described herein. In using such information or methods they should be mindful of their own safety and the safety of others, including parties for whom they have a professional responsibility.

To the fullest extent of the law, neither the Publisher nor the authors, contributors, or editors, assume any liability for any injury and/or damage to persons or property as a matter of products liability, negligence or otherwise, or from any use or operation of any methods, products, instructions, or ideas contained in the material herein.

ISBN 978-1-905763-07-8 (pbk)

Cover image courtesy of François Schuiten

Typeset by
Delta Typesetters, Cairo, Egypt
Email: hilali1945@yahoo.co.uk

British Library Cataloguing in Publication Data
A catalogue record of this book is available from the British Library

Library of Congress Cataloging-in-Publication Data
Comics in translation / edited by Federico Zanettin.
    p. cm.
  Includes bibliographical references and index.
  ISBN 978-1-905763-07-8 (pbk)
  ISBN 978-1-138-13887-2 (hbk)

1. Comic books, strips, etc.--Translating. I. Zanettin, Federico.

PN6714.C663 2008
418'.02--dc22

2007048678

Comics in Translation

Edited by Federico Zanettin

Comics are a pervasive art form and an intrinsic part of the cultural fabric of most countries. And yet, relatively little has been written on the translation of comics. *Comics in Translation* attempts to address this gap in the literature and to offer the first and most comprehensive account of various aspects of a diverse range of social practices subsumed under the label 'comics'.

Focusing on the role played by translation in shaping graphic narratives that appear in various formats, different contributors examine various aspects of this popular phenomenon. Topics covered include the impact of globalization and localization processes on the ways in which translated comics are embedded in cultures; the import of editorial and publishing practices; textual strategies adopted in translating comics, including the translation of culture- and language-specific features; and the interplay between visual and verbal messages. *Comics in translation* examines comics that originate in different cultures, belong to quite different genres, and are aimed at readers of different age groups and cultural backgrounds, from Disney comics to Art Spiegelman's *Maus*, from Katsuhiro Ōtomo's *Akira* to Goscinny and Uderzo's *Astérix*. The contributions are based on first-hand research and exemplify a wide range of approaches. Languages covered include English, Italian, Spanish, Arabic, French, German, Japanese and Inuit.

The volume features illustrations from the works discussed and an extensive annotated bibliography.

Contributors include: Raffaella Baccolini, Nadine Celotti, Adele D'Arcangelo, Catherine Delesse, Elena Di Giovanni, Heike Elisabeth Jüngst, Valerio Rota, Carmen Valero Garcés, Federico Zanettin and Jehan Zitawi.

Federico Zanettin is Associate Professor of English Language and Translation at the University of Perugia. In addition to comics in translation, his research interests include corpus-based translation studies and intercultural communication. He has published widely in these areas, and is co-editor of *Corpora in Translator Education* (2002), and of the journals *Translation Studies Abstracts and the Bibliography of Translation Studies* and *inTRAlinea*, an online journal of translation studies.

Contents

Acknowledgements

First of all, I would like to acknowledge the contributors to this volume, not only for their essays but also for their cooperation, patience and enthusiasm for this project. I am also particularly grateful to the people who helped in producing this volume: Mona and Ken Baker at St. Jerome Publishing for dealing with numerous requests on editorial matters and for always providing swift and detailed replies, and several colleagues who have been kind enough to review the essays and make suggestions for improving them. In particular, I would like to thank Dirk Delabastita and Gabriela Saldanha for their generous comments and support, and Andy Cresswell, Luciana Fellin, Patrick Leech, Martin Raybould, Chris Rundle, David Sheen, Dominic Stewart and Sam Whitsitt, who attentively proofread the essays at various stages and provided detailed comments. I would also like to thank François Schuiten for the image on the front cover, as well as the authors and publishers who graciously allowed us to reproduce the illustrations used throughout the volume. Finally, I am grateful to the women in my life, Nadia Pagani and Micol Zanettin, who with their support and love continue to help me to redefine perspectives and priorities on life and loving.

Federico Zanettin
August 2007

List of Figures

Credits

The author and the publisher are grateful to the copyright holders of the following material for permission to reprint images and text:

1 Comics in Translation: An Overview

FEDERICO ZANETTIN
University of Perugia, Italy

This article provides an introduction to comics, the translation of comics and the contents of the volume. It begins by offering a brief historical overview of comics, highlighting those aspects which may be especially interesting from a translation perspective, and an overview of different types of comics translation, from an inter- and an intra-semiotic perspective. This is followed by a discussion of the specificity of comics as an art form (the ninth art) and as a means of communication, and of its bearing on translation. The article ends with an overview of the literature on comics in translation, and of the contributions to the present volume.

In a socio-historical perspective comics have a precise time and place of birth: the end of the nineteenth-century, in the USA. While in many respects comics are not different from other forms of 'sequential art' (Eisner 1985) such as pre-historic graffiti, carved Roman columns, painted glass windows of medieval churches, eighteenth-century prints, or twenty-first century Web pages, "the history of comics is closely related to the emergence of mass-media, due to new means of mass repro-duction and an increasing readership of the printed media" (Mey 1998:136). More specifically, comics 'as we know them', began to appear in Sunday pull-out supplements in large print-run newspapers. This is in fact where the word comics itself originated: "Because of their exclusively humorous content, [the Sunday pull-out] supplements came to be known as 'the Sunday funnies', and thus in America the term 'comics' came to mean an integral part of a newspaper. [...] Later the word would encompass the whole range of graphic narrative expressions, from newspaper strips to comic books" (Sabin 1993:5). The birth date of comics is usually made to coincide with that of Yellow Kid, a character created by Richard F. Outcalt whose strips first appeared on the pages of New York newspapers in 1894 (see Figure 1.1, centre fold); this was not only one of the first comics to be printed in full colour and to contain dialogues within balloons in the pictures, but most of all "the first to demonstrate that a comic strip character could be merchandised profitably" (Olson, n.d.: online).

Within a few years 'the funnies' were joined by daily strips in black and white, and since the Sunday pages and daily strips created by early masters of American comics such as Winsor McCay and George Harriman (see e.g. Carlin et al. 2005), the history of comics in the world has evolved within different cultural traditions, but often bearing the mark of translation.

American comics rapidly travelled across the world and merged with other traditions of 'drawn stories'. The most famous European 'proto-comics' are perhaps those created by the Swiss teacher and painter Rodolphe Töpffer (1799-1846) (see Groensteen 1999, 2005a), who in 1837 published the first of a series of illustrated comedies in the form of booklets, and the German Wilhem Busch's (1832-1908) *Max und Moritz* illustrated stories in verse, which were published in 1865 and which directly inspired the American comic strip *Katzenjammer Kids*. However, most if not all European countries had a tradition of printed visual art (see Martín 2000 on Spanish protocomics, Pilcher and Brooks 2005 and Sabin 1993 on British protocomics, Bona n.d. and Gadducci 2004 on Italian protocomics), and drawn stories started to appear consistently in print at the beginning of the twentieth century, published mostly in magazines for children.

In the US, comic strips were not exclusively directed at children. Newspapers included both series which were read by the whole family, usually in Sunday pull-out sections, and others which were specifically targeted at adults, usually daily strips. In contrast, European drawn stories were perceived exclusively as children's literature and often produced for educational purposes rather than for entertainment. They were mostly meant to provide young readers with an introduction to the written world, and images were given a strictly subordinate role in the narration. Drawings were merely meant to illustrate written stories, as was seen fit in a conception of education which strongly underlined the primacy of the written word (Detti 1984). Accordingly, the register of the language used was that of written rather than spoken communication and, in contrast with American comics, at first (proto)comics in the rest of the world did not contain balloons, but only narrations written underneath the pictures.

Speech balloons began to appear only later in the twentieth century outside the United States, and can thus be considered a distinguishing feature of comics as an American form of visual narrative. In Japan balloons were first used in 1923 in the *Adventures of Shōchan* by Oda Shōsei and Kabashima Katsuichi (Orsi 1998:28); in France in 1925 in *Zig et Puce* by Alain Saint-Ogan (Fresnault-Deruelle 1990:30); in Italy from 1932, most notably in the translations of Walt Disney's *Mickey Mouse* and in those of Alex Raymond's *Flash Gordon* (Laura 1997).

In the 1930s the United States witnessed an explosion of comic strips, which also featured adventure themes drawn in a realistic style, and the rise of the comic book form: cheap publications in a format smaller than newspapers and containing usually 16 to 32 pages in colours. Comic books first appeared as collections of daily strips and then as periodical publications containing original materials, most notably the new superhero genre featuring costumed people with super powers, heralded by Joe Siegel and Simon Shuster's *Superman* (1938). For most of this and the following decade, translated American comics constituted the lion's share of comics published in European, South American and Asian countries, and spurred the growth of the art form, so that American conventions for comics gave a primary contribution to forging national comics traditions and industries.

The 'Golden Age' of American comics drew to a close in the 1950s when, after the highlights of the 1930s and 1940s, comic strips and books began to wane in quality if not in quantity. Comic book readers became less interested in the superheroes that had accompanied them during the war effort and turned their attention to comics dealing with crime, romance, exotic adventures featuring scantily dressed heroines, and horror. A moral campaign directed at protecting the population, and the youth in particular, against the bad influence of comics, as most notably depicted in the book *Seduction of the Innocent* by the American psychiatrist Fredric Wertham (1954), produced considerable social alarm (on horror comics and the anti-comics crusade see D'Arcangelo, this volume). Fearing and anticipating legislative measures, American publishers established their own 'Comics Code Authority', which enforced a very strict policy of self-censorship on contents. As a result, the flourishing production of comic books in the US was curbed; it began to regain ground only in the 1960s, though mostly restricted to syndicated humorous strips and superhero comic books targeting male adolescents.[1] Whereas rules and legislation controlling comics were similarly enforced elsewhere in the world in the 1950s,[2] the outcomes were different. Many European countries reacted to the diminishing stream of American comics with a surge in the publication of works by national authors. For instance, new national comic strips and books for children flanked those created under the Disney imprint, whose production moved almost entirely outside of the US, most notably to Italy and the Nordic countries.[3] European comic books and magazines contained not only the translations of American comics, but also stories by native authors which partly continued American adventure themes and genres and partly introduced new ones. In France, Belgium and Italy, which were perhaps the European countries where comics reached the widest readership as well as cultural recognition, comic books and magazines contained stories whose content and treatment of themes were not confined to child or adolescent imagery. In Italy in the 1960s, for instance, pocketbooks whose contents were crime, horror and explicit pornography became popular publications, joining classical adventure comic books, especially of the Western genre, on news-stands. Original comics, especially those in French, were also translated into other European languages, rivalling American ones.

The 1960s and 1970s witnessed also the establishment of a new type of comics addressed to educated adults rather than to a popular readership. This new type, most notably by Franco-Belgian, Italian and Argentinian authors, were usually first serialized in comic magazines and then collected in books. Such publications were characterized by a more pronounced authorial stance and the lack of periodicity, i.e. they were often complete stories rather than regular series, and the accent was on individual creators rather than standardized characters and plots. In the United States, underground comics (or commix) re-introduced adult contents (sex, drugs and politics being the main subject matters) in the late 1960s and 1970s, but comics fully resurfaced as a product for literate

---

[1] The 1960s are known as the 'Silver Age' of comics in the US, when a 'second generation' of superheroes, such as *Spider-Man* and *The Fantastic Four* (published by Marvel) joined ranks with 'first generation' characters such as *Superman* and *Batman* (published by DC).

[2] Comics have been the frequent target of censorship, which has particularly affected foreign comics, to the extent that, for example, American comics were banned by totalitarian regimes in Europe in the first half of the twentieth century, but also from the UK in 1955 under the Harmful Publications Act (Gravett 2006:3). Explicit censorship on the part of governmental bodies still dictates which comics are published in some countries (Zitawi, this volume), and mechanisms of self-censorship similarly operate a process of pre-selection in other countries (Baccolini and Zanettin, this volume).

[3] The Milan-based Disney Italy has been responsible since 2001 for managing the world market of Disney magazines (Occorsio 2006:9), and today Disney comics are produced for the most part in Italy: around 70% according to Castelli (1999: online) and Restaino (2004:145), while Occorsio has the Italian production at 50%, or 11,000 pages a year. Other main Disney comics-producing countries are Denmark, France, Spain and Brazil.

adults only in the 1980s. Since then, American mainstream publishers (DC and Marvel comics), together with a growing number of 'independent' publishers, began to produce new lines of 'graphic novels', a term adopted to create a new public image for comics and to signal that they had achieved 'grown-up status'.[4]

Meanwhile, in Japan the comics industry had been growing exponentially since the period following World War II into the single largest comics industry in the world. Today the business volume of comics in Japan is 50 times as big as that of the United States (the second largest) and takes up about 40% of all the printed material published in the country – as opposed to approximately 3% in the US (Pilcher and Brooks 2005:90). While the influence of translated American comics was clearly felt in the earliest period, Japanese comics, or manga, have developed into their own variety, which comprises a vast range of diverse genres targeted at specialized readerships. Japanese comics currently fall into five main categories, *shonen* ('boys'), *shojo* ('girls') *redisu* or *redikomi* ('ladies'), *seijin* ('adult erotica') and *seinen* ('young men'), subdivided into a myriad of sub-genres and covering just about every subject matter, from cooking to parenting for young hip mums, from table and computer games to business and sports, from religion to martial arts (Pilcher and Brooks 2005:93). Japanese comics have been translated in Asian countries since the 1960s, but remained practically unknown in the West until the 1980s. From the 1990s on they inundated Western markets. Currently manga represent around 50% of all comics published in translation in Western countries (Jüngst, this volume).

By and large we can distinguish between importing countries, where the production of native titles is paralleled by a sometimes even higher number of comics in translation, and exporting countries, where the market is covered mostly by internal production (Kaindl 1999:264). Superhero comics are distributed across the entire English speaking world, and they feature pre-eminently within comic books production not only in the US and Canada, but also in the UK, Ireland, Australia and India, among others (ToutenBD 2004), as well as in most of Europe and South America in translation. European comics are a small percentage of those published in the US, and usually belong to the 'graphic novel' category, whereas American comics are translated in large numbers in Europe and Asia, as well as elsewhere in the world.

American comics have exerted a lasting influence on world comics, not only because they have been and still are translated (or republished in other English speaking countries) in large numbers, but also because they have introduced genres and models (themes, drawing styles, visual conventions) which have been incorporated and developed within other national traditions. Japanese comics currently play a similar role. In Asian countries 'manga' have replaced 'comics' as a dominating cultural model and source of reference and inspiration (Ng 2003, Mahamood 2003), and both in Europe and America not only are original manga (in Japanese) sold in comic book stores, but native manga-style stories have started to appear along with translated publications (e.g. 'le

---

[4] The term 'graphic novel' first appeared in the 1960s, but it began to gain currency only after the publication of Will Eisner's *A Contract with God* in 1978 (see http://en.wikipedia.org/wiki/Graphic_novel). British authors such as Alan Moore and Neil Gaiman, together with the Americans Art Spiegelman and Frank Miller, have been instrumental in this new development.

nouvelle manga' movement in France, 'spaghetti manga' in Italy and 'Amerimanga' productions in the US; see Pellitteri 2006, Jüngst, this volume).

1. Aspects of Comics

Comics have undergone diverse historical and geographical developments, and some genres, often associated with a particular format, are more known and widespread in some areas than in others. As Pilcher and Brooks (2005:12) explain,

> Depending where you come from, most people's concept of comic books is either that of *Spider-Man* and *Batman*, 'juvenile' strips like *The Beano*, *Tintin* and *Astérix* or, more recently the all-encompassing term 'manga'... In some countries like Britain and Singapore, comics are regarded as a juvenile form of entertainment. In others such as France, they are a highly regarded form of expression – The Ninth Art – while in Japan, comics are so integral to its culture and society that it would be impossible to imagine the country without them.

Today, comics are published over the five continents. Almost every country in the world has its own comics industry, and each regional tradition has developed its own brands of them, including Africa, where new authors, most notably from Francophone Congo and Anglophone South Africa are now being brought to the general attention (Federici and Marchesini Reggiani 2002, 2004, 2006; Lent 2006). A typology of world comics, not to mention a presentation of the main authors and characters, is well beyond the scope of this introduction.[5] However, this section attempts a general overview of interrelated aspects such as genre, readership and publication/distribution form, since these may have a direct impact on comics in translation.

1.1 Genre

Depending on the theoretical framework adopted and on the context in which the term is used, comics have been variously termed a 'genre', 'medium', 'language', 'semiotic system', etc. For example, by 'language' of comics we could mean both the natural language in which the verbal component is expressed, or the 'grammar and semantics' of the medium/genre. The term 'genre' on the other hand, if broadly defined as a type of publication, may be used to distinguish comics from other printed products such as written or illustrated books. However, it would appear more appropriate to refer to the genres *of* comics rather than to comics *as* a genre. Over the years and across the world comics have in fact developed a whole range of genres which may well compare to those of written literature and cinema. Like most printed matter, comics are mainly produced and read for leisure or for educational purposes and can generally be categorized according to their primary function (entertainment vs. instruction). Most comics belong to fictional/narrative genres,

---

[5] See e.g. Horn (1976/1999), Restaino (2004), Pilcher and Brooks (2005) and various essays in the *International Journal of Comic Art* (since 1999) for a survey of different national traditions and authors. For further reference on the history and criticism of comics, see Spehner (2005).

but a variety of instructional and educational genres have been and are produced in different parts of the world, for different age groups and readerships.

While it is often not easy to trace clear boundaries between genres, we may distinguish among three main types of fictional (super-)genres, namely comedy, epics and tragedy. The first super-genre, comedy, is sometimes identified with the whole form, since, as pointed out above, historically the word comics refers to the American newspaper text type of humorous comics strips whose heroes were mostly 'funny animals' (e.g. Disney characters), children and pets. However, the super-genre of comedy includes also strips and books only targeted at adults and which range from gag and slapstick humour to political and social satire. The second super-genre, epics, includes a perhaps even wider array of genres, which have had varied success over time and are not equally represented in all countries. Popular genres include crime and detective fiction, horror, science-fiction, romance, war, sports, adventures in exotic scenarios and historical settings (from Africa to the American West, from the Japanese Middle Ages to the present), and erotica, as well as serious 'graphic novels'. The third super-genre, tragedy, is more recent (or less studied as such), and has perhaps been more developed in Japanese and American comics than in European ones (Groensteen 2005b).

Educational (or instructional) comics can be subdivided into 'technical' and 'attitudinal' (Eisner 1985:142). Comics designed to explicitly instruct young readers on subjects such as history, religion and politics, or on proper behaviour and adherence to moral rules, have existed since the beginning of the form. Comics are also being used as a source of material for education in general, including language teaching and learning. Non-fictional genres, both for children and adults, include – among other things – biography, autobiography and journalism, as well as non-narrative texts such as how-to manuals, philosophy textbooks (e.g. Osborne and Edney 1992) and essays on the language of comics (e.g. McCloud 1993). Educational comics, both 'technical' and 'attitudinal', seem to have a relevant role to play in developing countries, where they can often reach illiterate populations or groups speaking minority languages (Gravett 2006, Jüngst, this volume).

1.2   Readership

The form and content of comics may vary not only according to the age of the target readership they address – a first obvious distinction being that between comics for children and comics for adults – but also in relation to other target group variables such as genre/sex, occupation, etc. In the US, where comic books in the 1930s opened the market to young readers (Restaino 2004:121-125), the super-hero genre primarily addressing male adolescents still remains the mainstream production. In Japan, an extremely developed system of genres addresses various combinations of age, gender, social and occupational groups with different brands of comics. Furthermore, target readerships may overlap, so that, for instance, while some genres may be exclusively targeted at adults (e.g. comics involving violence, sex, or philosophy) it is rarely the case that comics addressed primarily to children, like all children's literature (Lathey 2006,

Oittinen 2006), do not imply an adult audience to some extent. Even within superhero comics of American origin or inspiration, some variations and subgenres have appeared which appeal primarily to an adult rather than to a younger readership.

A second aspect concerns the often assumed status of comics as para- or sub-literature, as opposed to 'serious', high-brow cultural products which supposedly appear only in written form. Comics have often been described as popular literature for poorly educated readers, repetitious mass products with no intrinsic artistic quality and written by anonymous hacks – if not as dangerous vehicles of moral corruption. Like many mass culture products, most comics are in fact based on stereotypical plots and characters which make for recognizable narrative structures (Eco 1994), and quite a few serial publications have met and meet low quality standards, being poorly written and drawn. While this would not be in itself a reason not to do research on comics (Fresnault-Deruelle 1990), it amounts to a blatant over-generalization. Comics production ranges in fact from 'low-brow' to 'hi-brow' and, as Restaino (2004:26) convincingly argues, some comics have the same complexity and require the same reading effort (and offer the same reading reward) as works by 'serious' prose writers such as James Joyce, Franz Kafka, Marcel Proust and Virginia Woolf.

Again, in different countries and times comics may primarily address a certain readership rather than another, and this may have implications for the way translated comics are perceived and the strategies used to translate (or not translate) them. For instance, Scatasta (2002) argues that whereas translations of 'low brow' comics literature, which represents the largest segment of readership, are dictated by the market and are generally target-oriented, translations of 'high-brow' comics literature are instead more source-oriented.

1.3   *Production and Distribution*

The allocation of genres and readerships both within and across regional productions is also mirrored by a variety of publication formats. In the US, the two most well known formats are the newspaper comic strip and the comic book. Comic strips are by necessity self-contained narrations, which are meant to be read on a daily or weekly basis. Among newspaper strips, humorous strips are usually self-conclusive, a series of variations on a restricted number of themes and situations ending up with a final gag, whereas adventure strips develop longer plots. Even adventure strips, however, to some extent have their own narrative structure: the first panel usually recalls the previous day's episode and the last panel introduces an element of suspense, so that each daily episode can be read in isolation. In many European and Asian countries comic strips as a newspaper text type are less widespread – or, as in Italy, almost unknown – and the preferred formats of publication are the comic magazine and the comic book. Stories are either printed in installments in anthological magazines – and the most successful ones are then reprinted in volumes – or they are published directly in book form. Popular series are published in self-concluding episodes or in installments, usually on a monthly basis, whereas 'graphic novels' are often published as 'stand-alone' volumes, in a variety of formats. As

Rota (this volume) notes, the publication format of comic books, rather than their genre, usually determines their allocation on the shelves of comic bookshops and bookstores. The typical American superhero comic book is a stapled periodical booklet containing a few dozen pages (including advertisements) of high-testosterone adventures printed in four colours on low quality paper, while graphic novels are usually longer (up to 200 pages) and contain non-serialized stories printed on good quality paper and glittering full colours, targeted at a readership on average older and more diversified than that of traditional comic book readers (mostly male teenagers). In Italy, the current most common format for popular comics is the 'notebook' or 'bonelli' format (from the name of the major Italian comic books publisher, Sergio Bonelli Editore), of around a hundred pages, printed in black and white. The typical French format is the album, hard bound, large (A4) paper size, 48 to 64 pages and in full colours, sold in bookshops and addressed to an upper-market readership. Manga are usually first published in monthly anthologies and then in smaller pocket-size books called tankōbon, consisting of 300-400 pages, all in black and white (and, of course, they are read from right to left and from top to bottom). A story can go on for a few thousands pages, perhaps in episodes, but many stories have a proper beginning and an end (see Raffaelli 1997 for a review of comic book formats). Popular comic books are based on fixed characters, whose adventures are often serialized by a team of script writers and draughtsmen who ensure continuity and periodicity. Other, often more 'intellectual' comics, are instead usually produced by a single author or pair, and although very successful characters may be featured in a series of adventures over the years, they are not periodical publications.

When comics are translated a change of genre, readership, publication format (or a combination of the three) may be involved which will then govern primary translation choices, as will become apparent in many of the articles contained in this volume. For example, a change in the form of production and distribution (e.g. serial to non-serial publication, publication in newspaper vs. publication in magazine) may lead to different translation strategies and audience design. When American comic strips such as George McManus's *Bringing up Father* (translated as *Arcibaldo e Petronilla*) were first published in Italy at the beginning of the last century on the pages of *Il Corriere dei Piccoli* and other similar magazines for children, the balloons were deleted and the images retouched, and rhymed sentences narrating the stories were added below each panel, in conformity with Italian drawn stories. Actually, the Italian word for 'comics', i.e. 'fumetti' – literally meaning 'balloons', shows how much this particular device was identified with the form visual narratives had developed in the United States. Notwithstanding the ban imposed on American comics by the Fascist regime in the second half of the 1930s,[6] the 'fumetti' were subsequently appropriated by Italian culture. A second example comes from the Italian translation of the first episode of Milton Caniff's *Steve Canyon*, which was originally published on a Sunday page in the US. The Italian weekly magazine *L'avventura* published as a first installment only the first 7 out of 11 panels of the original Sunday page, thus destroying the narrative tension of the original (Eco 1994:159).

---

[6] Disney comics were the latest to be banned because of Mussolini's liking for them (De Giacomo 1995).

The prototypical medium of comics is printed paper, either in the form of newspapers, magazines or comic books. However, since the 1990s comics have ventured onto the Internet, where they have found a congenial environment. This is because while on the one hand "computers make use of the imagery and of some of the conventions of the language of comics", on the other "comics can benefit from the immense possibilities offered by computer graphics" (Saraceni 2003:95). Some critics (most notably McCloud 2000) have argued that the electronic medium has the potential to transform the way comics are created and read. The Internet is presented as both the site of a radical aesthetic evolution and as a means to revolutionize distribution. On the one hand, by exploiting features of 'electronic canvases' such as scroll-down capabilities and hypertextual links, the electronic environment may change the form and mechanisms of production and consumption of comics. On the other, the global network may favour the creation of direct links between authors and readers, who would purchase webcomics through online transactions and bypass intermediaries. Other critics are more wary of the possibilities of the medium and simply maintain that "digital technology offers new avenues of aesthetic experimentation for comic artists" and that the Internet "has given some comic artists a modest prosperity that they would not have without the internet as a means of distribution" (Fenty et al. 2004:2). Print has remained the main form of publication for comics, while the Internet is used to distribute and archive comics already published in print such as strips syndicated in newspapers, and as an outlet for self-publication by a growing number of authors (see e.g. http://en.wikipedia.org/wiki/Webcomics, http://www.thewebcomiclist.com).

While an effect of online publication can be the worldwide availability of a comic in its original (albeit electronic) form rather than in translation, a development of interest to Translation Studies is the practice of scanlation. This consists in scanning, translating and distributing on the Internet unofficial electronic editions of manga, prior to publication in print. Scanlation and fansubs, the unofficial subtitled editions of anime (Japanese animation films), are usually tolerated by publishers and official distributors because of their promotional value, since scanlated manga and fansubs often effectively pilot commercial publication. While these practices are carried out by comics and anime fans – amateur translators who do not necessarily comply with prevailing professional norms for comics and cartoon translation – their choices orient the decisions of professional translators (Ferrer Simó 2005) and highlight the influence comics readers exert on shaping translation strategies (see Jüngst, this volume).

2.   Comics, Semiotics and Translation

One of the first mentions of comics in the literature on Translation Studies is probably to be found in Jakobson (quoted in Gorlée 1994:163): "however ludicrous may appear the idea of the Iliad and Odyssey in comics, certain structural features of their plot are preserved despite the disappearance of the verbal shape" (Jakobson 1960:350). Jakobson is here making reference to his well-known distinction between three kinds of translation, or "ways of interpreting verbal signs", namely, **intersemiotic translation** or **'transmutation'**, defined as "an interpretation of verbal signs by means of signs of nonverbal sign systems"; **interlingual translation**, or **'translation proper'**, defined as "an interpretation of verbal signs by means of other signs of another language"; and **intralingual translation**, or **'rewording'**, defined as "an interpretation of verbal signs by means of the same language" (Jakobson 1992 [1959]:145).

In Jakobson's definition, then, translation always involves the interpretation of verbal signs (i.e. natural languages) into other signs which can be verbal or non-verbal languages or sign systems. While Jakobson's exemplification of intersemiotic translation does not perhaps suggest a high consideration of comics, it defines them as a kind of non-verbal, multimedial [sic] language. Typical examples of transmutation are the translations from verbal language into visual languages, as in the plastic arts, architecture, painting, sculpture and photography; into auditive languages, such as music and song; into kinesic languages, such as ballet and pantomime; and into multimedia languages, such as cinema and opera (Jakobson also provides the example of "transposing *Wuthering Heights* into a motion picture"). According to Gorlée (1994:162), in the case of 'transmutation', the term 'translation' has to be intended metaphorically, since visual, kinesic and multimedial [sic] languages are 'artistic codes' and 'languages only in a metaphorical manner of speaking'.

Jakobson's model has been further elaborated, most notably by Toury (1986) and Eco (2001, 2003). Toury (1986) proposes a first-level distinction between intra- and intersemiotic translation. Within **intrasemiotic translation** a second-level distinction is posited between **intra-** and **inter-systemic translation**. This allows for the inclusion in the semiotic model not only of types of intersemiotic translation involving transmutation between verbal and nonverbal sign systems, but also between non verbal (or not exclusively verbal) 'languages' (in a metaphorical sense) such as, for example, music into film or comics into sculpture.

Starting from the consideration that Jakobson was using 'translation' in a metaphorical way as a synonym for 'interpretation', Eco (2003) proposes a typology of forms of **interpretation**, which include **interlingual interpretation**, or 'translation proper' as well as other forms of interpretation within or between other semiotic systems. Thus, **intrasystemic interpretation** includes rewording, that is 'translation' within natural languages (as in synonymy, paraphrase and comment) as well as 'translation' within other semiotic systems (e.g. scale reproduction in visual arts, changing a piece from major to minor in music), whereas **intersystemic interpretation** includes not only 'translation proper', but also **rewriting**, 'translation' between other semiotic systems and **adaptation** or **transmutation** (what Jakobson and Toury term 'intersemiotic translation').[7] According to this typology, we should ultimately regard 'translation proper' as an interpretative activity taking place between 'verbal systems', i.e. different natural languages. However, natural

---

[7] Eco posits also a third first-level category, that of interpretation by **'transcription'** (mechanical substitution). A further type of intrasystemic interpretation is **performance** (different interpretations of a song or different performances of a drama), while **parasynonymy**, which can be illustrated by amplifying the phrase 'that one over there' by pointing at the object with a finger, is a type of intersystemic interpretation which, like adaptation, involves a mutation in the semiotic continuum rather than in the substance (see also Torop 2002).

languages are not the only 'semiotic systems' which may be 'translated' (in a metaphorical sense), and semiotic systems such as music, painting, illustration and dance, as well as 'multimedia languages' such as cinema and theatre, can go through interpretative processes similar to those of verbal language.

Examples of transmutation involving comics abound, since comics can and have been adapted from and into a variety of other art forms, such as written literature, cinema (including animated cartoons), painting, music, song, sculpture, pantomime, etc. Especially fruitful has been the relationship between comics and cinema, and between comics and other visual languages, such as illustration and graphic design. Close relatives of comics are **cartooning** and **animated cartoons**, both of which make use of drawings. This relationship is underlined by the overlapping meaning of the terms used: thus in English 'cartoons' may refer to all three. Cartoons 'proper' differ from comics in that they consist of a single **panel** or **vignette**, although they are similar in that they share many of the same conventions, e.g. **speech balloons**, caricatural drawing style, **action lines**, and so on, and in fact many comic artists practice both forms. Animated cartoons (like all films) differ from 'comics' in that comics are based on ellipsis, so that the time of narration is independent from that of seeing/reading, while in motion pictures (including cartoons) time and vision coincide.[8] Animated cartoons and comics also have much is common, and the two forms have strong historical links and have influenced each other in both directions, for instance Walt Disney characters or *The Simpsons* by Matt Groening, which appeared first as animated cartoons, or the many 'anime' which Osamu Tezuka derived from his manga stories.[9]

The relationship between cinema and comics has been one of continuous interchange. On the one hand cinema has been for comics an endless source of plots, characters, faces and techniques, and many successful films have been adapted into comics or have generated some sort of comics sequel. On the other, filmic genres have been influenced by comics (see D'Arcangelo, this volume, on the influence of horror comics on cinema). Characters from comics have often been the source of both cartoons and films with real people, notably superhero comics, many of which have first been transposed into animated series and, especially in the last few years – thanks to special effects and computer graphics, into films featuring real actors (Barbieri 1991, Festi 2006).[10] The adaptation of a verbal narrative to a comic book (Baccolini and Zanettin, this volume, on Art Spiegelman's *Maus*) can also be seen as an example of transmutation.

A second type of 'comics in translation' is represented by comics which are republished as comics, rather than 'translated' into another semiotic environment. 'Republication' may however entail a number of different things. There are reprints, new editions and new versions of comics. Comics may be subject to 'rewriting' (in a metaphorical sense),

---

[8] In fact, the translation of cartoons has more in common with film dubbing and subtitling than with comics translation, since in moving pictures the verbal component is spoken rather than written.

[9] In Japanese, the word 'manga' may also refer both to 'comics' and 'anime' (a shortened borrowing for 'animated pictures').

[10] One particular form of 'comics' are the storyboards which are often used during cinema production. Eisner (1985:146) discusses storyboards as a type of instructional comics.

as comic characters and stories may change in time and space (e.g. new versions of the same Spider-Man story or 'parallel' versions of Spider-Man, both in America (Spider-Man 'classic', '2040', 'ultimate') and elsewhere (e.g. Japanese and Indian versions of Spider-Man), as can be seen from Figure 1.2 (centre fold).

When a comic is reprinted or republished, either in the same or in a different country/area, other semiotic systems are 'translated' besides verbal language (which may itself not be translated, as verbal text remains unchanged in most reprints). Not only might 'reprints' of the same stories be (partially) re-written and re-drawn, but a comic may be reproduced with a different page size and layout, different panels arrangement and reading direction, in colour rather than in black and white and vice versa, and different types of 'translation' may co-exit at different levels.

All the 'languages' used by comics can be 'translated' within and/or between semiotic systems. However, since translation takes place between texts rather than languages, it "does not involve comparing a language (or any other semiotic system) with another semiotic system; it involves passing from a text 'a', elaborated according to a semiotic system 'A', into a text 'b', elaborated according to a semiotic system 'B'" (Eco and Nergaard 1998:221). From a semiotic point of view, the translation of comics is thus concerned with different layers of interpretative activities, which can be variously conceptualized as inter- or intra-semiotic or systemic, depending on one's definition of system.

This volume is primarily concerned with the republication of comics in a country different from that of original publication, which usually involves translation between two natural languages. However, it seems important to stress that comics are primarily visual texts which may (or may not) include a verbal component, and that in the translation of comics interlingual interpretation ('translation proper') happens within the context of visual interpretation. Language is only one of the systems (in as far as we are happy with defining a language as a system) involved in the translation of comics, which both as 'originals' and 'translations' simultaneously draw on a number of different sign systems.

The translation of comics into another language is primarily their translation into another visual culture, so that not only are different natural languages such as English, Japanese, Italian or French involved, but also different cultural traditions and different sets of conventions for comics. In other words, the translation of comics does not only imply the interlinguistic (or intralinguistic) replacement of verbal material. Comics published in other languages may also undergo a number of changes which involve the interpretation of other sign systems, not just 'translation proper' between natural languages (Rota, this volume).

3.   The Language(s) of Comics

In semiotic terms, comics can be described essentially as a form of visual narration which results from both the mixing and blending of pictures and words.[11] That is, pictures and words are not only co-present in comics as the two ends of a scale which encompasses

---

[11] General studies which analyze comics mainly from a semiotic perspective include Fresnault-Deruelle (1990), Gasca and Gubern (1988), Barbieri (1991), McCloud (1993), Peeters (2000), Groensteen (1999).

iconic signs (the drawings) and symbolic signs (the words), but may be situated at various points along a continuum of communication practices (Saraceni 2003:13-35). Pictures can range from a maximum of realism, as in quasi-photographic representations, to a maximum of abstraction and iconicity, as in stylized 'cartoony' drawings. Words, on the other hand, do not only have a purely 'verbal' meaning but are also embodied with a visual, almost physical force. Words have graphic substance, forms, colours or layouts which make them 'part of the picture'. Not only can there be a calligraphic use of letters and words, but even lettering, as Will Eisner (1985:10) expresses it, "treated 'graphically' and in the service of the story, functions as an extension of the imagery". Furthermore, "[t]he interanimation of meaning between panels can affect the manner in which the reader blends the words and pictures in a particular panel. For instance, once a reader learns what a character or location looks like in one panel, the depiction in subsequent panels can become superfluous unless new actions or aspects are presented" (Duncan 2002:140). These mixes and blends may appear in different combinations and weight-ings according to the type, genre and target readerships of particular comics, and be modified in translation. For example, German publishers have used machine lettering for a long time, a sign of 'serious' writing, both in original and translated comics (Kaindl 1999, Jüngst, this volume).

Like cinema and theatre, comics are a syncretic semiotic environment, encompass-ing texts, media and discourses. In comics, different semiotic systems are co-present and interplay at different levels, and are culturally determined along dimensions of space and time. This multiplicity and heterogeneity of semiotic systems, referred to by Barbieri (1991) as the 'languages of comics', includes visual systems such as illustration, caricature, painting, photography and graphics; temporality systems, comprising written narratives, poetry and music; and mixed systems of images and temporality, i.e. cinema (from which comics derive techniques such as shot, angle, etc.) and theatre, inasmuch as in comics the characters are 'shown acting' and dialogues are 'performed'. Because of the possibility of representing the non verbal components of interaction (body language, facial expressions, use of space, etc.), dialogues in comics have a quality that is more akin to drama than to novels.

What differentiates comics from other forms of visual communication such as il-lustration, photography and painting is that comics are formed by the juxtaposition of at least two panels – which may or may not include words, in a sequence.[12] The narration is produced by the sequential gap between images, and the reader is left to fill in that gap with expectations and world knowledge: "the recognition by the reader of real-life people portrayed in the art and the addition of 'in-between' action are supplied by the reader out of his own experience" (Eisner 1985:140) or, as McCloud aptly puts it (Figure 1.3):

---

[12] It is in fact sometimes difficult to draw a precise line between a single vignette and a sequence. The white space between panels, ie. the 'gutter', may sometimes not be drawn even if it is understood to be there, or some strips may occasionally consist of only one panel. Conversely, sequential panels may in fact contain only one 'scene'.

I MAY HAVE DRAWN AN *AXE* BEING
RAISED IN THIS EXAMPLE, BUT I'M
NOT THE ONE WHO LET IT *DROP*
OR DECIDED HOW *HARD* THE BLOW,
OR *WHO* SCREAMED, OR *WHY*.

THAT, DEAR READER, WAS *YOUR*
SPECIAL CRIME, EACH OF YOU
COMMITTING IT IN YOUR OWN *STYLE*.

Figure 1.3: Scott McCloud, *Understanding Comics*, 1993, p. 68

The single **panel**, or 'frame' is the lower unit of meaning in comics (Horn 1976, Groensteen 2005a). However, in comic books as opposed to comic strips, the basic articulatory unit is the **page** (Fresnault-Deruelle 1990). Comic books are 'seen' before they are read, and 'reading' is in fact based on the tension between sequential narration and the use of layout pagination for creative effects (Peeters 2000:39). Peeters identifies different types of uses of the page, according to the relationship between the temporal/narrative and the spatial/visual dimensions. Visual and narrative aspects can be autonomous, with either one predominating. Narration predominates in 'conventional' uses, where each panel is of equal size and neatly separated from the adjoining ones by white spaces (the '**gutter**'). This is the case, for example, of the first American comic books, which were simply collections of previously published newspaper strips.[13] In 'decorative' uses the visual dimension predominates, in its pictorial or compositional aspects, and the page is read first as a picture.

In 'rhetorical' and 'productive' uses, the dimensions, layout, visual effects etc. of panels and pages are functional to the diegesis, rather than autonomous entities. The conventional 'grid' may be altered, and the potential of using the size and shape of panels for narrative or metalinguistic creativity had been in fact already fully exploited by Winsor McCay on the Sunday pages which narrated the *Adventures of Little Nemo* at the beginning of the twentieth century (Carlin 2005). Sometimes the gutter can be missing, and readers have to imagine an ideal segmentation of a page into panels; or part of a panel (e.g. a human figure or an object) can go over and beyond the border of a panel and

---

[13] In collections of narrative daily strips, the first panel of each strip was often modified to erase the 'summary of previous events'.

invade the space of an adjacent one ('**bleeds**'), or the border of an external panel may 'overflow' and coincide with the limit of the page. This last stylistic device is consistently used in manga (see Figure 1.4).

Figure 1.4: Kazuo Koike and Ryoichi Ikegami, *Crying Freeman*, 1986 (Italian edition by Granata Press, 1992)

As an example of how the interplay of verbal text and images in a page may affect (and be affected by) a translation, let us consider three different Italian translations of a page from Alan Moore and Dave Gibbon's *Watchmen* (Figure 1.5, centre fold).

Watchmen, written by Alan Moore (see D'Arcangelo, this volume, on Alan Moore), drawn by Dave Gibbons and coloured by John Higgins, is usually credited as one of the main contributions to American comics' 'coming of age' in the 1980s (the others being Art Spiegelman's *Maus* and Frank Miller's *Batman: The Dark Knight Returns*) and to the revitalization of the superhero genre (Sabin 1993). *Watchmen* was first published as a mini-series in 12 'chapters' by DC comics between 1986 and 1987, and in Italy between 1990 and 1991 as a series of pullout booklets, of the same format of the original American edition, attached to the comic magazine *Corto Maltese*. Both in the US and in Italy it was soon after published in book form. A second Italian translation (in volume form) was published in 2002 by Play Press, a small company specializing in American superheroes. Finally, it was published again as a volume by Panini in 2005 and distributed with the national newspaper *La Repubblica*.

The first chapter of the story begins with two detectives investigating the violent death of a character that was killed by being thrown out of a window from a tall building. The detectives are on the crime scene and are seen on page 4 exiting the building and discussing what course to give to the investigations. The construction of the page may seem at first sight rather 'conventional', with a standard, semi-fixed number of same-sized panels repeating itself page after page. However, when the page is 'read' graphically, it becomes apparent that two different 'narrative tracks' intermingle. The reconstruction of the events in the dialogues between the two investigators is accompanied by a visual flashback, a second 'narrative track' which is seen as if under a purple filter, its panels alternating with those of the main narrative track where things happen in 'real time'. The page is full of intra- and inter-textual references, both verbal and visual, e.g. the reference by one investigator to the 'knot-tops' in the first panel is followed by a peripheral view of one of these in the fifth panel; in the third panel we read some headlines from a newspaper stand, in front of which there is a boy wearing a 'winged' cap who reads a comic book, which are all elements functional to the narration; a new character, Rorshach, is mentioned in panel 6, and readers will later learn that this is the same person crossing the path of the two detectives wearing a sign in which the writing "the end is nigh" can be inferred. Through panels 2, 4 and 6, we follow the fall of the victim from outside the window and down to the street below. The point of view is that of a fixed camera, which starting from the middle of the top row in the page follows the body until it becomes a spot on the pavement. In the fourth panel, we can read an 'off-screen' comment made by one of the detectives, who is suggesting that the investigation should not be too widely publicized. The sentence in the box, "Well, what say we let this one drop out of sight?", thus acts also as a verbal commentary on the sequence shown in purple. In fact, "this one" may be taken to refer both to the investigation and to the body falling down the building.

The three Italian translations, by Stefano Negrini (1990/91), Alessandro Bottero (2002) and Gino Scatasta (2005), differ in a number of respects, including translation of the dialogues in balloons. The translations of the text in panel 4 are as follows:

- "be' che ne diresti se lasciassimo tutto nel dimenticatoio?" [lit. "well, what would you say if we left it all in oblivion?"] (Negrini)
- "beh, credi che sia meglio che tutto finisca nel dimenticatoio?" [lit. "well, do you think it is better that it all ends up in oblivion?"] (Bottero)
- "… sarebbe meglio lasciar **cadere** la cosa." [lit. "…it would be better to let this thing drop/fall."] (Scatasta)

In the translations by Negrini and Bottero, the idiomatic meaning and the spoken register effect of "let this one drop out of sight" are in some way recreated by recourse to the expression "leave/end up it all in oblivion, which however fails to reproduce the ambiguity provided by the dual verbal and visual reference of the original. The translation by Scatasta, on the other hand, avoids the pitfalls of rendering too closely the structure of the source verbal text, and by focusing instead on a visual reading of the page (Celotti, this volume) condenses the piece of dialogue around the central communicative function of the utterance, the ambiguity of the verb 'drop/*cadere*'.

A page is a unit of reading not only in the sense that each panel should be interpreted in the context of page layout and composition, but also in the sense that, in stories which last over several pages, each page should be interpreted in the sequential context of the page(s) preceding and following. The effects of pagination on reading, often exploited in comics for dramatic purposes, as when a splash action page in an adventure or superhero comic book opens after a page filled with 'regular' panels leading up to the action, are not unknown to works of written fiction, ever since they were put to use by Lawrence Sterne in *Tristram Shandy* (1759). In translated comics reading can be especially affected by a change of publication format (Rota, this volume). When *Watchmen* was translated in France, it was adapted to the French album format and published in six larger-sized volumes, with new 'classical' covers, thus changing the graphical proportions, narrative coherence and detailed structural construction of the original 'graphic novel' (Peeters 2000:61-63). A change in publication format may involve not only a change in the size and shape of the page, but also a change of the colours, which may be altered, added or subtracted (Jüngst, Rota, D'Arcangelo, Zanettin, all this volume), or in the reading direction, which may be reversed (Jüngst, Rota, Zitawi, all this volume). Comics can also be globally adapted to fit reading habits and expectations of target users. For example, the language of European comics is more literary than that of American ones (Sebastiani 2002), and their reading pace is usually slower (the rate of words to images is higher in American comics, (D'Arcangelo and Zanettin 2004, Zanettin, this volume). The reading pace is instead usually quicker in Japanese comics, where long sequences of pages without verbal content are anything but uncommon.

Comics have also developed a recognizable – at least to comics readers – set of conventions which, while already existing in visual art forms, proliferated in American newspaper strips and spread throughout the world, merging with indigenous traditions of visual narratives, and which have come to be seen as the 'articulatory grammar' of comics.

A first prototypical feature is the presence of **speech balloons**, i.e. bubbles containing verbal text in the form of direct speech to represent dialogues and thought. However, narrative text in **captions** may also be used, as well as alphabetic signs outside balloons and captions, as part of the drawings. Furthermore, while comics usually contain both images and words, the density of the verbal component in relation to images varies, to the point that some comics do not contain any words at all.

Other graphical and pictorial conventions have been developed to represent sounds, movements and other aspects of sensorial experience. Sounds are usually represented by **onomatopoeic words**, non-lexical strings of alphabetic symbols and punctuation marks (Valero Garcés, this volume). Movements are expressed through **motion lines**. Actions and concepts can be represented not only through (more or less) naturalistic pictures and words, but also through **'visual metaphors'** or **pictograms**, i.e. conventional stylized representations which are intertextually recognized, such as a saw to represent sleep or stars to represent pain in humorous comics (see Gasca and Gubern 1988 for a description of an extensive repertoire).

Most 'grammatical devices' such as speech balloons, onomatopoeia and visual metaphors are used in comics produced in many different cultures and can be seen as central to comics as an art form, while other features are perhaps less salient. However, there is not one single 'language' of comics, as each regional tradition has developed its own set of conventions and stylemes, as regards reading pace, drawing style, subject matter and themes. Each of these regional varieties of comics can thus be seen as a 'dialect' of the language of comics.

For instance, since Osamu Tezuka – a.k.a. the 'Japanese Disney' or 'the God of Manga' – who from the late 1940s revolutionized comics conventions in Japan by imposing his own drawing and narrative style, manga conventions have begun to distance themselves from those of Western comics. Tezuka brought the techniques of animated cartoons to comics, developing the pace of Japanese comics storytelling by increasing the number of panels used to narrate a story, which could go on for hundreds of pages. Another major difference between most Western and Japanese comics is the type of transition between panels. Whereas in Western comics 'action-to-action' transitions are the default choice, manga often make use of transitions such as 'moment-to-moment', 'subject-to-subject' and 'aspect-to-aspect', thus highlighting mood and sense of place rather than action (McCloud 1993:74-82). Mimicking the stylistic conventions of Disney cartoons, Tezuka also introduced a way of representing characters' faces, with large eyes, small noses, tiny mouths, and flat faces, which is now perceived as typically Japanese.

Other notable differences between manga and comics include the representation of dialogue and thought, movement, the proportions of the human figure and visual metaphors. For instance, in Western comics speech balloons are bubbles linked to characters by a pointer called 'tail', and thought balloons are cloud-like bubbles with a tail of increasingly smaller circular bubbles. In manga, tails are much less common for speech balloons, while the same convention used in American comics to represent thought is used to represent whispered dialogue instead (see Figure 1.4). An awkward or speechless moment is represented by an ellipsis over one's head. Movement is represented not only by speed lines, but also by 'background blurs', i.e. an overlay of straight lines to portray the direction of movements.

Furthermore, manga have their own repertoire of visual metaphors, for instance a white cross-shaped bandage to indicate pain, sweat drops to indicate bewilderment, nervousness, or mental weariness, throbbing veins in the upper head region to indicate anger or irritation, hatchings on the cheek to represent blushing. A character suddenly falling onto the floor is a typically humorous reaction to something ironic happening. All facial features shrinking, the nose disappearing, the character lifting off the floor and the limbs being multiplied as if moving very fast may symbolize panic or, if with larger facial features, comic rage.[14]

In the same way as American conventions (such as speech and thought balloons) have entered European and Japanese traditions, Manga conventions are now exerting a strong influence on American and European ones.

4.   Comics in Translation Studies Literature

About 30 years after the establishment of Translation Studies as an academic field, quite a large body of literature has been produced, widening the scope of the discipline to spoken and multimedia translation, and to other forms of intercultural communication. Many different translation products, processes and practices have been analyzed and discussed, and it seems therefore almost surprising that relatively little has been written on the translation of comics, which enjoy a wide readership and whose history is much intertwined with translation.[15]

In an overview of research dedicated to comics within Translation Studies, Celotti (2000:42-45; see also Kaindl 1999, Raskin 2004, Celotti, this volume) describes a situation

---

[14] For a list of manga-specific conventions, see 'Manga', Wikipedia (online) http://en.wikipedia.org/wiki/Manga.

[15] The relative paucity of studies dedicated to comics is, however, not unique to Translation Studies. As Eco (2005:36) notes, while those who review a novel (or a film) do not have to start with a legitimization of written literature, those who write about a comic (at least for the general public) often still preface what they have to say about them with apologetic statements about their cultural legitimacy. This is not because the discourse on comics is missing altogether from the public arena. Rather, on the one hand there is a poorly consolidated tradition of scientific and academic enquiry about comics which, as Eco suggests, may simply be due to the fact that many academics do not read comics, and are therefore unable to talk about them. On the other hand, a large part of the discourse on comics is taken up by fandom. The majority of writings about comics appear in news-stand publications, fan magazines and, increasingly, Internet channels such as discussion forums, blogs and fans' web sites, which often provide an enthusiastic but uncritical approach, coupled with an extreme attention to detail and a deep knowledge of the subject, including translation related aspects. Comics started to attract the interest of scholars from the 1960s onwards, most notably in Italy and France (see Horn 1976, Restaino 2004 and a number of forum articles in the *International Journal of Comic Art* for a history of comics criticism). However, more than a century after their generally acknowledged birth, and having not only spread throughout the world but also evolved into new and unforeseen directions, comics are increasingly gaining critical attention.

in which comics are mentioned only in passing in Translation Studies encyclopedias, dictionaries and textbooks, and they are not usually included in analytical indexes.[16] While in the last decade or so the number of publications on comics in translation has been consistently growing and diversifying, as can be seen from a quick glance at the dates of the about 150 items listed in the annotated bibliography found at the end of this volume, the picture described by Celotti is still by and large accurate.

In some studies (e.g. Hatim and Mason 1990:18-20, 202, Harvey 1995, 1998) comics are used in order to exemplify a type of translation procedure, strategy or orientation, for example when discussing the translation of puns or the technique of compensation. When not ignoring altogether the specificity of the art form, such studies focus exclusively on the verbal component of comics, thus treating them as if they were effectively written-only texts. The comics discussed in these studies, as well as in a large percentage of the research articles specifically dedicated to the translation of comics, are the French series *Astérix* and *Tintin*. The discussion often focuses on detailed linguistic aspects, analyzing the translation of features such as wordplays, proper names, onomatopoeia, citations, allusions, or the use of spoken language. *Astérix* and *Tintin* are amongst the most popular and translated comic series in the world, and having been translated into more than 50 languages offer rich material for research (Delesse, this volume). However, their 'overexposure' in Translation Studies literature may have contributed to creating or consolidating the perception that research on the translation of comics is almost exclusively concerned with humorous language and children's literature.

Comics are often presented as a type of multimedia text,[17] and implicitly or explicitly addressed within a '**constrained translation**' approach. According to Mayoral et al. (1988:362), constrained translation differs from non-constrained translation in that in the latter "in both SL and TL, the written language system is not accompanied by other systems and ... the message occupies only the visual channel". This circumstance "will condition our translation of the text" and "remove the condition of freedom which allows us, in isolated written prose, to approach the highest degree of dynamic equivalence in our translated text" (1988:363). While situating 'constrained translation' within an overall semiotic framework, such an approach exclusively focuses on 'translation proper', considering natural languages as the only 'systems' which are affected by translation. It is acknowledged that "non-linguistic systems ... must be considered by the translator", but they are regarded as "not specific objects of the translation process" (Mayoral et al. 1988:358).

According to Gottlieb (1998), comics, together with advertising and films, are polysemiotic texts, since they use visual and/or auditory channels in addition to the verbal

---

[16] The only exceptions mentioned by Celotti are two textbooks in Spanish, Santoyo Mediavilla (1987) and Rabadán (1991), which include a specific discussion on the translation of comics.

[17] However, while comics associate different semiotic systems (images and written text), they are visual narrations which only trigger the sense of sight (Groensteen 2001). It could be argued, therefore, that comics are not, strictly speaking, multimedia texts like films and theatre plays. Pellitteri (1998), on the other hand, contends that the images in comics trigger a multisensorial experience, in that they not only stimulate the sense of sight but also those of hearing, touch, smell and taste.

channel of communication which is exclusively used in monosemiotic texts (e.g. written books and radio programmes). Like film dubbing, comics involve isosemiotic translation in that the same channel is used, writing for comics and speech for film dubbing.[18] In the translation of films (including cartoons) the translation is constrained by both visual limitations (lip-synch for dubbing and legibility for subtitling) and temporal limitations. In translated comics time remains a prerogative of the reader, while translation is seen as constrained by visual limitations such as the space provided by balloons and captions and the interplay of visual and verbal signs.

As Celotti (this volume) argues (see also Yuste Frías 2001), two assumptions often underlie the 'constrained translation' approach: that written text inside speech balloons and boxes is the only component of comics which may change in translation, whereas everything else (more specifically, 'the pictures') remains unchanged (D'Oria and Conenna 1979:24, Mayoral et al. 1988:359, Würstle 1991:162), and that images have a 'universal' meaning (Rabadán 1991:296). Both these assumptions seem however to be misconceived.

Verbal language is not the only component of comics which gets translated, since visual components are often modified as well, as is amply demonstrated by many of the articles published in this volume and elsewhere. It is true that retouching the pictures, for example to remove or redraw unwanted elements or to modify the size and shape of balloons, involves extra costs for the publishers, and that commercial considerations are usually at a premium, especially as far as 'popular' comics are concerned. However, other social factors may intervene which justify such expenses, for example the prevailing conventions for comics in a country or area (see, for example, the removal of balloons from American comics in early twentieth-century Italy), direct or indirect censorship (Kaindl 1999, Zanettin 2007, Zitawi, this volume), or specific cultural and/or promotional agendas (D'Arcangelo, this volume). Furthermore, current technologies have changed the way comics, especially comics in translation, are produced. Traditionally, the translator would provide the publisher with a printed translation of the verbal content, which would then be reviewed by an internal editor and handed to the letterer. After having scratched away the original text from the balloons in the films with a razor blade, the letterer would write the translation by hand in the empty balloons before the films went to the printing press. Today the translation is received as a text file, and lettering is usually done with the help of a graphics programme, by erasing the original text and importing the translated dialogues in the area of the balloons on the graphic file. If need be, the original handwritten characters can be scanned and reused as fonts in a translated comic book, and dialogues can be 'shrunk' to fit into balloons. Not only lettering, but also other graphic adaptations involving the retouching of pictures have been made simpler and less expensive by computer technology (Valero Garcès, this volume). Furthermore, modifications involving a change in publication format, use of colours, page layout, panels composition, etc. may even involve saving on costs, as happens for

---

[18] Film subtitling instead involves diasemiotic translation, since a different channel is used (writing rather than speech).

instance when a comic book originally printed in colour is printed in black and white (D'Arcangelo, this volume), or when translated text is typewritten rather than handwritten (Zanettin, this volume).[19]

As for the supposedly universal nature of images, it seems clear that visual cultural references, citations and allusions may well represent 'cultural bumps' (Leppihalme 1997) and be subjected to different translation strategies. Anthea Bell (n.d.: online), for instance, explains how a pun based on the interplay of text and images in an *Astérix* panel was translated by reframing both verbal and visual context, for target readers who are less familiar with the visual citation:[20]

> This drawing parodies the dramatic painting by Géricault of the notorious incident when a number of seamen were set adrift on a raft to die; their place is taken, in the Asterixian rendering, by the pirates who are constantly having their ship scuttled by the Gaulish heroes [...] In the French, the pirate captain is exclaiming, '*Je suis médusé!*' = 'dumbfounded' – from the Gorgon Medusa whose gaze turned the beholder to stone, but with reference here to the ship called La Méduse whose raft and seamen were painted by Géricault. The solution, in English, was to use a pun on Géricault/ Jericho (by Jericho!) instead – the pun itself was the idea of a friend of the translators, who then worked it in by pointing up the artistic connotations with a rueful: 'We've been framed.' To give a further clue to the pun, space in the frame, bottom right, was used to add a footnote: 'Ancient Gaulish artist', which is not present in the French.

Like verbal communication, visual communication relies on shared cultural assumptions. In his celebrated analysis of the first page of *Steve Canyon* by Milton Caniff, Eco (1994 [1964]:138, 163) suggests that Italian readers of the Italian translation would not read visual clues in the same way that American readers would. Not only would they not be able to understand that the hero is an aircraft pilot because of missing verbal clues (military slang), but they would probably also attribute to Steve Canyon's 'brunette' secretary a familiar rather than an exotic connotation. The interpretation of visual signs by the readers of a comic in translation is affected not only by possible alterations (retouching or removal) of (part of) the picture, but also by 'typographical' changes such as those involving format (e.g. lettering, colour, reading direction, etc.). For instance, whereas the first manga published in the West were 'flipped' to conform to Western reading habits, most of them are now printed in the original right-to-left reading direction (Jüngst, Rota this volume). Barbieri (2004) argues that this 'philological' approach can in fact alter the perception of manga by Western readers. Images are not symmetrical, and the disposition of bodily masses on the panel affects their interpretation, which is often culture-specific. For instance, while in the Western figurative tradition a movement is perceived as fluent and effortless if going from left to right and as difficult if going in the opposite direction, the reverse is true in the Japanese figurative tradition. Thus,

---

[19] I would like to thank Andrea Ciccarelli of Saldapress for providing details on editorial practices concerning the process of publishing a translated comic.

[20] On cultural allusions in Astérix, see Rivière (2001).

'reading' the images in the 'original' direction (from right to left) not only conflicts with the direction in which the words are read (from left to right), but alters the perception of the stream of actions portrayed.

Finally, as seen in section 1.3 above, specific comics conventions do not always coincide in different comics cultures. For example, the 'same' convention can be interpreted in different ways in 'comics' and 'manga', e.g. cloud-shaped balloons can represent either thought (in comics) or whispering (in manga).

By looking at the translation of comics from a strictly linguistic perspective and focusing exclusively on the verbal text, many studies thus regard comics translation as a special case of interlingual translation, constrained – or at best 'supported' (Gottlieb 1998) – by visual or technical limitations.

Other studies call for a closer integration between linguistic analysis and a wider sociocultural and semiotic outlook. Most notably, Klaus Kaindl (1999)[21] has proposed that comics translation practices should be analyzed within their social context of production and reception and has suggested a taxonomy of aspects of comics which may be modified during the translation process. According to Kaindl, Bourdieu's concepts of 'agent', 'field' and 'habitus' may help in providing a viable descriptive framework to account for the social dimension of this practice. Thus, for example, while early American comics were mainly situated in the journalistic field, "European comics have developed along different lines and are primarily rooted in the literary field" (Kaindl 1999:270). Furthermore, Kaindl draws up a translation-relevant anatomy of comics, based on a systematic account of features of translated comics vis-à-vis the originals. These include typographical signs (font type and size, layout, format), pictorial signs (colours, action lines, vignettes, perspective), and linguistic signs (titles, inscriptions, dialogues, onomatopoeia, narration). Each of these elements may be subjected to strategies of change such as replacement (the standard option for linguistic signs), deletion, addition etc.

The translation of comics is different from 'translation proper' not only because words co-exist with non-verbal systems, but also because verbal language in comics is only part – if sometimes the only visible part (i.e. overt translation) – of what gets translated. From a descriptive stance, however, while the analysis can be focused only on the translation of the verbal component, it cannot dispense with an examination of how words interplay with pictures in the co-construction of meaning. If we want to compare what readers in different countries do when they read the 'same' comics, we must also take into account the changes that affect comics as visual texts, and as semiotic and cultural artefacts.

5. **Contents of This Volume**

The first part of the volume deals with rather general aspects of the translation of comics, while the contributions in the second part are each focused on a more specific case study. The article by Nadine Celotti outlines a semiotic perspective for the study of the

---

[21] This article was based on a PhD dissertation (Kaindl 1999), which later grew into a full monograph focused on comics in translation (Kaindl 2004). Unfortunately, both works are only available in German.

translation of comics, adopting the point of view of the translator, who is seen as a semiotic investigator. Celotti defines comics as "a narrative space where pictorial elements convey meaning, not less than verbal messages, over which they often have primacy" and advocates a move away from the constrained approach. She argues that the primacy of pictorial elements over verbal messages should not be seen as a constraint, nor translators of comics as subject to the 'tyranny' of visual messages. Rather, she emphasizes the role of the visual component in comics and the importance of 'reading' the images together with the verbal messages in order to interpret – and translate – them. She first suggests that translators should distinguish four different 'loci' of translation, namely balloons, titles, captions and linguistic paratext. She then discusses the different ways in which the linguistic paratext, i.e. verbal messages within the drawing, can be dealt with in translation. Finally, she shows how the different types of interplay between visual and verbal messages in comics can affect their translation.

While Celotti draws her examples mainly from Franco-Belgian comics (translated into Italian), Heike Elisabeth Jüngst's contribution deals with the translation of manga, currently the largest segment of translated comics in the world. Jüngst deals specifically with manga translated into German, but her analysis can be extended to most Western countries. She provides a detailed historical overview of how the strategies applied to the translation of manga have changed over the years, and describes some of the translation strategies used for dealing with both verbal and visual text in manga. An important factor which has conditioned manga translation practices is fan culture: manga readers "want their manga to look Japanese, and this extends to some linguistic as well as pictorial aspects". For example, translated manga are now mainly published in the right-to-left original reading direction; Japanese loanwords are retained for aesthetic purposes, and words that describe realia are explained rather than translated. Referring to Nida's classic distinction between formal and dynamic equivalence, Jüngst argues that 'formally' equivalent' translations seem now to be the prevailing norm for manga, to the effect that a translated manga may almost look more Japanese than the original.

Valerio Rota draws attention to the importance of an analysis of the cultural contexts in which (translated) comics are published, and looks at how the geographical origin of a comic book may influence expectations relating to it. Since authors conceive their works (story length, graphic techniques, genre, etc.) keeping in mind how and where they will be published, publication formats have an important impact on the quality of comics, the attitude of readers and the periodicity of their publication. Rota distinguishes between four main comic book formats, typical of the American, French, Italian and Japanese comics industries, and argues that a modification of the size, proportions and characteristics of the original format through editorial processes in the receiving country substantially alters the original work, with important consequences for the reception of translated comics. Like Celotti, Rota points out that a distinction between text and pictures may be misleading and that written text should be treated like a graphic element of the page. The 'texture' of comics, that is "the complex structure resulting from the interweaving of texts and pictures", is presented to the target culture after a process of adaptation which takes into consideration both the expectations and tastes of the new cultural context, and the features of the work to be translated. Either domesticating or foreignizing strategies (Venuti 1995) can be adopted, and a comic book can be adapted to the local format, kept in the same format of the original, or presented in a third format, different from both the original and the local ones. Rota argues that, since the formats of publication which characterize each geographic area clearly appear before the eyes of the reader, translated comics can be seen as the tangible proof of the 'experience of the foreign' highlighted and wished for by Antoine Berman.

The contributions in the second part of the volume deal with the translation of comics belonging to quite different genres and aimed at readers of different age groups (e.g. children vs. adult readers), social class and culture (e.g. 'popular' vs. 'quality' comics). Language pairs and translation directions involved include English, Italian, Spanish, Arabic, French, German, Japanese and Inuit. All based on first-hand research and on thoroughly documented data, the articles exemplify a wide range of approaches.

Raffaella Baccolini and Federico Zanettin analyze the foreign editions of *Maus* by Art Spiegelman, the account of his father Vladek's experience during the Shoah. The authors argue that translation is a central feature in *Maus*, both in a metaphorical and a technical sense. They use the term 'translation' to describe Spiegelman's attempt to deal with a traumatic experience by using words and images which adapt, condense and transform Vladek's tape-recorded story into graphic narrative, in the mixed form of Spiegelman's own account of himself. Translation is also thematized in the graphic novel by the shift in the language spoken by Vladek in the past (Polish translated into standard English) and in the present (broken English). Vladek's broken language is the 'language of telling', which succeeds in representing the traumatic experience of the Holocaust and at the same time mirrors the impossibility of making sense of it. The article discusses how this has been one of the most problematic aspects involved in the publication of foreign editions of *Maus*, and focuses in particular on two Italian translations.

Taking up Kaindl's (1999) suggestion that research on comics should be based on sociological grounds, Adele D'Arcangelo carries out a contrastive analysis of the American and Italian traditions of horror comics. Against this backdrop, the Italian editions of the episodes of *The Saga of the Swamp Thing* written by Alan Moore are analyzed in terms of editorial policies. Whereas in the US the episodes written by the British author were published by DC Comics as an attempt to revitalize a series which had lost its popularity over the years, in Italy they were presented by Magic Press as a graphic novel (i.e. a 'unitary work' by a precise author), as part of a wider cultural and publishing project. D'Arcangelo argues that this editorial operation has actually improved Alan Moore's fame in the target culture, and that through its publishing policies Magic Press successfully managed to act as an agent of cultural innovation, bringing about a change in the expectations of the target community of readers.

A detailed account of the Arabic language comics market and of the editorial practices of publishers in Egypt and in the United Arab Emirates also forms the background of Jehan Zitawi's analysis of Disney comics in Arabic translation. Zitawi examines a sizable corpus of Disney comics translated into Arabic, together with their English source texts, within the framework of Brown and Levinson's politeness theory. She identifies three main translation strategies followed in translating Disney comics, which contain many sketches that could be construed as face threatening to Arab readers. Potentially offensive written and visual materials are handled by translators, publishers and official censoring bodies according to the politeness strategies they believe most appropriate for Arab readers. For example they can manipulate comics by deleting romantic, sexual or religious references ('don't do the Face Threatening Act' strategy), or by replacing them with 'euphemistic' alternatives ('do the Face Threatening Act on record with mitigation'), or they can retain them unaltered ('do the Face Threatening Act on record with no mitigation'). Zitawi shows, however, that both the 'Arab translator' and the 'Arab reader' are composite and plural entities rather than monolithic ones. Accordingly, editorial practices may vary considerably, so that Disney comics produced and distributed in the more conservative Gulf States contain more modifications and deletions than those translated in Egypt.

While dealing with very different types of comics, the next three articles all make reference to globalization/localization as a useful conceptual tool for the analysis of comics in translation. Jüngst deals with the translation of a rarely investigated genre of comics, namely educational comics. While most educational comics are not meant for translation, some of them are designed for plurilingual distribution and are thus 'globalized', for instance by avoiding the use of culture-specific elements in the pictures. Other comics are instead only later 'localized', i.e. stripped of their original characterizing features and adapted to a new target group. The problem of conveying special factual knowledge in a popularized shape is certainly often an issue when translating educational comics, but translation decisions and strategies also depend to a large extent on social and political factors. Educational comics in translation can in fact be published by public institutions such as the EU, or by private ones, be they multinational companies or non-profit and political organizations. They can be directed to a minority language group in a multicultural territory, e.g. Spanish-speaking people in the US or Inuit people in Canada, or to a specific target group in a different country, e.g. Japanese educational comics for girls (*shojo-manga*) in Germany, or for a specific educational purpose, as in the case of Astérix comics translated into Latin.

Zanettin suggests that the translation of comics may be usefully investigated within a localization framework, understood in its broadest sense as the adaptation and updating of visual and verbal signs to a target locale. Different actors are involved in the process, in addition to the translator proper, and 'translation' in the sense of 'replacement of strings of natural language' is only a component of the localization process. This approach is illustrated through discussion of the production processes which lead to the publication of a number of comics in translation, with examples from comics translated from and into English and Italian. As a case study, Zanettin then discusses three different Italian translations of a 1961 French comic book, an episode of the *Blueberry* Western saga by Charlier and Giraud. Each edition of *La pista dei Navajo* is the result of a localization process involving the modification of both verbal and visual sign systems and is designed for different receiving audiences, in terms of age-group and cultural background.

Elena Di Giovanni discusses the foreign translations of the *Winx Club* animated cartoons and comics. This is an Italian production primarily targeting young girls, which revolves around the adventures of a group of fairy teenagers. Both cartoons and comics are translated and distributed worldwide, and enjoy a wide popularity and commercial success. According to Di Giovanni, the *Winx Club* success story can be seen as an instance of resistance to multimedia globalization through translation, in that the Italian producers' management and supervision of all English versions of the *Winx Club* products ensures an overall control of the translation process. The English translations, even though they are usually performed by English native speakers, often reveal traces of the original Italian. While these can occasionally be perceived as inadequate or awkward, they effectively stand out as an alternative 'voice' running against the tide of translation from English into countless target cultures, and act as a vehicle for a minor language and culture which can positively influence a redefinition of media-generated cultural traffic.

The last two articles in this collection are concerned with two somewhat more 'traditional' topics, i.e. the translation of onomatopoeic sounds and inscriptions and the translation of humorous language. Carmen Valero Garcés' article deals with onomatopoeia and unarticulated language in Spanish comic books, comparing original and translated Spanish production. She first provides an overview of previous research on the subject, and then discusses her own data, consisting of a corpus of comics translated into Spanish from American English and a corpus of original Spanish comics. Her discussion is supplemented by the results of a questionnaire concerning the use of onomatopoeias by Spanish authors. The data show that, as regards the translation of onomatopoeic sounds, two main translation strategies are applied in Spain. In the case of sounds produced by animals, unarticulated sounds produced by humans, and sounds used to show feelings or attitude, English onomatopoeias are replaced by Spanish equivalents. When English onomatopoeias are used to represent 'mechanical' sounds, they are instead usually retained. However, many onomatopoeic sounds now feel as though they are part of the Spanish language even though they were originally borrowings from English, and English onomatopoeias are largely used even in comics originally written in Spanish.

In her article on the translation of proper names, onomastic puns and spoonerisms, Catherine Delesse investigates the British translations of the two well known French comic series *Astérix* and *Tintin*. Both series were extremely challenging for the translators, since they often play on linguistic devices such as polysemy, homophony, paronymy and metathesis for humorous effects. Delesse describes the various strategies used by the two teams of English translators, who often resorted to 'generalized compensation'. Both teams were very creative and used both linguistic and visual resources to recreate target texts whose coherence is sometimes greater than that of the original texts.

The last contribution, by Zanettin, consists of an annotated bibliography on the translation of comics. An abstract is provided for most publications listed.

As far as possible, visual documentation is provided for all the examples discussed, either within each article or in the centre fold in the case of illustrations in colour. Obtaining copyright permissions was a complex matter. While a consolidated practice of 'fair use' allows for the quotation of short extracts from written texts (usually up to 400 words) in scholarly works, all 'quotations' from visual texts such as comics at present require permission from copyright holders. Most publishers and authors gracefully agreed to allow free republication, but some never replied to our letters of request, others asked for a (sometimes substantial) fee, while still others (notably Disney) denied permission without any apparent reason. Leonard Rifas and Scott McCloud,[22] who own the copyright for some of the images which appear in this volume, remarked that 'quoting' a panel or two should be considered 'fair use'. It is hoped that this may become a consolidated practice in the future, thus facilitating a deeper understanding of comics in translation and a smoother circulation of ideas.

6. Conclusion

This volume is mainly addressed to researchers and students working in institutions specialized in translation studies, translator training and intercultural communication and to scholars of comics. However, because of the variety of cultural contexts and approaches involved, the volume should also appeal to scholars working in other fields, such as literary and cultural studies.

    The articles in this volume provide only a partial account of comics in translation, as it touches upon just a few genres, types and aspects. Considering the pervasiveness of comics (and cartoons), which not only appear in large print runs in newspapers, magazines and books, but also form part of the general cultural fabric and are in a relation of reciprocal exchange with many social activities and cultural artefacts (e.g. films, advertising, design, computers, etc.), the study of comics in translation is certainly still an underdeveloped area, especially if compared with that of other art forms such as cinema, of which comics are coeval. However, it is hoped that this volume may help towards a wider understanding of this social practice.

References

Primary Sources
Koike, Kazuo and Ryoichi Ikegami (1986-88) *The Crying Freeman*, Tokio: Shogakukan [*Crying Freeman*, Bologna: Granata Press 1992/93].
McCloud, Scott (1993) *Understanding Comics*, Northampton, MA: Tundra.
Moore, Alan, Dave Gibbons and John Higgins (1986/87) *Watchmen*, New York: DC Comics [*Watchmen*, Milano: Rizzoli/Milano Libri 1993; Play Press 2002; Panini/La Repubblica 2005].
Osborne, Richard and Ralph Edney (1992) *Philosophy for beginners*, New York: Writers & Readers.
R. F. Outcault's The Yellow Kid: A Centennial Celebration of the Kid Who Started the Comics (1995) Northampton, MA: Kitchen Sink Press.

Secondary Sources
Barbieri, Daniele (1991) *I linguaggi del fumetto*, Milano: Bompiani.

---

[22] Personal communication with the author and Heike Elisabeth Jüngst.

------ (2004) 'Samurai allo specchio', *Golem – L'indispensabile*, n.8, novembre 2004 (online) http://www.golemindispensabile.it/Puntata43/articolo.asp?id=1688&num=43&sez=51 1&tipo=&mpp=&ed=&as= (Accessed 8 February 2006).

Bell, Anthea (n.d.) 'Astérix - What's in a name', *LiteraryTranslation.com*, *The British Council Arts* (online) http://www.literarytranslation.com/usr/downloads/workshops/asterix.pdf (Accessed 30 January 2007).

Bona, Luigi (n.d.) *Appunti sulle origini e sulla storia del fumetto italiano*, Fondazione Franco Fossati (online) http://www.lfb.it/fff/fumetto/storia/st_it_010.htm (Accessed 30 January 2007).

Carlin, John (2005) 'Masters of American Comics: An Art History of Twentieth-Century American Comic Strips and Books', in John Carlin, Paul Karasik and Brian Walker (eds) *Masters of American Comics*, New Haven & London: Yale University Press, 25-175.

------, Paul Karasik and Brian Walker (eds) (2005) *Masters of American Comics*, New Haven & London: Yale University Press.

Castelli, Alfredo (1999) *America on my mind. Italian Comics and the Industry of Imagination. A short history of comics in Italy* (online) http://www.bvzm.com/english/eng_set.html (Accessed 30 January 2007).

Celotti, Nadine (2000) 'Méditer sur la traduction des bandes dessinées: une perspective de sémiologie parallèle', *Rivista internazionale di tecnica della traduzione* 5:41-61.

D'Arcangelo, Adele and Federico Zanettin (2004) 'Dylan Dog Goes to the USA: A North-American Translation of an Italian Comic Book Series', *Across Languages and Cultures* 5(2):187-211.

Detti, Ermanno (1984) *Il fumetto tra cultura e scuola*, Firenze: La Nuova Italia.

De Giacomo, Francesco (1995) 'Quando il duce salvò Topolino', *If. Immagini e fumetti* 4, Epierre.

D'Oria, Domenico and Mirella Conenna (1979) 'Sémiologie d'une traduction: Astérix en italien', *Equivalences: Revue de l'Ecole Supérieure de Traducteurs et d'Interprètes de Bruxelles* 10(1):19-38.

Duncan, Randy (2002) 'The Weaver's Art: An Examination of Comic Book "Writing"', *International Journal of Comic Art* 4(1):134-142.

Eco, Umberto (1994 [1964]) *Apocalittici e integrati. Comunicazioni di massa e teorie della cultura di massa*, Milano: Bompiani.

------ (2001) *Experiences in Translation*, Toronto: University of Toronto Press.

------ (2003) *Dire quasi la stessa cosa. Esperienze di traduzione*, Milano: RCS Libri.

------ (2005) 'Hugo Pratt. All'ultima storia capì: Corto Maltese sono io', *La Repubblica*, Domenica 7 Agosto 2005, 36-37.

------ and Siri Nergaard (1998) 'Semiotic approaches', in Mona Baker (ed.) *The Routledge Encyclopedia of Translation Studies*, London & New York: Routledge, 218-222.

Eisner, Will (1985) *Comics as sequential art*, Tamarac, Florida: Poorhouse Press.

Federici, Sandra and Andrea Marchesini Reggiani (eds) (2002) *Africa Comics. Antologia delle migliori storie a fumetti del Premio Africa e Mediterraneo*, Bologna: Edizioni Lai-momo.

Federici, Sandra and Andrea Marchesini Reggiani (eds) (2004) *Africa Comics 2003. Antologia del Premio Africa e Mediterraneo*, Bologna: Edizioni Lai-momo.

Federici, Sandra and Andrea Marchesini Reggiani (eds) (2006) *Africa Comics 2004-2005. Antologia del Premio Africa e Mediterraneo*, Bologna: Edizioni Lai-momo.

Fenty, Sean, Trena Houp and Laurie Taylor (2004) 'Webcomics: The Influence and Continuation of the Comix Revolution', *ImageText* 1(2) (online) http://www.english.ufl.edu/imagetext/archives/volume1/issue2/group/ (Accessed 30 January 2007).

Ferrer Simó, María Rosario (2005) 'Fansubs y scanlations: la influencia del aficionado en los criterios profesionales', *Puentes* 6:27-43.

Festi, Roberto (ed.) (2006) *Cinema & Fumetto. I personaggi dei comics sul grande schermo*, Trento: EsaExpo.

Fresnault-Deruelle, Pierre (1990) *I fumetti: libri a strisce*, Palermo: Sellerio [Italian trans. by Daniela De Agostini and Maurizio Ferrari; originally published in 1977 as *Récits et Discours par la Bande*, Paris: Hachette].

Gadducci, Fabio (2004) 'Notes on the Early Decades of Italian Comic Art', *International Journal of Comic Art* 6(2):30-77.

Gasca, Luis and Román Gubern (1988) *El discurso del comic*, Madrid: Catedra.

Gorlée, Dinda L. (1994) *Semiotics and the Problem of Translation*, Amsterdam & Atlanta, GA: Rodopi.

Gottlieb, Henrik (1998) 'Subtitling', in Mona Baker (ed.) *The Routledge Encyclopedia of Translation Studies*, London & New York: Routledge, 244-248.

Gravett, Paul (ed.) (2006) "No laughing matter. Cartoonists take issue", *New Internationalist* 307 (March 2006):2-15.

Groensteen, Thierry (1999) *Système de la bande dessinée*, Paris: PUF.

------ (2001) 'Fumetto e teoria in Francia e Belgio. Intervista a cura di Fabio Bonetti', *FM* 26(3) (online) http://www.fucine.com/network/fucinemute/core/index.php?url=redir. php?articleid=424 (Accessed 30 January 2006).

------ (2005a) *La bande dessinée. Une littérature graphique*, Toulouse: Milan.

------ (2005b) 'Orrore del vuoto. Il sentimento tragico dell'esistenza del fumetto', in Daniele Barbieri (ed.) *La linea inquieta. Emozioni e ironia nel fumetto*, Roma: Meltemi.

Gubern, Román (1972) *El lenguaje de los cómics*, Barcelona: Península.

Harvey, Keith (1995) 'A Descriptive Framework for Compensation', *The Translator* 1(1):65-86.

------ (1998) 'Compensation', in Mona Baker (ed.) *The Routledge Encyclopedia of Translation Studies*, London & New York: Routledge, 37-40.

Hatim, Basil and Ian Mason (1990) *Discourse and the Translator,* London & New York: Longman.

Hernández-Bartolomé, Ana Isabel and Gustavo Mendiluce-Cabrera (2004) 'Audesc: Translating Images into Words for Spanish Visually Impaired People', *Meta* 49(2) (online) http://www. erudit.org/revue/meta/2004/v49/n2/009350ar.html (Accessed 30 January 2007).

Horn, Maurice (1976/1999) (ed.) *The World Encyclopedia of Comics*, New York: Chelsea.

Jakobson, Roman (1960) 'Concluding statement: Linguistics and poetics', in Thomas A. Seabok (ed.) *Style in language*, Cambridge, MA: MIT Press, 350-377.

------ (1992 [1959]) 'On linguistic aspects of translation', in Rainer Schulte and John Biguenet (eds) *Theories of Translation. An anthology of Essays from Dryden to Derrida*, Chicago & London: The University of Chicago Press, 144-151.

Kaindl, Klaus (1999) *Übersetzungswissenschaft im interdisziplinären Dialog. Am Beispiel der comicuebersetzung*, Doctoral Dissertation, University of Vienna.

------ (1999) 'Thump, Whizz, Poom: A Framework for the Study of Comics under Translation', *Target* 11(2):263-288.

------ (2004) *Übersetzungswissenschaft im interdisziplinären Dialog*, Tübingen: Stauffenburg.

Lathey, Gillian (2006) 'The Translator Revealed: Didacticism, Cultural Mediation and Visions of the Child Reader in Translators' Prefaces', in Jan Van Coillie and Walter P. Verschueren (eds) *Children's Literature in Translation: Challenges and Strategies*, Manchester: St. Jerome, 1-16.

Laura, Ernesto G. (1997) *Gli anni de 'L'Avventuroso'*, Firenze: Nerbini.

Lent, John (2006) 'The Richness of African cartooning: A Secret Far Too Long', *International Journal of Comic Art* 8(1):71-113.

Leppihalme, Ritva (1997) *Culture Bumps: An Empirical Approach to the Translation of Allusions*,

Clevedon: Multilingual Matters.

Mahamood, Muliyadi (2003) 'Japanese Style in Malaysian Comics and Cartoons', *International Journal of Comic Art* 5(2):194-204.

Martín, Antonio (2000) *Apuntes para una historia de los tebeos*, Barcelona: Glénat.

Mayoral Asensio, Roberto, Dorothy Kelly & Natividad Gallardo (1988) 'The Concept of Constrained Translation. Non-Linguistic Perspectives of Translation', *Meta* 33(3):356-367.

Mey, K.-A. L. (1998) 'Comics', in Jacob Mey (ed.) *Concise Encyclopedia of Pragmatics*, Amsterdam: Elsevier, 136-140.

McCloud, Scott (1993) *Understanding comics*, Northampton, MA: Tundra.

------ (2000) *Reinventing Comics*, New York: Paradox Press.

Ng, Wai-ming (2000) 'A comparative study of Japanese comics in Southwest Asia and East Asia', *International Journal of Comic Art* 2(1):44-56.

------ (2003) 'Japanese elements in Hong Kong comics: History, Art and Industry', *International Journal of Comic Art* 5(2):184-193.

Occorsio, Eugenio (2006) 'Dai detersivi a Mickey Mouse la parola d'ordine è 'localizzazione", *La Repubblica, Affari e Finanza*, 10 luglio 2006, 9.

Oittinen, Riitta (2006) 'No Innocent Act: On the Ethics of Translating for Children', in Jan Van Coillie and Walter P. Verschueren (eds) *Children's Literature in Translation: Challenges and Strategies*, Manchester: St. Jerome, 35-45.

Olson, Richard D. (n.d.) *R. F. Outcault, The Father of the American Sunday Comics, and the Truth About the Creation of the Yellow Kid* (online) http://www.neponset.com/yellowkid/history.htm (Accessed 30 January 2007).

Orsi, Maria Teresa (1998) *Storia del fumetto giapponese. Primo volume. L'evoluzione dall'era Meiji agli anni settanta*, Venezia: Musa.

Peeters, Benoît (2000) *Leggere il fumetto*, Torino: Vittorio Pavesio Edizioni.

Pellitteri, Marco (1998) *Sense of comics*, Roma: Castelvecchi.

------ (2006) 'Manga in Italy. History of a Powerful Cultural Hybridization', *International Journal of Comic Art* 8(2):56-76.

Pilcher, Tim and Brad Brooks (2005) *The Essential Guide to World Comics*, London: Collins & Brown.

Rabadán, Rosa (1991) *Equivalencia y traducción*, León: Universidad del León.

Raffaelli, Luca (1997) *Il fumetto*, Milano: Il saggiatore.

Raskin, Lydia (2004) 'Interférences dans la traduction français-espagnol de la bande dessinée humoristique', in Emilio Ortega Arjonilla (ed.) *Panorama actual de la investigación en traducción e interpretación*, Granada: Atrio (CDROM, Vol. 3), 411-419.

Restaino, Franco (2004) *Storia del fumetto. Da Yellow Kid ai Manga*, Milano: UTET.

Rivière, Stéphane (2001) 'Les allusions culturelles dans Astérix' (online) http://www.mage.fst.uha.fr/asterix/allusion/allusion.html (Accessed 30 January 2007).

Sabin, Roger (1993) *Adult Comics. An Introduction*, London & New York: Routledge.

Santoyo Mediavilla, Julio César (1987) *El delito de traducir: Teoría y crítica de la traducción: antología*, Barcelona: Universitat Autònoma de Barcelona.

Saraceni, Mario (2003) *The language of comics*, London & New York: Routledge.

Scatasta, Gino (2002) 'La traduzione dei fumetti', in Romana Zacchi and Massimiliano Morini (eds) *Manuale di traduzione dall'inglese*, Milano: Bruno Mondadori, 102-112.

Sebastiani, Alberto (2002) 'La lingua nella realtà composita dei fumetti', *Quaderni dell'Osservatorio Linguistico* I-2002:316-346.

Spehner, Norbert (2005) 'Bibliographie internationale sélective des études sur la bande dessinée', *Belphégor* 1(5) (online) http://etc.dal.ca/belphegor/vol5_no1/it/main_it.html

(Accessed 30 January 2007).

Torop, Peeter (2002) 'Translation as translating as culture', *Sign Systems Studies* 30(2):593-605.

Toury, Gideon (1986) 'Translation', in Thomas Sebeok (ed.) *Encyclopedic Dictionary of Semiotics*, vol. 2. Berlin: Mouton de Gruyter, 1107–1124.

ToutenBD (2004) 'Dossier. Zoom sur la BD Indienne' (online) http://www.toutenbd.com/article. php3?id_article=988 (Accessed 30 May 2006).

Van Coillie, Jan and Walter P. Verschueren (eds) (2006) *Children's Literature in Translation: Challenges and Strategies,* Manchester and Kinderhook: St Jerome.

Venuti, Lawrence (1995) *The Translator's Invisibility: A History of Translation,* London & New York: Routledge.

Würstle, Régine (1991) 'Äquivalenzprobleme bei der Übersetzung multimedialer Texte. Zur Übersetzung der Comics *Les Frustrés* von Claire Bretécher', in Christian Schmitt (ed.) *Neue Methoden der Sprachmittlung,* (Pro Lingua; 10), Wilhemsfeld: Verlag, S., 149-170.

Yuste Frías, José (2001) 'La traducción especializada de textos con imagen: el cómic', in Departamento de Traducción e Interpretación (ed.) 'El traductor profesional ante el próximo milenio' *II Jornadas sobre la formación y profesión del traductor e intérprete,* Villaviciosa de Odón (Madrid): Universidad Europea CEES, 4 (CD-ROM).

Zanettin, Federico (2007) 'I fumetti in traduzione: approcci e prospettive di ricerca', in Vittoria Intonti, Graziella Todisco and Maristella Gatto (eds) *La traduzione. Lo stato dell'arte / Translation. The State of the Art,* Ravenna: Longo, 137-150.

2 The Translator of Comics as a Semiotic Investigator

NADINE CELOTTI

University of Trieste, Italy

Comics are a narrative space where both pictures and words convey meaning and jointly create the story, with the translator "reading" the meaning of the pictorial elements and their different relationships with the verbal messages – for example whether the relationship between them is one of complementarity or dialogue. This article distinguishes between four loci of translation, or different areas of comics where verbal messages appear: balloons, captions, titles and linguistic paratext (verbal content within pictures, e.g. inscriptions, road signs, newspapers and onomatopoeia). It especially focuses on the translation of the linguistic paratext, a locus which shows a high level of variability in terms of whether the verbal message is translated or not. A range of different strategies used by translators are identified and discussed, stressing the need for the translator to pay attention to all kinds of interplay between visual and verbal messages, and to approach the translation of comics as a semiotic experience.

> *It isn't about captions nor illustrations but about a real complementary relationship between the readable and the visible, two instances, each taking its own part in the narrative. (Benoît Peeters 1993:26)[1]*

It is taking Translation Studies a long time to recognize the specificity of comics: a narrative space where pictorial elements convey meaning, no less than verbal messages, over which they often have primacy. Comics are "narrative[s] with a visual dominant" (Groensteen 1999:14). Today, the literature on the translation of comics is quite fragmented and confines itself mainly to linguistic features like onomatopoeia, cultural allusions and puns, or remains focused on a specific comic series like *Astérix*, *Tintin* or *Dylan Dog*. For a long time, comics have been completely ignored as an object of investigation in their own right. Recent dictionaries and encyclopedias of Translation Studies (e.g. Shuttleworth and Cowie 1997, Baker 1998) do not even have an independent entry on comics. Shuttleworth and Cowie (1997:109-110) refer to them only once in their entry on 'Multi-medial Texts' (formerly Audio-medial texts), described as:

> A term used by Reiss to refer to a subsidiary text-type which supplements Reiss' basic text typology. The multi-medial category consists of texts in which the verbal content is supplemented by elements in other media; however, all such texts will also simultaneously belong to one of the other, main text-types. [...] Songs, comic strips, plays, and writing for radio or television are all examples of this type.

In fact, Katharina Reiss, who first investigated the intricate relationships between text-type and translation (Reiss 1971), explicitly included comics among 'multi-medial' texts

---

[1] All translations from French by the author, unless otherwise stated.

in her 1984 revised typology (Reiss and Vermeer 1984). Since this categorization has gained currency, the accent on the medium has often contributed to emphasizing the constraints that these supplementary languages involve. The debate on comics in translation has been characterized by a view of the presence of the balloons as a limitation to the freedom of translators, operating in much the same way as lip synchronization in dubbing.

A specific concept has even been created within Translation Studies for the translation of multimedia text, i.e. 'constrained translation'. The 'constrained translation' approach dates back to the 1980s, but it is still has some currency today:

> We here define constrained translations as translations that are, for practical or commercial reasons, spatially limited, such as, for instance, advertisements with brief and catchy slogans, cartoons, comics and subtitles [...] They [comics] are limited spatially in that translations must fit into balloons or panels, and in that they have a specific objective. (Grun and Dollerup 2003:198)

This concept of the picture as a constraint often goes hand in hand with the concept of the universality of the picture. As Kaindl (2004:183) suggests, it is like a belief in the existence of a visual Esperanto. Pictures are seen as a universal visual language, as not having a cultural meaning, as can be seen in this statement by Rabádan (1991:296):

> Iconical medium: the picture, the universal code that restricts and imposes limitations on the linguistic expression – the local code – in this case of constrained translation.

While Shuttleworth and Cowie present comics as a multimedia text type, in the first edition of the *Routledge Encyclopedia of Translation Studies* (Baker 1998) comics are mentioned in entries such as 'compensation' and 'semiotic approaches'. In order to explain the technique of compensation, the author of the first, Keith Harvey, refers to the translation of puns in an English translation of an *Astérix* story. It seems no coincidence that many articles on the translation of comics have dealt with the issue of puns, as if they were one of the main characteristic of comics. In the entry on 'semiotic approaches', Umberto Eco and Siri Nergaard state that semiotics "can provide tools and suggestions [...] also for the countless translations of mass-communication texts which often involve more than one semiotic system [...] such as television programs, film, advertising, comic strips, and so on" (Eco and Nergaard 1998:220).

This approach leads us to focus on the specificity of comics as a form of sequential art (Eisner 1985), in which the simultaneity of the visual and the verbal languages generates the diegesis. This could be a decisive step forward and away from the constrained translation approach, so that the visual message is no more seen as a "tyranny" (Cary 1986:54), but instead "read" together with the verbal language in order to grasp the globality of meanings.[2] This approach has not yet achieved a large consensus; only a few works

---

[2] See also Yuste Frías (2006) for critical reflections on the concept of 'constrained translation' in the field of children's literature, in which verbal language and iconic language often co-exist.

analyze comics using semiotic tools. For instance, Celotti (1997, 2000) calls for a 'parallel semiological perspective'. The term is taken from the French linguist Pottier (1992:21), who states that such as perspective combines "all the semiotic systems which are used in parallel with the linguistic system. The one more frequently found is without doubt visual illustration (drawing, picture, photo)". More recently, Kaindl (2004) has proposed that the translation of comics should be approached from a 'multimodality perspective', which attempts a systematic analysis of how different semiotic resources such as language, image, sound and music are given meaning through their mutual interdependence.[3]

In this article, I wish to outline a semiotic approach to the translation of comics, distancing myself from the concept of constrained translation and challenging also the conception of the universality of the picture. I will extend what Ducrot (1991) said about words to pictures: no picture is 'innocent'. Each visual sign conveys meaning, therefore I will avoid using the common expression 'non verbal' when referring to visual elements in order to stress its autonomous life as a concept, or its own semiotic identity, and not to describe it through a negation. I would like to show how the specificity of comics affects the manner of translating and how visual language can be a resource rather than a constraint for the translator.

The translation of comics also brings up other important issues linked to cultural, economic, political, and (indeed) psychoanalytical factors (Tisseron 2000) which can affect the success of comics in different countries. It is well known that several comics cross the border into different countries with considerable difficulties, not only because of a 'good' or a 'bad' translation. For instance it is hard to find Hugo Pratt's *Corto Maltese* in the UK or works by Tronchet in Italy. The very popular and successful Italian series *Dylan Dog*[4] has been a real failure in France after three attempts at different periods (1987, 1993, 2001) with different publishers (Lug, Glénat, Hors Collection). Comics are cultural products, and each culture conceives comics in its own way: size, periodicity, prices, layout of pages, colours and so on, all components which can be markedly different. For instance, in France the so called "48CC" (48 pages, cartonné, colours) format is seen as a French specificity (Pomier 2005:48), whereas the Bonelli Comics (16x21 cm) as an Italian preference, and in the US the monthly 32-page colour comic book is more common (Rota 2004:2, this volume). Comics also have a different cultural status in different countries. For instance, "U.S. comics have lagged far behind their European and Japanese counterparts in both popularity and cultural acceptance" (McCloud (2000:65). And within Europe, for instance in France, where comics occupy a large section in bookshops and libraries, they are given greater consideration than in Italy, where they are usually distributed on news stands and are perceived mainly as a product for children or adolescents which can even influence them negatively and lead them away from 'True Literature'. Italian adult

---

[3] Video, films, websites, advertisements and computer games are the text types mainly investigated within a multimodality perspective, whereas comics and cartoons do not really seem to have attracted much attention, even if they are occasionally mentioned, as in Baldry and Thibault (2006:34): "Cartoons are a well-known example of multimodal narratives, a good demonstration, of how meaning making depends on the integration of semiotic resources".

[4] See e.g. Eco (1998:15-16), who refers to Dylan Dog as a 'cult product'.

comics, like Hugo Pratt's or Milo Manara's, belong more to an intellectual niche and are often confined to comic shops.

Another cultural factor which can exert some influence on the way comics are translated is 'political correctness', sometimes leading to the deletion of visual messages of violence or of verbal insults. Some comics adopt their own system of ethics: for instance, in Disney comics no one smokes, shoots or goes fishing; Morris's Lucky Luke's cigarette has been changed into a blade of grass, first in Sweden and then in most countries. Economic aspects, like copyright problems, can also bring about a change in the way a character is named or visually represented.[5]

All the aspects discussed above would seem at first glance to be mostly a concern of the publishers, who decide how to sell their comics as a product to the market. Often publishers prefer to conform to the values currently dominating in their culture. For instance, they may 'domesticate' the format of a comic book or its thresholds (using the terminology of Genette 1987), and such changes constitute one of the most evident features of cultural adaptation. Publishers may ask the translator to carry out a 'cultural adaptation', but translators of comics, like all translators, are social beings, dealing with a socially determined practice (Kaindl 1999), and can negotiate the appropriate translation strategies with their publishers. Faced with many visual signs belonging to a specific culture, translators need to choose between a domesticating and a foreignizing perspective. In most cases, while visual signs will be carried through in a translation with all their cultural connotations, verbal signs will change into another 'foreign' language. Therefore, in order to avoid lack of homogeneity between words and pictures or a cultural gap it seems important for a translator of comics to define her or his translation project (Berman 1995). And here the importance of a semiotic approach becomes clear. In fact, in the case of comics, reading has to be understood in a wider sense than that in which the term is commonly used since, as Eisner (1985:7-8) suggests, "the reader is required to exercise both visual and verbal interpretive skills".

In the following section I will attempt to illustrate the richness of meaning in the visual language in comics, because the linguistic work of the translator cannot start without reading the iconic language.[6]

1.   Visual Messages

While drawings take up a considerable part of the visual space, they do not make up the whole of the visual message. In fact the visual message is composed of a variety of elements, each of which conveys meaning and lends rhythm to the narration: layout,

---

[5] In the American version of the Italian comic *Dylan Dog*, the name of one of the main characters, Groucho Marx, has been changed to Felix and his characteristic moustache has been deleted, in order to avoid using copyrighted images. See Rota (2001) and D'Arcangelo and Zanettin (2004).

[6] Basic references for any translator for understanding the essence of comics include *Comics and Sequential Art* by Eisner (1985), *Système de la bande dessinée* by the French scholar Groensteen (1999) and *Understanding Comics* by McCloud (1996); the latter is an essay in comic book format. In this article, I am primarily concerned with the translation of Western comics. See Jüngst (this volume) and Rota (this volume) for a discussion of specific aspects involved in the translation of Japanese comics.

size and shape of panels, strips and pages, balloons and gutters, colours, lettering, etc., features which together create an iconic "solidarity" (Groensteen 1999:21), generating the "sequential fixed pictures" narrative: the essence of comics.

A reader, and a translator even more so, first approaches a comic book as a sequence of visual messages. The first visual messages that the translator meets are the thresholds, i.e. the front cover, the flyleaf and everything else that may come before the first page of the story. The translator then takes a 'sequential glance' at the first page in order to perceive the narrative rhythm. The organization of space is semantically dependent on the narration, and the different page layouts are "mapped out from a given semantic content" (Groensteen 1999:107).[7] For instance, "[l]ong narrow panels that create a crowded feeling enhance the rising tempo of panic" (Eisner 1985:33). In *Astérix* and *Tintin*, narrow and long vertical panels are often used for a character standing up, while large and horizontal panels for a character lying down. The shape of a panel may also be used to convey a specific meaning. For instance, a panel shaped like a cloud is used to express an idea or a recollection, or a panel without contours to suggest wide spaces. The gutter fundamentally participates in the rhythm and needs to be read as well, since "the heart of comics lies in the space between the panels where the reader's imagination makes still pictures come alive!" (McCloud 2000:1).

Having gained a first global perception, the translator stops at each single panel, the minimum unit of comics (Groensteen 1999), and attempts to grasp the visual and verbal solidarity. She or he has to pay attention to every visual sign in order to detect its contribution to the global meaning. For example, a balloon shaped like a cloud means that what is inside forms part of interior monologue and is not spoken out loud, while overlapping balloons are used to convey the speed of verbal interactions. Lettering is also a meaningful resource since it involves both a visual and verbal dimensions.

The example in Figure 2.1 (centre fold) illustrates how a misreading of the visual elements may result in a substantial alteration of meaning in translation. In the *Le Petit Spirou* story by Tome and Janry, a friend of the main character (who only appears in the last panel) threatens to use black magic against his schoolmates if they don't give him their ice-creams. As a demonstration, he moulds the mashed potatoes in his plate in the shape of the school porter, and after uttering a magical formula hits the sculpture with a fork, at which point the porter also jumps as if she were hit by something. In the Italian translation, the words that are 'drawn' in the second balloon in panel B3 (i.e. third panel in row 2) have been treated as if they were only a visual message and left in French, presumably because the translator understood the words in the panel ("Fée gaff cetat wa ratt pah ton kou!") to be meaningless, whereas they can in fact be read (or rather, heard) as a call out to Spirou to strike with his slingshot: "Fais gaffe, c'est à toi, rate pas

---

[7] Several typologies (e.g. Peeters 1998, Groensteen 1999) have been proposed to describe different page layouts. Peeters (1998) discusses four main types: the conventional layout, where panels are all of the same size; the decorative, where premince is given to esthetical considerations; the rhetorical and the productive layout, where the organization of the panels in the page is functional to the story. Groensteen (1999:114-119) agrees with Peeters' typology, but distinguishes between regularity and irregularity in a page, and between discretion and ostentation.

ton coup!", literally "Be careful it's your turn don't miss it!"). The humorous effect is thus lost in the Italian translation.

Furthermore, the translator also has to decide whether a written message placed outside the balloon is more visual than verbal. Therefore another important step for the translator is to pinpoint where the verbal messages lie in order to identify the 'locus' of translation.

2.   Verbal Messages: Loci of Translation

The aim of the translator should be to translate all verbal messages, but in reality not all of them will be translated in comics. Four different areas of verbal messages can be identified – each of them with its own function, which means that potentially there could be four loci of translation, but for one locus there is a high level of variability as concerns whether the verbal message will be translated or not.

1.   **Balloons**. The balloon is the main but not the only place where written 'spoken' language is to be found. The verbal message usually represents the spoken mode, i.e. a character speaking aloud in the first person, and it usually has to be translated.

2.   **Captions**. The 'sacred' text at the top or bottom of the panel, usually in the third person, grants the narration a literary dimension (Groensteen 1999:30). It usually marks changes in time and space, but it can also include commentaries connected with the pictures. Figure 2.2, for instance, illustrates Francesco Tullio Altan's characteristic legends, which function as 'voice off' comments.
In the first panel, Colombus says in the balloon: "What foolish and arrogant people! What a filthy world! And do you know who will change it, Mario?", and the caption comments: "Vanquished, he philosophises". In the second panel Colombus says: "You see? It isn't going to be you". Mario replies: "Sorry" and the caption comments: "He makes the most of his erudition". In the third panel Colombus says: "but me neither...", the comment in the caption is: "But deep down, he is good at heart".

3.   **Titles**. It is well known that one of the main functions of titles is to be attractive, and they are often changed during their journey from one country to another. Changes in titles in films can be seen as a prototypical example. But they can also be maintained, and in this case they reveal their origin and may provide an exotic touch. For instance, the title of Baru's French comic *L'autoroute du soleil* (lit. "Motorway of the South") has not been translated into Italian, a choice which is coherent with the global foreignizing strategy of the translator, as we shall see later.

Therefore, besides having to translate titles linked to their function as attention-getter, the translator should also be aware of the possible connection between the title and the visual messages.

Figure 2.2: Altan, *Colombo*, 2003, p. 30

4.   **The linguistic paratext**. The verbal signs outside the balloon and inside the draw-ing: inscriptions, road signs, newspapers, onomatopoeia, sometimes dialogues, and so on. I choose to call them 'linguistic paratext', as suggested by Margarito (2005), follow-ing Genette. The paratext can have both functions, visual and verbal, and the translator should decide which of these to give priority to. For the translator it could be useful to distinguish the written messages from those which play a fundamental part in the progress of the diegesis from the others. A panel will often contain a letter or newspaper headline which is an integral part of the story, and which has to be read if the story is to be followed. In such cases the translator really has no choice but to translate it. There are other paratexts which can tell us about the social, cultural or geographic context or can make use of jokes or puns. In these cases the translator has to choose from a range of strategies, which are discussed below.

3.   The Different Strategies of Translation for the Linguistic Paratext

If the first three loci of translation always require a translation of the verbal message, the fourth locus presents a high degree of variability. The translator has a range of at least six different strategies for this locus. The verbal message can be:

a) translated
b) translated with a footnote in the gutter
c) culturally adapted
d) left untranslated
e) deleted
f) a mix of (some of) the above

First of all it has to be said that the choice of a procedure also involves, in a way, an eco-nomic dimension because of the costs involved in changing the drawing.

The first strategy is often followed especially when the verbal message – such as pages of newspapers, letters or signs – plays an explicit part in the diegesis, as though its function were similar to that of a balloon. For example, in the French comic by Zidrou and Fournier, *Les Crannibales: l'aile ou la cuisse*, a panel contains a letter ("Chère voisine, Merci de veiller sur notre maison…", lit. "Dear Neighbour, thank you for keeping an eye on our house…") which is addressed to one of the main characters, who needs to read it in order for the story to unfold. In such a case the linguistic paratext must be translated.

At times, however, when the verbal message which is crucial to the story is deeply embedded in the drawing, the translator may resort to a footnote. For instance, in Baru's *L'autoroute du Soleil* a topical page ending a chapter of the graphic novel only contains a close-up of a poster on the wall of a room, over which one of the characters has scrawled the words "Va te faire foutre", the only verbal message in the panel. In the Italian translation, the footnote "Vaffanculo!" (lit. "Fuck off") is added in the gutter below the panel. At other times the verbal message becomes an iconic message, whose translation within the drawing would be excessively intrusive. In the Italian edition of a story by Cabanes, translated as *Gli anni giovani*, a French verbal message is drawn as a flash of lightning in the sky. Here again the translator has provided an Italian translation in a footnote in the gutter, while the visual message is left unchanged inside the picture.

The third strategy, cultural adaptation in the paratext, is generally found when the translator decides to adopt an overall domestication strategy. In the Italian translation of Tronchet's comic series *Jean-Claude Tergal*, the main character has been given an Italian name, *Domenico Tergazzi*, and the translator has culturally adapted other names, including those in the paratext. In a panel (Figure 2.3), the sign in front of a bar, "Chez Raoul" (lit. "Raoul's", Raoul being a French forename), has thus been translated as *Bar Juventus*, after the name of an Italian football club.

Figure 2.3a: Tronchet, *Jean-Claude Tergal*, Tome 3, 1993, p. 40

Figure 2.3b: Tronchet, *Domenico Tergazzi*, 1992, p. 36

Messages written in the paratexts are sometimes left in the source language. Some have a function which is more visual than verbal, as though they had become drawings like wall graffiti or advertising billboards, and their non-translation does not give rise to any semantic gap – they serve as a reminder of the story's setting. Some of these messages, however, may produce a kind of translational non-coherence if left untranslated. In Marjane Satrapi's autobiographical graphic novel in French, *Persepolis*, for instance, one panel (2000:104A1) represents the author reading a newspaper in Tehran. Whereas in other panels it can be clearly seen that the newspaper is written in Persian, here the author decided to show the title of the page she is reading in French. This title, "martyrs du jour" (lit. "martyrs of the day"), is left in French in the Italian translation.

Another strategy consists in deleting the linguistic paratext. In Tronchet's *Au bonheur des drames*, a panel shows two characters reading the menu outside a pizza restaurant. Above them, a sign reads "PIZZERIA", and below "chez Francina et Jean-Claudio". Together with the Italian word "pizzeria", two names ending in -*a* and -*o* give a connotation of "italianity" to the restaurant. In the Italian edition the name of the pizzeria has been removed, perhaps because the translator decided that it would not have the same connotation for the Italian reader.

Finally, there is the policy of mixed strategies, consisting partly in translating or adaptating and partly in deleting or retaining the linguistic paratext, as Figure 2.4 from Tome and Janry's *Le Petit Spirou* illustrates. In the translated Italian text, the names on the spine of the books in the French original have been deleted (La Fontaine), retained (Tintin, Perrault, Grimm), and culturally adapted (Andersen rather than Segur).

Figure 2.4a: Tome et Janry, *Le petit Spirou*, "Merci Qui?", 1994, p. 7

Figure 2.4b: Tome et Janry, *Il piccolo Spirù*: "Grazie di che?", 1997, p. 7

It is clear that on the one hand, translating through adaptation or deletion could mask aspects of the source text. On the other hand, not translating at all could create a gap in the meaning and interrupt the diegesis. Not all the features have the same 'weight', which needs to be assessed case by case, especially for the linguistic paratext.

In any case, faced with this range of strategies, the translator should choose on the basis of her or his overall aim – either adapt the comic to the target culture or allow its origin to show through. The Italian translation of *L'Autoroute du soleil* remains firmly rooted in its French origin, suggesting that the translator followed a general foreignizing strategy in all the loci of translation: all the messages in the paratext – licence plates, road signs, and names of bars – are left in French, the title is in French and proper names have not been changed. When a translation is necessary for comprehension purposes, a footnote is added in the gutter. This adds up to a coherent overall strategy which does not obstruct the flow of the story and is in line with the 'sociological' genre of comics which aims to recount the adventures of marginalized people in French society. The Italian translation of Tronchet's *Jean-Claude Tergal présente ses pires amis* reflects an entirely different choice. All cultural references have been adapted: titles, names and signs have all been Italianized.

The paratextual locus of translation can be highly challenging for the translator. Strategies which retain the otherness of the source text must in all events reflect a conscious choice as much as strategies of cultural adaptation (when the iconic message does not reveal the culture of origin, as is often the case in sci-fi comics), and not be the result of a thoughtless act of omission.

Once the loci of translation have been clearly identified, the translator has to pay attention to the different types of interaction between the two meaning-making resources, the visual and the verbal.

4. The Interplay between the Visual and the Verbal Message

In his famous work on the rhetoric of image, Roland Barthes (1982) pointed out two functions of the verbal message in relation to the iconic message: the anchoring function (*ancrage*) and the relaying (*relais*) one. Since any image is polysemic, a verbal key is needed in order to 'anchor', to fix the sense of the image. The linguistic message, usually through a caption, will guide us to its interpretation. In comics, the anchoring function is not always involved, since the meaning of a panel can be understood without any verbal guide. In so-called silent comics, for instance, there are no words at all. Instead, the relaying function represents the core of narrative in comics, since "here the word (more often a piece of dialogue) and the image are in a complementary relationship; words are fragments of a more general syntagm in the same way as images, and the unity of the message is created at a higher level: the level of the story" (Barthes 1982:32-33). Habitual readers of comics easily deal with this basic complementary interaction of visual and verbal messages, but those who are not educated to read comics, as could be the case with non-specialized translators, should not forget always to read both messages and not only the verbal one. This may seem obvious, but it has to be said that many translation errors stem from the translator's failure to read the interconnection between the verbal and visual messages. Other kinds of interconnection which convey meaning in comics exist (Groensteen 1999:155-159). One such interconnection, which I will call 'conversational interplay', seems to me especially relevant from the point of view of the translator. This involves meaning being conveyed by a sort of conversation between the visual message and a verbal message placed in one, or more, of the four loci of translation: balloon, caption, title and paratext. This interplay, which I would like to illustrate with some examples, manifestly reasserts that images convey meaning and should not be seen as constraining features.

The first example comes from *Les cousins Dalton*, an episode of the French comic series *Lucky Luke* by Morris. In one panel, the Daltons, who are four inseparable and stupid gangsters whose criminal ventures always fail thanks to Lucky Luke, all shoot at an empty can of beans, which is lying on the ground right in front of them. This happens after several vain attempts to hit the can as it is thrown in the air. In the next panel a hand is shown holding up the can, with just one hole in it, while one of the Daltons (a balloon with a tail pointing outside the panel) says "Ah! tout de même" ("At long last"), thus implying that after several attempts with their guns the Dalton cousins have finally been successful. The Italian translator rendered the expression as "Ah! di nuovo" ("Ah! Again"), suggesting the opposite meaning. Here, the meaning of the verbal message located inside a balloon is completed by the visual message, which the translator has apparently failed to interpret.

The interplay between balloon and visual message can also be used to generate humour. It is often based on the combination of metaphorization/de-metaphorization processes, a tricky strategy for a translator. An example which illustrates the humorous effect produced by the play on signs depending on a multimodal combination can be found in Kaindl (2004): a picture shows a man who breaks free from his chains while another character comments in a balloon "Il est déchaîné", playing with the two levels, the literal one ("he's free from his chains") and the metaphorical one ("he is beside himself with rage"). The translation of such "visual puns" (Zanettin 1998) requires particular inventiveness.

The interplay with the balloon-visual message can also be based on a culture-specific feature such as the meaning of gestures. For instance, a raised thumb is generally understood to mean OK. This gesture, however, has at least four other meanings besides the North-American one,[8] one of which is "pax" (or "truce!") in the context of children's games in France. The gesture often appears in Franco-Belgian comics when an exhausted character appeals for a break.

In the last panel of page 11 of *Astérix en Hispanie*, by Uderzo and Goscinny, a Roman soldier is lying on the ground after a series of blows inflicted on him by Obelix, and he raises his thumb to ask for a respite, without any accompanying verbal message. The non-French reader of a translation may be misled into thinking that the Roman soldier is giving the OK sign (Yuste Frías 1998), unless a footnote is added to explain the meaning of the gesture. The same gesture appears in a story by Margerin, published in Italy as *Quando l'amore bussa alla porta* (lit. "When love knocks on the door"). In order to gain a respite after a fight, one character raises his thumb (*pouce* in French), this time also saying *pouce!* (truce!). This echo around the word *pouce* and the image of the raised thumb has been lost in the Italian translation where "pouce" was translated as "basta" ("enough").

The translator also needs to be particularly aware of the possibility of a close connection between the title and the visual messages. For instance, in *Les Crannibales: l'aile ou la cuisse* by Zidrou and Fournier, one story is entitled "îles flottantes" (lit. "floating islands"), which in French also refers to a cream dessert. Thus there is an interplay between the literal interpretation, reinforced by a panel in which one of the characters shows a picture with a floating island in it, and the culinary interpretation, as the story revolves around food. Since in many languages the dessert is not known or has a different name, when translating the title it may be difficult to retain both of its meanings.

When deciding on a translation strategy, the translator should also consider whether there is any connection between visual messages and the written message in the paratext. This kind of interplay often occurs when onomatopoeia coexists with the picture of the event or action referred to, since onomatopoeic sounds are not always 'universal' (see Valero Garcés, this volume). For example, in French comics the sound of a slap is written as the French word for "slap", i.e. "baff" (Figure 2.5).

In Italian comics, for instance in Hugo Pratt's *Corto Maltese* stories, the sound of a slap is instead often represented by the Italian word for slap, i.e. "schiaffo!", or with its abbreviation "schiaff!" or "schiaf!". In the French translation of the *Corto Maltese* story translated as *Conversation mondaine à Moululhe*, the Italian onomatopoeia is left unchanged.

Another, more elaborate kind of interplay occurs between three features creating a sort of trilogue: the visual message with two areas for verbal messages. In Figure 2.6, a

---

[8] In Japan: 1. a male friend 2. five; 'Up with the Basques!' in the Basque Country and north-west Spain; 'nothing doing' in western Punjab. See Morris (1997:275).

Figure 2.5: Maëster, *Soeur Marie-Thérèse des Batignolles* – Tome 4, 1994, p. 8

panel from a *Le petit Spirou* story, a man has a pee standing up on a pan and the text in the first caption comments that he enjoys himself pretending to be a "lance d'incendie" (a "fire hose"); the onomatopoeia in the drawing (*pin pon*) is meant to represent the sound of a fire engine. The three messages interact with each other to generate humour. The Italian translation, in which the onomatopoeia is not translated, fails to engage the reader in the trilogue, thus creating a comprehension gap.

Figure 2.6a: Tome et Janry, *Le petit Spirou*, 1994, p. 4

Figure 2.6b: Tome and Janry, *Il piccolo Spirù*, 1997, p. 4

The 'conversational interplay' can take place not only within a panel but also across panels. Paratextual inscriptions may enter into an intertextual relationship with the text in the balloons in different panels and across different pages. For example, the word *Charité* (literally, charity) is used in this way in Maëster's *Soeur Marie-Thérèse des Batignolles* (Figure 2.7). A man begs for money in the Paris underground and asks for "charité", then two panels later he shouts the word to a nun, who punches him and says she does not want to give money because "on est pas encore arrivé à "la charité"" (lit. "We haven't got to "charity", yet"). Finally a sign shows that *charité* is the name of an underground station in Paris, *La Charité*. The interplay between these different loci of translation may pose a serious challenge to the translator in terms of maintaining intertextual coherence.

Figure 2.7: Maëster, *Soeur Marie-Thérèse des Batignolles* – Tome 3, 1992, p. 8-9

More examples could be provided to illustrate other forms of interplay, but my point here is only to stress the relevance of the issue for the translator, who has to struggle not only with linguistic features, but also with all the visual language and its complex interplay with the verbal messages. The language of comics can be extremely stimulating not only for authors who want to explore its richness and creativity, as for example illustrated by the experimental work of the Oubapo project,[9] but also for translators.

5. Conclusion

Translating comics can be a challenging and stimulating experience. The translator is required to achieve harmony and coherence between the iconic message and the verbal message, paying attention both to the interconnections between pictures and text and those between the various loci of translation. At times the iconic language parades its origins so stridently that the translator is warned off the option of cultural adaptation. Rather than a question of constraint or 'tyranny' of the picture, this is an expression of the meaning-making function of the visual message. The choice of translation strategy has immediate repercussions both on the paratext and on how, and whether, to translate proper nouns, onomatopoeia and cultural allusions.

By way of conclusion, I would like to welcome the translator of comics as a semiotic investigator faced with a multimodal text with two meaning-making resources rather than with a text constrained by the pictures. And I would suggest that Eisner's thought about reading comics as "an act of both aesthetic perception and intellectual pursuit" (1985:8) could be extended to translating comics.

References

Primary Sources
Altan, Francesco Tullio (2003 [1976]) *Colombo*, Roma: La Repubblica-Panini Comics.
Baru (1995) *L'autoroute du soleil*, Tokyo: Kodansha [Italian translation by Anastasia Casoni, *L'autoroute du soleil*, Roma: La Repubblica-Coconino Press, 2006].
Cabanes, Max (1994) *Gli anni giovani*, 1a puntata, *Blue*, anno IV, n°36.
Goscinny, René and Albert Uderzo (1969) *Astérix en Hispanie*, Paris: Hachette.
Maëster (1992) *Soeur Marie-Thérèse des Batignolles*, "Dieu vous le rendra", Paris: Fluide Glacial.
Maëster (1994) *Soeur Marie-Thérèse des Batignolles*, "Sur la terre comme au ciel", Paris: Fluide Glacial.
Margerin, Frank (1981) *Quando l'amore bussa alla porta*, Metal Hurlant 1, March 1981.
Morris (1986) *Lucky Luke*, Les cousins Dalton, Belgique: Dupuis.
Pratt, Ugo (1984) *Corto Maltese, Conversation mondaine à Moululhe*, Paris: Casterman.
Satrapi, Marjane (2000-2003) *Persépolis*, Paris: L'association [Italian translation by Cristina Spar-agana and Gianluigi Gasparini, *Persepolis*, Roma: La Repubblica-Panini Comics, 2005].
Tome et Janry (1994) *Le petit Spirou*, "Merci Qui?", Dupuis [Italian translation by Luca Basenghi, *Il piccolo Spirù*: "Grazie di che?", Scandiano: Edizioni Bande Dessinée, 1997].
Tronchet (1993) *Jean-Claude Tergal présente ses pires amis*, Tome 3 Paris: Fluide Glacial [Ital-ian translation: "Domenico Tergazzi presenta i suoi peggiori amici", *Totem Comic*, n° 105, November 1992].
------ (1994) *Au bonheur des drames*, Tome 4, Paris: L'écho des Savanes/Albin Michel [Italian translation: "La famiglia Scalogni", *Totem Comic*, n°119, June 1993].
Zidrou et Fournier (2000) *Les Crannibales : l'aile ou la cuisse*, Belgique: Dupuis.

---

[9] *Oubapo, Ouvroir de Bande Dessinée Potentielle*, a clear reference to the more famous OULIPO. Since 1997, four issues of the Oubapo have been published by L'association in Paris.

Secondary Sources

Baker, Mona (ed.) (1998) *Encyclopaedia of Translation Studies*, London & New York: Routledge.
Baldry, Anthony and Paul J. Thibault (2006) *Multimodal Transcription and Text Analysis*, London: Equinox.
Barthes, Roland (1982) 'Rhétorique de l'image', in *L'obvis et l'obtus*, Paris: Seuil.
Berman, Antoine (1995*) Pour une critique des traductions: John Donne*, Paris: Gallimard.
Cary, Edmond (1986) *Comment faut-il traduire?*, Lille: Presses Universitaires de Lille.
Celotti, Nadine (1997) 'Langue et images en présence: des espaces langagiers pluriels comme moment de réflexion pour la traductologie contemporaine', in *L'histoire et les théories de la traduction*, Berne et Genève: ASTTI et ETI, 487-503.
------ (2000) 'Méditer sur la traduction des bandes dessinées: une perspective de sémiologie parallèle', *Rivista Internazionale di Tecnica della Traduzione* 5:41-61.
D'Arcangelo, Adele and Federico Zanettin (2004) 'Dylan Dog Goes to the USA: A North-American Translation of an Italian Comic Book Series', *Across Languages and Cultures* 5(2):187-210.
Ducrot, Oswald (1991) *Dire et ne pas dire : principes de sémantique linguistique*, 3rd ed. corrigée et augmentée, Paris: Hermann.
Eco, Umberto (1998) 'Umberto Eco e Tiziano Sclavi. Un dialogo', in Alberto Ostini (ed.) *Dylan Dog. Indocili sentimenti, arcane paure,* Milano: Eudisis Edizioni, 13-32.
------ and Siri Nergaard (1998) 'Semiotic approaches', in Mona Baker (ed.) *Encyclopaedia of Translation Studies*, London & New York: Routledge, 218-222.
Eisner, Will (1985) *Comics and sequential art*, Tamarac, Florida: Poorhouse Press.
Genette, Gérard (1987) *Seuils*, Paris: Seuil.
Groensteen, Thierry (1999) *Système de la bande dessinée*, Paris: PUF.
Grun, Maria and Cay Dollerup (2003) "Loss' and 'gain' in comics', *Perspectives: Studies in Translatology* 11 (3):197-216.
Harvey, Keith (1998) 'Compensation', in Mona Baker (ed.) *Encyclopaedia of Translation Studies*, London & New York: Routledge, 37-40.
Kaindl, Klaus (1999) 'Thump, Whizz, Poom: A Framework for the Study of Comics under Translation', *Target* 11(2):263-288.
------ (2004) 'Multimodality in the translation of humour in comics', in Eija Ventola, Charles Cassily and Martin Kaltenbacher (eds) *Perspectives on Multimodality*, Amsterdam: John Benjamins, 173-192.
Margarito, Maria Grazia (2005) 'En accompagnement d'images... d'autres images parfois (notes sur des apartés de la BD)', *Ela* 138(avril-juin):243-255.
McCloud, Scott (1993) *Understanding Comics. The invisible Art*, Northampton, MA: Tundra.
------ (2000) *Reinventing Comics*, New York: Paradox Press.
Morris, Desmond (1997) *Le langage des gestes*, Paris: Marabout [French translation of *Body Talk*, London: Jonathan Cape, 1994].
Peeters Benoît (1993) *La bande dessinée*, Paris: Flammarion.
------ (1998) *Case, Planche, Récit*, Paris: Casterman.
Pomier, Frédéric (2005) *Comment lire la bande dessinée*, Paris: Klincksieck.
Pottier, Bernard (1992) *Sémantique générale*, Paris: Presses Universitaires de France.
Rabádan, Rosa (1991) *Equivalencia y traducción*, León: Universidad de León.
Reiss, Katharina (1971) *Möglichkeiten und Grenzen der Übersetzungskritik. Kategorien und Kriterien für eine sachgerechte Beurteilung von Übersetzungen*, Munich: Max Hüber.
Reiss, Katharina and Hans Vermeer (1984) *Grundlegung einer allgemeinen Translationstheoris*, Tubingen: Neimeyer.

Rota, Valerio (2001) *Nuvole migranti. Viaggio nel fumetto tradotto*, Mottola: Lilliput.

------ (2004) *La marca dello straniero*, Mottola: Lilliput.

Shuttleworth, Mark and Moira Cowie (1997) *Dictionary of translation studies*, Manchester: St. Jerome.

Tisseron, Serge (2000) *Psychanalyse de la bande dessinée*, Paris: Flammarion.

Yuste Frías, José (1998) 'El Pulgar Levantado: un buen ejemplo de la influencia del contexto cultural en la interpretación y traducción de un gesto simbólico', in F. Félix Fernández and E. Ortega Arjonilla (eds) *II Estudios sobre Traducción e Interpretación*, Málaga: Universidad de Málaga y Diputación Provincial de Málaga, Vol. I, 411-418.

------ (2006) 'La pareja texto/imagen en la traducción de libros infantiles', in Ana Luna Alonso and Silvia Montero Küpper (eds) *Tradución e Politica editorial de Literatura infantil e xuvenil*, Vigo: Servizio de Publicacións da Universidade de Vigo, 267-276.

Zanettin, Federico (1998) 'I fumetti e traduzione multimediale', *inTRAlinea* 1 (online) http://www.intralinea.it/volumes/eng_open.php?id=P156 (Accessed 20 September 2006).

3   Translating Manga[1]

HEIKE JÜNGST
University of Leipzig, Germany

The translation of manga occupies a special position within the translation of comics in general. This is due to several factors, among them the difference in style and visual language between manga and Western comics, the chequered publication history of manga in Western languages and the strong interest in (and influence on) manga translations exerted by fan groups. Translating manga confronts the translator with decisions about the reading direction, the question of whether to leave, to imitate or to translate onomatopoeia and the question of if and where to insert footnotes. Some of these decisions involve the use of the Japanese alphabets in an otherwise translated text, and the unique visual language of manga makes footnotes a more natural decision than they would be in translations from one Western language into another. The history of manga translation over the past years shows how translation strategies moved from adapting texts so that they would fit into the target cultures' existing markets for comics to special translation strategies reserved for manga, which preserve the cultural specificity of the texts.

Manga, that is Japanese comics, have become the largest segment of translated comics in the Western world. For instance, whereas the German comics market was dominated by translations from English and French until the 1990s, translations from Japanese have taken priority over translations from all other languages since then.

This article will take a historical outlook at how the idea of what constitutes a good manga translation has changed over the past decades. These changes will be demonstrated by analyzing the choice of titles that were actually translated over the years, with a special focus on the early years of manga translation, and the strategies used in translating the text and adapting (or not adapting) the pictures. There will be a focus on fan groups and their ideas of proper manga translation and a mention of manga offspins such as pseudo-manga and manga competitions. These topics are interesting because in contrast to readers of other texts, manga fans are highly critical of the translations they read, no matter whether they speak Japanese or not. Manga do of course present the translator with all the problems comics translation in general generates, plus some extras that are due to the complex semiotic structure we find in many manga.

In order to classify the changes which happened to manga translation over the years, Nida's distinction between formal equivalence and dynamic equivalence may prove useful. Some of the most interesting changes in manga translation have happened on the scale between these two kinds of equivalence. According to Nida (1964:159):

---

[1] This article is an extended and updated version of Jüngst (2004).

> Formal equivalence focuses attention on the message itself, in both form and content … A gloss translation of this type is designed to permit the reader to identify himself as fully as possible with a person in the source-language context, and to understand as much as he can of the customs, manner of thought, and means of expression.
>
> A translation of dynamic equivalence aims at complete naturalness of expression, and tries to relate the receptor to modes of behavior relevant within the context of his own culture; it does not insist that he understand the cultural patterns of the source-language context in order to comprehend the message.

That is, in a 'retrospective' translation the target text mirrors all the properties of the source text (formal equivalence); in a 'prospective' translation the target text is designed in such a way that it fulfils the intended communicative function for the target culture (dynamic equivalence) (Nord 1998:142). Nida himself concludes these definitions by saying that "between the two poles of translating … there are a number of intervening grades" (1964:160).

Although Nida refers to verbal text, his definition can be applied to the analysis of pictures in translation as well. The strategies applied to verbal text and pictures may differ in the translation of one and the same manga, as will be demonstrated below. One of the basic decisions involved here is the question whether or not the pictures and the reading direction should be reversed ('flipped') in the translated version.

The techniques used for manga translation have changed over the years. There is a constant, albeit gradual movement from dynamic to more formal equivalence. It can be seen in the treatment of the pictures, the onomatopoeia, and sometimes the verbal text. The examples below, starting with the first manga ever translated into German, will serve to demonstrate this change and to explain the connection between the changes in translation techniques and the rising popularity of manga in the West. Although many of the observations pertain mainly to Germany (with the exception of *Hadashi no Gen*, where I have included ample information about the translation into English),[2] many social and semiotic factors dealt with in this article are relevant for the translation of manga across the Western world. Moreover, there will be frequent mention of anime, Japanese animated films, whose fate is closely linked to that of manga.

1. Historical Overview

Although there are efforts to trace the existence of manga back to historical Japanese drawings, these efforts are not more convincing than comparable European theories which state that cave paintings are in fact early comics. Manga are a relatively young genre, a genre of the twentieth century, and they only really began to enjoy their present

---

[2] I would like to thank Leonard Rifas, one of the American initiators of the project, without whose help and generosity I could never have located the information about Project Gen.

status after World War II (Schodt 1986, Berndt 1995). Today, manga are extremely popular; the 2004 sales volume was 254.9 billion yen.[3] They are highly specialized as far as target groups are concerned: We find manga for all age groups and almost all special interest groups. In contrast to Western comics, which seem to appeal mainly to male readers (Lecarne 2000:20), manga also cater to the needs and wishes of a female readership. Manga are therefore not a target-group restricted phenomenon.[4]

It is important to note that not every European or American publisher of comics was automatically interested in allowing manga into their market. They had their own artists and did not want to share the market with newcomers. In the 1950s and 1960s, *Jungle taitei* (*Kimba the White Lion*) by Osamu Tezuka was the first anime, Japanese animated cartoons, to appear in the US and France.[5] Whereas manga began to be important in the US in the late 1980s, it took them several years longer to find big audiences in Germany, and whereas *Kozure ōkami* (*Lone Wolf and Cub*) by Gōseki Kojima and Kazuo Koike enjoyed an enormous success in the US from 1987 on, it was not translated into German until 2003 (Bouissou 2000:4-7).

In Germany, manga made their entrance through several backdoors. There were animation co-productions between Japanese and German TV stations in the early 1970s, several years before the first manga were actually translated into either English or German. In 1972/73, Germany and Japan realized their first anime co-production, based on the *Wickie* books by the Swedish author Runer Jonsson (Dodker-Tobler 1986:250). The series was successful, although some people claimed that its artistic quality was poor, and it was followed by several German-Japanese co-productions such as the immensely popular animated version of the Swiss children's classic *Heidi* (*Arupusu no shōjo Haiji*). Comic books accompanying it were drawn by German artists in Germany (Cuypers 1986:84), a custom which prevailed also in France (Bouissou 2000:5).

This shows that the rules for anime were slightly different from those for manga. The first manga to reach the West was Keiji Nakazawa's *Hadashi no Gen* (1971; first translated editions early 1980s, and a work of art meant for an audience who would not watch children's anime). Until 1995, manga were a kind of literature only the 'initiated' would read, that is adult comic readers who were looking for something new and interesting. The term 'manga' was unrecognizable to anyone except people who actually spoke Japanese or those who were exceptionally avid comic readers. A comic reader interviewed in Germany in 1993 still considered it necessary to explain to the reporter what manga were and what they were like (Sonnenschein 1993:70). Up to then, many

---

[3] This figure sounds enormous, but in fact manga sales in Japan have dropped over the past years. This is not a sign of decreasing popularity but rather of the increasing popularity of new-used bookstores where readers can buy manga cheaper only days after they go on sale (anon. 2005).
[4] The division is not so much between manga readers and those who do not read manga but between normal manga readers and those who form part of fan cultures. These so-called **otaku** are not considered the norm.
[5] *Kimba* was joined later by the little robot *Tetsuwan atomu*, renamed Astro and redesigned for compliance with the Comics Code for an American audience (Fujishima 154, quoted in Bouissou 2000:4). And whereas some anime were popular in the Roman part of Europe (see the list in Bouissou 2000:5), they did not yet reach Germany.

of the manga that were actually published were published by small presses that only comics fans would know (Phillipps 1996:193). In 1995, the interest of these specialists culminated in the publication of an article on manga in the German comics fan and research publication *Comixene*. In this article, Joachim Kaps, who then worked for the German comics publisher Carlsen, speaks of a dozen or so manga available in German (Kaps 1995:9). Some ventured so far as to speak of a manga boom (which looks strange after the real boom manga had some years later), whereas others classified the interest in manga as a fad which would soon pass.

Today, the growing global market for manga is what makes manga publishing worthwhile in Japan (anon. 2005). In 2004, the sales turnover of the German publisher Carlsen was 27.1 million Euro, with 50% comics and 70% of the comics turnover manga (Wahl 2005).

1.1 *Hadashi no Gen*

Whereas the animated TV series in German-Japanese co-production were addressed at children, the first manga translated into English,[6] and also the first manga translated into German, was considered a manga for grown-ups, at least in Germany. *Hadashi no Gen* by Keiji Nakazawa is an eyewitness account of the Hiroshima bombing. Nakazawa first wrote a short version which appeared as *Ore wa mita* (*I saw it*) in the Japanese boy's weekly *Shonen Jump* in 1972. Nakazawa was then encouraged to write a long version, which appeared in *Shonen Jump* from 1973 to 1975 (*I saw it*, inside back cover).

Nakazawa's books on *Gen* were meant for Japanese children but did not only appeal to young readers. They were discovered by no-nukes and peace movements in the West in the late 1970s and early 1980s. One of the translators of the English version, Leonard Rifas, himself an author and publisher of educational comics, wrote an account on how *Gen* came to be translated (Rifas 2004:139; emphasis in original):

> My motivation in republishing Nakazawa's manga was partly to encourage opposition to nuclear weapons, but I published Nakazawa's work *in comic book format* primarily to advance my agenda of promoting comic books as a powerful medium for educational and political-organizing projects.

The translation history of *Gen* both into English and into German is complex. The English versions started with translations published by Rifas' own one-man company EduComics, but were later taken over by publishers such as Penguin Books and Last Gasp (Rifas 2004). This means that *Gen* transcended the sphere of comic book publishers. However, the first step was translation by a group of interested volunteers called Project Gen, a process which Rifas describes as an expression of the "globalization from below"-phenomenon.[7]

---

[6] There was probably an earlier manga translation available in the US, as Leonardo da Sá writes in the Comics Scholars list, 12 December 2003 (Rifas 2004).
[7] Rifas here refers to the term coined by Brecher, Costello and Smith in *Globalization from Below: The Power of Solidarity* (Rifas 2004).

Rifas describes how he first learned about *Hadashi no Gen* and asked Project Gen in Tokyo for permission to republish the book in English, and in the process became the "fourth member" of the group.[8] However, as *Hadashi no Gen* is a very long manga, Rifas then decided to start by publishing *Ore wa mita* (Rifas 2004:141):

> After publishing two issues of *Gen of Hiroshima*, serializing the first 104 pages of the *Barefoot Gen* story, I finally learned that Nakazawa had drawn an earlier work, *Ore wa mita*, in 1972, which told a complete, unfictionalized, autobiographical story of the bombing in comics format, and which was short enough to republish in one issue. At that point I dropped the serialization of *Hadashi no Gen*, and took on the very ambitious project of publishing Nakazawa's *Ore wa mita* as *I SAW IT* in full-color, American comic book format.

Meanwhile, in Germany, *Hadashi no Gen* was published by Rowohlt. Rowohlt is one of the leading publishing houses in Germany, normally associated with the German editions of Sartre and Camus and also with political publications. *Gen* appeared in one of Rowohlt's paperback imprints, *rororo aktuell*,[9] reserved for political pamphlets, often written by members of the Peace Movement or of Greenpeace. This publication decision singled out *Hadashi no Gen* from all the other comics Rowohlt published, in fact from all the comics published in Germany up to then. The publishers did not call *Barfuß durch Hiroshima* a comic, but a "Bildergeschichte gegen den Krieg", a "picture story against the war", thus avoiding associations with popular comic series such as *Superman* or *Mickey Mouse*. The choice of the imprint also meant that children would not buy the book (or that grown-ups would not buy the book for children). Thus, the target group changed.[10]

The publication decision rested on the fact that *Hadashi no Gen* is an eye-witness report of the Hiroshima bombing; an interest in using the comics format as such for educational purposes as we find it with Rifas did not play a role here. In his preface to the German edition, one of the translators, Hans Kirchmann, criticizes Japan for its culture of obedience and warns Germany against following the Japanese model (Nakazawa 1982, n. pag.). This must be seen in the context of the early 1980s, when Japan's enormous economic success frightened Europe, as well as the German 1968 student revolt tradition of disobedience. The artistic quality or the 'otherness', the 'Japaneseness' of the manga, did not play a role in the publication decision. Kirchmann almost apologizes for the fact that German readers might find the pictures strange (n. pag.). The combination of cute pictures and a truly horrible story, which is so typical of many manga, was new to German readers.

The violence depicted in *Gen* was something which also worried Rifas. He entered

---

[8] Between 1978 and 1979, Project Gen published English editions of the first two volumes of *Hadashi no Gen*. The print runs were extremely small, 8,000 copies for the first volume and 5,000 copies for the second volume (Rifas 2004).

[9] This is interesting insofar as Rowohlt also published paperbacks by critical German cartoonists and comics authors who were connected to the 1968 student revolt, namely Marie Marcks and Chlodwig Poth. However, their books appeared in a special imprint devoted to cartoons.

[10] Rifas, too, cautioned the readers against giving the book to children (Rifas 2004).

into correspondence with Fredric Wertham, a researcher interested in violence in comic books who had written the enormously influential *Seduction of the Innocent*, a book that warns against exposing children to violence in comic books. Wertham replied to Rifas that he did not object to depictions of violence "with a clearly stated purpose of being against it" (Rifas 2004:142), but he did not like the finished book (Rifas 2004).

The German translation is "from the English and Japanese by Hans Kirchmann and Kumiko Yasui" (my translation). The book reads front to back, which means that the pictures had to be rearranged ('flipped') as they originally followed the Japanese back-to-front and right-to-left reading direction. Onomatopoeia is in German. However, the slogans on political banners remain in their mostly Sino-Japanese (**kanji**) shape throughout the book and are explained in footnotes. Otherwise, no changes have been made. The English edition used is that of Project Gen.

Rifas, on the other hand, made other adaptations (2004:145):

> ... flipping Japanese manga art left-to-right, reshaping the dialogue balloons for horizontal text, and relettering the pages was expensive and time-consuming. In the case of Nakazawa's work I had also made the expensive (and controversial) decision to add shading screens to the story to make it look more familiar to American comics fans, who were used to either four-color comics, or black and white comics with a full range of gray tones.

Still, *Hadashi no Gen* was no commercial success and did not reach beyond a certain readership. Bouissou traces what he calls "the failure of *Barefoot Gen*" back to a variety of reasons (2000:7):[11]

> The memories of an A-bomb survivor were no comic material in the eyes of Westerner [sic!], for whom fantazy [sic!] is what the comics are all about. Also, the A-bomb experience, which lies at the core of the postwar collective psyche in Japan and earned Gen a tremendous success at home, was not shared by the Western audience. Furthermore, Nakazawa's narrative relies upon a grossly exaggerated [sic!] – even grotesque – graphical expression of feelings and emotion. This technique is typical of many manga, but the Western audience is not accustomed to it, and deemed it out of place in such a tragic story.

However, the authors of the German preface noticed these problems too, and found that the readers could overcome them. Twenty years later, *Hadashi no Gen* finally reached a larger audience with the newly translated four-volume edition in German which has profited from the general interest in manga. The new translation is generally regarded as far superior to the 1982 translation (Fiedler, forthcoming) and is much better where the visual quality is concerned. It uses machine lettering, which may have to do with the serious aspect of the story as it does not remind German readers too much of entertaining comics they may have read.

---

[11] *Hadashi no Gen* was also not particularly successful in France (1983 and 1990) and in England (1989, despite being published by a mainstream publisher, Penguin Books) (Bouissou 2000:6).

1.2 Nihon Keizai Nyūmon

The next manga to reach Germany was, again, a text for grown-ups. *Nihon Keizai Nyūmon* by Ishinomori Shotarō is an uncommon but interesting choice for a translation. As the titles *Japan GmbH* (German) or *Japan Inc.* (English) show, it is a comic that deals with questions from business and economics. In Germany, the book was published in 1989 by Rentrop, a publishing house which specializes in these fields, not by a comics publisher. *Nihon Keizai Nyūmon*, despite its artistic and informational merits, was not designed to be a long-seller. The topic is the Japanese economy in the 1980s, and the interest the comic arouses today is merely historical. There are, however, some interesting translation decisions that can be observed in *Nihon Keizai Nyūmon*: The pictures have been flipped, but the onomatopoeia in katakana has been flipped with the pictures, so that they cannot be read even by those who can read Japanese (Berndt 1995:36). In fact, they are reduced to their aesthetic status, and of course the phenomenon of all characters being left-handed is manifest here too (examples from other manga can be found in Kaindl 1999b). The book is not available anymore.

1.3 Genji Monogatari

Probably one of the strangest publication histories of manga in Germany is connected with *Genji Monogatari*, Yamato Waki's manga version of the classical eleventh-century Japanese novel.[12] The editor, Charlotte Olderdissen, actually founded Okawa for the sole purpose of publishing a German version of this manga. She was not particularly interested in manga as such but found that *Genji Monogatari* stood out from all the other manga and merited translation (Phillipps 1996:205). Unfortunately, the project never extended beyond the first volume, Charlotte Olderdissen has died in the meantime and the publishing house does not exist anymore.

The idea of 'Japaneseness', of a 'foreign' text, was an important factor when it came to choosing translation strategies. The *Genji Monogatari* was originally written by Murasaki Shikibu, a Japanese lady at the court of the emperor. It is one of the classical texts of Japanese literature, which means that the Japanese target group for the manga, unlike the German target group, would know the original text (Phillipps 1996:205). In order to help the German readers understand what was going on in the condensed text of the manga, the translators, Keiko Sato and Hedi Hahn, supplemented the German edition with numerous footnotes. The onomatopoeia remained in the Japanese katakana alphabet (see below) and was also explained in footnotes. Other footnotes deal with culture-specific features such as ranks at the Court of the Emperor or with artistic conventions the reader might not recognize. Phillipps criticizes the inconsistencies of this method (1996:206), but readers who chose to buy this manga will actually have been interested in this kind of additional information. *Genji Monogatari* has a high-brow feel

---

[12] The manga was published in Germany in 1992 by Okawa Verlag (Berndt 1995:12, Phillipps 1996:204-207) and has not been reissued since.

to it. The circulation was small, and the interested readership was probably a history of art readership rather than a comics readership.

1.4 *Akira*

Whereas the translations of *Hadashi no Gen*, *Genji Monogatari* and *Nihon Keizai Nyūmon* were addressed at highly specific target groups outside the comics fan scene, *Akira* was the first manga translated into German that was deliberately addressed at manga readers. As with the translation of *Hadashi no Gen*, the translation of Katsuhiro Ōtomo's *Akira* was an international phenomenon, although both comics were translated for a small and highly specialized audience of comics fans (Helbling 2001).[13]

The first volumes of the German version were published in 1991 by Carlsen, at the same time as the French version (1991-1997), three years after the American version (starting in 1988) and ten years after the comic had been published in Japan.[14] They failed to create a boom reaching beyond the comics scene, but *Akira* turned into a long-seller. In Germany, the copies of the 1991 edition (and reprints) were available well into 2001. Later German editions of *Akira* are different in style, but on the whole *Akira* must be seen as an international success rather than as a home success (Schilling 1997:174, quoted in Bouissou 2000).

Bouissou describes how *Akira* is constructed in a way which makes it suitable for global distribution (Bouissou 2000, passim). In fact, *Akira* is not as 'foreign' as either *Hadashi no Gen* or *Genji Monogatari*. It is highly dynamic, more so than many European or American series, but there is no clash between violent action and cute characters (as in *Hadashi no Gen*) and the semiotic features can be interpreted without outside help (unlike *Genji Monogatari*). But there are influences which go beyond that, such as the friendship between Ōtomo and the French comics artist Moebius, and Ōtomo himself says that he has been influenced by *Star Wars* (Bouissou 2000:21). The style is somewhere in-between:

> Ōtomo himself is very internationally minded … He drew some of the fourteen cover-pages for the hardbound editions along the aesthetical criterions of European BD, some others according to American taste, and some in a more Japanese style (Akira, vol. 14 [French edition]). (Bouissou 2000:22)

> *Akira* is an incredible patchwork of Western and Japanese pop culture images, peppered with references to the contemporary history – from Hiroshima to UN Peace Keeping … Nevertheless, *Akira* retains a strongly "exotic" flavour, which explains his success abroad. (Bouissou 2000:26)

---

[13] Bouissou (2000:1) comments that the French readership the publishers had in mind "targeted well-educated high-income urbanites at a time when manga were still considered cheap stuff for children or semi-illiterate teenagers", and this also applies to readerships elsewhere in the West. Note the difference that manga were not considered anything of that kind in Germany at that time – there were virtually no manga for children, all the manga translated up to Akira were manga for adults. Still, the target group for Akira translations was the same in all three countries.
[14] There were Spanish and Italian editions in 1991 too, and the comic was translated into several more languages (Bouissou 2000:22).

The 1991 German version of *Akira* uses the American version, flipped and coloured, as a basis. Using picture material not originally from Japan but from a third country later became a standard feature of manga translation. Although the colouring is seen as a breach of etiquette by today's manga purists in Europe, the colours chosen are appropriate and the colouring does not clash with the style (Rota, this volume). An example is provided by a comparison between Figure 3.1a (centre fold), the recent German version of *Akira* (sold as "original version" in German bookshops), and Figure 3.1b (centre fold), the coloured version: It is still left to right, there are English onomatopoeia, but it is now black and white.

2.   The First Successful Series

None of the manga mentioned so far changed the German comics market. Although German comics publishers like Carlsen and Ehapa never gave up on manga,[15] the real change came to Germany when the first **shōjo manga** or girl's manga appeared on the shelves. This did not happen until the mid to late 1990s. In 1995, Berndt could still rightly claim that shōjo manga did not play a role on the German market (1995:37).

The manga boom hinged on the publication plus anime on TV marketing of two series, Akira Toriyama's *Dragon Ball* and Naoko Takeuchi's *Sailor Moon*. Whereas *Dragon Ball* is an action-packed **shōnen manga**, a manga for boys, *Sailor Moon* is a shōjo manga, a manga for girls, or more precisely, a magic girl manga, where girls discover their secret second identity and have to save the world. In contrast to the manga published in Germany before, these two series are addressed at children. Most adults do not like them, and many 'serious' manga fans who like *Akira* would never touch them. *Sailor Moon* created an even more important impact than *Dragon Ball*, as comics for girls had been a rarity up to then and as the comics sector now suddenly opened to a whole new readership (Böckem and Dallach 2002).

These two series shaped the general perception of manga in Germany in the way in which *Mickey Mouse* or *Superman* shaped the general perception of comics. People who do not read manga will at least have seen these manga in bookshops or will have come across pictures from the anime versions in TV magazines. The same people will probably never have heard of *Akira* or *Hadashi no Gen*. Thus, for many Germans *Dragon Ball* and *Sailor Moon* represent the prototypical manga in both drawing style and content. The huge-eyed, long-legged girls of *Sailor Moon* constitute one prototype, the cuddly, crazy characters from *Dragon Ball* constitute the other. In the mind of the non-manga reader, both are normally mixed into a kind of supermanga-prototype.

Both series were published in Germany before the first manga monthlies featuring various series had started to appear. They were consequently published in the Japanese **tankōbon** format, a pocketbook format with approximately 200 pages per volume. Normally this is only done with series which have been successful in a monthly manga magazine, but these magazines only reached Germany much later,

---

[15] There is a German Ehapa version of *Appleseed* from 1994, as well as a few efforts to publish manga from various publishers (Kaps 1995).

in 2001. The books were in black and white, and the spines of the tankōbon formed a picture if you placed them next to each other on your bookshelf. So far, everything was very Japanese. In the late 1990s, when *Sailor Moon* enjoyed particular popularity, some episodes were also available in a classic Western comic book format (soft paper covers, 68 pages, full colour).

However, the translation techniques used differ considerably. *Sailor Moon*, which was published by Ehapa, was translated from Japanese into German via relay languages. The reading direction of all the volumes in the German edition is European standard: front to back, left to right. *Dragon Ball*, on the other hand, was translated directly from Japanese, and the reading direction remained unchanged from the Japanese original: back to front, as in the case of the *Genji Monogatari* manga.[16] According to the publisher, there were several reasons why the reading direction had not been changed. Firstly, there is the claim that this practice offers higher authenticity, a claim which is still today reprinted on the first page of every manga published by Carlsen. Secondly, the former director of the Carlsen comics section, Joachim Kaps, mentioned in an interview that various Japanese publishers demanded that the reading direction should not be changed (Kaps 2001).[17] The readership quickly made the claim of authenticity their own, and the knowledge that "real manga" have to be read back to front became insider knowledge. Only adults who did not know any better would open the manga the wrong way round. If Böckem and Dallach (2002) claim to have interviewed a girl who read a whole manga the wrong way round, this seems less than believable.

Both series enjoyed an enormous success. They all but saved the clapped-out business of comics publishing in Germany and even made the founding of new publishing businesses possible. The 18 *Sailor Moon* volumes as well as the 42 *Dragon Ball* volumes sold well. Until 2001, *Dragon Ball* sold 3 million copies in Germany (Sawatzki 2001).

3. Manga, Fan Groups and Translation Decisions

Manga has developed into a fan culture phenomenon of considerable size. Teenagers do not only read manga and watch anime. Like their Japanese counterparts, some of them take part in cosplays (events where the participants dress up as manga characters) whereas others draw fan art and participate in competitions.[18] There are also various special magazines about manga and anime.

Although there are by now numerous manga by German artists, translations from the Japanese dominate the market. Translations of manga from other languages, e.g. **Amerimanga** translated from the English, are quite rare. Korean comics, **manhwa**, are

---

[16] The first volumes of *Sailor Moon* were translated from English into German by Georg Tempel, the later volumes were translated from French into German by Fritz Walter. *Dragon Ball* was translated from Japanese into German by Junko Iwamoto-Seebeck and Jürgen Seebeck, the team who had already translated *Akira*. The publisher was Carlsen, as with *Akira*.

[17] Calculation of costs is not mentioned. Interestingly, using the Japanese reading direction is not always cheaper, as the picture material is not always imported directly from Japan, but e.g. from France, and has to be re-flipped in some rare cases (*Banzai!* 9/2005:253).

[18] The biggest of these competitions in Germany, held in connection with the Leipzig Book Fair, attracts thousands of competitors.

rapidly gaining popularity though. Manga fans are conscious of the fact that they are reading translations. Some of them learn Japanese, but as very few schools in Germany offer courses in Japanese, this is normally a private effort with a high drop-out rate. However, they expect the translations to give them something which is as much like the original as possible. The idea that there will always be losses and gains in comics translation, as expressed by Grun and Dollerup (2003), is not one these readers would be pleased with.

As mentioned before, today's German translations of manga have found their place on Nida's scale between formal and dynamic equivalence, and it is a unique place. The target group wants a basically formally equivalent translation. They want their manga to look Japanese,[19] and this extends to some linguistic as well as pictorial aspects. The reading direction of the pictures is the same as in the Japanese original, there are no added colours and no added shades. However, as will also be shown below, there can be additions to or subtractions from the pictures, although these have to do with legal prescriptions rather than with a communicative function for the target group. And, of course, the reading direction of the verbal text must be left to right.[20] When the German version of *What's Michael?* (a funny manga about a cat; the original readership are adult cat lovers) was published in European reading direction, the publisher, interviewed by an insider magazine, had to provide an explanation to what was seen as almost a breach of etiquette. The publisher had been planning to reach cat-loving audiences all over Germany, not necessarily manga readers only. When this failed, the series was published in the German manga monthly *MangaPower*, in Japanese reading direction (rl 2002c).

The verbal text is in normal German; Japanese syntax and phrasing are not imitated except in some cases where they are used in order to enhance the Japanese feeling (see below). Therefore, one could claim that the verbal text is in large parts translated in a dynamically equivalent style. Many manga are not as highly culture-specific as a first look might suggest. Many manga stories borrow from universal narratives; the target groups, teenagers in two highly industrialized, well-off countries, do not differ in every respect imaginable. There is no need to be formally equivalent in every single respect.

Absurd though it may sound, it is precisely the decision for a nearly formally equivalent translation which fulfils the intended communicative function in the target culture, something associated with the more dynamically equivalent translation above. One of the communicative functions of manga is, in fact, to make the reader look like a manga connoisseur.[21] Other communicative functions fulfilled by manga such as entertainment could be fulfilled as effectively if the pictures were flipped and thus the macro reading

---

[19] This is in accordance with what Schodt observed of manga translations: "No matter how well translated, many [manga] are still very 'Japanese' in story, visual style, and pacing" (Schodt 1996:30).

[20] Top to bottom Latin script actually works right to left too, but no one has gone that far yet.

[21] How closely the target group read their manga can be seen from a letter to the editor in the German manga monthly *Banzai!* The reader had noticed that one of the pictures was the wrong way round and had mused over a possible meaning. This provided a most interesting insight into translation practice in the world of German manga. The editor answered that the pictures came to Germany by way of France. As they had been flipped for left-to-right reading for the French audience, they had to be 're-flipped' to the original Japanese reading direction for German readers. During this process, one picture had remained unflipped, as the attentive reader had noticed.

direction reversed along with the micro reading direction of the verbal text.

Many of the processes that are typical for fan demands in manga translation can be found in **scanlation** (or scanslation) practices. Scanlation is a process by which pages from Japanese manga are scanned and then translated and presented on the Internet by manga fans. Scanlation is not legal but generally tolerated (Deppey 2005, O'Hagan 2006, and en.wikipedia.org/wiki/Scanlation). The scanlator code of honour demands that only manga that have not yet been published in the target language may be scanlated, and there are indeed publishers who tolerate scanlation as a basis for target-group research (Yang 2004). Basically, fans choose manga they want other people to read for scanlation. The practice is related to that of **fan subs**, subtitling of anime by fans. Scanlation seems to have originated in the US in the late 1990s, but again precise dates are difficult to come by. Numerous web sites in various languages give advice on how to produce a good scanlation.

4.   Aspects of Manga translation

The following aspects are typical of manga translation rather than of other kinds of comics translation. They have to do with the specific problems the language transfer poses as well as with the visuals.

4.1 Attractive Loanwords

For those who do not speak Japanese, a short description of the Japanese writing system may be helpful. Japanese uses four different kinds of writing. Firstly, there are the two Japanese syllable alphabets, **hiragana** and **katakana**. Hiragana is used mainly for structures such as verb endings, but it is the alphabet Japanese children learn first, so that books meant for young children are also printed in hiragana. Katakana, the edgier of the syllable alphabets, is used for loanwords, certain kinds of onomatopoeia and sometimes for a kind of effect which resembles the use of italics in a Roman script. Secondly, there are **kanji**, Chinese characters, of which 1945 are officially used in Japan. In books for older children, kanji are used, but they are explained in a small hiragana type called **furigana**. In books for adults, furigana are only used for kanji that are rarely used. Sometimes, Roman script is used as well, mainly for decorative purposes. Of course, kanji take up less space than Roman script would, but they cannot be printed in a very small type, as this would reduce legibility. The role these alphabets play in translation has changed over the years, as will be seen below.

One of the most interesting and actually quite entertaining problems when translating manga is the use of loanwords in Japanese. There is a tendency to use loanwords just for effect, for example because they sound beautiful or look elegant. The meaning of these loanwords is often secondary or not important at all. These loanwords do not look grotesque in a Japanese text, but they do so as soon as the text is translated into the language the loanwords come from.

English and German are the main sources for attractive loanwords. Often, these loanwords are only used to provide a catchy title. This is true of *Weiß Kreuz* ("White Cross") or *Weiß Kreuz Glühen* ("White Cross Glow"). But there is also a more interestingly motivated use of loanwords, as with the vocabulary connected with the psyche and the nervous system in *Neon Genesis Evangelion*, which is mainly in German (*Banzai!* 17/2003:99).

What happens with loanwords like these which make sense in a certain context in translation is obvious: they blend in and vanish, unless the translator uses a footnote in order to inform the reader that this particular word was German in the Japanese original. However, loanwords which are only used for their beautiful sound do not blend in and look even stranger in a text that is in their language of origin.

An interesting loanword effect can be seen in Figure 3.2, from *Xxxholic*. The "exotic feel" of the Roman letters in the Japanese version gets lost in the German version. Interestingly, this is also a manga which uses machine lettering in the speech balloon German version, probably due to the fact that this is cheaper than hand lettering, but tries to make up for this by using a variety of typefaces. However, using italics for the speech balloon text throughout must be considered non-typical.

There is a rather recent Japanese anime and manga which uses German loanwords for names and which has a preference for using loanwords in a way which sounds strange to the German ear. The German title *Meine Liebe* (My Love) is used for the original Japanese version. The country in which *Meine Liebe* takes place is called "Kuchen" (cake), one of the counts is the Count of Marmelade, one of the cities is called "Erdbeer" (strawberry). In a review of the Japanese version in a German special magazine which appeared before a German translation of the manga was available, the reviewer predicted that a German audience would burst with laughter if the names were kept in their original form (pk 2005c:54). The manga came out in January 2006 and the translators decided to keep the German words. It does sound very strange, as there is a strong element of unwanted humour.

Moreover, there is the problem of transcription. In contrast to the example above, loanwords are normally transcribed into Japanese, a task for which the katakana alphabet is used. Katakana cannot represent all the sounds from English or German, and consequently, the translated version in Roman letters can either use the original form of the loanword, or else it can use a transcript from katakana. The latter is not normally done. The series *Furūtsu Basuketto* (short: *Furuba*) is published in Germany with its title in the 'correct' English spelling *Fruits Basket* (*Daisuki* 1/2003:12). The same is true for the title of the manga *Vagabond*, which would otherwise spell *Bagabondo* (see Figure 3.4). Severe problems with the transcription of Czech words from katakana into Latin script can be witnessed in the German version of Naoki Urusawa's *Monster*: Obviously, the translator did not take the pains to check the original Czech spelling, but used a simple letter-by-letter transliteration.

However, sometimes other translation strategies are used. A very strange decision was taken in the case of the German title of Miyazaki's film *Howl's Moving Castle*. The film is based on an English children's book, and Miyazaki used the original name of one of the characters, Howl, which in Japanese would be spelled "Hauru". So far, this is not particularly problematic, as the Japanese audience know how to spell this name in Roman letters. However, the German distributor of the film, Universum Film, decided to call Howl "Hauro". They claimed that this would give a Japanese touch to the name – which does not make sense at all, as the story does not even take place in Japan (pk 2005d:11). This example not only shows how strange the treatment of loanwords in manga and anime can be; it also demonstrates how the notion of 'Japaneseness' has become the chief concern of many who work in the field and who prepare texts for German readers, to the point where the German version is more Japanese than the original.

Figure 3.2a: CLAMP, *xxxholic* 1, 2003, p. 33

Figure 3.2b: CLAMP: *xxxholic* 1, 2004, p. 33 (German translation: Claudia Peter)

4.2 *Onomatopoeia*

Onomatopoeia is part of the picture. Translating it means retouching the whole picture, a costly and time-consuming process. Therefore, onomatopoeia may simply be left in

Figure 3.3a: CLAMP: *xxxholic* 1, 2003, p. 17

their original language (Schmitt 1998:268). In many cases, the reader will be able to form an impression of the sound.

Many of the onomatopoeic sounds we find in German translations of manga are neither in German nor in Japanese (see also Phillipps 1996:196). Manga which take the English translation as a basis for a German translation normally do not replace the

English onomatopoeia, as is the case with *Akira*. Another good example of this trend is Rumiko Takahashi's *Ranma ½* where the English translation formed the basis for the German translation. English onomatopoeia seem to find more favour in Germany today than German onomatopoeia anyway. But sometimes, the reader is faced with an

Figure 3.3b: CLAMP *xxxholic* 1, 2004, p. 17 (German translation: Claudia Peter)

unmotivated mix of onomatopoeia from various languages. In the German version of Clamp's *Magic Knight Rayearth*, we find the French-looking "vroum" (1999:51), the English "flaaash" (1999:119) and the German "trippelditrapp" (1999:32). The use of this mix seems completely unmotivated.

The use of onomatopoeia in translation can be very creative. In the example in Figure 3.3, the word "nack" used in the bottom left panel of the German version seems to be an addition to the German language. "Zoosh" in the upper left panel looks English rather than German.

Japanese is a language that is particularly rich in onomatopoeia even in everyday speech (Fukuda 1993:7). Many books on manga mention onomatopoeia (e.g. Schodt 1986, Mangajin 1993:38-39), and many authors are quite fascinated by the range of possibilities the use of Japanese onomatopoeic offers. Therefore, an obvious choice is not to translate the onomatopoeia but to transcribe them. As onomatopoeia is motivated, even readers who do not speak Japanese may get an idea of the sound the particular onomatopoeia is meant to convey. The German version of Sadamoto and Gainax's *Neon Genesis Evangelion* is full of them, e.g. "klim" for spectacles falling onto the floor (1999:48) or "tada tada" for the sound of the subway (1999:58).

4.3 Use of Japanese Alphabets

At first it seems obvious that everything that is in a Japanese script, including onomatopoeia, has to be translated. Whereas most comics readers are perfectly able to decipher English onomatopoeia like those in the examples given above, Japanese onomatopoeia is in katakana. Basically, the translator is faced with three possibilities: translate the onomatopoeia, transcript the onomatopoeia or leave them as they are. We have seen examples of the first two possibilities in the analyses above.

The latter possibility does not seem to make sense at first. However, in the light of a formally equivalent translation, the look of the text may play a part, and consequently, this possibility is also sometimes chosen. Katakana look very Japanese, therefore authentic, and therefore they may please the audience. Moreover, even manga readers who gave up on learning Japanese may have got so far as to master the katakana alphabet and may feel comforted that their efforts have not been completely in vain. Some of the early translations use katakana with explanations, e.g. Waki's *Genji Monogatari*. In this case, the katakana were meant for a grown-up audience with an interest in Japanese culture.

Carlsen has published a whole group of manga addressed at a young readership, where the katakana remain unchanged as well as unexplained. All of the manga in question were written by Hayao Miyazaki, and two of them are coloured **fuirumu komikkusu** or **anime manga** where a replacement of katakana would be complicated and expensive.[22] *Spirited Away – Chihiros Reise ins Zauberland* [*Sen to Chihiro no kamikakushi*] is a manga meant for young children, as can be seen from the Japanese edition where complex kanji are explained in furigana (Miyazaki 2001b). Young German readers may either have been puzzled or become interested, or simply have accepted the use of

---

[22] These comics are made up from cells from the animated film to which speech balloons are added.

katakana for the onomatopoeia as part of the manga style.[23]

Other words printed in Japanese alphabets in *Spirited Away* are explained in footnotes, depending on their importance, e.g. the text on the goodbye card Chihiro is given by her friends (Miyazaki 2002, I:5) or the "No Entry" sign on a door (Miyazaki 2002, I:116). It is important for the reader to know that Chihiro and her friend Haku walk through a door which says "No Entry", and the text on the goodbye-card plays an important part in Chihiros rescue. Shop signs remain untranslated and simply form part of the backdrop. One page (p. 128) which appears in the German version of the film comic is completely identical to the Japanese original, except for a footnote which contains the German translation of the sign. This kind of translation decision is rare, but it is the only way to make sense of what happens as the magic Yubaba works on Chihiro's name only works in kanji.

Despite this, the decision to leave onomatopoeia in katakana and to leave them unexplained looks like a new trend in manga for older readers but cannot yet be confirmed. The German version of Inoue Takehiko's *Vagabond* (2002) has all onomatopoeia in katakana, in a beautiful calligraphic script. Leaving the onomatopoeia in katakana can therefore be a decision which adds to the aesthetic quality of the translated manga, not just to some kind of authenticity. It is interesting to see the way calligraphic script is used on the covers of the German edition (see Figures 3.4 and 3.5). On the front cover, the title is printed over the calligraphic original title, whereas on the back cover, the calligraphic style of the original is imitated. The English title is used for the German version, so that *Vagabond* (German: Vagabund) remains a loanword.

4.4 Explaining Japanese Words

As with other texts in translation, it sometimes makes sense to explain words that describe realia rather than translate them. This was done in *Genji Monogatari*, as described above.

However, there are other reasons why Japanese words might remain in their original form. Again, the clamouring for authenticity comes to mind, but of course we are also faced with a kind of exoticism. This is particularly true as those words which remain in Japanese in manga translated into German could be replaced by their German equivalent, or else could be left out, as is the case with many honorifics. However, it is honorifics which sound very Japanese to the Western ear and which are also used in all kinds of films that deal with or take place in Japan, above all the famous *-san*.

Daisuki, a German shōjo-manga magazine, uses Japanese honorifics throughout and offers explanations in footnotes when these honorifics first appear in a given episode of a series. Along with "-san" (Daisuki 1/2003:25), there is "-kun" (1/2003:26; for boys and young men), "-sensei" for a teacher (1/2003:30), and, as these are manga for girls, we find many instances of the diminutive "-chan" (1/2003:27) which girls tend to use when addressing each other.

---

[23] Joachim Kaps of Tokyopop Germany emphasizes this approach: The aesthetic quality of the katakana onomatopoeia matters (personal communication).

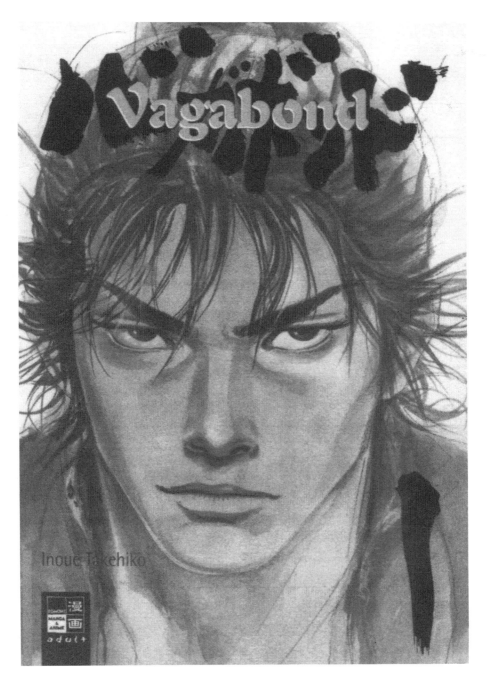

Figure 3.4: Inoue Takehiko, *Vagabond*, 2002, German Edition, Front Cover

Sometimes, whole phrases are quoted in Japanese, even though there is no reason for this translation choice other than exoticism. Kitoh's *Naru Taru* sometimes uses footnotes

Figure 3.5: Inoue Takehiko, *Vagabond*, 2002, German Edition, Back Cover

or explanations right after the Japanese expression – ("Ippon! One point for me!" My trans. ["Ippon! Punkt für mich!"] Kitoh 2002, vol. 5:42); however, expressions such as "Gochisoo-sama!", spoken by father and daughter at the dining table (Kitoh 2002, vol. 7:70), are left unexplained. Often, the words are made unambiguous by the pictures. However, this is a rather uncommon strategy. Explaining expressions by repeating them in the speech balloons takes up much space, and space is always restricted in comics translations.

4.5 Pictorial Content

Sometimes, pictorial elements of a comic are changed in translation. *Deletio*, "removal of texts or pictures" (Kaindl 1999a:277), is the most obvious and most common of these categories. It often refers to pictorial elements which might offend readers (Schmitt 1998:269) and sometimes to cultural elements the target group might not be familiar with (Schmitt 1997:644-645). Other changes include adaptations of pictures made necessary by rearranging the reading direction. Phillipps (1996:203) has the example of a clockface which shows the wrong time after flipping the picture, and such problems have become obsolete with the tendency to leave the reading direction unchanged.

In the translation of manga into German, *deletio* is, if not common, at least well-documented. It is often said that manga contain particularly violent or pornographic pictures, but this is not true for every genre of manga. Often, such manga are meant for an adult readership who can decide for themselves if they want such content. However, sometimes manga are translated for a different readership. This decision may quite simply be wrong, as with *Naru Taru* by Mohiro Kitoh. The drawings look quite cute; the heroine of the manga is a young girl called Shiina who is accompanied by a star-shaped dragon. This set-up sounds like that of any manga for children. However, *Naru Taru* is not meant for children. At the very latest from volume five, the series is dominated by violent illustrations; some of them violent and pornographic at the same time. Whereas the first volumes of the German translation were directed at a young audience, the books are marked "adult" on the spine from volume four on.[24] The blurbs of the first volumes let the reader expect a sweet and light-hearted story. Whereas the first two books have a kind of tone which seems unsuitable for children, but where it is difficult to pin down the actual problem, the later volumes have displays of bloody murder. It did not help much to try and alleviate the character of the pictures by adding underwear to cover a female character (Kaindl's category of *adiectio*) or to delete the giant hand of a monster (rl 2002b). The original picture is cruel, but the retouched picture does not make much sense.

As the publishers had originally marketed the manga for a young target group, they tried to add extra text in order to make it palatable. Volume five has a case of bullying at school. Here, the vengeance is bloody, and adding an epilogue on **ijime**, schoolyard bullying, looks helpless (Kitoh 2002, vol. 5). The epilogue contains information about bullying, including addresses of German organizations which would help the victims (a practice we normally find in educational comics). There are also explanations about the

---

[24] Prospective German buyers might not even know the word; it is not part of general German speech.

different perception of violent drawings in Germany and Japan, as if the publisher felt uneasy about the whole series. Although the German *Naru Taru* exists in this unhappy limbo, it was not discontinued; by now, all volumes have been published.

Substituting culture-specific elements in the pictures is not common in manga, no matter how foreign things may look. Susanne Phillipps lists certain pictorial symbols in manga non-Japanese readers would not be familiar with (1996:196), but these normally remain unchanged in the translated versions, and manga readers normally obtain the necessary knowledge from books, manga magazines or the Internet. As in Japonism, the different visual character is part of the attraction. Sometimes, there is a cultural mix. In the US, Koike and Kojima's *Kozure Ōkami* carries covers by American artist Frank Miller. Miller himself has written **Amerimanga** (*Ronin* appeared from 1983 onwards; Horn 1999:534), and although he is not particularly popular in Germany, the covers are also used for the German version of *Kozure Ōkami*, as is, strangely enough, the English title *Lone Wolf and Cub*.

It is very rare that pictorial elements have to be removed or exchanged because of legal rules. Still, it happened with Hiroaki Samura's *Blade of the Immortal*. The hero wears a swastika on his kimono. Printing swastikas, no matter in which direction they point, is forbidden by German law,[25] and consequently, the manga could not be distributed in Germany in its original form (Helbling 2001). The matter has been settled by now, and the swastika has been changed into a cross in the German version. Unfortunately, this might again be seen as a symbol, which now carries different associations. A swastika which appeared on a kimono sleeve in *Bronze Zetsuai* was changed into an abstract symbol in the German translation.

4.6 Material Appearance

Japanese manga have a material appearance which is different from that of their Western counterparts. Manga magazines, featuring several series, can have the size of a telephone book; manga magazines appearing in Germany are much slimmer. Apart from the fuirumu komikkusu, manga are printed in black and white on cheap paper. Fuirumu komikkusu are printed on heavy, glossy white paper in Japan (Loveday and Chiba 1986:159), and the same paper quality is used for the German translations (e.g. *Mononoke*, *Spirited Away*).

German publishers have come to imitate the format, although not necessarily the paper. Whereas the first edition of *Akira* had **bande dessinée** size and looks, the new edition (same length, but in only six volumes) looks decidedly more Japanese. It is telephone-book size, the quality of the paper is not quite as good as that of the first edition, and the print is black and white.

A manga which retains much of the original visual aspect is Hayao Miyazaki's *Nausicaä* (Miyazaki 2001). It is one of the manga where the onomatopoeia has remained in katakana. Moreover, the material appearance is untypical for a comic printed in Germany. The paper is rough and grayish. The Japanese custom of sometimes using cheap, coloured

---

[25] The fact that in this case the swastika appears in a Buddhist context also does not matter.

paper for manga (Loveday and Chiba 1986:159) has not caught on in Germany. So far, the only manga printed on coloured paper is Yoshida's *Banana Fish* (2003), and in this case the paper is of good quality. The colour of the paper, yellow, refers to the title of the manga.

In 2001 Carlsen and Egmont started the manga magazines *Banzai!*, followed by *MangaPower* early in 2002.[26] The magazines imitate the Japanese format, with episodes from several series by several authors. Both magazines are back-to-front, including verbal text pages written in German by German authors, where the right page has to be read before the left page. Ersatz-authenticity actually stops at one point: the spines of *Banzai!* (like those of some tankōbon series) form a picture if you have not missed an issue and if you put them in a row on the shelf. However, the books in this row must be arranged left to right, with number one at the utmost left. Japanese readers would rather arrange their books right to left, as can be seen from Japanese publishers' catalogues.

A definite change takes place with the text in the speech balloons. It is normally hand-lettered in the German versions, as it would be in a French or American comic. Japanese manga use machine type. Hand lettering would be too difficult to read; machine type offers better reading in smaller typefaces.

In summary, it can be said that strategies of dynamic equivalence have been and are being replaced by strategies feigning authenticity and formal equivalence. This is true for every aspect of manga translation. The ideal of formal equivalence, however, can never be reached completely: The very different visual aspect of Japanese and Roman alphabets and the fact that the Roman verbal text will always run counter to the reading direction of the flipped pictures makes this impossible.

5. Imitation, Pseudomanga and Cultural Exchange

With the popularity of manga came the interest of fans to draw their own manga. Manga by non-Japanese artists are often termed **pseudomanga**, or, in accordance with the artist's provenance, Amerimanga or Euromanga. Becoming a **mangaka**, a manga artist, has become a job today's German children dream of, and thousands of amateur mangaka try their luck in one of the big manga competitions. Japan has partly replaced the US as a source for popular culture – interesting reflections on this can be found in Briese (2002) and in Schodt (1996:31). The first German pseudomanga appeared in 2001, and the number of artists who draw pseudomanga has increased dramatically. German pseudomanga always run back to front. "Japanese reading direction" is one of the prerequisites if you want to hand in a manga, e.g. at the *Manga Talente* competition. An interesting use of pseudomanga were the German advertisements for the Japanese car brand Mazda in 2001, executed by the German pseudomanga artist Sascha Nils Marx in purest Japanese manga style (they were exhibited at the Frankfurt Book Fair 2001 and ran in a number of magazines in the same year).[27] German efforts to produce pseudomanga are, as can

---

[26] *Banzai!* was discontinued in December 2005, after fifty issues.
[27] On the other hand, Jürgen Seebeck's *Bloody Circus* is difficult to classify as a pseudomanga. The author wrote

be seen, much later than Amerimanga efforts such as Ben Dunn's *Ninja High School* (on these see Schodt 1996:326-328). Interestingly, many Germans who draw pseudomanga are of Asian origin.

Manga have also sparked off an interest in the Japanese language and culture as such. The manga *Hikaru no go* (serialized in *Banzai!*) created an interest in the game of go. In fact, there has been a huge go-playing section at the Leipzig book fair for the past two years, close to the manga and comics stalls. In letters to the editor directed at manga magazines, Japanese loanwords mark the author as insider. *Konnichiwa* or *ohayō* (good morning) have become the standard greetings. Manga readers call themselves **otaku**, although the word has the negative connotation of being too much of a fan in Japanese.

6. Conclusion

The translation of manga into German has a short but already chequered history. We find all kinds of strategies between almost pure formal equivalence and dynamic equivalence. Today, there is a clear preference for an attempt at formal equivalence. This has to do with the readership manga have managed to find, a readership who like their manga to look as 'Japanese' as possible. This idea of 'Japaneseness' concentrates on the visual appearance, as many readers will not be able to judge the formal equivalence quality of the translated verbal text. This preference may lead to strange translation decisions where the translation tries to look more Japanese than the original. Strategies such as flipping the pictures in order to provide easier left-to-right reading or colouring the pictures in order to make them look more Western are not used anymore today. At the same time, the rejection of these strategies made manga translation quicker, easier and cheaper. This has also contributed to the rise of manga. From a tiny segment of comics translation, the translation of manga has in fact become its main branch.

However, changes may well be afoot. Manga have been joined by their Korean counterpart, **manhwa**. In the last few years, manhwa have slowly become as acceptable to manga readers as manga themselves. Manhwa come in the same styles and genres as manga. However, Korean is written from left to right, which means that manhwa have European reading direction. In contrast to the idea of 'Japaneseness' connected with manga and the interest in the Japanese language and culture which derived from it, there has so far not been a comparable movement concerning the Korean language and culture. Moreover, **manhua** from Taiwan have also found their readership. No comics addict will have the time to learn three languages, which are incidentally not even related.

As Joachim Kaps from Tokyopop Germany states, the idea of manga as specifically Japanese may become outdated soon. Young manga readers seem to accept manga conventions as typical for a specific kind of comic, not as something imported from another culture (personal communication). It seems as if manga has finally found its place in the German universe of comics.

---

the comic in Japanese and translated it into German, but the artistic techniques used could be traced back to the *bande dessinée* as well as to manga.

References

Primary Sources

Banzai! (2001 –) Hamburg: Carlsen (monthly).

CLAMP (1999) *Magic Knight Rayearth. 6: Starke Herzen* [German translation by Antje Bockel] Hamburg: Carlsen.

------ (2003): *xxxholic*, vol. 1. Tōkyō: Kodansha [*xxxholic* 1. Köln: Egmont Manga und Anime, 2004, German translation by Claudia Peter].

Daisuki (2003 –) Hamburg: Carlsen (monthly).

Fujishima, Kosuke (2002) 'Oh! My Mini-Goddess', *MangaPower* 3, Berlin: Egmont Manga und Anime, 459-469.

Kitoh [Kitō], Mohiro (2002 – 2006) *Naru Taru*, 12 vols., Berlin: Egmont Manga und Anime.

Kobayashi, Makoto (2001) *What's Michael?, 1. Alles für die Katz'* [What's Michael?, German translation by Stefan Zeidenitz], Berlin: Egmont Manga und Anime.

Koike, Kazuo and Goseki Kojima (2000 –) *Lone Wolf and Cub* [*Kozure Ōkami*], Milwaukie, OR: Dark Horse Comics.

Labs, Robert (2001a) *Dragic Master*, Hamburg: Carlsen [German manga].

Manga Power (2002 –) Berlin: Egmont Manga und Anime (monthly).

Marx, Sascha Nils and Stefan Voss (2002) *Naglayas Herz* [Naglayas Heart], Berlin: Egmont Manga und Anime.

Miyazaki, Hayao (2001a) *Nausicaä aus dem Tal der Winde* [*Kaze no tani no Naushika*] [Nausicaa from the Valley of the Winds, German translation by Junko Iwamoto-Seebeck and Jürgen Seebeck], 4 vols., Hamburg: Carlsen.

------ (2000) *Prinzessin Mononoke. Der Comic zum Film* [*Film Comic Mononoke Hime*] [Princess Mononoke Film Comic, German translation by Junko Iwamoto-Seebeck and Jürgen See-beck], 4 vols., Hamburg: Carlsen.

------ (2001b) *Sen to Chihiro no kamikakushi*, 5 vols., Tōkyō: Tokuma Shoten.

------ (2002-2003) *Spirited Away – Chihiros Reise ins Zauberland* [*Sen to Chihiro no kamikakushi*, German translation by Nina Olligschläger], 5 vols., Hamburg: Carlsen.

Nakazawa, Keiji (1982a) *Barfuß durch Hiroshima. Eine Bildergeschichte gegen den Krieg* [*Hadashi no Gen*] [Barefoot Gen/Gen of Hiroshima, translated from English and Japanese into Ger-man by Hans Kirchmann and Kumiko Yasui], Reinbek: Rowohlt (rororo aktuell).

Nakazawa, Keiji (2004) *Barfuß durch Hiroshima* [translated from Japanese into German by Nina Olligschläger], Hamburg: Carlsen.

------ (1982b) *I Saw It!* [*Ore wa mita*], San Francisco: Educomics [The English version is a coop-eration between Leonard Rifas, Alan Gleason, Yuko Kitaura, Fred Schodt, Mizue Fujinuma, Rebecca Wilson, Guy Coldwell and Tom Orzechowski].

Ōtomo, Katsuhiro (1991-1996) *Akira* [German translation by Junko Iwamoto-Seebeck and Jürgen Seebeck], 20 vols., Hamburg: Carlsen (ComicArt).

------ (2000-2001) *Akira* German translation by Junko Iwamoto-Seebeck and Jürgen Seebeck], 6 vols., black and white, Hamburg: Carlsen.

Sadamoto, Yoshiyuki and Gainax (1999) *Neon Genesis Evangelion. 3: Weiße Narben* [German translation by Antje Bockel], Hamburg: Carlsen.

------ (2001) *Neon Genesis Evangelion. 6: Fourth Children* [German translation by Antje Bockel], Hamburg: Carlsen.

Samura, Hiroaki (2002) *Blade of the Immortal 1* [German translation by Christine Steinle], Berlin: Egmont Manga und Anime.

Seebeck, Jürgen (2000) *Bloody Circus* [Originally written in Japanese, translated into German by the author himself], Hamburg: Carlsen.

Shirow [Shirō], Masamune (1994-1996) *Appleseed* [translated from English into German by Georg W. Tempel], 10 vols., Stuttgart: Ehapa/Feest.

Shotaro [Shōtarō], Ishinomori (1989) *Japan GmbH – Eine Einführung in die japanische Wirtschaft* [*Nihon Keizai Nyūmon*] [*Japan Inc.*, translated by Akiko-Elisabeth Burian], Bonn: Rentrop.

Sōshi, Sen (2001) *Einführung in die Teezeremonie. Erstes Kapitel*, [*Chakai nyūmon*] [*An Introduction into the Japanese Tea Ceremony*, German translation by Christian Dunkel], Berlin: Mori-Ōgai-Gedenkstätte der Humboldt-Universität zu Berlin.

Takahashi, Rumiko (1999) *Ranma ½. 1. Die wunderbare Quelle* [translated from English into German by Frank Neubauer], Stuttgart: Feest Comics.

Takehiko, Inoue (2002) *Vagabond*. Vol. 1 [German translation by Holger Hermann Haupt], Berlin: Egmont Manga und Anime.

Takeuchi, Naoko (1998-2000) *Sailor Moon* [translated from English into German by Georg W. Tempel resp. French into German by Fritz Walter], 18 vols., Stuttgart (later Berlin): Ehapa.

Toriyama, Akira (1997-2001) *Dragon Ball* [German translation by Junko Iwamoto-Seebeck and Jürgen Seebeck], 42 vols., Hamburg: Carlsen.

Waki, Yamato (1992) *Genji Monogatari. Asakiyumemishi* [*The History of Genji*, German translation by Keiko Sato and Hedi Hahn], Böblingen: Okawa.

Yoshida, Akimi (2003) *Banana Fish 1* [German translation by Christine Roedel], Nettetal-Kaldenkirchen: Planet Manga.

Secondary Sources

Anon. (2002) 'Manga-Talente 2002', *Banzai!* 8:8-9.

----- (2005) 'Industrial Report: Japanese Publishing Industry', *JETRO Japan Economic Monthly*, July 2005 (online) http://www.jetro.go.jp/en/market/trend/industrial/pdf/jem0507-2e.pdf (Accessed 9 April 2006).

Berndt, Jaqueline (1995) *Phänomen Manga*, Berlin: Edition q.

Böckem, Jörg and Christoph Dallach (2002) 'Manga Chutney', *Spiegel Online* 24 June 2002 (online) http://www.spiegel.de/kultur/gesellschaft/ (Accessed 9 April 2006).

Bouissou, Jean-Marie (2000) 'Manga Goes Global' (online) http://www.ceri-sciences-po.org (Accessed 15 November 2005).

Briese, Brigitte (2002) 'Editorial', *Bulletin Jugend und Literatur* 32(8):3.

Cuypers, Jari and Klaus Strzyz (1986) *Comic Zeichen Buch*, Berlin: Gerald Leue.

Deppey, Dirk (2005) 'Scanlation Nation: Amateur Manga Translators Tell Their Stories', *The Comics Journal Online Edition* (online) http://www.tcj.com/269/n_scan.html (Accessed 8 May 2006).

Dodker-Tobler, Verena (1986) 'Zeichentrickfilm und Comics aus medienpädagogischer Sicht' [Animated Film and Comics from a Media Education Perspective], in Alphons Silbermann and H.-D. Dyroff (eds) *Comics and Visual Culture: Research Studies from Ten Countries*, München, New York, London and Paris: Saur, 248-253.

Fiedler, Sabine (forthcoming) '*Nudpieda Gen – Hadashi no Gen* in an International Speech Community'.

Fukuda, Hiroko (1993) *Flip, Slither & Bang. Japanese Sound and Action Words*, Tōkyō: Kodansha International.

Grun, Maria and Cay Dollerup (2003) '"Loss" and "gain" in comics', *Perspectives* 11(3):197-216.

Helbling, Brigitte (2001) 'Und das Herz macht dodom' [And the Heart Beats dodom], *Kölner Stadt-Anzeiger*, 25/26 August, Section Moderne Zeiten, n. pag.

Horn, Maurice (1999) *The World Encyclopedia of Comics, Second Edition*, Philadelphia: Chelsea House.

Jüngst, Heike (2004) 'Japanese Comics in Germany', *Perspectives: Studies in Translatology* 12(2):83-105.

Kaindl, Klaus (1999a) 'Thump, Whizz, Poom: A Framework for the Study of Comics under Translation', *Target* 11(2):263-288.

------ (1999b) 'Warum sind alle Japaner Linkshänder?' [Why Are the Japanese All Left-handed?], *TEXTconTEXT* 13(3):1-24.

Kaps, Joachim (1995) 'Mangamania. Japanische Comics erobern den deutschen Markt' [Japanese Comics Conquer the German Market], *Comixene* 11 (June/July):9-11.

------ (2001) 'Carlsen Comics' Joachim Kaps im Comicgate Exklusiv-Interview. Interview by Fritz Saalfeld' (online) http://www.comicgate.de/int_jokaps.htm (Accessed 8 September 2005).

Lecarme, Philippe (2000) 'Raisons et déraisons d'un refus', *Les cahiers pédagogiques* 382:19-20.

Loveday, Leo and Satomi Chiba (1986) 'Aspects of the Development Toward a Visual Culture in Respect of Comics: Japan', in Alphons Silbermann and H.-D. Dyroff (eds) *Comics and Visual Culture: Research Studies from Ten Countries*, München, New York, London and Paris: Saur, 158-184.

Mangajin's Basic Japanese through Comics (1993) New York and Tokyo: Weatherhill.

Nida, Eugene (1964) *Toward a Science of Translation*, Leiden: Brill.

nk [Nadine Kubbe] (2001) '*Angelic Layer* – Erwecke Deinen Engel' [Angelic Layer – Awake Your Angel], *Animania* 42:40-41.

Nord, Christiane (1998) 'Das Verhältnis des Zieltextes zum Ausgangstext' [The Relation Between Target Text and Source Text], in Mary Snell-Hornby, Hans G. Hönig, Paul Kußmaul and Peter A. Schmitt (eds), *Handbuch Translation*, Tübingen: Stauffenburg, 141-144.

O'Hagan, Minako (2006) 'Teletranslation Revisited: Futurama for Screen Translators?', Paper presented at the *Marie Curie Euroconference on Audiovisual Translation Scenarios, 1 May 2006, University of Copenhagen*.

Olderdissen, Charlotte (1992) 'Vorwort', Waki 1992, *i*.

Phillipps, Susanne (1996) 'Manga für ein deutschsprachiges Publikum: Möglichkeiten der Übertragung von Text-Bild-Verbindungen' [Manga for a German Audience], *Japanstudien* 8:193-210.

pk [Petra Kilburg] (2005a) 'Spieglein, Spieglein an der Wand' [Mirror on the Wall], *Animania* 1-2:44-46.

------ (2005b) 'Miyazaki & Moebius', *Animania* 4:89-91.

------ (2005c) 'Von Marmelade und Kuchen ...' [Of Marmelade and Cake], *Animania* 6:52-55.

------ (2005d) 'Sophies Reise ins Zauberschloss' [Howl's Moving Castle], *Animania* 8-9:10-14.

Rifas, Leonard (2004) 'Globalizing Comic Books from Below: How Manga Came to America', *International Journal of Comics Art* 6(2):138-171.

rl [Ricky Leibold] (2002a) '*Hallo Kurt* – Ein Hund für alle Fälle' [Ohayō Spaku], *Animania* 47:46.

------ (2002b) '*Naru Taru* – Ein Stern für Shiina' [Naru Taru – A Star for Shiina], *Animania* 46:66.

------ (2002c) '*What's Michael?* Expeditionen ins Reich der Stubentiger' [What's Michael? Expeditions into the World of Pet Cats], *Animania* 47:53.

Rommens, Aarnoud (2000) 'Manga Story-telling/showing', *Image [&] Narrative* 1 (Cognitive Narratology) (online) http://www.imageandnarrative.be (Accessed 30 November 2005).

Sato, Keiko and Hedi Hahn (1992) 'Vorwort', in Waki 1992, *i*.

'Scanlation', in *Wikipedia, the free encyclopedia* (online) http://en.wikipedia.org/wiki/Scanlation (Last modified 25 April 2006; Accessed 8 May 2006).

Schmitt, Peter A. (1997) 'Comics und Cartoons: (k)ein Gegenstand der Übersetzungswissenschaft?' [Comics and Cartoons: A Topic Unsuited for Translation Studies?], in Horst W.

Drescher (ed.) *Transfer. Übersetzen – Dolmetschen – Interkulturalität*, Frankfurt/Main etc.: Lang, 619-662.

------ (1998) 'Graphische Literatur, Comics', in Mary Snell-Hornby, Hans G. Hönig, Paul Kußmaul and Peter A. Schmitt (eds), *Handbuch Translation*, Tübingen: Stauffenburg, 199-269.

Schilling, Mark (1997) *The Encyclopedya of Japanese Pop Culture*, New York: Weatherhill.

Schodt, Frederic (1986) *Manga! Manga! The World of Japanese Comics*, Tokyo: Kodansha International.

----- (1996) *Dreamland Japan. Writings on Modern Manga*, Berkeley, CA: Stone Bridge Press.

Sonnenschein, Sabine (1993) 'Statements von Comic-Fans: Heimkino zum Blättern' [Comic Fans' Statements], *Medien Concret* 1, *Special Issue: Comics*: 68-70.

sr [Sabine Rudert] (2005) 'Nachwuchs-Fieber' [Newcomer-Fever], *Animania* 4:30-32.

Wahl, Yuriko (2005) 'In Deutschland grassiert das Manga-Fieber', *Stern.de* (online) http://www.stern.de/unterhaltung/comic/541655.html?nv=cb (Accessed 17 June 2005).

Yang, Jeff (2004) 'Asian Pop Manga Nation: No longer an obscure cult art form, Japanese comics are becoming as American as apuru pai' (online) http://sfgate.com/cgi-bin/article.cgi?file=/g/archive/2004/06/14/manganation.DTL (Accessed 8 May 2006).

4 Aspects of Adaptation

The Translation of Comics Formats

VALERIO ROTA
University of Bari, Italy

Comics all over the world are not only published in different languages but also in different formats, such as comic book, album, tankōbon, etc. When translated, comics may retain their original format or be adapted to the publishing conventions of the target culture. However, often the graphic elements of comics make cultural adaptation difficult and expensive for publishers. Drawing on the theories of Antoine Berman and Lawrence Venuti, it is argued that translated comics cannot help but reveal their foreign origin, and that their 'domestication' is virtually impossible without a marked departure from the original work. Examples discussed include translations of Japanese, American and European comics.

Comics have a relevant role in the publishing industry. With sales figures which very often reach hundreds of thousands of copies per title (and even millions, in the case of best sellers like *Astérix* or some Japanese magazines), the importance of comic publications is not to be underestimated.

Translated comics cover a good part of this industry. This is also due to the fact that translating a comic is undoubtedly less expensive than producing it from scratch and publishing it. Zanettin and D'Arcangelo (2004:187-188) point out how, despite the great quantity of existing translated comics in many countries, the number of studies on comics in translation are very limited, and they mainly deal with aspects such as the translation of puns, proper names, interjections, etc., from a purely linguistic perspective or, adopting a more semiotic approach, also considering the relationship between text and pictures (see Celotti, this volume, for a more detailed discussion).

However, a distinction between text and pictures may arguably be misleading. For instance, Scott McCloud (1994:9) describes comics as "[j]uxtaposed pictorial and other images in deliberate sequence, intended to convey information and/or to produce an aesthetic response in the viewer". In his definition, McCloud does not use the formula 'image plus text', as other scholars usually do; indeed, comics are not the mere product of the juxtaposition of words and pictures, but something more complex. McCloud simply mentions "other images": a definition in which all kinds of texts in comics must be included. Text is treated like a graphic element of the page; it is firstly a picture, then a text. Indeed, the text is subordinated to images; evidence of this is the existence of comics without words: Masashi Tanaka's *Gon* in Japan, for instance; or Lewis Trondheim's *La Mouche* in France.[1] Moreover, Scott McCloud talks about 'the viewer' instead of 'the

---

[1] Other examples of comics without words include some short episodes of Gianfranco Berardi's and Ivo Milazzo's *Ken Parker*, collected in the volume *Il respiro e il sogno*, and the Korean comic *Eden* by Jung Choel, published by Sai Comics in 2004; moreover, a collection of wordless comics entitled *No words* was published between 1998 and 2000 by the Italian publishing house Phoenix and meant for international distribution.

reader', clearly underlining the position, function and role of texts in comics: they are not simply a comment on the picture, but are an integral part of it. Texts in comics are not the mere transcription of the characters' speeches: they are a graphic representation of them. Before being something to be read (i.e. texts), they are something to be seen: pictures themselves, which contribute to the visual equilibrium of the page. In fact, their graphic peculiarity comes before their textual quality. Far from being a mere 'simulation' of sounds and speech, balloons and onomatopoeic texts are graphic devices which can be (and are) employed to provoke specific effects on the reader. That is, words in comics are first of all employed to represent and evoke feelings through the modulation of elements like their size, shape, colour and disposition in space, all of which are graphic and extratextual elements. Even the colour and shape of balloons, which are the physical containers of words, contribute to the creation of particular effects. All these elements pave the way for the effect of the text itself; that is, words as such play their role only subsequently, when their graphic quality has already created a certain atmosphere in the mind of the reader. It is true that there have been some attempts at realizing comics without pictures, employing words and punctuation only (see, for instance, Shane Simmons' *Longshot Comics*, Figure 4.1), but, even in these cases, notwithstanding the effort of employing symbols only, avoiding the use of iconic elements, the spatial disposition of letters, words, sentences and punctuation signs are of utmost importance. Moreover, the use of non-textual elements like panel borders and other lines is always strictly necessary; these characteristics therefore reveal the graphic essence even of these 'text-only' comics.

Figure 4.1: Shane Simmons, *Longshot Comics*, 1993[2]

Texts and pictures in comics, then, are so tightly interwoven that they cannot be distinguished from each other or, worse, separated. Even tentative attempts at distinguishing symbolic items (words, texts) from iconic items (pictures, images), although useful in some respects, are not free from risks, as there cannot be a clear separation between these two aspects.

Analyzing translated comics from a cultural point of view instead of adopting a semiotic or a linguistic one may be extremely fruitful and useful in giving new impulse to the development of research in this field.

---

[2] See http://www.eyestrainproductions.com/es/movies_in_longshot.php?choice=dumbdumb.

1. **Formats³**

In Italian comic bookshops, publications are not ranged by genre (science fiction, action, comedy, detective stories…), but rather by nation: French comics, American, Italian, Japanese, etc. In other words, the geographical origin of these publications influences their arrangement on the shelves of comic bookshops. Since this does not happen with text-only books, the reason must lie in the cultural specificity of comics. Different cultures produce different kinds of comics: the size and contents of publications, for historical and practical reasons, vary from nation to nation, accommodating to the tastes and expectations of the different reading public. Cultural differences emerge not only in the different ways in which comics are conceived, in the layout of pages, strips and panels, and in the way of employing the graphic and narrative techniques available, but also in the preference for black and white or colour stories, in their length, in the size of publications, and even in their price and their periodicity. These are all signals of a different attitude and expectation towards this form of art, and a different way of enjoying it.

Each comic-producing culture has developed a favourite format in which comics are published. What follows is a list of the 4 most common formats currently used. It must be noted that, while the size of a format remains nearly always the same (with possible minor variations of a few centimetres), pagination may vary noticeably. An approximate range of the number of pages is given in each case:

– **comic book**: 17x26cm, 32 to 80 pages, soft-cover (stapled or square-bound), full-colour, periodical (usually monthly or bi-monthly). These generally contain a short episode (22-24 pages) of a longer, ongoing story, usually to be continued in the following issue, although special issues and annuals may contain longer, self-contained stories. This format was used for the first time in the 1930s in the US to collect reprints of daily strips that had originally appeared in newspapers; it was later employed to publish brand-new stories. Since 1938 (year of publication of *Action Comics* #1, containing the first appearance of Superman, the character created by Jerry Siegel and Joe Schuster), the comic book has been the favourite format in which super-hero stories are published. Super-hero titles are usually centred on a single main character, or a group of characters. Many independent (non-superhero) North-American comics are also published in this format, in black and white rather than in colour. The most common comic book is a 32-page installment containing a 22-page story, with the remaining pages being dedicated to ads and various features, like the letters page. These publications were sold in ordinary news stands for many years; however, in the late '70s a parallel direct market of comic-only (and comic-related merchandise) shops developed, thus providing new opportunities: for instance, the direct market fostered the development and diffusion of trade paperbacks (thicker, square-bound volumes collecting reprints of complete story arcs) and graphic novels (hardcover or paperback volumes containing a brand-new story), which are also sold in ordinary bookstores. Each comic book series

---

³ The analysis takes into consideration stand-alone comics publications, such as books or comic periodicals, leaving out comic strips published in newspapers or other forms of publication.

is handled by different teams of artists, although the same team may retain the artistic direction of a title for very long runs: for instance, the work of Stan Lee and Jack Kirby on the *Fantastic Four* magazine lasted over 100 issues.

–   ***album***: 23x30cm, 32 to 80 pages (though the most common pagination is 48 pages), hard-cover, full-colour, non-periodical. The album is the favourite format in the French market: humour as well as adventure stories are published in these large, 'giant-sized' volumes, sold in ordinary bookstores. Albums generally contain a long, self-contained story. Titles may focus on a single hero or hero-like main character (Jean Van Hamme's and William Vance's *XIII*, Morris's *Lucky Luke*, Herge's *Tintin*) or groups of characters (Edgar-Pierre Jacob's *Blake et Mortimer*), but they may also be more general (Serge Le Tendre's and Régis Loisel's *La quête de l'oiseau du temps*, Joann Sfar's and Lewis Trondheim's *Donjon*). Recently, some small quality labels (L'Association publishing house, for instance) have experimented with alternative formats to the classic albums: David B's *L'ascension du haut mal* is a 6-volume autobiographical work published in giant-sized, black-and-white, soft-cover albums; Marjane Satrapi's best seller *Persepolis*[4] has been published in a 17x24cm format, in black and white; the volumes that make up Fabrice Neaud's *Journal*, published by Ego Comme X, have a markedly different number of pages (112 for volume one, 72 for volume two, 376 for volume three, and so on), and beside the classic, ordinary colour albums published by Dargaud, Lewis Trondheim's series *Lapinot* includes a special black-and-white volume of 512 pages, published in an alternative format by L'Association. Unlike North-American comic book series, French series published in albums are usually entirely produced by the same authors, from the first to the last episode. For this reason, albums are not published on a regular basis, and even many years can elapse between two issues: for instance, E.P. Jacobs produced eight volumes of his *Blake et Mortimer* series in twenty-six years.

–   ***bonelliano***: 16x21cm, 96 to 160 pages, soft-cover (square-bound), black-and-white, periodical (usually monthly or bi-monthly).[5] The *bonelliano*, named after the Sergio Bonelli Editore publishing house and sold in newsstands along with newspapers and other periodicals, is the most common format in which serial Italian comics are published. It appeared in the 1950s as collections of reprinted comic strips, and was later employed to publish self-contained 96-page adventure stories, rather similar in flavour to those published in French adventure albums (in fact, European comics readers generally prefer long and self-contained stories instead of short stories or cliff-hanging episodes). Titles are centred on main characters (*Tex, Zagor, Dylan Dog, Martin Mystère, Nathan Never*). Due to the large quantity of pages per series published monthly, each title has to be handled by many teams of artists.

–   ***tankōbon***: 12x18cm or 13x18cm (or other sizes), from a minimum of 176-192 to more than 400 pages, soft-cover (square-bound), black-and-white, non-periodical (although

---

[4] Marjane Satrapi, of Iranian origins, emigrated to France in 1994 where, encouraged by David B., she began to write her own biography in comics form.
[5] This format has also been defined by Luca Raffaelli (1997) as 'formato quaderno' (literally, 'notebook format'), although the name *bonelliano* or 'formato Bonelli' is far more common.

many series are published on a bi-monthly basis). In fact, the term *tankōbon* (meaning collection book) does not denote a specific format, but simply a volume collecting episodes of a Japanese comic series which, generally speaking, has previously appeared in periodical magazines. The most common *tankōbon* volumes are 12x18cm per 192 or 208 pages, or 13x18cm per 238 or 256 pages, but there are countless other sizes: for instance, Katsuhiro Ōtomo's *Akira* was published in 18 x 26 cm, 358-page *tankōbon* volumes. Japanese series are first published in short episodes on a weekly or monthly basis in phonebook-sized magazines, and later collected in *tankōbon* volumes. These episodes, once collected, generally form a single, uninterrupted narration; thus, the six volumes that make up *Akira* form a long story of over 1800 pages. There are, however, some Japanese series made up of many short, self-contained stories (Osamu Tezuka's *Blackjack*, or Monkey Punch's *Lupin the 3rd*, for instance). Another derivative format is the *widebon* (wide book), which collects reprints of *tankōbon* series in thicker, 400-page volumes. Japanese comic series are the work of a single author, but due to the enormous number of pages (20-22) to be produced per week, the main author employs a staff of artists who finish off the work, drawing details, backgrounds, applying cross-hatchings, and completing the job.

This list is clearly not exhaustive, nor does it presume to cover all possible formats in each country analyzed. There are other formats, for types of comics such as the Italian *neri*, i.e. a pocket-sized format (12x17cm, with minor variations) in which many popular crime (*Diabolik*) and erotic stories are published; or the French *petit format* (13x18cm, 128 pages, square-bound, printed on bad-quality paper), used for the periodical publication of translated Italian serials and, unlike albums, sold at newsstands.[6]

Arranging comics by geographical origin in comic bookshops is not a simple matter of convenience and saving space. Unlike other kinds of works, comics have a determinate physical and spatial element, i.e. the page, with a specific size, which influences the formats in which comics are published. Conversely, the size of the page is influenced by the size of the publication that is going to contain it: in fact, authors of comics conceive their works keeping in mind how and where they will be published. The format is not simply the size in which comics are printed: it strongly influences the quality of comics (story length, graphic techniques, genre), their enjoyment and how they are conceived (a mere piece of entertainment, a cultural product), the periodicity of their publication (and consequently the rhythm of narration, although in an indirect way). Besides revealing the history of comics in a given cultural setting, formats have important effects on the production of comics, on their style, and also on the attitude of readers towards this form of art. The page, then, imposing artistic restrictions and potentialities, is not just an incidental feature, but rather a fundamental creative element in comics. This element, with its proportions and its characteristics, cannot be easily modified in translation through editorial processes without altering the original work substantially; therefore, changing the size of the original publication is an operation which has important consequences for the translated comic and its enjoyment

---

[6] One study of comics which takes into consideration formats of publication is Raffaelli (1997).

2.   Translating Formats

Given that the text of comics has graphic qualities, it follows that the translation of a comic does not only involve the linguistic but also the graphic side of it. Texts in comics are visual elements of the page; therefore, pages and pictures themselves actually need 'translation'. Even wordless comics are not exempt from this rule: formats may (and sometimes must) be altered and manipulated in order to adapt the comic to other cultures and other reading publics.

Very often, the success of a translated comic depends on the way in which it is edited. A publishing house has to make some important choices in the phase of adaptation[7] of the foreign comic to the target culture. Obviously, these choices are made according to various priorities. For instance, if the reading public of a given country prefers colour stories, the publisher can decide to colour a comic which was originally in black and white, or to shrink a magazine-sized comic into a pocket-sized format, in order to render it more appealing; or, by contrast, if the target reading public gives priority to respecting the original work, the publisher can decide to leave the comic as it is.

The text of comics (or, better, its 'texture', that is the complex structure resulting from the interweaving of texts and pictures) is presented to the target culture after a process of adaptation has been undertaken, a process which has to take into consideration the expectations and tastes of the new cultural context, and at the same time has also to preserve, as much as possible, the features of the work to be translated. However, the current tendency of European publishing houses is to manipulate and alter comics to be translated as little as possible, for economic as well as cultural reasons: every manipulation comes at a cost; moreover, more attentive readers do not tolerate alterations of the original works unless they are strictly necessary.

In 'translating' the format, three main possibilities are available:

–   adaptation to a local format;
–   retention of the original format;
–   adoption of a third format, different from both the original and the local ones (in any case, this implies a heavy manipulation of the original work). This is the case, for instance, of the already mentioned *petit format*, used in France for the publication of translated Italian comics.

As is the case with many forms of art (Berman 1984; Venuti 1995), even in the field of comics two main translation (or, better, adaptation) strategies may be adopted: domesticating and foreignizing.[8]

---

[7] With the term 'adaptation' I mean the whole process of transferring a comic from one culture to another. This process includes not only the translation, but also all kinds of modifications that the patronage (i.e. the entity which has the power to 're-write' cultural works; see Lefevere 1992) may decide to apply to them.

[8] The two terms 'domestication' and 'foreignization' were coined by Lawrence Venuti, on the basis of a distinction made by Schleiermacher in 1813. He defines domestication as "an ethnocentric reduction of the foreign text to target language cultural values" (1995:20), while foreignization is a process that allows the original work to resist integration and to maintain its features.

2.1 Foreignizing Translation Strategies

The comic keeps, as far as possible, its original cultural and editorial characteristics; the format is preserved, thus clearly revealing the foreign origin of the comic. In the case of Far Eastern comics, even the original direction of reading (from right to left) is maintained. This strategy is mainly adopted in countries (like Italy, France, and Spain, for instance) where the reading public has developed an awareness of the artistic importance of comics and where, consequently, drastic alterations of the original works (a domesticating strategy) would not be viewed in a favourable light.

The most common and evident result of the adoption of a foreignizing strategy is the preservation of the original format, i.e. the size in which the comic was conceived and published. This may seem a quite obvious measure for a form of art in which the size of the page is a fundamental element; however, it does not appear so when one remembers that, due to commercial and practical reasons, comics (which are often not considered artistic products) have very often been heavily altered in foreign editions to meet the tastes of different cultures and reading publics. For instance, Superman comics in Italy were first published in the 1930s and 1940s in the *giornale* format (newspaper-sized, in the pages of *L'Audace* magazine, where the character was named "Ciclone": Vaccari 1999), then in the 1950s and 1960s in a *libretto* (pocket-sized) format (where he was called "Nembo Kid"), and finally, in the late 1960s and the 1970s, in their original comic book format. That is, over the course of the years Superman comics have been published and translated in Italy following the most common and popular formats of each period. The original comic book format was adopted only when the awareness of the Italian reading public began to grow, at a moment when comics in Italy were beginning to be considered a genuine form of artistic expression instead of mere entertainment for children (see, for example, Umberto Eco's *Apocalittici e integrati*, published in 1964).

The foreignizing strategy implies only minor adjustments of the original format. In the case of serial comics, for instance, a different number of pages, or a variation in the periodicity of the publication (in comparison to the original one), is considered a perfectly acceptable variation of the characteristics of the original publication.

Foreignizing strategies may or may not involve the adaptation of graphics. Thus, in the comic to be translated there can be graphically rendered textual elements that may or may not be adapted: onomatopoeia, the titles of the stories, and the like. The most obvious thing to do is to prepare a translated version of these texts and modify printing films to insert the translations in the graphics. Sometimes, these textual elements are considered an integral part of the graphics, and altering them is hardly tolerated by the mainstream reading public. Therefore, some Italian publishing houses keep the titles of the stories graphically unaltered, simply putting a translation of them at the bottom of the page. However, this and similar procedures are in many cases mainly dictated by economic concerns; appealing to the tastes of the public, who eventually appreciate this policy, can be simply considered a bonus.

The application of a foreignizing strategy normally has the advantage of maintaining many of the features of the original work. Sometimes, however, keeping the original format without applying any form of adaptation may lead to a failure from the commercial point of view as well as from that of preserving the comic in another culture. The first Italian edition of Neil Gaiman's *The Sandman* provides an obvious example of this. The Italian translation rights of this American serial were bought at the beginning of the 1990s by Comic Art, a publishing house which tried many editorial formats: at first, *The Sandman* was published in single episodes in an anthological magazine; then, in a 32-page comic book entitled *Sandman*, identical to the American edition; finally, in thicker books collecting more or less two and a half episodes each. All these attempts proved to be failures; in particular, the most disastrous was the one most similar to the original edition: 32-page books, containing a 24-page episode each, a format which did not satisfy Italian readers and, more importantly, did not allow them to appreciate the complexity and depth of Gaiman's work. The translation rights of *The Sandman* were later acquired by Magic Press, which published it in deluxe volumes containing a complete story arc in each, sold through the Italian direct market like graphic novels. This edition was in line with the tastes of the Italian public, and the comic became a fairly good seller. American readers generally like stories in short installments, with story arcs usually developing over a long stretch of time; by contrast, European readers prefer long and complete stories. This explains why the publication of volumes containing complete story arcs was an ideal solution for introducing *The Sandman* in Italy.

2.2 Domesticating Strategies

Comics are published in a form which fits the tastes of the target reading public. The most obvious case of domestication involves the publication of a foreign comic in the local format, notwithstanding the characteristics of the original publication. The domesticating strategy is mainly adopted in culturally dominant countries (the US, for instance) either generally or, in particular cases, for stylistically similar products (e.g. some adventure comic book stories and South-American comics that are very similar in flavour to European adventure serials, published in Italy in *bonelliano* format).

In European countries techniques pertaining to a domesticating strategy, such as reassembling panels and pages to adapt them to a different format, colouring stories originally conceived to be published in black and white, and other similar manipulations, are not easily tolerated by the reading public, as they are considered disrespectful of the original work, unless they are carried out (or, at least, edited) by the authors themselves.

The domesticating strategy does not normally imply a change simply in the original format; this change may be (and very often is) accompanied by many alterations of the original comic. Sometimes, the strategy does not involve the format at all, but simply leads to one or more other alterations. Here is a list of potential alterations which may be applied to comics translated from a domesticating perspective:

– *shrinking or magnification of pages and panels*. This is the most common procedure when a foreign comic is adapted to fit a different format. An example of shrunk pages can be found in the Italian translation of *The Savage Sword of Conan*, a giant-sized North-American magazine which was published for more than 80 issues in the smaller *bonelliano* format by the Italian publishing house Comic Art, from 1986 to 1994. Conversely, examples of magnification of pages can be found in the many translations of Japanese comics published in the US in the 1980s and the 1990s, where the original small *tankōbon* format was enlarged to fit the comic book format.

– *colouring of black-and-white comics, or publication of colour comics in black and white.* Examples of these alterations can once again be seen in Japanese comics published in the US in the 1980s, when the original works published in black and white were coloured for the North-American market; other examples include the Italian black-and-white comic *Il Comandante Mark* published in Greece in full colour in the magazine *Peripeteia,* and, conversely, the successful reprints of classic colour super-hero stories sold in the Spanish market in black and white.

– *mutilation of texts.* This procedure is often a consequence of altering the original format to a smaller one. In fact, the translated text of comics always needs to undergo some adjustments: in translation, texts generally tend to become longer than the original, thus making it difficult to insert in the physical space of the balloons. The translator carries out a preliminary adaptation of the text, by choosing the shortest synonyms and omitting, as far as possible, non-functional words. The degree of reduction also depends on the skill of the letterer, who writes texts in balloons by hand or mechanically. Moreover, the original letterer works directly on panels, which are usually larger than the printed page; by contrast, the letterer of the translated edition must work on printing films, which are of the same size as the printed page. Thus, because of the high level of skill needed to write long texts in small spaces, every translated comic risks being a reduction of the original text.[9] The Italian translation of *XIII* by Eura Editoriale, for instance, keeps the original album format of this famous French series by William Vance and Jean Van Hamme, but the Italian publisher was nevertheless obliged to reduce the quantity of translated texts to make them fit the narrow space available in balloons (Rota 2001:142-143). However, in the case of shrunk formats, the mutilation and simplification of texts is not just a risk but, rather, a necessity. The example in Figure 4.2a is taken from an issue of the Italian version of *The Savage Sword of Conan,* compared to the American original (Figure 4.2b) which was published in magazine format. In a further translation by Panini Comics (Figure 4.2c), in the same *bonelliano* format, the text has been likewise shortened and adapted. The comparisons clearly show that in both cases the loss of textual information is quite considerable.

– *re-arrangement of pages and panels.* This is one of the most devastating types of alteration, since it disrupts the graphic equilibrium of the page originally established by the artist. When the proportions between the original format and the new one are too different, publishing houses may decide to re-arrange the panels in order to fit the new format. An example of this is the Italian edition of *El Eternauta,* an Argentinian comic by

---

[9] Computer lettering, which makes it possible to calibrate the size of fonts, has now minimized this problem considerably (Scatasta 2002).

Figure 4.2a: Roy Thomas and John Buscema, *La Torre dell'Elefante*, Comic Art,
November 1987, p. 8
Lit.: "Here it is, looming against the sky… // the Tower of the Elephant! // Above,
the great jewel glitters among the stars."

Figure 4.2b: Roy Thomas and John Buscema, *The Tower of the Elephant*, Marvel Comics,
November 1977, p. 10

Héctor G. Oesterheld and Francisco Solano Lopez, which uses a classic vertical format instead of the original horizontal one.[10] This procedure is easier when the comic has a regular arrangement of panels on the page, and panels are in a quadrangular form, but is pratically impossible with bleed-art pages or non-quadrangular panels (as typical of Japanese comics). In some extreme cases, the re-arrangement may require the mutilation of art or the adding (in rare cases) of new art to complete the page.

–   *omission of pages and panels*. Single panels (with a consequent, necessary re-arrangement of the remaining panels) or entire pages can be omitted in order to fit the story in publications with a lower number of pages (see Zanettin, this volume for an example of this).

Figure 4.2c: Roy Thomas and John Buscema, *La Torre dell'Elefante*, Panini, Novembre 1996, p. 6
Lit. "The Tower of the Elephant. // One wonders why it is so named. // Above, great jewels glitter beneath the stars."

–   *cultural or political censorship*. Alterations may be undertaken for cultural or political reasons. Form a domesticating perspective, when a foreign cultural element is considered too 'strange' for the target cultural environment, one may decide to eliminate it, or replace what is considered a 'disturbing' element with a more familiar one. A good example of cultural censorship can be found in the first North-American translation of *Uruseiyatsura*, a Japanese humorous comic by Rumiko Takahashi. In the very first episode of this series Ataru, one of the main characters, is scared by the sudden appearance of an *oni*, a traditional Japanese demon. In the Japanese tradition, *oni* are kept away by beans,

---

[10] For more information on the Italian and original versions of *El Eternauta*, see Pesce (2000) and Raffaelli (2003:8).

just as garlic is said to keep away vampires in Western folklore. Ataru throws a handful of beans in the face of the *oni*, in an attempt to chase it away. In the US translation of the comic, however, the beans were re-drawn and replaced with candies, and the *oni* was turned into a monstrous Halloween mask: Ataru, then, in the US version simply tries to use candies to keep away a more familiar (for the American public) Halloween-masked character.

Another case of cultural graphic censorship comes from the super-hero comics translated in France. A 1950 French law prevents the depiction of violence, crime, ugliness and immoral behaviour in periodical publications for young people. Thus, over the years many French publishers have systematically censored North-American comics which were considered too scary for French children, eliminating violent sequences and re-drawing the appearance of ugly characters (Jannequin *et al.* 1994). Zitawi (this volume) discusses other examples of cultural censorship.

Likewise, political censorship tends to obliterate the presence of political elements and references, from the text as well as from the graphics of comics. In the first issue of *The Amazing Spider-Man* (March 1963), the villain named Chameleon steals some top-secret plans and consigns them to the occupants of a "red sub", with a clear symbol of hammer and sickle on it, which surfaces on the waterfront to meet him. This type of scenario was very common in US comics in the Cold War period. In the first Italian edition of that story by Editoriale Corno (April 1970), however, the symbol of hammer and sickle was erased from the picture of the submarine, thus avoiding political references in an entertainment comic.

Another example, regarding text only, can be found in the Italian translation of issue 256 of *The Incredible Hulk*. This story, which was published in the US in February 1981, saw the debut of an Israeli super-heroine named Sabra. In the Italian translation published in 1989 (*Fantastici Quattro* 8, Star Comics), this name was changed into "Saba": at that time, the word "Sabra" grimly recalled the concentration camp in which many Palestinians and Lebanese people were killed in September 1982. No connection with the massacre could have been intended by the author Bill Mantlo, who wrote the story one year before this event; however, the Italian editor decided to modify the name and explain the reasons for this decision in an introduction to the story.

2.3   The Translation of Western Comics formats

European readers of comics generally prefer long and self-contained stories; in France, as well as in Italy, long and self-contained stories are produced and published with great success. However, both France and Italy prefer translated stories from such countries as Japan and the US, where comics are published in short episodes: in fact, the different formats in which comics stories are published in France and Italy constitutes an obstacle to their translation. Popular[11] French comics stories are published in deluxe colour albums,

---

[11] 'Popular' in that the comic, with its easy narrative and graphic style, appeals to the tastes of a large part of the reading public, thus selling a large number of copies.

whereas Italian readers are used to *bonelliani*, which are cheaper, smaller, black and white periodical publications. Nevertheless, their content is more or less the same: a long and self-contained story. Adaptation to formats other than the original one is very difficult: the stories are specifically conceived for their original format, and a drastic adaptation would compromise their quality. As a consequence, despite the fact that the stories share similar features, few Italian comics are published in France, and vice versa.[12]

However paradoxical it may appear then, popular French series today have fewer chances of being published in Italy than more sophisticated products: their deluxe album format makes them too expensive for those Italian readers who like popular stories, and their contents are not 'intellectual' enough to arouse the interest of more demanding readers who look for high-brow products. Italian publishers thus prefer to choose sophisticated French comics for translation rather than popular ones: they cannot risk disappointing readers by publishing 'ordinary' stories in a deluxe and expensive format. Italian readers expect to find a different kind of comic in a different format: finding in an expensive, hard-cover album what can be found in a cheaper *bonelliano* (i.e. a popular, self-contained comics story) would be disappointing for them.

However, there are other reasons why it is practically impossible to transform a French popular comic into an Italian popular publication: a French series cannot be published on a regular basis, as there would soon be no more stories available for publication; moreover, the care required to produce a French album does not match the exigencies of a periodical publication, usually subject to deadlines. Italian readers are used to one story per month: a longer wait between two episodes would easily lead to disaffection.

North-American serial comics are published in France and Italy in periodical publications, identical in size to the original ones. The only difference is in the number of pages: French and Italian editions of American comics usually have 48 or 80 pages, collecting two or three stories (even from different series) in a single issue. This expedient measure compensates for the different time required to read a comic book, which is shorter than the reading time required by an album or a *bonelliano*. Another frequent expedient is to collect an entire story arc of a single series, thus presenting a complete story, in a thicker volume. In this case, the number of episodes per publication may vary: from a minimum of two to twelve or more episodes. A rich apparatus of introduction and notes, which helps the reader to retrace the original edition of the stories and to learn some biographical information about the authors, usually accompanies these translations.

North-American comics, then, are presented to the European reading public in an appealing form. More importantly, the original format is preserved: the foreign origin of these comics can thus be easily identified. The comic book format immediately informs

---

[12] Raffaelli (2006:219) confirms this thesis, and also tries to give an explanation of it: "gli italiani vogliono affezionarsi a un personaggio di cui leggere storie lunghe e frequentemente (una volta al mese, come, appunto, per gli albi Bonelli, ma anche quelli Eura, Star Comics o delle Edizioni If). I francesi invece vogliono maggiore varietà di titoli e l'evento, l'albo che arriva ogni anno" (Italian readers look for characters of whom to grow fond, and read long stories frequently (once a month, as it happens with Bonelli books, and also with Eura, Star Comics and Edizioni If publications). By contrast, French readers look for a wider variety of characters, and 'the event', the book coming once a year).

readers that they are going to read something different from what they usually find in the 48-page giant album or in the 96-page pocket-sized *bonelliano*. European readers are thus able to recognize these publications as containing comics stories coming from a different cultural context, with graphic and narrative styles different from those associated with European comics, and are prepared to find in these publications a different product from those which they usually find in *bonelliani* or in albums.

These mechanisms explain the situation described at the beginning of section 2: the arrangement of comics in Italian shops on the basis of their format is not dictated by simple logistics. Formats are not just a typographical and editorial convenience; they tell the history of comics in the cultures that have produced them. A different format implies a different panel division, different graphic techniques, narrative rhythm, content, and so on: ultimately, it implies a different artistic outcome. Through formats, readers are able to recognize the origin of the comic that they are going to read, and they already know its general characteristics: for instance, a *bonelliano* reveals the presence of a long adventure story in black and white, while a comic book format usually implies a colour episode of a super-hero story.

3.   The Translation of Japanese Comics Formats

Japanese comics offer a very specific example of the problems relating to the translation of comics, and a good summary of the issues involved.

Europe and the US discovered Japanese *manga* in the late eighties. Japan can count on an enormous production of cartoons and comics, mainly directed at the internal market. In fact, the seventies saw a massive importation of **anime** (Japanese cartoons) into Europe, which were broadcast on State and private TV channels. Alfredo Castelli (1983) states that in the years 1976-1982 almost the entire Japanese catalogue of TV cartoons (which went back to around 1962) was imported into Italy. It was a real cultural invasion: thirty years of Japanese animated productions were broadcast in Europe in an extremely brief space of time; moreover, the utter novelty of these products (which reflected a completely different and distant culture, conceived for a Japanese audience and not planned for exportation), had a tremendous impact on European viewers' imagination. Strangely enough, in this period of indiscriminate importation from Japan, very few Japanese comics (which are the primary source of inspiration for anime) were translated for publication in Europe.

In 1986-87, First Comics and Eclipse Comics began to translate some Japanese comics for the North-American market (Kazuya Kudo's and Ryoichi Ikegami's *Mai the psychic girl*, Sanpei Shirato's *Kamui*, Masamune Shirow's *Appleseed*, Kazuo Koike's and Goseki Kojima's *Lone wolf and cub*, Kaoru Shintani's *Area 88*, and other titles), with only limited success. The domesticating strategy adopted (comic book format, sometimes in colour) was not ideal for these comics, whose narrative rhythm did not match the few pages offered by the comic book format, and whose massive use of cross-hatchings and chiaroscuros did not suit colour.

Manga captured the attention of a larger public thanks to the edition of Katsuhiro Ōtomo's *Akira* by Marvel Comics in 1988, which, luckily, had no format problems (the size of the original *tankōbon* was 18x26cm, practically identical to the 17x26cm of a comic book); moreover, the excellent colours used by Steve Oliff for the North-American edition perfectly matched the graphic style of the author, which used little cross-hatching. Thus, notwithstanding the domesticating process it went through, this edition was much appreciated, and the US version of *Akira* is well known in other Western countries as well. For the first time, an important publishing house presented a Japanese comic in the US, arousing interest in this kind of cultural product; from that moment on, the demand for *manga* in the North-American market steadily increased.

In the 1990s, Europe began to import Japanese comics on a regular basis; however, the materials published on the European market came exclusively from North-American publishing houses. This dependence on North-American adaptations was due to two main reasons. The first was economic and practical: Japanese comics translated in the United States were already graphically adapted for a Western public; the second depended on translation rights arrangements: Japanese publishing houses believed that quality would be best safeguarded if further Western editions were based on the already supervised and approved North-American editions. Nevertheless, European publishing houses, although using the material from US editions, in many cases preferred to restore some of the features which had been altered in those editions in order to produce a closer version to the original Japanese. In the case of censorship, the original was restored (see the example of the *oni* transformed into a Halloween mask, already mentioned in paragraph 3.2, which was brought back to its original state by Granata Press for the Italian edition of that episode of *Uruseiyatsura*); or, in the case of coloured editions, black and white was restored (see, for instance, the Italian edition of Kia Asamiya's *Gunhed*, published in Italy by Granata Press in black and white on the basis of the coloured US edition). This tendency to bring the comics back to their original status indicates a different European attitude towards comics, both on the part of publishers and on the part of the reading public. Jüngst (this volume) offers a detailed discussion of manga translation in Germany.

3.1 The Inversion of Pages

An important issue related to Japanese comics is the inversion of pages. The Far Eastern direction of reading, which goes from right to left, requires a mirrored inversion of pages to restore the Western sense of direction (from left to right). Some Japanese authors, who considered the inversion of pages an intolerable alteration, even refused to grant translation rights for their works. Tempted by the enormous commercial potential of Japanese titles, some Italian publishing houses considered translating Japanese comics while keeping the direction of reading unaltered, in order to obtain the translation rights of these series. Notwithstanding the initial perplexity of some, this initiative proved a great success: readers were willing to alter their direction of reading and learn a new one, in order to read their favourite *manga*. Today, many Japanese comics are published in Europe without inverting their pages; even those titles that are not subject to restrictions from their authors are often left untouched, firstly for economic reasons (not inverting pages means saving time and money), and secondly because readers prefer it this way: keeping the original direction of reading is considered respectful to the original work.[13]

The question of whether non-inversion is really a form of respect for Japanese comics is currently being debated. Barbieri (2004), among others, argues that it is rather the other way round: Western readership is accustomed to 'scanning' all kind of images from left to right; therefore, non-inverted panels in Japanese comics convey a different meaning if observed by a Western eye. A quick movement, for instance, is perceived as slow by a European reader if not inverted in mirror-fashion; or a violent kick may turn into a simple trip. Moreover, in a non-inverted comic, images run from right to left while texts run from left to right, thus slowing down the normal reading pace. The reading habits of Western readers (moving from left to right), Barbieri writes, are different from the reading habits of Far Eastern readers: these customs, consolidated by years of individual practice and transformed into collective practices, apply not only to the reading of written texts, but also to the reading of images. Barbieri cites as evidence an ongoing doctoral research project in semiotics which, in analyzing and comparing Western and Far-Eastern paintings, shows how painted volumes, following the direction of reading of each culture, are placed in different positions: the interpretation of images, then, is strictly dependent on the direction in which they are 'read'. Images in manga are thus 'written' in a 'language' suitable for Japanese eyes; it is necessary to 'translate' pages by inverting them in order to allow Western eyes to 'read' the same visual meaning. It seems, then, that the philological accuracy of non-inverted manga does not result in equivalence: in this case, the foreignizing strategy apparently misses its target.

However, what counts most is that the European reading public is firmly convinced that reading a non-inverted translated manga is the best way to appreciate it. But mirror inversion of pages does raise a number of issues. The first general consequence of inversion is the transformation of all characters into left-handers; moreover, many actions change their direction (actions made from left to right are turned into right-to-left actions, and vice versa). This situation may sometimes create some important problems. For instance, it is known that *samurai* followed a strict code of honour called *bushido*, whose rules obliged them never to hold their sword with their left hand. Unfortunately, inversion transforms what for samurai was a profound source of shame (i.e., swords held in left hands) into a rule.

A similar cultural issue related to inversion can be found in *Mugen no junin*, a samurai comic by Hiroaki Samura published in the US by Dark Horse (translated as *Blade of the*

---

[13] Many passionate European readers of comics (particularly manga readers) have developed intolerance towards what, for them, are unnecessary alterations of comics in translation: for instance, they do not tolerate graphic or textual censorship, they point out translation mistakes and discuss the quality of translated editions on Internet forums. Today, many European publishing houses have adopted a policy intended to satisfy these demanding readers: graphic elements (such as titles and other graphically rendered texts, which should be translated) are often left unaltered; cultural differences are explained in introductory articles or in footnotes; pages of Japanese comics are not inverted; even Japanese onomatopoeia are sometimes not adapted.

Immortal) and in Italy by Comic Art and Panini Comics (under the title *L'Immortale*). The main character, Manji, wears a kimono with a swastika on its back (one of the meanings of *manji*, in Japanese, is 'swastika'). The swastika with arms oriented anticlockwise is a Buddhist symbol, which was later adopted, in a version with clockwise-oriented arms, by Nazism. In a hypothetical inverted Western version of this comic, then, Manji would happen to wear a Nazi symbol instead of a Buddhist one. For this reason, the Italian version of this manga was published in non-inverted form; moreover, a new left-to-right version for the North-American market was prepared under the supervision of the original author, in which single panels were inverted instead of the whole page.

3.2 Japanese Comics: the Experience of the Foreign

Japanese manga depict a culture that is very distant from the Western context. Manga richly exploit Japanese culture and openly draw from folklore and traditions. Japanese comics frequently talk about classic demons and monsters (*oni, tengu, kappa*) or legends (*Urashima Taro, Yuki Onna*), and many manga characters are *ninja* or *samurai*. A domesticating strategy would have serious problems in handling all these 'alien' cultural elements, and surely it could not hide them. Similarly, a foreignizing strategy would leave Western readers puzzled before unknown and obscure cultural references.

For these reasons, many western editions of Japanese comics need rich textual introductions or, in some cases, even glossaries, to make the comprehension of Japanese cultural elements easier for European and North-American readers. For instance, the first Italian edition of *Sanctuary* by Sho Fumimura and Ryoichi Ikegami, published by Granata Press, is a manga about a *yakuza* gangster and a politician; this was enriched by a long and detailed introduction on Japanese politics written by Federico Colpi, in which the complex relationship between the *yakuza* (Japanese criminal organization) and Japanese political parties was brilliantly explained and clarified: unlike the Italian *mafia*, the Japanese *yakuza* acts openly in Japanese society, and its members are tolerated by the police unless they flagrantly violate the law. In the later reprint of *Sanctuary* by Star Comics, no introduction was offered, and many Italian readers of this edition found the plot absurd and appalling, as they were not able to recognize the profound differences between the *mafia* and the *yakuza*.

Glossaries are sometimes necessary to explain some untranslatable terms related to Japanese history and culture. The US and Italian editions of Kazuo Koike's and Goseki Kojima's *Kozure Okami* (*Lone wolf and cub*), a famous *samurai* series, are supplemented by a substantial appendix in which the meaning of terms like *ronin, seppuku* and *dotanuki* are explained. The same is true of Keichiro Ryu's and Tetsuo Hara's *Hana no Keiji*, a manga set in Medieval Japan, where glossary entries in the Italian edition by Star Comics explain the meaning of historical terms like *kabukimono, Sengoku jidai, daimyo*, as well as some units of measurement like *koku* or *shaku*.

These versions, then, adopt a foreignizing strategy, but at the same time try to avoid disorienting the reader by providing some cultural coordinates.

Even in translated editions, Japanese comics display their 'foreignness' in a patent way;

that is, their foreign origin cannot be hidden. Pages that run from right to left, their peculiar graphic and narrative styles, and the totally different culture which permeates them, make the application of a domesticating strategy totally ineffective. In short, Japanese comics are an example of how alterity overcomes any other element in translation. This is in no way limited to Japanese comics, but can be applied to the translation of all comics: although Far Eastern comics translated in Europe undoubtedly present an extreme case of recognition of alterity, the origin of every translated comic can be easily identified.

4.   Translated Comics and Alterity

In such a peculiar form of art as comics, the alterity of a foreign work emerges in an extremely evident way. The graphic styles of the different 'schools' (European, American and Japanese, to mention the most important and most exported), the layout of pages, the formats of publication which characterize each geographic area, all clearly appear before the eyes of the reader, who is able to detect without difficulty the origin of a comics publication. In short, translated comics seem to be the tangible proof of the 'épreuve de l'étranger' (the 'experience of the foreign') highlighted and wished for by Antoine Berman (1984).

Berman opposes literal translation with translation *ad sensum*, ethnocentric translation with ethical translation. He defines as *ethnocentric* that translation in which "on doit traduire l'œuvre étrangère de façon que l'on ne 'sente' pas la traduction", so as "la traduction doit se faire oublier" (Berman 1999:35; lit. 'one must translate the foreign work in a way that does not 'sense' the translation'). This vision of translation, based on the restitution of mere meaning, implies a hierarchy between the languages involved in the process, and a submission of the source language to the target language. Berman proposes instead an *ethical* translation, suggesting that "l'acte éthique consiste à reconnaître et à recevoir l'Autre en tant qu'Autre" (Berman 1999:74; 'the ethical act consists in recognizing and receiving the Other as Other'). These theories find supporting evidence in the translation of comics: it is impossible to 'domesticate' the original work in order to adapt it to other formats of publication without altering its essence, and it is likewise impossible to disguise it in order to hide its foreign origin.

The analysis of translated comics shows how one can overcome the present tendencies of the publishing industry which, denounced by Lawrence Venuti (1995; 1998), is inclined to 'flatten' translated texts in the search for an idealized 'readability' (in concert with usually tight publishing deadlines and the intellectual laziness of readers).[14] European readers of comics readers the radical differences in imported comics stories and are prepared to accept them. The resistance offered by comics to drastic adaptations aimed at hiding their origin underline how it is possible, and even necessary, to conceive of translation as the recognition of and respect for other cultures, rather than their assimilation into a standardized image.

---

[14] Venuti specifically analyzes the US publishing industry, but his analysis can be extended to other cultural contexts; for instance, even the Italian publishing industry generally adopts domesticating strategies in the translation of narrative texts.

References

Primary Sources

Asamiya, Kia (1989) [*Gunhed*, Tokyo: Kadokawa Shoten (*Gunhed*, Italian translation by Sandra Murer, *Zero* 24-27, Bologna: Granata Press, 1992].

Berardi, Giancarlo and Ivo Milazzo (1993) *Ken Parker. Il respiro e il sogno*, Milano: Parker Editore.

Bonelli, Gianluigi and Aurelio Galeppini (1948 ---) *Tex*, Milano: Sergio Bonelli Editore.

Castelli, Alfredo and Giancarlo Alessandrini (1982 ---) *Martin Mystère*, Milano: Sergio Bonelli Editore.

Choel, Jung (2003) *Eden*, Seoul: Sai Comics.

David, B. (1996) *L'ascension du haut mal*, Paris: L'Association.

EsseGesse (1970) *Il Comandante Mark*, Milano: If Edizioni.

Fumimura, Sho and Ryoichi Ikegami (1990) *Sanctuary*, Tokyo: Shogakukan [*Sanctuary*, Italian translation by Sandra Murer and Federico Colpi, *Zero*, 18-39; *Z Star* 30-37, Bologna: Granata Press, 1992; *Sanctuary*, Italian translation by Rieko Fukuda, Bosco: Star Comics, 2000].

Gaiman, Neil and Sam Kieth (1989) *The Sandman*, New York: DC Comics [*Sandman*, Italian translation by Luca Boschi, *Horror* 12-13, Roma: Comic Art, 1991].

Giussani, Angela and Luciana Giussani (1962 ---) *Diabolik*, Milano: Astorina.

Hergé (1929) *Tintin*, Bruxelles: Casterman.

Jacobs, Edgar-Pierre (1946 ---) *Blake et Mortimer*, Paris: Dargaud.

Koike, Kazuo and Goseki Kojima (1970) *Kozure Okami*, Tokyo: Studio Ship.

Kudo, Kazuya and Ryoichi Ikegami (1986) *Mai the psychic girl*, Tokyo: Shogakukan.

Le Tendre, Serge and Régis Loisel (1983 ---) *La quête de l'oiseau du temps*, Paris: Dargaud.

Lee, Stan and Jack Kirby (1961 ---) *Fantastic Four*, New York: Marvel Comics.

------ (1962 ---) *The Incredible Hulk*, New York: Marvel Comics.

Lee, Stan and Steve Ditko (1962 ---) *The Amazing Spider-Man*, New York: Marvel Comics; "Spider-Man" 1 (March 1963) ["L'Uomo Ragno" 1, Milano: Editoriale Corno, 1970].

Mantlo, Bill and Sal Buscema (1981) *The Incredible Hulk* 256, "Power in the Promised Land!" [*L'incredibile Hulk*, "Potere nella Terra Promessa", Italian translation by Pier Paolo Ronchetti, *Fantastici Quattro* 8, Bosco: Star Comics, 1989].

Medda, Michele, Antonio Serra, Bepi Vigna and Claudio Castellini (1991 ---) *Nathan Never*, Milano: Sergio Bonelli Editore.

Monkey Punch (1967) *Lupin Sansei*, Tokyo: Chuokoron-sha.

Morris (1949 ---) *Lucky Luke*, Paris: Dargaud.

Neaud, Fabrice (1996 ---), *Journal*, Paris: Ego Comme X.

Nolitta, Guido and Gallieno Ferri (1961 ---) *Zagor*, Milano: Sergio Bonelli Editore.

Oesterheld, Hector German and Francisco Solano Lopez (1958) *El Eternauta*, Buenos Aires: Ediciones Record.

Ōtomo, Katsuhiro (1982) *Akira*, Tokyo: Kodansha [*Akira*, English translation by Jo Duffy, New York: Marvel Comics, 1989].

Ryu, Keichiro and Tetsuo Hara (1990) *Hana no Keiji*, Tokyo: Shueisha [*Keiji il magnifico*, Italian translation by Rieko Fukuda and Anna Maria Moggi, Bosco: Star Comics, 1999].

Samura, Hiroaki (1994) *Mugen no junin*, Tokyo: Kodansha [*L'Immortale*, Roma: Comic Art, 1997].

Satrapi, Marjane (2000/03) *Persepolis*, Paris: L'Association.

Sclavi, Tiziano and Angelo Stano (1986 ---) *Dylan Dog*, Milano: Sergio Bonelli Editore.

Sfar, Joann and Lewis Trondheim (1998) *Donjon*, Paris: Delcourt.

Shintani, Kaoru (1979) *Area 88*, Tokyo: Shogakukan.

Shirato, Sanpei (1964) *Nippuu Kamui Gaiden*, Tokyo: Shogakukan.

Shirow, Masamune (1985) *Appleseed*, Tokyo: Seishinsha.

Siegel, Jerry and Joe Schuster (1938 ---) *Action Comics (Superman)*, New York: DC Comics.

Simmons, Shane (1993) *Longshot Comics Book One: The Long and Unlearned Life of Roland Gethers*, San Jose: Slave Labor.

Takahashi, Rumiko (1980) *Uruseiyatsura*, Tokyo: Shogakukan [*Lum – Perfect Collection* 1, English translation by Gerard Jones, San Francisco: Viz Communications, 1989].

Tanaka, Masashi (1992 ---) *Gon*, Tokyo: Kodansha.

Tezuka, Osamu (1973) *Black Jack*, Tokyo: Akita Shoten.

Thomas, Roy and Barry Windsor-Smith (1970 ---) *Conan the Barbarian*, New York: Marvel Comics.

Thomas, Roy and John Buscema (1977) *The Savage Sword of Conan* 24, New York: Marvel Comics [*Conan il Barbaro* 13, Roma: Comic Art, 1987; *Conan Chiaroscuro* 1, Italian translation by Gino Scatasta, Modena: Panini Comics, 1996].

Trondheim, Lewis (1992) *Lapinot et les carottes de Patagonie*, Paris: L'Association.

------ (1995) *La mouche*, Paris: Seuil.

Van Hamme, Jean and William Vance (1984-2007) *XIII*, Paris: Dargaud [*XIII*, *Euracomix* 52, Milano: Eura Editoriale, 1992].

Secondary Sources

Barbieri, Daniele (2004) 'Samurai allo specchio', *Golem l'indispensabile* 8 (online) http://www.golemindispensabile.it/Puntata43/articolo.asp?id=1688&num=43&sez=511&tipo=&mpp=&ed=&as= (Accessed 15 December 2005).

D'Arcangelo, Adele and Federico Zanettin (2004) 'Dylan Dog Goes to the USA: A North-American Translation of an Italian Comic Book Series', *Across Languages and Cultures* 5(2):187-211.

Berman, Antoine (1984) *L'épreuve de l'étranger*, Paris: Gallimard.

------ (1999) *La traduction et la lettre ou L'auberge du lointain*, Paris: Seuil.

Castelli, Alfredo (1983) 'Manga', *Eureka* 11/12:4-16.

Eco, Umberto (1964) *Apocalittici e integrati*, Milano: Bompiani.

Jannequin, Jean-Paul and Bernard Joubert (1994) 'L'avventura della Marvel in Francia', *Marvel Magazine* 1:126-128.

Lefevere, André (1992) *Translation, Rewriting, and the Manipulation of Literary Fame*, London: Routledge.

McCloud, Scott (1994) *Understanding Comics. The Invisible Art*, New York: Harper Collins.

Pesce, Marco (2000) 'Eternauti vecchi e nuovi', *Prospettiva Globale* (online) http://www.prospettivaglobale.com/PuntiVista/02.htm (Accessed 15 December 2005).

Raffaelli, Luca (1997) *Il fumetto*, Milano/Paris, Il Saggiatore/Flammarion.

------ (2003) 'Chi è l'Eternauta', *I classici del fumetto di Repubblica* 29:5-12.

------ (2006) 'La formula Bonelli non è esportabile', in Vittorio Spinazzola (ed.) *Tirature '06*, Milano: Il Saggiatore/Fondazione Mondadori, 217-221.

Rota, Valerio (2001) *Nuvole migranti. Viaggio nel fumetto tradotto*, Mottola: Lilliput Editrice.

Scatasta, Gino (2002) 'La traduzione dei fumetti', in Romana Zacchi and Massimiliano Morini (eds) *Manuale di traduzione dall'inglese*, Milano: Bruno Mondadori, 102-112.

Vaccari, Marcello (1999) 'Ciclone', *L'angolo dell'archeologo* 1 (online) http://associazioni.monet.modena.it/glamazonia/articoli/archeo1.htm (Accessed 15 December 2005).

Venuti, Lawrence (1995) *The Translator's Invisibility: A History of Translation*, London: Routledge.

------ (1998) *The Scandals of Translation: Towards an Ethics of Difference*, London: Routledge.

5 The Language of Trauma
Art Spiegelman's Maus *and its Translations*

RAFFAELLA BACCOLINI
University of Bologna, Italy

FEDERICO ZANETTIN
University of Perugia, Italy

This article examines the way in which foreign editions of Art Spiegelman's Maus, *which narrates in comic book form the story of his father's experience during the Shoah – as narrated to Art by him in later years – have dealt with one of the central themes of the book, namely the (un)translatability of trauma. The impossibility of telling is countered by an insistence on accuracy and detail, as well as the admission that language fails to convey the emotional distress associated with trauma. The current study focuses on the role of language and translation both in the English and in foreign editions. It first looks at translation as representation of an experience in the form of a narrative, in this case a comic book. One way through which Spiegelman succeeds in the telling of trauma without making sense of the Holocaust is represented by the role of language, particularly the choice to characterize the language of telling – his father's speech – with broken English. Spiegelman's concern with detail and accuracy can also be seen in his direct involvement in the translation of his work. The article discusses the translations of* Maus *into a number of languages and cultures, and considers how the use of broken language is carried over in the translations. More specifically, the focus is on comparing the translation into Italian by Cristina Previtali with a previous edition translated by Ranieri Carano.*

This essay analyzes Art Spiegelman's classic graphic novel *Maus*, which deals with his father's experience during the Shoah,[1] a work which has received numerous prizes and won much recognition even within academia. The aspect that has most attracted critics' and scholars' attention is, naturally, the author's treatment of the Holocaust (see, for example, Witek 1990:96-120, Orvell 1992, Hirsch 1992-93, Tabachnick 1993, Iadonisi 1994, Rothberg 1994, Cory 1995, Doherty 1996, Lowenstein 1998, Young 1998, Geis 2003, McGlothlin 2003, Elmwood 2004, Chute 2005). A crucial issue in the debate about Holocaust literature is the question of the representability and translatability of trauma into words and images – that is, the crisis of representation and language that often follows a traumatic experience. The impossibility to tell – the divide that is often created between survivors and witnesses and those that have not experienced an event – is accompanied by an imperative to account and pass on one's story, the desire to translate one's life to others. Such impossibility to tell is countered, paradoxically, by an insistence on accuracy and detail as well as the admission of the failure of language.

---

[1] Although we are aware of the unfortunate sacrificial connotation attached to the term 'Holocaust', we will use it interchangeably with the more appropriate Hebrew 'Shoah', since Holocaust is the most widely accepted term both in common and scholarly usage.

Language fails to convey the emotional distress associated with trauma; trauma resists language; and yet only a most accurate telling can begin to write trauma.

In this essay, we focus on the role of language and translation with regard to the telling of trauma both in the English and in foreign editions. The term 'translation' will thus be used to describe the articulation of feelings and physical pain in verbal form; the narrativisation of one's own life history; the editing of such a history into the mixed form of Spiegelman's own account of himself and his father; and finally the re-representation of the graphic novel in Italian. We first look at translation as representation of an experience in narrative form, in this case a comic book: having recorded in a series of oral interviews the story of his father's experience in the concentration camps (and much more), Spiegelman went on to condense, arrange and translate that wealth of information into what Will Eisner has defined as 'sequential storytelling' (1985). Spiegelman's original material, more than 40 hours of recorded conversation with his father, is translated on the page in a continuous movement between past and present – the story recorded and the telling of the story itself. One way through which Spiegelman succeeds in the telling of trauma without making sense of the Holocaust concerns the role of language in his writing. In particular, the choice to characterize the language of telling – his father's speech – with broken English generates a displacing effect that, in turn, becomes an apt representation of the foreignness and senselessness of the Holocaust experience (Rosen 2003).

Spiegelman's concern with detail and accuracy can also be seen in his direct involvement in the translation of his work. We discuss below the translations of *Maus* into a number of languages and cultures and consider how the use of broken language is carried over in the translations. More specifically, we attempt a comparison between the translation into Italian by Cristina Previtali (2000) and a previous edition translated by Ranieri Carano (1989-1992).

1.   Translating Trauma

In an ironic comment, Spiegelman himself has reflected on how 'naturally' trauma seems to come to him: "after all, disaster is my muse!" (Spiegelman 2004:n.p.). When we talk about trauma – the term comes from the Greek word for 'wound' – we refer to "a disordered psychic or behavioral state resulting from mental or emotional stress or physical injury" (Webster online). The medical definition of trauma, then, refers to a serious and acute injury or wound. From the psychological and psychiatric points of view, trauma refers to a disruptive, extreme experience that has belated mental and physical effects and symptoms, such as the occurrence of flashbacks, nightmares, depression, numbness and fits of panic. Such an experience shakes the foundations of one's beliefs and shatters one's world view: it "indicates a shattering or cesura in experience which has belated effects" (La Capra 2001:186). According to Dominick La Capra, trauma is a shocking experience that "disarticulates the self and creates holes in existence" (2001:41). Despite the fact that the perception of trauma varies depending on an individual's history and culture, in the new life that is created after a trauma there is no order or control. As Terrence Des Pres states, "[w]here men and women are forced to endure terrible things at the hand of others – whenever, that is, extremity involves moral issues – the need to remember becomes a general response. ... Survival and bearing witness become reciprocal acts" (1980:29).

The literature of trauma – what La Capra calls "writing trauma" as distinguished from "writing about trauma" (2001:186) – "holds at its center the reconstruction and recuperation of the traumatic experience" (Tal 1996:17).[2] Such writing, however, is also actively engaged in a dialogue with its readers, in the attempt to tell, explain, and recreate an experience that, by its very definition, "lies beyond the bounds of 'normal' conception" and is thus unimaginable (ibid.:15). Being mediated by language, textual representations "do not have the impact of the traumatic experience", and they therefore usually address the impossibility to narrate traumatic events (ibid.). The wound created by a traumatic episode also entails a crisis of representation: how can trauma be narrated when it often refers to an extreme and overwhelming event that was not fully grasped as it occurred? How can language best convey an experience and its lasting effects that often defy language itself? The same words "hold different realities" for survivors and bystanders (Wiesel 1990:33). Moreover, with regard to physical pain, Elaine Scarry has noted that pain, often inexpressible and incommunicable, "does not simply resist language but actively destroys" the victims' voices (1985:4).

Writing trauma is then a difficult attempt to come to terms and "work through" (to borrow Sigmund Freud's words) the shattering of one's world, in the hope of regaining control over one's emotions and memories. But such a working through often becomes, in turn, a reflection on the inadequacy of language in conveying the experience in question. Moreover, reflection on the possibility of language in the face of loss and trauma is often accompanied by the presence of another conflict: the risk of turning trauma and violence into a spectacle and the fear of exploiting the suffering. Guilt, disillusion, resentment, fear of exploitation and of being misunderstood accompany the need nonetheless to remember and speak.[3] This complex enterprise ultimately reveals that it is only rarely that literature provides comfort or healing; rather, it offers an attempt to shape the way in which one's experience is written into history. To tell History without making room for the personal stories seems to tell it all wrong.

However, if traumas can be devastating and upsetting, they can also be opportunities for change. The literature of trauma asks its readers to participate; it is literature that works by shocking and wounding readers, often by way of identification. Bearing witness, in Kalí Tal's words (1996:7), is

> an aggressive act. It is born out of a refusal to bow to outside pressure to revise
> or to repress experience, a decision to embrace conflict rather than conformity,

---

[2] Depending on one's definition of trauma, literature dealing with traumatic events can refer exclusively to the writing of survivors and victims or, in a broader sense, also to writing by people (relatives, in particular) indirectly involved in trauma, but experiencing terror ensuing from the memory of trauma. In the latter case, one definition is 'family' or 'quiet trauma' (see Kaplan 1).

[3] The representation of the Holocaust is a highly controversial issue among European and American critics. For an overview of different positions, see Baccolini (2003).

to endure a lifetime of anger and pain rather than to submit to the seductive pull of revision and repression. Its goal is change.

The very act of translating a traumatic experience into language becomes a new creation, a critical activity, an instance of bearing witness, and a way of ensuring the survival of one's memories. For it is true, as Walter Benjamin says in 'Theses on the Philosophy of History', that "every image of the past that is not recognized by the present as one of its own concerns threatens to disappear irretrievably" (1992:V, 247). In this process, this literature also invites readers to go beyond the initial shock or wound and "work toward the more subtle work of articulating the haunting presence of trauma in everyday life" (Harad 2003:online).

When dealing with trauma, then, writers need to find specific strategies to account for such complexity. A common feature of trauma literature is the awareness of the very complexity surrounding trauma and its representation. Writing trauma insists on the failure of communication, accepts the inadequacy of language, openly discusses them, and yet, at the same time, tries to capture the unimaginable through an almost maniacal attention to detail. Accuracy becomes a central strategy to counter what cannot be accurately described nor imagined. Nicolas Dames finds in 'the traumatic' the most authentic form of memory, the opposite of 'the nostalgic'. Dames's claim is interesting not so much for what he says about authenticity – after all it has been noted that witness literature is not important in terms of *factual* events but rather in terms of *felt* experience – but for

Figure 5.1: Art Spiegelman, *Maus II*, 1991, p. 16

what he identifies with the traumatic: i.e., "the particular, the accurate, the connected, the unwilled, the unpleasant" (2001:74). Although it is difficult to generalize about trauma literature – because people react to a traumatic event differently – one way to deal with writing trauma is to try to communicate what is unimaginable and disturbing through accurate, precise details.

The dilemma of not knowing, together with the impossibility of understanding, pervades Spiegelman's book, as explicitly shown at the beginning of the second volume of *Maus* in the conversations between Art and his wife (Figure 5.1) and Art and his psychoanalyst Pavel, also a camp survivor (see *Maus* II:40-ff.).
The panels explicitly show Spiegelman's angst about his fraught project. For him, Anja's lost diaries – which his mother wrote for him and his father burned in a moment of depression and despair after his wife committed suicide (see Figure 5.9) – become the book's metaphor for the irretrievability of the Holocaust experience, against which his attempt can only pale in comparison.

But Spiegelman is also careful to make the point that there can be no understanding of the Holocaust (Figure 5.2). The series of panels serves the purpose of showing the gap in communication and understanding between trauma survivors and others. But it also provides an example of how to avoid imposing meaning on the Nazi genocide. 'Normal' logic cannot apply to the world of the concentration camps: Art's disorientation invites readers to abandon all expectations of meaning and logic. This is the point of Vladek's comment: it is not just that those who did not experience the camps cannot understand what it was like, the Holocaust itself defies comprehension.

Figure 5.2: Art Spiegelman, *Maus II*, 1991, p. 64

Another point Spiegelman gets across is the fear that once the relevant experience has been revealed, nothing really changes. This fear is explicitly mentioned by Art's psychoanalyst, when he helplessly states that knowing and understanding do not necessarily bring about change (Figure 5.3).

Moreover, knowing and trying to understand – as partial and limited as they can be – do not even allow for healing. As Vladek recounts the hanging of some friends with whom he dealt in black market affairs, time does not seem to have changed his feelings (Figure 5.4).
Even more importantly, Spiegelman seems to say that art also does not provide a cure for trauma. Showing his father some sketches of his book, including the episode of the hanged black market Jews, Vladek's response is once again the same (Figure 5.5).

Figure 5.3: Art Spiegelman, *Maus II*, 1991, p. 45

Figure 5.4: Art Spiegelman, *Maus I*, 1986, p. 84

Figure 5.5: Art Spiegelman, *Maus I*, 1986, p. 133

And yet, even though the translation of trauma does not seem to allow for much healing, according to Robert S. Leventhal (1995:online),

> traversing the breach between past and present, Father and Son, language and image, manifest and latent, Spiegelman's *Maus* bears witness to the process of bearing witness, and the technical and technological requirement of writing and tape-recording in order to produce a narrative of the trauma and thereby alleviate the symptomology of depression and withdrawal that is the danger of a past left to fester as an unhealed wound.

2. *Maus* and the Process of Translating Vladek's Narrative

It took Spiegelman thirteen years and a couple of trips to Auschwitz to complete the story of his family, and of his father's terrifying journey through the camps in WWII in particular. Between 1972 and 1979 he interviewed his father; he then started working on the strips in the 1980s, publishing the first volume, *Maus: A Survivor's Tale*, in 1986. The first volume of *Maus* was translated into eighteen languages (Safran Foer 2005:297). The second volume, *Maus: And Here My Troubles Began*, was published in 1991, and following the award of the Pulizter Prize in 1992 (as the first comic book to win that literary competition), Spiegelman's autobiographical account of life as the child of Holocaust survivors went on to become a classic and to make a major contribution to changing the perception that "comic books are brightly colored adventure stories mass-produced for children" (Witek 2004:online).

In 1994 Spiegelman published *The Complete Maus*, a CD-ROM which details the design process of the comic book, and which contains digital images of all the pages of the novel together with large samples of the materials used as a basis (transcripts of the interviews with Vladek, pictures and maps, drawings) and other accompanying materials. Interviews with the author, samples of other works, and other marginalia and appendices offer "an exploration of the production and reception of the comic" and highlight "the awareness of its own constructedness and self-reflexivity" (Anderson and Katz 2003:160). Navigating through the hypertext, it is possible to follow the process which started from the audio recordings of the interviews of Vladek Spiegelman and their transcriptions, and from the drafts and sketches by Art, and led to the creation of the graphic novel. In an audio commentary, Spiegelman explains how page layout and drawings were often the result of a long and laborious study aimed at recovering every detail of his father's experience (point of view, maps) and how the original interviews, which did not follow a chronological order, where re-worked into a chronological narrative. This aspect is condensed in a panel where Art asks Vladek to keep his story straight (Figure 5.6).

Figure 5.6: Art Spiegelman, *Maus I*, 1986, p. 82

The main narrative frame of the book is the present time of writing, within which the narration of Vladek and Art's conversations is embedded. These episodes contain Vladek's tale, but the chronology of the events told has been reconstructed. When the events narrated by Vladek are visually represented, rather than told in the dialogues between father and son, Vladek's narration is shown as captions contained within square boxes, placed outside the main drawing (Figure 5.7) or in the gutter; balloons, on the other hand, are used for the dialogue among characters.

Figure 5.7: Art Spiegelman, *Maus I*, 1986, p. 136

Vladek's narration is thus constructed like a series of flashbacks, where the events and characters represented are commented upon by the off-screen voice of the narrator. The filmic metaphor is in fact suggested at the beginning of the first chapter, when Vladek starts his narration. The lower left half of the page is occupied by a larger than usual and borderless panel, in which Vladek is shown pedalling, with a large movie poster in the background of the famous Rudolph Valentino film *The Sheik* (Figure 5.8).

The distinction between these two different planes of narration is not only rendered through this visual device, but is also given a different verbal representation. In fact, while Vladek's narrative voice is at times almost taken whole from the transcriptions, and closely represents the language variety used by him, a type of 'broken English' spoken by Jewish immigrants of Polish origin, the dialogues between the characters, which would have taken place in Polish, are in standard English. In other words, direct speech is in broken English, while reported speech is 'translated' by Spiegelman from Vladek's broken English into standard English (see Figures 5.7 and 5.8).

Maus is both a collective and individual work – or even, as has been suggested, a "collaborative autobiography" (see Iadonisi 1994) consisting of the father's memories

Figure 5.8: Art Spiegelman, *Maus I*, 1986, p. 13

mediated by the son's perceptions. Spiegelman himself underlines this aspect of his work: "*Maus* is not what happened in the past, but rather what the son understands of the father's story. [… It is] an autobiographical history of my relationship with my father, a survivor of the Nazi death camps, cast with cartoon animals" (quoted in Young 1998:670). *Maus*, then, has been seen as a "narrative hybrid" that makes room for history and memory: not the Holocaust as it actually occurred but the histories that Spiegelman, like many other second generation people, has heard or read over the years (Young 1998:669). In this light, Spiegelman's mother's lost diaries become a central image in the book (see Figure 5.9). They represent the irretrievable, what has been lost and cannot be recovered. They are a symbol of the impossibility of recovering, adequately portraying, and understanding the trauma of the Holocaust. According to Saul Friedlander's distinction, they represent "deep memory", i.e., "that which remains essentially inarticulable and unrepresentable, that which continues to exist as unresolved trauma just beyond the reach of meaning" as distinguished from "common memory", i.e., "that which 'tends to restore or establish coherence, closure and possibly a redemptive stance'" (quoted in Young 1998:666-67). It is in the nature of *Maus*'s historical narrative hybrid – with its visual and verbal devices – that common and deep memory find representation.[4]

In Spiegelman's work, the strategies that are most congenial to the author in order to come to terms with the complexity of his father's language and the narrative structure and to capture the complexity of telling trauma are: the medium itself, the comics; the extensive research and documentation which led to visual and verbal accuracy; and the role of English and of Vladek's variety of it.

As John Carlin argues, Spiegelman "uses the language of comics to help us feel what cannot be said or seen about the real horrors of genocide" (2005:134). The mixture of words and images is particularly conducive to the collapsing of past and present, personal

---

[4] Spiegelman's works deal with two traumatic events that are commonly considered as a watershed: the Shoah and the 11 September 2001 World Trade Center attack. Spiegelman's most recent work, the 'elliptical essay' *In the Shadow of No Towers*, also tries to capture the complexity of the events by juxtaposing personal and collective experiences and by showing how "past and present bleed into each other" ('An Interview': 2005 online). For Spiegelman, the main similarity between *Shadow* and *Maus* is that he found himself "at the intersection where personal history and world history cross" ('Off the Page' 2004:online). Although he initially thought to "capture what happened to [him] that day", show what he had seen "directly", and contrast that with the "media reality", the project also ended up resonating "with the nature of the ephemeral and the eternal – what it is to have something that was never meant to last, like a newspaper, and something meant to last forever, like the pyramids or the World Trade Center towers" (Spiegelman, quoted in Leopold 2004:online). The nature of the ephemeral and the eternal is, to a certain extent, present also in Spiegelman's *Maus* and its attempt to translate trauma: the need to counter the passing of time and the force of oblivion with the story of his father, the desire to understand, and the recognition of the impossibility of full recovery and adequate portrayal of trauma can be seen as another attempt to reproduce the relationship between these two terms. The book presents itself as another narrative hybrid, one that includes an introduction, ten comic strips, and an appendix that explains and reprints the original classic comic strips that are worked in Spiegelman's panels. As in *Maus* with Anja's diaries, in *Shadow* the difficulty of representing the skeleton of the north tower glowing just before it collapsed symbolizes the irretrievability of trauma. Spiegelman's recent work has not received as much attention yet. One of the reasons may be the fact that Spiegelman's take on the WTC attack has included criticism of the Bush administration at a moment when criticism of American politics was synonymous with being 'unpatriotic'. This has resulted in a controversial work that was considered more suited for a European public, was therefore turned down by prestigious journals like *The New York Review of Books*, and found a publishing venue in the US only on the pages of a minor Jewish periodical – *Forward* (Farkas 2002:125, 127).

Figure 5.9: Art Spiegelman, *Maus I*, 1986, p. 158

and collective, and can better attempt to capture the trauma that mind and eye cannot imagine. According to Leventhal, "In *Maus*, the image is never left to stand alone, but is always caught up in the differential between narrative, image, dialogue and reflection. In this manner, an opening or aperture for critical thinking on the transmission of past trauma is created" (1995:online). Spiegelman says of comics that "as a medium [they] are really about choreographing time" (quoted in Baker 2004:online); they are "about time made manifest spatially, in that you've got all these different chunks of time – each box being a different moment of time – and you see them all at once. As a result you're always, in comics, being made aware of different times inhabiting the same space" (quoted in Silverblatt 1995:35).[5]

Spiegelman's description above of comics and their ability to make readers "aware of different times inhabiting the same space" is fundamental also to understanding the recurrence and persistence of trauma. In fact, in *Maus*, the collapsing of past and present is rendered in various ways that involve the mixture of words and images, at times mostly language, and elsewhere predominantly images: from the opening frames, where

---

[5] As mentioned, both *Maus* and *In the Shade of No Towers* are examples of hybridity. *Maus*, in particular, is a difficult book to catalogue as regards 'genre': as Hillary Chute has noted, "this book is fictional and non-fictional; modernist and postmodernist; esoteric and popular; universalizing and particularizing; representational and non-representational; narrative and experimental" (2005:online). Spiegelman's distress at finding his book placed in the Fiction Best Seller List of the *New York Times Book Review* is by now a well-known fact. Members of the Pulitzer Prize committee were similarly "befuddled by a project whose merit they could not deny but whose medium they could not quite categorize" (Doherty 1996:69).

young Art's friends' "cruelty" becomes the pretext for a tirade on friendship on Vladek's part (*Maus* I:5-6), through dialogue, as for example when Art tells Françoise of his Zyklon B fantasy (*Maus* II:16), to "silent" images as when Vladek, Art, and Françoise drive through a wood in the Catskills where several bodies hang from the tree (*Maus* II:79).

The point of the opening panels is to show how pervasive the memory of the Holocaust is for both Vladek and Art. The book is divided between sequences that show Vladek and his family in the past before Art's birth and others that show Vladek and his family in the present, including Art and his wife Françoise and Vladek's new companion, Mala, also a Holocaust survivor. The opening pages are the only instance of the past that includes Art as well. In them we see a ten-year-old Art skating with friends, falling, and being made fun of by them. A crying Art goes to his father, apparently in search of comfort, whereas the episode allows Vladek to hint – as seems to be typical – at his past in the camps (Figure 5.10). The opening suggests that memories of the Holocaust were

Figure 5.10: Art Spiegelman, *Maus I*, 1986, p. 6

part of Art's education – suggesting also, however, that Art's life has been permanently shaped by the experience of his parents.

In other instances the pervasiveness of Holocaust memories is more openly discussed and recognized by the author himself. In a series of exchanges with his wife, Spiegelman addresses the question as he remembers his child's nightmares (Figure 5.11).

Figure 5.11: Art Spiegelman, *Maus II*, 1991, p. 16

In this dialogue, Spiegelman clearly appears as a "survivor" himself, not of the primary trauma, but as E. Ann Kaplan would say, of "family" or "quiet trauma". Similarly, in another strip, as Françoise and Art hear Vladek moaning in his sleep, we understand how apparently "normal" life with Holocaust memories must have been for Art. To a fearful Françoise who inquires about the noise, Art replies, "Oh, nothing – just Vladek… He's moaning in his sleep again. When I was a kid I thought that was the noise all grown-ups made while they slept" (*Maus* II:74).

In yet other instances, however, the persistence of Holocaust memory is silent, or simply drawn. This is the case in a panel which shows Art, his wife and his father driving through a wood in the Catskills, as Vladek responds to Art's enquires about some prisoners' revolt in Auschwitz. As he remembers the fate they encountered, that is that they all got killed, we see the bodies of the four girls hanging from the trees (Figure 5.12).

In another case the panels juxtapose, once again, present and past: the time represented is the present, but the drawings explicitly allude to what David Rousset (1947) called the "concentrationary universe". At the beginning of chapter 2 of *Maus II*, the panel shows a depressed Art sitting at his drawing table on a pile of dead bodies. Outside his window there's a concentration camp watch-tower (Figure 5.13).

This panel and those following allow the author to discuss his mixed and guilty feelings over his possible exploitation of the Holocaust, anticipating a debate that will become central years later in books such as Norman G. Finkelstein's *The Holocaust Industry*. In a way, the silent imagery can also be seen as an example of the meticulous accuracy that characterizes Spiegelman's work, including research, documentation, and follow-up attention to issues such as publication formats and translation. Also in the realm of the visual, diagrams and maps shape the narrative, as when Vladek explains how to sew a boot (*Maus* II:60), or ten pages later, when he explains the layout of the crematoria

Figure 5.12: Art Spiegelman, *Maus II*, 1991, p. 79

Figure 5.13: Art Spiegelman, *Maus II*, 1991, p. 41

(*Maus* II:70). As Stephen E. Tabachnick has observed, "the boot diagram prepares us for the crematorium diagram: the first explains a technical process that most people simply do not know about while the second describes a technical process that most people cannot even imagine" (1993:158). Or again, when the crematorium in the last panel of page 69 (*Maus* II) enters the panel above it, and the smoke of Art's cigarette becomes, simultaneously, the smoke of the crematorium (Figure 5.14).

Details allow Spiegelman to come close to representing the unimaginable and to collapsing the past into the present, as when Vladek is drawn on the ground in the shape of a David's star (*Maus* I, 80), or when Vladek and Anja walk on a swastika-shaped road – with the clear suggestion that wherever they would go they would go toward danger (Figure 5.15).[6]

Figure 5.14: Art Spiegelman, *Maus II*, 1991, p. 69

---

[6] Another example of accuracy is the section describing a family reunion (Maus I:74-75): while the grown-ups are discussing the dangerous, recent events, the kids at the table, Richieu and Lolek, are scolded by Anja and her mother, respectively – one for spilling food on the tablecloth and the other for reading at the table. It is an example of silent narrative that often goes unnoticed. It is also a way of condensing information that Spiegelman was given in the oral interviews.

Figure 5.15: Art Spiegelman, *Maus I*, 1986, p. 125

Some criticism has been levelled at the choice of using the language and conventions of comics to deal with the theme of the Holocaust.[7] However, paradoxically the animal metaphor can also be seen as an attempt to be as accurate as possible in the face of the dilemma of untranslatability. By depicting the Jews as mice and the Germans as cats, Spiegelman draws on the tradition of "funny animal comics" and at the same time subverts it, in that he is not only consistent with the Nazi propaganda of the times, which featured Jews as the vermin of society, but he is also authentic. Because he did not experience the Holocaust firsthand, any representation that attempts to be more realistic would look inauthentic. Linked to this, the insertion of real pictures (his brother Richieu's, the author and his mother's, his father's) contributes to undermining the animal metaphor.[8] The horror of racial theory is not supported by the metaphor, rather it is dismantled and denounced through it. As Adam Gopnik has noted, the use of the animal metaphor suggests "the condition of human beings forced to behave as animals" as well as the sense that "this story is too horrible to be presented" (quoted in Tabachnick 1993:158). Spiegelman himself explains this point: "If one draws this kind of

---

[7] In the CD-ROM interview, Spiegelman (1994b) recalls how in Germany he was asked whether he did not think that drawing the Jews as mice was "in bad taste", to which he replied, "No, I think the Holocaust was in bad taste".
[8] On the use and function of Holocaust pictures in *Maus*, see Hirsch (1992-93).

Figure 1.1: R. F. Outcault and E. W. Townsend, 'McFadden's Row of Flats',
New York Journal, 18 Oct. 1896

Figure 1.2: Five different versions of Spider-Man

Figure 1.5: Alan Moore, Dave Gibbons and John Higgins, *Watchmen,* 1986, p. 4

Figure 2.1a: Tome et Janry, *Le petit Spirou*, 1994, p. 13

Figure 2.1b: Tome et Janry, *Il piccolo Spirù*, 1997, p. 13 (Italian translation: Luca Basenghi)

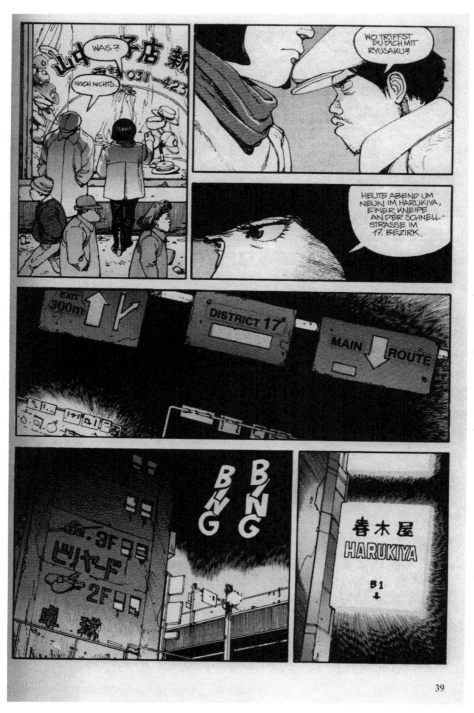

Figure 3.1a: Katsuhiro Ōtomo, *Akira*, vol. 1, 2000, p. 39 (German translation: Junko Iwamoto-Seebeck and Jürgen Seebeck)

Figure 3.1b: Katsuhiro Otomo, *Akira* vol. 1, 1991, p. 39 (German translation: Junko Iwamoto Seebeck and Jürgen Seebeck)

Figure 6.1a: Alan Moore, John Totleben and Tatiana Wood, *Swamp Thing Book 3 The Curse. The Nukeface Paper, part 1,* 2000, p. 5

PROLOGO:

Mentre la sua amata dorme, la creatura della palude siede nel fuoco rosa senza fiamme che è il crepuscolo e sorveglia i suoi territori.

Ad oriente, i fattorini dei giornalai si sono stufati a metà del loro giro di consegne, buttano con discrezione i giornali avanzati e dicono all'edicolante che deve aver sbagliato il conto. I titoli monotoni danzano su di un vento tiepido, erbe monocrome che rotolano attraverso sempre meno luce.

Lui osserva i fogli dei giornali sbattere come enormi falene, paralizzate dal loro stesso peso, mentre zoppicano goffamente tra gli alberi neri. Le loro pagine sono piene di tragedie obsolete e di volti abbandonati; tutta l'isteria attentamente registrata di un mondo a cui lui più non appartiene.

Dietro di lui, la sua amata borbotta tre sillabe sommerse dai sogni, ma non si sveglia, e lui è felice sotto lo scurirsi di un cielo vulcanico. La palude li sommerge. E' il loro cosmo umido, e i problemi del mondo distante non sembrano nulla più che le conversazioni bisbigliate di folli lontani...

Figure 6.1b: Alan Moore and John Totleben, *Swamp Thing. La maledizione. Il carteggio Nukeface, Ia parte*, 2006, page 1 (Italian translation: Leonardo Rizzi)

Figure 9.3a: Charlier and Giraud, *La pista dei Navajos*, Crespi Editore, 1971, p. 47

Figure 9.3b: Charlier and Giraud, *La pista dei Navajos*, Alessandro Editore, 2005, p. 45

Figure 9.4a: Charlier and Giraud, *La pista dei Navajos*, Crespi Editore, 1971, p. 13

Figure 9.4b: Charlier and Giraud, *La pista dei Navajos*, Edizioni Nuova Frontiera, 1982, p. 11

Figure 9.4c: Charlier and Giraud, *La pista dei Navajos*, Alessandro Distribuzioni, 2005, p. 11

Figure 9.5a: Charlier and Giraud, *La piste des Navajos*, Dargaud, 1969, p. 27

Figure 9.5b: Charlier and Giraud, *La pista dei Navajos*, Crespi Editore, 1971, p. 29

Figure 9.6a: Charlier and Giraud, *La piste des Navajos*, Dargaud, 1969, p. 40

Figure 9.6b: Charlier and Giraud, *La pista dei Navajos*, Crespi Editore, 1971, p. 42

Figure 9.8a: Charlier and Giraud, *La pista dei Navajos*, Edizioni Nuova Frontiera, 1982, p. 12

Figure 9.8b: Charlier and Giraud, *La pista dei Navajos*, Alessandro Distribuzioni, 2005, p. 12

Figure 9.7a: Charlier and Giraud, *La pista dei Navajos*, Edizioni Nuova Frontiera, 1982, p. 4

Figure 9.7b: Charlier and Giraud, *La pista dei Navajos*, Alessandro Distribuzioni, 2005, p. 4

Figure 10.1: The Winx Club

Figure 10.2: Giorgio Pezzin, Michele Lilli, Juliette and Luca dell'Annunziata, 'I Ragazzi di Fonterossa', *The Winx Club Magazine*, 3, 2004, p. 35

Figure 11.2: Bill Watterson, *Calvin y Hobbes,* 1994 (Spanish translation: Gabriel Roura)

Figure 11.3: Midam, 'Kid Paddle', *El Pequeño País*, November 22, 2006, p. 1

Figure 12.2a: Goscinny and Uderzo, *Astérix chez les Bretons*, 1966, p. 21

Figure 12.2b: Goscinny and Uderzo, *Asterix in Britain*, 1970, p. 21 (English translation: Anthea Bell and Derek Hockridge)

stuff with people it comes out wrong. And the way it comes out wrong is, first of all, I've never lived through anything like that … and it would be counterfeit to try to pretend that the drawings are representations of something that's actually happening. I don't know what a German looked like who was in a small town doing a specific thing. My notions are born of a few score of photographs and a couple of movies. I'm bound to do something inauthentic" (quoted in Witek 1990:102).

In order to capture the complexity of his father's traumatic experience, Spiegelman also foregrounds the issue of language. In the debate surrounding Holocaust literature, an attempt has been made to assess the significance of specific languages (see Ezrahi 1980). While Yiddish and German are the languages that have been most affected since they are "the languages of the victim and persecutor", English has not been considered 'fit' because, being "of little significance in the camps and ghettoes, [it] has a marginal standing, making it an 'outsider' and marking it with 'autonomy' and 'purity'" (Rosen 2003:123). English can at best be a translation.

In *Maus*, on the other hand, Spiegelman makes the English language a theme. If English is not traditionally a language of Holocaust testimony, it becomes so by the particular use that Spiegelman makes of it and the effect it has on its (American) readers. As mentioned above, there is a contrast between the fluent, colloquial English used to represent the languages of Europe as spoken by their native speakers and Vladek's broken English in the present (the language of telling). Vladek's linguistic characterization separates him from other survivors (e.g. Mala and the psychoanalyst) who speak fluent English even in the present, and marks Vladek's tale as an individual story. Thus, even though Mala in reality "speaks with a thick accent but her actual language is quite good", Spiegelman chooses not to characterize her speech as broken English: her thick accent, in fact, "wasn't an issue" (see Spiegelman's Interview in Previtali 2000:177). According to Alan C. Rosen, "Vladek's 'tortured, visualized prose' … is not only meant to represent an English-speaking 'foreigner' but is also meant to torture English into being a foreign language" (2003:129). It is therefore this very quality of 'foreignness' that makes English a language of testimony. In fact, "[b]y fracturing Vladek's English and by making it the most foreign language in *Maus* …, Spiegelman uses it to convey the foreignness of the Holocaust itself" (Rosen 2003:129). Through Vladek's broken English, Spiegelman "articulates the incommensurability between past and present. … Paradoxically, it is not the representation of events of the Holocaust itself that is most foreign to the American readers of *Maus*; it is rather *the telling* about the Holocaust, the testimony, that carries the burden of everything that is foreign" (Rosen 2003:130-131).

3.   Translating *Maus* into Other Languages

Such linguistic characterization has indeed proven to be one of the most problematic aspects of the publication of foreign editions of *Maus*. Spiegelman himself has been aware of the issues involved in translation and has been very keen to collaborate with foreign translators and publishers. In an audio interview included in the *Maus* CD-ROM,

Spiegelman discusses how foreign editions did not receive the same attention or critical praise in all countries. According to him, for instance, the comic book did not receive much attention in Japan, possibly both because of its topic – "Jews are totally exotic"– and because of its going against reading conventions for comics in that country (Spiegelman 1994b). Compared to western comics, Japanese comics require a rather shorter reading time, since they usually contain many pages with very few or even no words. *Maus*, which is very dense even by western standards as regards the proportion of text to the images, is "too dense" for Japanese readers, who are used to comics where "the panel to panel movements are almost like looking at the frames of a film" (Spiegelman 1994b; our transcription).[9] In other countries, such as Hungary, Sweden, and Denmark, *Maus* was also not very successful, and was never published in full.

It could be argued that the perception of Spiegelman's work in the receiving cultures influenced its translation, indeed the very possibility of its translation. In Israel, for instance, *Maus* was never published, even though a publisher had initially worked on the project and the work had been partly translated. This situation, an instance of the primary norms (Toury 1995) which determine what gets and what does not get translated, can be ascribed to a form of resistance on the part of the target culture to the treatment of the themes of identity and memory in *Maus*.

In a 2005 interview, Marianne Hirsch, whose writings on *Maus* were instrumental in giving the comic book academic recognition, reports on a course she co-taught the previous year at Dartmouth and at the University of Tel Aviv about memory of the Holocaust in Israel and the US. *Maus* was among the texts chosen for discussing memory and national identity, and it provoked heated discussion: "some of the students in Israel were just bursting to talk about how troubling they found the book. Especially the professor, but also some of the students" (Kuhlman 2005:online). Pointing out that *Maus* has not been translated into Hebrew, Hirsch tries to explain how controversial its reception could be in Israel: "I think that being in Israel, picking up a book that has a swastika on the cover, no matter what the book is about, is really searing ... the cover was painful and offensive to some of the class members and those students could not get beyond that shock to talk about it further" (Kuhlman 2005:online).

According to Spiegelman, the difficulties experienced with the Israeli edition may be explained partly with the representation of Jews as mice and partly with the viewpoint from which the story is told:

> The image of a mouse is very difficult in Israel. They like to think of themselves as at least cats. I think it's more a military culture so the idea of being a mouse is a problem. ... The other thing, and again, that's just my guess, is that in most works about this period, especially in the ones that have come to popular culture to some degree, Israel is the happy ending of the story. In *Schindler's List* it is the happy ending, everywhere ... And then in the historical culture you see that the Jewish

[9] However, as Spiegelman remarks elsewhere on the foreign translations of *Maus* (Interview in Previtali 2000:173), "for some reason that I don't know, the Korean edition goes well. I don't understand... I really don't understand".

continuity is there and whatever. And in my book Israel is more or less irrelevant. Because a small cameo appears through a surviving uncle, but it has nothing to do with the central line of the story and all ends up in America with the rather unhappy happy ending. (Spiegelman Interview in Previtali 2000:176)

Maus was not only regarded as a potentially controversial work because of its subject and its form – including the derogatory connotations often attached by the general public to comic books – but also because it was potentially liable to legal litigations. Among the characters in *Maus* there are two cousins of Vladek who are depicted as members of the Jewish police. While the Israeli edition was being prepared, Spiegelman discovered that in fact one of them, Haskel, was in the Jewish police, but the second one, Pesach, was not:

> Well, it actually turns out … one of them, Haskel, was a Jewish policeman, but Pesach, his brother, was a hang-around, but he wasn't a Jewish policeman. His son, Pesach, survived the war, he's the one that's crying in the bunker. I didn't even know that he was alive. But after the book came out it eventually worked its way to him and we communicated. He was very upset that his father should be portrayed wearing a Jewish policeman's hat. Menachem Spiegelman was Pesach's son. Pesach died, Haskel survived, Haskel raised him. He was therefore very unhappy to see Haskel portrayed … I think rather neutrally, but being a Jewish policeman is not seen as a positive thing anywhere, and certainly in Israel. He felt it was necessary in the book to enter much more positive information about how many people Haskel really helped in the ghetto. And Israeli law, as I understand, is such that libel doesn't stop at the grave, it's the people of memory. So that my publisher became terrified by this cousin of mine and my cousin really wanted to just become a collaborator on the book, and just rework it with me not just in that section but in places where he had no business even mentioning anything. The result was this kind of real mess, I kept begging him, leave the book as it is, I don't care in a way if it's true or not. It is interesting to know that Pesach wasn't a Jewish policeman, but that's not really important, what's important is that Vladek thought he was a Jewish policeman. And if anything at that time when I was to communicate with him, I was still thinking of having a Roshamon section at the end of the book that would indicate further than I did the problems of memory. (Spiegelman 1994b)

The controversial nature of the book is not the only reason it was not published in Israel. In the same interview, Spiegelman comments on the problems associated with translating the verbal content:

> In the Israeli edition, …, I couldn't get a translator to deal with the fact that my father speaks in broken English and this is central to the book, and it's a central problem for any translator. How do you get Vladek's English to sound like an immigrant's English without caricaturing into some kind of shtick Yiddish? Which is not. If anything, it is more like Polish grammar transposed. And in Israel I just wasn't able to get a translator to be willing to deal with broken Hebrew. … well,

he sounds like he's arrived off the boat ten minutes ago because there's no such thing as broken Hebrew, which I know is impossible. But I just couldn't get it to happen. (Spiegelman 1994b)

In a later interview, Spiegelman makes the same point, this time with reference to the publisher rather than to the translator. According to Spiegelman, the publisher

> ... refused, refused to make any concession to Vladek's broken language. And I would argue with him and said "Look, there are a lot of people from other countries here in Israel. I'm sure some of them come from Poland. Why can't you just find somebody who can echo that language?" "Oh, no, no!", he said, "In Israel everybody speaks good Hebrew". "That sounds ridiculous", I said. He said "Oh yes, yes" because otherwise it just sounds like they are as greenhorns who just arrived. (Spiegelman Interview in Previtali 2000:175)

This complex problem here seems to involve also the issue of cultural and linguistic identity, the way it is constructed and perceived inside Israel, and the way it is received and recognized outside it. Hebrew is a learnt language for many of its citizens with a recent history of immigration and, for a relatively long period, there was little agreement on one formal linguistic standard, as regards grammar, lexis and pronunciation (Even-Zohar 2005). According to Myhill (2004:209), "Israeli Hebrew has not (yet) developed a variety of clearly distinguished sociolects or geographical dialects as exist in other languages". Spiegelman's disbelief, then, may be well-grounded when considering that for many Holocaust survivors who emigrated to Palestine, like for instance Vladek's brother, Hebrew was not a native tongue. Many diaspora Jews might have easily found themselves in Israel in a linguistic situation similar to that of Vladek after he emigrated to the US. Itamar Even-Zohar (2005) reports an anecdote of an old apple selling woman who, at the beginning of the 1950s, addresses passers-by in a Tel Aviv street with broken Hebrew; when exhorted by a Yiddish speaker to speak "plain Jewish [Yiddish]", she replies "what can we do, uncle, we are after all in exile!" (2005:online). It seems that it is not so much that Vladek's broken English is impossible to translate "because there's no such thing as broken Hebrew", but rather that Hebrew is perceived by its speakers as a marker of identity which cannot allow for linguistic variation.

Spiegelman was also deeply involved with both the German and the French translations.[10] Françoise Mouly, Spiegelman's wife and a French native speaker, collaborated with the translator of the French edition. Spiegelman himself followed the German translation: "The German one, I went through several translations and even fired my first publisher, and resold the book, because after several translations from the first publisher I was getting nowhere" (Spiegelman 1994b). Some of the problems with the

---

[10] One problem with most foreign translations was the technical constraint posed by the size of the balloons. In the panels in *Maus* "every eighth of an inch has been accounted for" (Spiegelman 1994b), so that balloons cannot be redrawn and the length of the text must be the same in each language. As in most languages the length of the translated text tended to exceed that of the original English, it often "became necessary to choose which subordinate meaning or clause might be left out" (Spiegelman 1994b).

reception of *Maus* in Germany are also anticipated in the opening pages of the second volume (Figure 5.16).

Figure 5.16: Art Spiegelman, *Maus II*, 1991, p. 42

The Polish translator was instead himself dissatisfied with the way he rendered Vladek's language, which was Polish throughout, but in which the standard variety spoken by Vladek in the past contrasted with the broken Polish of the present. A further problem in the Polish edition was the representation of Poles as pigs, an image which – as may be expected – did not give rise to positive feelings in the target readership (see Interview in Previtali 2000:172-173, 176).

3.1 The Italian Translations

An analysis of all foreign editions of *Maus* is beyond the scope of this article, which considers the Italian translations instead in some detail. In particular, we concentrate on the key aspect of rendering Vladek's broken English. A first Italian translation, by Ranieri Carano, was published in installments (following the original publication in the comic magazine *Raw*) in the Italian comic magazine *Linus*, then with considerable success, first as separate volumes (1989-1992) and then as a single volume by the publisher Rizzoli (1995).[11] In 2000, however, *Maus* was re-published by Einaudi, a major publisher

---

[11] A second edition came out in 1997. All references are to this second edition.

of literary works, in a new translation by Cristina Previtali. This new translation was the result of a number of concomitant factors: the translation rights with Rizzoli expired in 1999; the (future) translator had read *Maus* both in English and in its first Italian translation, and had decided to base her degree thesis (Previtali 2000) on a new translation of Spiegelman's work. Previtali then contacted Spiegelman who, dissatisfied with the first translation was more than happy to actively participate in the new translation project, which eventually led to the publication by Einaudi.

A central problem for the translator concerns rendering Vladek's linguistic characterization not only without ending up with a caricature Yiddish, but also maintaining its function as the "language of telling". Figure 5.17a illustrates the type of translation adopted by Carano in the first Italian edition, while Figure 5.17b illustrates the translation by Previtali (with reference to Figure 5.7 in English).

Figure 5.17a: Art Spiegelman, *Maus*, 1997, p. 136 (Italian translation: Ranieri Carano)

For ease of comparison, the original English and Italian translations are provided in parallel columns in Table 5.1.

Figure 5.17b: Art Spiegelman, *Maus,* 2000, p. 134 (Italian translation: Cristina Previtali)

Spiegelman	Carano	Previtali
Maybe we should try my father's old house. The janitor has known our family for years.	Forse è meglio provare vecchia casa dei miei. Portiere conosce mia famiglia da anni.	Potremmo provare nella vecchia casa di mio padre. Il portiere conosce la mia famiglia da anni.
Let's try. We've got to get off the streets before dawn!	Proviamo. Dobbiamo non essere più in strada prima di alba.	Proviamo. Dopo l'alba non potremo più stare in strada!
I was a little safe. I had a coat and boots, so like a Gestapo wore when he was not in service. But Anja – her appearance – you could see more easy she was Jewish. I was afraid for her.	Io ero abbastanza protetto. Avevo giaccone e stivali come uno di Gestapo fuori servizio. Ma Anja ... oh, potevi vedere facilmente che lei ebrea. Avevo paura per lei.	Io ero un po' protetto. Avevo giaccome e stivali come quelli di Gestapo fuori servizio. Ma Anja – suo aspetto – era più facile vedere che lei è ebrea. Temevo per lei.

Table 5.1: Maus, p. 136: an original panel and two Italian translations compared

The dialogue between Vladek and Anja, supposedly in Polish, is translated in standard colloquial English in Spiegelman's original panel, while the narrator's voice in the caption is in broken English. In Carano's translation, both dialogue and narration are in broken Italian, which is created by deleting articles (e.g. "Portiere conosce mia famiglia da anni", lit. "Janitor has known my family for years", instead of the correct "Il portiere conosce la mia famiglia da anni", lit. "The janitor has known the my family for years") and the copular "be" ("lei ebrea", lit. "she Jewish", instead of the correct "lei era ebrea", lit. "she was Jewish").[12] Previtali's translation differentiates instead between the language of the dialogues, rendered in standard Italian, and the "off-screen" narration, which is in broken Italian (e.g. "lei è ebrea", "she is Jewish", instead of the correct "(lei) era ebrea", lit. "(she) was Jewish").

In Carano's translation, Vladek's broken Italian is characterized mostly by missing articles, the marked presence of personal pronouns (usually omitted in Italian) and the omission of copular "be". In this translation, not only does Vladek's broken variety of language spill over to other characters in his tale of his life in Poland, but also to his partner Mala, who is made to speak the same variety of broken Italian even when her conversations with Art are reported. For example, a comparison between the content of the balloon in Figure 5.18a and its translations by Carano (Figure 5.18b) and Previtali (Figure 5.18c), respectively, shows that Carano starts the sentence with a personal pronoun and does not use the indefinite article "un" in front of "miserabile" (pauper). Previtali's translation is instead in standard Italian.

Figure 5.18a: Art Spiegelman, *Maus I*, 1986, p. 132

---

[12] Carano chooses to translate in broken Italian even the one instance in which Vladek explicitly speaks Polish in the present, thus making Vladek's languages always 'broken'. Compare the translation by Carano (*Maus* 257A1-257A2) with *Maus II* 99A1-99A2, where Vladek's Polish sentence in the balloon is accompanied by a translation in fluent English in the gutter.

Figure 5.18b: Art Spiegelman, *Maus*, 1997, p. 132 (Italian translation: Ranieri Carano)

Figure 5.18c: Art Spiegelman, *Maus*, 2000, p. 130 (Italian translation: Cristina Previtali)

In Carano's translation, the dialogues in Vladek's tale are also characterized by a lower degree of formality. For example, in Figure 5.19b, in Carano's translation Mrs. Kawka (the Polish charater) does not use the courtesy title "Mr" (compare Carano's "D'accordo, Spiegelman" with Previtali's "D'accordo, Sig. Spiegelman"), and addresses Vladek using the informal second person form instead of the formal third person (compare Carano's "ricorda" with Previtali's "ricordi"). In this example, besides the usual deletion of articles, some inaccuracies can be detected both at the lexical level ("barn" becomes "capanna", lit. "hut/shack") and grammatical level ("you must say" becomes "devo dire", lit. "I must say").

In her thesis, Previtali (2000) details instead how she systematically reconstructed a specific variety of broken Italian, aiming to reproduce the linguistic features and cultural connotations of Vladek's broken English. In an interview with Previtali, Spiegelman had described his father's language thus:

there's some Yiddish words and Polish structure and probably every once in a while something from Germany would be there… because the part of Poland he came from was Silesia. Sometimes it was Germany and sometimes it was Russia, so it's specific to that. But for me it was only intuition. It was like Vlaked language. It wasn't Polish, it wasn't Russian, it wasn't English it wasn't anything, just Vladek's language, so ... (Interview in Previtali 2000:171)

Figure 5.19a: Art Spiegelman, *Maus I*, 1986, p. 139

Figure 5.19b: Art Spiegelman, *Maus*, 1997, p. 139 (Italian translation: Ranieri Carano)

While Art Spiegelman reconstructed his father's narration from the audio recorded sessions without an explicit linguistic analysis ("to me it was just intuition"), Previtali was able to observe a number of regularities which characterize Vladek's divergence from the norm of standard English. As far as syntax and grammar are concerned, these include for example the use of "what" instead of relative pronouns such as "who, that" for anaphoric reference, a divergent use of verb tenses, and prepositions.

Previtali found a model for her "broken Italian" in the writings of Moni Ovadia, actor, playwright, singer, and composer who since the 1990s has been drawing the attention of the wider Italian public to the Jewish musical and cultural traditions. In his shows and in his writings Ovadia, himself of Jewish-Hungarian origins and coming from a multi-lingual family, has been using a variety of language based on the Italian learnt in Milan by an American Lubavitsch rabbi of Polish origin and who had Yiddish as his mother language. Previtali also tried to systematically apply features of the Italian spoken by immigrants of Polish origin. These include the use of "chi/quale" ("what"/"which") with the function of anaphoric relative pronoun, a divergent use of prepositions (paralleling similar features in Vladek's broken English) and the omission of articles. In consultation with Spiegelman and in order to avoid too strong an association between Vladek's lan-guage (in translation) and the "shtick Yiddish" created by Ovadia, the translator refrained from applying marked phonetic features such as dropping double consonant sounds (Previtali 2000:151-153).

Figure 5.19c: Art Spiegelman, *Maus*, 2000, p. 137 (Italian translation: Cristina Previtali)

Vladek's vocabulary is mostly that of standard American English, with a number of Yiddish words included. These were mostly retained in Previtali's translation, with the assumption that they would be recognized by readers familiar with them through the works of Ovadia and other literary works by Jewish-American writers translated into Italian. However, when the translator deemed that a Yiddish word was too unusual and the context would not offer enough clues to its meaning, she added a gloss in Ital-ian (Figures 5.20 and 5.21). On other occasions Yiddish words were replaced by Italian equivalents, because space constraints did not allow for the insertion of a gloss (Previtali 2000:147-150):

Figure 5.20a: Art Spiegelman, *Maus I*, 1986, p. 96

Figure 5.20b: Art Spiegelman, *Maus*, 1997, p. 96 (Italian translation: Ranieri Carano)

Figure 5.20c: Art Spiegelman, *Maus*, 2000, p. 94 (Italian translation: Cristina Previtali)

Figure 5.21a: Art Spiegelman, *Maus II*, 1991, p. 47

Figure 5.21b: Art Spiegelman, *Maus*, 1997, p. 205 (Italian translation: Ranieri Carano)

Figure 5.21c: Art Spiegelman, *Maus*, 2000, p. 203 (Italian translation: Cristina Previtali)

In Carano's translation, on the other hand, Yiddish words seem to have the function of adding an exotic element to the ungrammatical variety of language spoken by Jewish characters. In Figure 5.20b, Vladek tells Art on the telephone that Mala "mi fa meshugah", literally "makes meshuga to me" – a rather incomprehensible expression, whereas Previtali (5.20c) not only adopts Ovadia's spelling of the word but also encases it in a structural frame (the underlying idiom "mi fa diventare matto", "makes me crazy") which allows the reader to understand the Yiddish word in context ("mi fa diventare meshugga"). In Figure 5.21b, not only is the chief of the tinmen made to speak in broken Italian, but the word "drek" is translated as "Yiddish", which apparently only serves the purpose of adding a touch of "local colour" to the dialogue. In Previtali's translation (5.21c), the Yiddish word is instead retained and accompanied by an Italian equivalent gloss ("spazzatura", lit. "garbage").

Spiegelman's project did not stop with the publication of the graphic novel in English, but continued with the publication of the CD-ROM and of the foreign editions of *Maus*. The Italian edition by Einaudi was the result of a close collaboration between translator and author, who not only demanded that the book be published in the same size and format as the American edition (Previtali 2000:86) but also closely followed the translation work itself. At the request of Spiegelman, the new Italian edition of *Maus* includes a translator's note, which, again at the request of the author (Previtali 2000:155), occupies the fourth page of *Maus*, after the two introductory pages and the cover of the first chapter, in place of the dedication, which is placed on the first title page before the copyright statement.[13]

Maus's complex structure, separating apparently "translated speech" from apparently "untranslated" narrative, where the latter is "broken" in the sense of being imbued with exile, trauma and non-assimilation, is one of Spiegelman's most effective strategies to translate what is unrepresentable. The foreign editions of *Maus* add yet another layer of complexity. In this respect, the different strategies employed by the two Italian translators, regardless of any assessment of translation quality, further testify to the crisis in representation and language that often follows trauma.

4.   Conclusion

With *Maus*, Spiegelman has created a story that is compelling in its portrayal of the Holocaust and in its consistent analysis of the hazards and gaps in the reconstruction of history. Through the structuring of narrative, sensitive use of language, and a detailed yet simple visual strategy, *Maus* does not divide the past from the present and future, but constantly calls attention to the way they collapse into each other. Translation is a central feature in *Maus*, both in a metaphorical and a technical sense. Bearing witness to the unrepresantability of trauma, *Maus* attempts to translate Vladek's terrifying experience for audiences that are mostly 'foreign' to it. By rendering Vladek's tale through a comic book, Spiegelman also operates a kind of intersemiotic translation: he adapts, condenses and transforms Vladek's tape-recorded story into graphic narrative. But translation is also thematized by the shift in the language spoken by Vladek in the past and in the present. Vladek's broken English generates a displacing effect that succeeds in representing trauma without making sense of the Holocaust and becomes, thus, the language of telling.

The linguistic varieties in *Maus* – Vladek's broken English in the present, his and others' fluent English in the past representing native European languages, the fluent

---

[13] This seems a recurrent pattern in Spiegelman's work. The Italian translation of his more recent *Shadow*, also by Previtali, was subject to similar requests. Initially published by the newspaper *La Repubblica*, Spiegelman withdrew publication because the newspaper did not retain the same size of the original publication and reduced it to a two-page format within the pages of its magazine, *Il Venerdì di Repubblica*. The publication of *Shadow* was resumed on the pages of the journal *Internazionale*, which complied with the author's requests.

English of the present of the narration – stand in a complex relationship which may be altered when the language is changed, i.e. when the text is translated. The problems posed by the role of language and translation seem indeed to be a primary concern of the author, and are even referred to in the book itself (see Figure 5.16),

As far as the Italian editions are concerned, by eliminating any difference between the language of reported and direct speech in Vladek's narrative, Carano's translation alters the relation which holds between verbal and visual elements in the original as well as the tension between past and present, between the story recorded and the telling of the story itself. In Carano's translation Vladek's broken English becomes, on the one hand, a "Jewish" language, the shtick Yiddish Spiegelman wanted to avoid, while on the other, it is also the language of the past, as all characters in Europe, including Germans and Poles, speak with a broken Italian. Paradoxically, Carano's version recreates the less defined language characterization found in the three-page story which appeared in 1972 in *Funny Animals*, the earliest publication of the *Maus* project (see Spiegelman 1994a). There, broken English is not only the language of Vladek's past and present, but also that of all European Jews.

In the reviews of the new edition by Einaudi (see press review in Previtali 2000:201-219), Previtali's translation is positively acknowledged without any discussion of the differences between this and the previous translation. It is difficult to know to what extent a translation may shape the perception of Spiegelman's *Maus* in 'foreign' cultures. In several countries, *Maus* has not been received at all because it was not translated, and these countries' histories are such that an extensive English readership does not exist. In Israel, *Maus* was not translated but, as Spiegelman himself noted (Interview in Previtali 2000:175), it could be at least read in English. In other countries it was translated but with little success; in other countries yet – primarily, Italy, Germany and France – it was translated and has entered the cultural debates within those areas. Although the changes brought about by Previtali's translation seem to have gone largely unnoticed, the re-publication of *Maus* in Italy was able to rekindle interest in it and draw further attention to Spiegelman's complex verbal and visual narrative, a narrative that has described the self-contained world of the camps without making the Shoah comprehensible.

References

Primary Sources
Spiegelman, Art (1973-1991) *Maus. A Survivor's Tale*, New York: Pantheon, 2 vols. [*Maus*, Italian translation by Ranieri Carano, Milano: Rizzoli, 1997; *Maus*, Italian translation by Cristina Previtali Torino: Einaudi, 2000].
Spiegelman, Art (1994a) *The Complete Maus CD-ROM*, New York: Voyager.
Spiegelman, Art (2004) *In the Shadow of No Towers*, New York: Pantheon.

Secondary Sources:
Anderson, John C. and Bradley Katz (2003) 'Read Only Memory: Maus and its Marginalia on CD-ROM', in Deborah R. Geis (ed.) *Considering* Maus: *Approaches to Art Spiegelman's "Survivor's Tale" of the Holocaust*, Tuscaloosa & London: University of Alabama Press, 159-174.

Baccolini, Raffaella (2003) "A place without pity': Images of the Body in Cynthia Ozick's 'The Shawl", in Vita Fortunati, Annamaria Lamarra and Eleonara Federici (eds) *The Controversial Women's Body: Images and representations in Literature and Art*, Bologna: Bononia University Press, 223-243.

Baker, Kenneth (2004) 'Art Spiegelman gets pointed with his pen, whether it's writing about Sept. 11 or Republicans. But don't call him a political cartoonist', *SFGate.com*, 15 October (online) http://www.sfgate.com/cgi-bin/article.cgi?f=/c/a/2004/10/15/DDGHB97QB037. DTL (Accessed 20 May 2006).

Barnes&Noble.com (2005) 'An Interview with Art Spiegelman', 24 October 2005 (online) http://search.barnesandnoble.com/booksearch/isbninquiry.asp?z=y&ean=9780375423 079&pwb=1&displayonly=ITV (Accessed 15 April 2006).

Benjamin, Walter (1992) 'Theses on the Philosophy of History', in *Illuminations*, trans. Harry Zohn, London: Fontana, 245-55.

Carlin, John (2005) 'Masters of American Comics: An Art History of Twentieth-Century American Comic Strips and Books', in John Carlin, Paul Karasik and Brian Walker (eds) *Masters of American Comics*, New Haven & London: Yale University Press, 25-175.

Chute, Hillary (2005) 'Literature Narrative Structures in *Maus*', *Indy Magazine* (online) http://64.23.98.142/indy/winter_2005/chute/index.html (Accessed 20 May 2006).

Cory, Mark (1995) 'Comedic Distance in Holocaust Literature', *Journal of American Culture* 18(1):35-40.

Dames, Nicholas (2001) *Amnesiac Selves: Nostalgia, Forgetting, and British Fiction, 1810-1870*, Oxford: Oxford University Press.

Des Pres, Terrence (1980) *The Survivor. An Anatomy of Life in the Death Camps*, Oxford: Oxford University Press.

Doherty, Thomas (1996) 'Art Spiegelman's *Maus*: Graphic Art and the Holocaust', *American Literature* 68(1):69-84.

Eisner, Will (1985) *Comics and Sequential Art*, Tamarac: Poorhouse Press.

Elmwood, Victoria A. (2004) "Happy, Happy Ever After': The Transformation of Trauma Between the Generations in Art Spiegelman's *Maus: A Survivor's Tale*', *Biography* 27(4):691-720.

Even-Zohar, Itamar (2005) 'Who Is Afraid of the Hebrew Culture?', in *Papers in Culture Research* 2005 (online) http://www.tau.ac.il/~itamarez/works/papers/papers/ps-revised.pdf (Accessed 3 June 2006).

Ezrahi, Sidra DeKoven (1980) *By Words Alone: The Holocaust in Literature*, Chiacago & London: University of Chicago Press.

Farkas, Alessandra (2002) 'L'11 settembre? Non chiamatelo Olocausto', *Sette* 45 (7 November): 124-127.

Geis, Deborah R. (ed.) (2003) *Considering* Maus: *Approaches to Art Spiegelman's "Survivor's Tale" of the Holocaust*, Tuscaloosa & London: University of Alabama Press.

Harad, Alyssa (2003) 'Resisting Crisis: Trauma, Pedagogy and Survival', *S&F Online* 2(1) (online) http://www.barnard.columbia.edu/sfonline/ps/printaha.htm (Accessed 20 May 2006).

Hirsch, Marianne (1992-93) 'Family Pictures: *Maus*, Mourning, and Post-Memory', *Discourse* 15(2):3-29.

Iadonisi, Rick (1994) 'Bleeding History and Owning His [Father's] Story: *Maus* and Collaborative Autobiography', *CEA Critic* 57(1):41-56.

Kaplan, E. Ann (2005) *Trauma Culture: The Politics of Terror and Loss in Media and Literature*, New Brunswick: Rutgers University Press.

Kuhlman, Martha (2005) interview with Marianne Hirsch on *Maus, Indie magazine* Winter 2005 (online) http://64.23.98.142/indy/winter_2005/kuhlman_hirsch/index.html (Accessed 20 May 2006).

La Capra, Dominick (2001) *Writing History, Writing Trauma*, Baltimore: Johns Hopkins University Press.

Leopold, Todd (2004) 'Sketches of the Apocalypse', *CNN.com*, 9 September (online) http://edition.cnn.com/2004/SHOWBIZ/books/09/09/art.spiegelman/?eref=yahoo (Accessed 20 May 2006).

Leventhal, Robert S. (1995) 'Art Spiegelman's *MAUS*: Working-Through the Trauma of the Holocaust' (online) http://www3.iath.virginia.edu/holocaust/spiegelman.html (Accessed 20 May 2006).

Lowenstein, Andrea Freud (1998) 'Confronting Stereotypes: *Maus* in Crown Heights', *College English* 60(4):396-420.

McGlothlin, Erin Heather (2003) 'No Time Like the Present: Narrative and Time in Art Spiegelman's *Maus*', *Narrative* 11(2):177-98.

Merriam-Webster Online, 'Trauma' (online) http://www.m-w.com/dictionary/trauma (Accessed 20 May 2006)

Myhill, John (2004) *Language in Jewish Society. Towards a New Understanding*, Clavedon, Buffalo & Toronto: Multilingual Matters.

Orvell, Miles (1992) 'Writing Posthistorically: *Krazy Kat, Maus*, and the Contemporary Fiction Cartoon', *American Literature History* 4(1):110-128

Previtali, Cristina (2000) *MAUS di Art Spiegelman. Una traduzione in italiano*, Scuola Superiore di Lingue Moderne per Interpreti e Traduttori, Università di Bologna, Degree dissertation.

Robinson, Tasha (2004) 'Art Spiegelman', *The A.V. Club* (29 December) (online) http://www.avclub.com/content/node/23319 (Accessed 20 January 2006).

Rosen, Alan C. (2003) 'The Language of Survival: English as Metaphor in Art Spiegelman's *Maus*', in Deborah R. Geis (ed.) *Considering* Maus: *Approaches to Art Spiegelman's "Survivor's Tale" of the Holocaust*, Tuscaloosa & London: University of Alabama Press, 159-174.

Rothberg, Michael (1994) "We Were Talking Jewish': Art Spiegelman's *Maus* as 'Holocaust' Production', *Contemporary Literature* 35(4):661-687.

Rousset, David (1947) *The Other Kingdom*, trans. Ramon Guthrie, New York: Reynal & Hitchcock.

Safran Foer, Jonathan (2005) 'Breakdownable', in John Carlin, Paul Karasik and Brian Walker (eds) *Masters of American Comics*, New Haven & London: Yale University Press, 290-299.

Scarry, Elaine (1985) *The Body in Pain: The Making and Unmaking of the World*, Oxford: Oxford University Press.

Silverblatt, Michael (1995) 'The Cultural Relief of Art Spiegelman', *Tampa Review* 5:31-36.

Spiegelman, Art (1994b) 'I enjoyed reading the reviews of *Maus* in different countries', Audio Interview, in Art Spiegelman (1994a).

Tabachnick, Stephen E. (1993) 'Of *Maus* and Memory: The Structure of Art Spiegelman's Graphic Novel of the Holocaust', *Word & Image* 9(2):154-62.

Tal, Kalí (1996) *Worlds of Hurt: Reading the Literatures of Trauma*, Cambridge: Cambridge University Press.

Toury, Gideon (1995) *Descriptive Translation Studies and Beyond*, Amsterdam: John Benjamins.

washingtonpost.com (2004) 'Off the Page: Art Spiegelman', 26 October 2004 (online) http://www.washingtonpost.com/wp-dyn/articles/A42271-2004Oct18.html (Accessed 20 May 2006).

Wiesel, Elie (1990) 'To Believe or Not to Believe', in *From the Kingdom of Memory*, New York: Summit.

Witek, Joseph (1990) *Comic Books as History: The Narrative Art of Jack Jackson, Art Spiegelman, and Harvey Pekar*, Jackson: University Press of Mississippi.

------ (2004) 'Imagetext, or, Why Art Spiegelman Doesn't Draw Comics', *ImageTexT: Interdisciplinary Comics Studies* 1(1) (online) http://www.english.ufl.edu/imagetext/archives/v1_1/witek/index.shtml (Accessed 20 August 2006).

Young, James E. (1998) 'The Holocaust as Vicarious Past: Art Spiegelman's *Maus* and the Afterimages of History', *Critical Inquiry* 24:666-99.

6 'Slime Hero from the Swamp'

The Italian Editions of Alan Moore's Horror Saga the Swamp Thing

ADELE D'ARCANGELO
University of Bologna, Italy

This article examines the Italian editions of the American horror comic book series the Swamp Thing. In particular, it considers the episodes written by Alan Moore, which were first published as a series in the 1980s in the US by DC comics (later republished in the 1990s as a graphic novel), and in Italy from 1990 to 2006 both in comic book and in graphic novel format (by Comic Art and Magic Press). Following an overview of the development of the horror genre in American and in Italian comics, the analysis will focus on the episodes written by Alan Moore, which were much appreciated by both readers and critics. The discussion considers social, economic and literary aspects of comics, and points out areas of distance and/or encounter between source and target poles at the levels of editorial policies, readership and culture.

My analysis aims at discussing the editorial route a horror comic, namely the *Swamp Thing*, went through in the Italian editorial market. I will offer my example as a case study which I hope will be useful in understanding how the translation of comics as a special mass communication medium is subject to special rules that need to be taken into consideration when trying to understand successful or unsuccessful editorial policies in a target culture. My approach will be to consider the case of the *Swamp Thing* mainly as an editorial example of good quality translation that has also been successful on a commercial level for Magic Press, who is still publishing it in Italy. As pointed out by Klaus Kaindl (1999:285),

> [i]t should be the aim of future studies to carry out investigations of translations on a textual and an intertextual level, with textual studies focusing on particular translation strategies at a given time or in a given culture adopted by one or several publishing companies.

Kaindl (1999:269) offers a classification of translation-relevant elements of comics and refers to Bourdieu's concepts of field, habitus, and agents of cultural production to remind us that

> [c]omic strips were initially published in the so-called yellow press, mainly in order to arouse interest as a novelty and induce people to buy the paper. In most of the strips, form and content were thus determined by that pole of the journalistic fields which was primarily oriented at economic capital, i.e. at boosting sales. The general practices and structures of the journalistic fields also shaped the production of the comic strips, including the issue of ownership. Whereas in the literary

field, the author of a work generally also has the rights to it, the ownership of comic strips is usually with the newspaper or press syndicates.

If, on the one hand, the question of ownership has mainly remained the same up to the present, so that even acclaimed authors such as Alan Moore still do not own the copyright of their works published by DC and Marvel majors, on the other hand, it is true that the general attitude towards comics has changed since the 1980s. As a result, a number of authors writing comics have started to become as famous as the artists drawing them, thus ensuring popularity for the series they created, not only in terms of sales but also in terms of critical attention.[1] This new attitude towards comics could be analyzed by referring once again to Bourdieu (1980) when he asks "who creates the creator?", meaning that in the production of "cultural goods", it is the publisher (in the case of written production) who is the "'person' able to proclaim the value of the author he defends and in whom he, above all, 'invests his prestige' acting as a 'symbolic banker' and offering as security all the symbolic capital he has accumulated" (Bourdieu 1986:133).

However, in my analysis I wish to underline how in the case of the *Swamp Thing*, published by the Italian Magic Press, there are a number of elements that need to be considered in order to understand whether this particular editorial operation has actually improved Alan Moore's fame in the target culture, and whether Magic Press could be considered the "creator of the *Swamp Thing* creator" within the world of Italian comics. As Lawrence Venuti states (2000:482), in translation processes

> [t]ranslation never communicates in an untroubled fashion because the translator negotiates the linguistic and cultural differences of the foreign text by reducing them and supplying another set of differences, basically domestic, drawn from the receiving language and culture to enable the foreign to be received there. The foreign text, then, is not so much communicated as inscribed with domestic intelligibilities and interests. The inscription begins with the very choice of the text for translation, always a very selective, densely motivated choice.

In this article, I would like to argue that *Swamp Thing* was a case of an extremely successful translation process, where by 'translation' I am not simply referring to the linguistic transposition of a text, but also to the graphic and editorial strategies that made such success possible. I will start my analysis with an overview of horror comics in the US and in Italy which I believe will be useful to understand the status of this particular genre in the Italian editorial market, because in the last two decades of the twentieth century, cultural attitudes towards comics in Italy have undergone a process of transformation in which Magic Press played a crucial role.

---

[1] These considerations are particularly true for US comics. The situation in those years was different in European countries such as Italy and France, as well as in Japan.

1.   Horror Comics in the US and in Italy

Before focusing on the Italian edition of the *Swamp Thing* it may be useful to provide a brief overview of the genre to which this series belongs. Part of the success in terms of sales and of critical response for the Magic Press edition of *Swamp Thing* is arguably due to the fact that horror as a genre has often – if not always – been given special attention by important authors, artists and critics in the US. From the very first examples of rewriting the classics of gothic literature to the production of the 1980s, the interaction between the literary canon and the achievements of comics in the field have always been evident. Many of the horror genre titles in the history of comics have become outstanding successes, and both writers and authors have been able to collaborate in a specific direction, e.g. often using black and white graphic expression, which is absolutely not the standard in the US comics culture. As a consequence, many products of the genre are still quoted today in the history books of comics as the pinnacle achievements of their time in terms of both graphic and narrative expression. This is one of the reasons why horror comics have been extremely influential in American culture at large. For example,

> [m]any of the horror novelists and movie directors of the late 30 years have been influenced by the horror comics of the 1950s, from George Romero (*Night of the Living Dead*) to Stephen King (*Creepshow*). The horror comics of the 1950s, and their influences, have been absorbed into mainstream popular culture through the movies and television series of the 1980s and 1990s. (Benton 1991:5)

Furthermore, the horror genre has always had considerable appeal for young readers, and this is also why it has often drawn the attention of both sociologists and moralists, who were quick to initiate campaigns of censorship against its production.

Finally, it is also important to stress that authors and critics have often reported the excellent quality of Italian production in this field. Claudio Peroni, who launched *Psycho*, one of the two horror magazines published in Italy in the 1960s (see below), has stressed the potential expressivity of this genre that is specially intended for adult readers.

> The greatest satisfaction for me was producing horror comics, because in this way I gained the opportunity both of having fun and of telling tales for adults. Yes, because I think horror stories are nothing but fairytales for over 18-year-old people, who can read them without fearing to be judged as children. (Peroni and Raucci 1999: online; my translation)

Perhaps another reason why horror comics have been so successful in achieving a high standard of quality in Italy has to do with the fact that horror films were extremely popular, especially in the 1970s, when home-made horror films competed with American productions. Films by the Italian director Dario Argento, for instance, are considered cult examples of this genre in the US – where it is notoriously difficult for European movies to attract the attention of a large audience – and even more so in Japan. As Fabio Bonetti argues, cinematographic techniques were influenced by horror comics, which acted "as an example of an independent genre that was often to be found on the margins of the mainstream, but maybe for this same reason was able to survive several editorial developments and changes during the last fifty years" (Bonetti 2001: online; my translation).

In fact, the production of Italian horror comics started in the 1960s and gained momentum with *Dylan Dog* (see below), a series that since its launch has been at the top of the bestseller list on the Italian market.

1.1   *From Werewolves and Vampires to Swamp Things: American Horror Comics*

According to Mike Benton, it was through the crime genre that the horror form was first introduced in comics (Benton 1991:9). Violent accounts of famous crimes and stories of homicidal criminals usually enjoyed huge success from the 1930s onwards, and the genre reached its peak in 1948 when the first elements of horror and terror were added in an effort to retain the interest of readers. Stories were mainly adaptations of short stories or novels from the British and American tradition. These publications were not yet properly 'comics', looking more like hybrid productions in which narration was still supported by captions rather than by balloons. The first American horror comic is considered to be *The Hunchback of Notre Dame*, based on the novel *Notre-Dame de Paris* by Victor Hugo (drawings by Dick Briefer); it was issued in 1936. Four years later, Briefer presented the first series that took its inspiration from Mary Shelley's *Frankenstein*, but in this case the *New Adventures* of the 'Monster' were set in twentieth-century New York. In the 1940s, the series *Classic Comics* (later called *Comics Illustrated*) came out with several novels and transpositions of short stories which included a more faithful version of *Frankenstein*, a revised version of *Dr. Jekyll and Mr. Hyde* by R. L. Stevenson, and a number of short stories by E. A. Poe. Even the very first number of the first series completely dedicated to horror – *Adventures into Unknown* (1948) – would start with an adaptation of Horace Walpole's *The Castle of Otranto*. That same year, *The Spirit, by* Will Eisner, would present a graphic version of two classic short stories: *The Empty House* by Ambrose Bierce, and *The Fall of the House of Usher* by Edgar Allan Poe.

Gradually, the number of horror comics increased, and in the late 1940s a few horror stories also appeared in some adventure and superhero comics. In 1947, a comic book entitled *Eerie* – which rapidly went on to become a successful series in a short time – was issued by Avon Comics. The success of the horror formula in those years was definitely born out by the publishing policy of Marvel Comics, which is to say, it comes as no surprise for Captain America to change to a horror version in *Captain America's Weird Tales*. In 1948, a horror story entitled *Zombie Terror*, with a Wonder Woman type heroine, was published by a family-owned comic books company called Entertaining Comics. Today, EC comics are still considered the best of the genre produced in those years. EC publications were soon exported to Europe, where they were so influential that horror films changed according to the style of the comics themselves. EC publications were the first example of a comic book genre which was to influence the genre of film making so significantly (King 1981:29-57).

One major characteristic of EC comics was that each issue of the three famous series *Haunt of Fears, The Crypt of Terror* and *The Vault of Horror* (all first released in 1950) presented four different stories in which there was no recurrent hero. The only types that were present in each issue were the three narrators, the 'Vault Keeper', the 'Crypt Keeper' and the 'Old Witch'. These three characters would invite their readers to follow them into brand new regions of terror, where hardly any supernatural element would be present. The cases of terror were for the most part caused by problems of a psychotic nature which could apply to any kind of family, race or age.[2] In these stories the text still tended to prevail over the images and narration would always progress on a literary level:

> for those who had an open enough mind, these brief stories could clarify how some classic themes could be treated with the same accuracy and depth both by literature and by comics, but unfortunately open minded people were not too many in McCarthyist America. (Cantucci n.d.: online; my translation)

It was probably the huge popularity these comic books gained in just a few years that attracted the attention of the censors. The realistic settings of EC comics were certainly the first element that provoked campaigners, who started to accuse EC and other comics of circulating harmful reading among young people and children. The campaign against comic books was started in the US by the then eminent psychiatrist Fredric Wertham, who attacked all EC comics as well as Marvel's superhero series, leading a crusade which culminated in the creation of the Comics Code Authority (1954).[3]

Martin Barker offers an outstanding analysis of this moral campaign against comics, which he also shows as having had strong political motivations both in England and in the US. Barker's conclusion about the campaign which brought about the censorship of EC and other 'harmful publications' was that campaigners felt that American and British ideology and culture could be in danger. Comics were dangerous because they had a strong appeal for young people and children, who were the representatives of the Nation's future (Barker 1984).[4]

New horror magazines expressively targeted for adult readers, and which therefore did not have to strictly conform to the guidelines of the Code Authority, started to be

---

[2] Among the best episodes we might quote *There Was an Old Woman* and *The Handler*, which focus on the inconvenience of being undertakers, both rendered with great macabre expressivity by Graham Ingels – a veteran of the genre; *The Small Assassin* and *Let's Play Poison* drawn by George Evans and Jack Davis, in which we come to know how children might reveal themselves to be little monsters. Jack Davis also interpreted *The Black Ferris* in which some classic themes of the genre were first presented (haunted castles in amusement parks for instance). Joe Orlando was the artist who presented the most poetic text, *The Lake*, an intimately human story in which the love story between two children was to last forever, overcoming limitations such as time and death.

[3] The Comics Authority Code was imposed in 1954, following a stream of comic books and magazines dealing with horror subjects. Wertham wrote a famous text on the bad influence horror comics could have on children. *Seduction of the Innocent* (1954, New York: Rinehart & Company) was used by the US Senate, the press, etc. as the basic manifesto of the campaign against comics.

[4] The suppression of EC comics, however, was to give them a special fame which was kept alive by contemporary readers of the comics in those days and by collectors who kept copies of the series. In comic bookshops both contemporary reprints and old original issues for collectors are now available.

published about 10 years later, at the end of the 1950s. The new readers, of course, were most probably the same readers of the EC series, who had developed an interest in the genre, and were now adults.

In the late 1950s, horror comics were particularly influenced by the fear of an imminent nuclear war. Gigantic mutant monsters generated from atomic explosions at nuclear test sites invaded cinemas and comic books of the late 1950s and early 1960s. Among the comics published during this period, one series was comparable in fame to past EC production. This was entitled *Creepy*, and like the EC series, its stories were presented by a host, 'Uncle Creepy'. But while the EC stories were usually contemporary tales of horror told in realistic settings, *Creepy* tended to be more gothic in atmosphere and settings.[5]

Once again this revival also took inspiration from the relationship between horror and literature. *Creepy* and *Eerie* – both published by James Warren – occasionally presented transpositions of Ray Bradbury's novels as well as stories by Edgar Allan Poe, and it was especially in the revised versions of famous novels that new, realistic graphic techniques were experimented with, often giving a grotesque interpretation to the stories.

In 1971, a revised Comics Code was introduced in the US. Some of the restrictions against horror comics were lifted, and by 1975 there were – besides the coloured versions – 23 black and white horror comic books available on the market, many of which were reprints of the 1950s pre-code horror comics that had been revised and made bloodier for new 1970s readers. Among the artists who collaborated in the production of the *Creepy* and *Eerie* series of those years are names such as Jerry Grandenetti, Bernie Wrightson and Richard Corben, all of whom contributed to the high artistic quality reached at that time. Horror was actually one of the few comics genres that would leave the authors a certain freedom of expression, which authors and artists – who had trained themselves through collaborating mainly on fanzines and underground magazines – certainly cherished.

It was particularly when the EC and Warren series published their reinterpretation of the classics that they experimented with graphic innovations concerning page-size, and especially in the usage of shadowing and brush, a characteristic that would become typical of the horror comics production for adults. During the 1970s, some classics of gothic literature matched the Avant-garde narrative of comic books in those stories that were specially aimed at an adult readership, while later in the 1980s a new trend of horror was to start gaining the attention of readers. Characters were to become more complex and psychologically frail in the description of their mostly human qualities even when they were not human at all. An example of the high quality attained by horror comics in the 1980s is Alan Moore's *Swamp Thing*, which is still considered the best horror comic ever produced. *Swamp Thing* set the standard, and was to become a touchstone to which authors of the 1990s would refer in trying to find inspiration for new productions in the field.

---

[5] The huge success of *Creepy* soon sparked the launch of a new publication, *Eerie*. In it, stories were also introduced by a narrator, 'cousin Eerie', and were inspired by 1930s horror film settings and characters. Stories were often published in black and white in an attempt to be as faithful as possible to Hollywood horror cult filmography of the past.

1.2   From Werewolves and Vampires to Investigators of Nightmares: Italian Horror Comics

Until 1986, when *Dylan Dog* was first launched, Italy had felt little attraction for the Gothic atmosphere of horror comics. The first horror comics published in Italy were actually EC stories, occasionally printed – between the late 1950s and the beginning of the 1960s – as single episodes alongside other series, though they never really gained much attention and did not match the success achieved in other European countries. That horror comics did not develop into a tradition in those years was probably because of the popularity of other competing genres, such as western and detective comics. Italian 'horror comics' in those days were often a mixture of genres, with an emphasis on crime and pornography.

At the end of the 1960s, however, the leading publisher, Mondadori, brought out an Italian translation of *Creepy* and *Eerie* as a paperback series – *I racconti dello zio Tibia e del cugino Ossa* [6] (1968), which was signalled a new interest in this genre.

In 1969 the magazine *Horror* was launched by Sansoni Editore in Milan, and was intended to set the standard for a new genre of 'quality products' for the Italian school of horror comics. *Horror* was not as successful as the authors and publishers had wished, but it was still able to attract the attention of a number of fans. The stories had a very concise tone and were impressively agile in their montage. Themes included classical stories of vampires and werewolves as well as more original ones dealing with fantastic settings and the subconscious mind.

Horror, soon to be joined by the similar magazine *Psycho,* also presented a series of literary masterpieces which had been re-interpreted by a leading author of that time, Dino Battaglia. Battaglia took inspiration from writers such as Hoffmann, Poe and Lovecraft in analyzing human anguish and psyche mysteries. The author was able to give an extremely original version of classic short stories in which his text and illustrations interacted in a dazzling combination. The technical achievements reached at the time by black and white drawings gave a special, mature glamour to the final product.[7]

After the moderate success of the 1960s, more than twenty years had to pass before horror would again become a proper genre in the Italian comics tradition. *Dylan Dog*, the British Investigator of Nightmare, created by Tiziano Sclavi and published by Sergio Bonelli, was first issued in 1984 and soon became a major hit of the genre.[8] Its

---

[6] Lit.: The Tales of Uncle Tibia and Cousin Bone. The series consisted of three volumes, published under the following titles: *Le spiacevoli notti dello zio Tibia* (Lit.: The Unpleasant Nights of Uncle Tibia), *Zio Tibia colpisce ancora* (Lit.: Uncle Tibia hits Back) and *Mezzanotte con zio Tibia* (Lit.: Midnight with Uncle Tibia). In 1972 Mondadori also published some of the adaptations of Ray Bradbury's novels first issued by EC comics during the 1950s.

[7] *Psycho*, launched by Claudio Peroni and published by Editrice Naka, was to have a special appeal for readers because of its reference to Hitchcock's film. The new magazine was very similar to *Horror* in terms of content, format and number of pages. In addition, many of the authors collaborating on *Horror* would start working for *Psycho* as well; the publishers and editorial boards did not object because the competition had a positive effect and both magazines improved their quality (Peroni and Raucci 1999: online). The editorial experience of *Psycho* was brief, but not because of economic reasons. The publisher thought the magazine was not in line with other Editrice Naka's publications, which were meant more for young target readers.

[8] On the American translations of *Dylan Dog*, see D'Arcangelo and Zanettin (2004), Rota (2001).

success spawned new horror series which, however, have been unable to replicate its achievements.

2.   The Saga of the *Swamp Thing*

A comparison of the evolution of horror comics in the US and in Italy might give us some clues as to how to explain the specific success of the *Swamp Thing* in the two countries. In this section, the evolution of the American series will be analyzed in some detail. In the sections which follow, I will examine how the Italian publishing company, Magic Press, was able to dedicate part of its editorial programme to the publication of 'Alan Moore's ABC' – his entire production – and how this strategy was successful in familiarizing Italian readers with the acclaimed British author and his outstanding production.

2.1   *From the Swamp to Stardom*

"Politics notwithstanding, how did we get a vampire in the White House? After seventeen years, the US Comics Code Authority[9] lifted some of its restrictions against horror in comics and allowed vampires and werewolves to be used in comic books published after January 1971" (Benton 1991:71). This is how Mike Benton introduces the readers of his *Illustrated History of Horror Comics* to the new wave of horror comics that would be produced starting from 1971, and in which a range of well-known horror characters (mainly vampires, werewolves and Frankenstein-like monsters) were paralleled by a number of new kinds of creatures of a more unknown, though generally human nature, such as Gerry Conway's *Man Thing* (published by Marvel), who was the first 'slime hero from the swamp' (Benton 1991:71). But another 'thing' was also rising from the swamp in the 1970s: only a month after Marvel's publication of Conway's *Man Thing*, the *Swamp Thing* appeared in a DC Comics episode (*House of Secrets* # 92 June 1971), in an original story written by Len Wein and drawn by Berni Wrightson (Benton 1991:72). But starting from 1972, the character was given his own comic book, which gained considerable success and was published until 1976 when the series was first suppressed (it was finally republished in 1982). But it was not until issue # 21, 1984, that the series finally became famous and known throughout the world as the best horror series not only of the 1980s but of all time. The 1982 series (up to #20) was selling about 17,000 issues a month, and DC was considering whether to suppress it when the editorial board decided to ask British comic book writer Alan Moore, who was then starting to achieve a certain success in the field of comics, if he would collaborate on its renewal (Benton 1991:74). Alan Moore accepted and wrote 'The Anatomy Lesson', in which the Swamp Thing is believed to be dead and hibernates in a special laboratory, owned by a General from

---

[9] The new code was revised due to pressures from publishers who wanted to compete with black and white horror magazines operating outside the code, but also to allow comic books to address some social issues prohibited under the 1954 code (Benton 1991:71).

the Army. The General asks Jason Woodrue (the so called Floronic Man – a well known character from DC universe) to do research on the biological secrets of the monster, as he hopes to commercially exploit any possible scientific finding. Woodrue, himself a victim of genetic mutation, accepts the offer, hoping also to find an answer to his own problems. After an accurate autopsy (the anatomy lesson of the title), Woodrue makes an exceptional discovery: the Swamp Thing is not a man transformed into a vegetable monster, but is a plant from the swamp, which, having absorbed the bio-regenerating fluid experimented with in Alec Holland's laboratory, has also absorbed the botanic researcher's human conscience lying at the bottom of the swamp, therefore transforming itself into a sort of anthropomorphic vegetable with a conscience:

> In some ways, his (Moore's) merits are those of the finest tradition of comics: his ear for dialogue, his talent for concise, clear storytelling, his unerring sense of pace and timing. In other ways he and his collaborators, Stephen Bissette and John Totleben, pretty well lead the field, especially in building a sense of terror. You'll find a hint of this on the first page of 'The Anatomy Lesson', a promise gruesomely kept by the finale of the story. But it's the uncompromising radicalism of 'The Anatomy Lesson' that announces most clearly this team is a force to be respected. There surely can't be many writers who, having taken over an established character, would begin by demonstrating (in the autopsy scene) that the character has never made sense as he was presented and is in fact something far less human than even he himself believed. Moore, Bissette and Totleben take the Swamp Thing apart in order to rebuild him. (Ramsey Campbell, introduction to *Saga of the Swamp Thing*)[10]

In the end we find out the Swamp Thing is not Alec Holland, but a plant whose fate has been that of only experiencing an illusion of its humanity. This is how Alan Moore describes the idea that was to give fame not only to the *Swamp Thing* DC series, but to the comics writer himself:

> I had started to win a few awards over here for things like *V for Vendetta* … but it was much better to be given a comic that was on the verge of cancellation. … (I) killed him off in the first issue! People stood for it because it was a dopey premise. The whole thing that the book hinged upon, was there was this tragic individual who is basically like Hamlet covered in snot. He just walks around feeling sorry for himself. That's understandable, I mean I would too, but everybody knows that his quest to regain his lost humanity, that's never going to happen, because as soon as he does that the book finishes. Even the most naïve reader is surely aware of that. So, I thought, let's turn it around and make that not an issue anymore. Let's see what's interesting about being a vegetable creature. You could make him kind of a swamp god, you could make him a kind of an elemental force, you could also use him to talk environmental issues. There were actually quite a lot of applications that you could give to this big, kind of animate manure pile! You

---

[10] Alan Moore's second series of *Swamp Thing* is also referred to as *Saga of the Swamp Thing*.

know, composte heap. We did kind of a tour of America where we would take in some of the standard horror tropes, vampires and werewolves, and turn them into things that were social problems in America at the time ....[11]

The following episode ('Swamped' #22 1984) was to sell 100,000 copies, which represented about five times that of the standard sales for the series.

2.2   The Author and His Work

Alan Moore is one of the best known comic books' authors. Born in 1954 in the UK, where he still lives, he started writing comics at the age of 25, clearly influenced by the American Underground production. His work was published in the magazine *Sound*, and later on he collaborated with other British magazines such as *Dr. Who*, *2000 AD* and *Warrior*. In the 1980s Moore joined DC Comics, introducing new elements to the then static reality of US comics. Moore's groundbreaking work on *Swamp Thing* would lead to the inception of the 'Vertigo' imprint which, operating under this name in order to separate itself from the more mainstream, family-friendly DC Comics image, started publishing stories aimed at a more mature audience.

It would be difficult to write a summary of how the *Swamp Thing* series developed in Moore's hands. As is the case with most of his productions, Alan Moore's writing is too dense and deep in significance to be described in simple terms. One example of the level of intertextuality involved and Moore's ability to play with different levels of language use should suffice. In # 32 1985, the bayou where the *Swamp Thing* lives is visited by aliens coming from an outside world. The episode is called 'Pog' and it is a clear tribute to Walt Kelly's strips *Pogo*, published in the 1940s. However, the little opossum created by the fantasy of Kelly has become an alien, and while he speaks with his sweet friends in the distinguished dialect of the Okefenokee bayou, he now lives on a planet which very much resembles the Swamp Thing's bayou. The little alien is doomed to wander across the cosmos, together with his friends, because the planet they lived on ('The Lady' is how they call it) has been invaded by a violent race that has killed off every inhabitant of the planet, except for a tiny group whose space shuttle lands in Louisiana. As soon as the aliens see the water, they believe they have found a familiar environment. In particular, the crocodile-like alien (Albert the Alligator in Kelly's series) will soon jump into the water while his little friend Pog is with the Swamp Thing, who will explain to him how that place is also invaded by creatures (human beings) who don't show any respect for it. The end of the story is particularly moving. Two terrestrial alligators kill the alien crocodile who was happily bathing and who ran towards them as if he had found new friends. Tiny little Pog cries for his friend near the gigantic Swamp Thing before restarting his journey through the stars. In this episode, Moore invents a completely new language

---

[11] BBC Radio 4 broadcast *Chain Reaction* interview transcript by Jonah Weiland, 27 January 2005, http//www. comicbookresources.com. The interview was conducted by Stewart Lee, a well known stand-up comedian and radio-TV programme writer, creator of the hit musical *Jerry Springer: the Opera*.

for the alien visitors to planet Earth, using terms that refer to the vegetable world. When the little alien Pog meets the Swamp Thing he addresses him by saying 'You're made out of the same *ingreenients* as the Lady. You must be her *guardiner* or such.' As Annalisa Di Liddo points out in relation to Alan Moore's work:

> The parody elaborated on the language until it gets distorted, corresponds to the deformation of the graphic sign – another form of parody, expressed through the excess and the redundancy that constitute its fundamental characteristics, as if the author would like to signal, throughout this emphasis both on deformation and on the metamorphic quality of the protagonist and of the narration, that the *Swamp Thing* can be read as a metaphor of the comic book itself, a blob-like creature, which has an extraordinary capacity of absorbing all stimulus from the environment surrounding it, feeding itself with its own never-ending mixing and re-aggregation of different elements. (Di Liddo 2006:66-67, my translation)

The mixing of elements on the one hand, and the extraordinary level of integration between text and image on the other, is what makes this horror series special and sets it apart from any other kind of production ever presented. Alan Moore's brilliant, new idea was graphically interpreted by two outsider artists, Stephen Bissette and John Totleben (the colourist was Tatiana Wood), who were all able to create the exact atmosphere that would match Moore's elaborate texts. The results were soon evident and not only on a commercial level. Critics would also start paying attention to the series and to its author who would soon be considered as one of the most acclaimed and influential authors in the world of American comics, and whose creativity had greatly contributed to the revaluation of comics as a media by mainstream culture (see e.g. Pilcher and Brooks 2005:41, Restaino 2004:158-159).[12]

In 1990 Moore left DC Comics (because of disagreements on merchandizing copyright issues) and started his own publishing company, which he called Mad Love. This experience soon came to a halt, however, and in the mid 1990s it seemed as if Moore had been superseded by new authors working for DC Comics, such as Neil Gaiman, Jamie Delano and Grant Morrison. Moore decided, nonetheless, not to go back and work for DC, and together with some of the best comics writers of those years – such as Neil Gaiman, Frank Miller and Dave Sim – he started a collaboration with graphic innovator and media entrepreneur Todd Mc Farlane at Image. The Image editorial project had the courage to break the DC-Marvel monopoly through a new concept of comics publishing, where the graphic element was given more consideration. Moore carried on working

---

[12] Apart from *The Swamp Thing*, other recognized masterpieces include *V for Vendetta*, a desperate and cold narration in an anti-Utopia British-style; *Watchmen*, a revisionist graphic novel in which world famous Marvel superheroes have to cope with human problems and ethical issues, thus missing all elements that made them super (see the Introduction to this volume); *Brought to Light: Shadowplay*, denouncing the atrocities that the CIA perpetuated in Latin America; *From Hell*, a meticulous reconstruction of the life and 'works' of Jack the Ripper; *A Small Killing*, a minimalist tale of lost innocence in which it is possible to detect some autobiographic elements; *The League of the Extraordinary Gentlemen*, a story that takes place in 1898 in a fictional world where all of the characters and events from literature (and possibly the entire stock of fiction) coexist (Lorenzon 2001).

for Image, and at the very end of the 1990s he gave birth to such new, excellent series as *Tom Strong*, *Promethea* and *The League of Extraordinary Gentlemen*, whose popularity soon allowed him to regain the pivotal position he had held earlier in the world of comics' stardom (Lorenzon 2001).

3.   Publishing Policies and Magic Press

Very often, if not always, the success of a translated comic series depends on the format in which it is published (Rota 2003, this volume). Not long ago, comics were mostly localized, i.e. adapted to the specific target culture. Thus, for example, comics originally in black and white would often be coloured in the US, while coloured US products would be printed in black and white in Italy, often in order to reduce costs. All of this has changed in recent years, perhaps also because of the increasing critical attention given to comics. For instance, as is well known, manga are published in black and white in Japan. When they were translated and published in America for the first time, the Americans wanted them in colour. The colouring process, however, erased the graphic effects of the screening and shadowing, resulting in a bad quality graphic sign. Japanese authors, who own the copyrights of their works, threatened to withdraw their titles if they continued to be published in coloured editions (Rota 2003). While printed in black and white, the first Italian editions of Japanese comics – like their American counterparts – were printed as mirror images, in compliance with the Italian reading direction. Once again, some of the main Japanese authors decided not to sell copyrights of their works unless the original reading direction was maintained and, once again, they had their way. The profession of comics author (*manga-ka*) is held in high esteem in Japan, and here again Bourdieu comes to mind in his stress on the relation between cultural authorship and economic powers.

Reading manga in an 'inverted' (i.e. original Japanese) direction was especially appreciated by young fans who considered the novelty as part of the cultural experience of diversity made possible by reading a Japanese comic book (Rota 2003, Jüngst, this volume). This editorial experience of alterity had excellent results, especially as regards sales. When economic demands coincide with cultural trends, as is often the case with contemporary comics production, this encounter can generate successful adaptations.

In the essay 'Production of Belief', Bourdieu (1986:138) considers the opposition between

> 'commercial' and non 'commercial', as an opposition between small-scale and large-scale ('commercial') production, between the deferred, lasting success of classics and the immediate, temporary success of best sellers; between a production based on denial of the 'economy of profit' (sales, target, etc.) which ignores or challenges the expectations of the established audience and serves no other demand than the one it itself produces, but in the long term, and a production which secures success and the corresponding profits by adjusting to a pre-existing demand ... Thus the opposition between 'genuine art' and

'commercial' art corresponds to the opposition between ordinary entrepreneurs seeking immediate economic profit and cultural entrepreneurs struggling to accumulate specifically cultural capital, albeit at the cost of temporarily renouncing economic profit.

It seems that the editorial policy of Magic Press corresponds exactly to this analysis by Bourdieu. Magic Press was established in Rome in 1990 as an editorial service agency, and in 1994 it started publishing after editors Pasquale Ruggiero and Francesco Cinquemani joined the company. The first publications were superhero comics distributed on newsstands, which ensured significant economic gains. Then, having obtained copyrights from DC for its Vertigo imprint, Magic Press stopped distribution on newsstands and concentrated on the "*fumetterie*", the comic bookshop market, which in the mid-1980s was still in an embryonic state in Italy. This policy proved to be particularly successful and ensured profits that allowed the publisher to start considering other possible cultural investments and new projects, such as releasing newsstands' products together with products created mainly for *fumetterie*, specializing in quality comics. The precarious economic situation in which Magic Press was founded required an attentive economic management with regard to editorial policies as well as policies relating to distribution. Accurately choosing the material to be published and having the right distribution networks was essential in order to guarantee the image of a newborn publishing company which wanted to be known as a quality press in the field, on the one hand, while avoiding dangerous capital dispersion on the other. The aim was to establish a basis for sustaining long term editorial projects. The choice of publishing prestigious titles that are very different in genre and intended target readership, as for instance the *Star Wars* series or the prestigious volumes of Gaiman's *Sandman*, has to be seen as a step towards this company's consolidation strategy.

Magic Press diversified its editorial production along two lines. The first was based on large print runs sold on newsstands, to guarantee a large readership (examples include *Il Corvo presenta*; *X-Files* and *Star Wars*, which started with a print run of 30,000 copies); the second was based on graphic novels by American avant-garde authors, sold in *fumetterie*, and aimed at a more restricted number of readers who would appreciate titles that were sold at unpopular prices (the number of copies to be distributed in comic bookshops in this case was approximately 5000 per volume on average, a number that would in any case guarantee profits). Magic Press was then able to aim at a market that was at that time not fully developed in Italy, create products expressly made for the comic bookshops, and finance the entire operation through the economic profits gained from newsstands sales. Moreover, distribution in the *fumetterie* did not have to respect rigid editorial datelines which were required for newsstands, thus allowing Magic Press to consider the results of each single publication before deciding to start the next (Saltarelli 2006). Among the products explicitly designed for comic bookshops was Neil Gaiman's *Sandman*, which was to become a kind of touchstone for the whole Italian market. For historical, economic and distributional reasons the series was issued in the US in the typical American comic book format: 24 pages published on a monthly basis to support a serial structure based on the *cliffhanger effect*. It was conceived as a collection of stories in several episodes linked by the same plot. Magic Press decided to publish *Sandman* in graphic novel format, closer to the original intentions of the author (Saltarelli 2006). The operation was successful, and in recent years Magic Press has enlarged and diversified its production to include Japanese, Italian and French comics.

The new conception of comic books format was soon to become a standard in Italy, and it is in this specific format that the saga of the *Swamp Thing* is still published at present.

4.   The Italian *Swamp Thing*

As often happens with successful comic series, the Italian editorial story of the *Swamp Thing* is quite complex. Copyright was first obtained from DC by Comic Art, a publisher based in Rome which published mostly 'classic' comics in book format to be sold mainly in newspaper stands. Comic Art was relatively successful in publishing important series in comic book format, using quality paper and often creating brand new covers.[13]

According to Alessio Danesi (of the editorial board of Magic Press), one of the problems with the Comic Art publication of the *Swamp Thing* was that before being launched as an independent title, the series was first published in *Horror*, a magazine dedicated to the horror genre which might be considered a tribute to the homonymous title published at the end of the 1960s. Soon after, episodes of the *Swamp Thing* in colour were included in the anthological magazine *DC Comics Presents*, together with a number of other Vertigo series (Morlacchini n.d.). Then, between 1990 and 1995 Comic Art published twelve new issues of the *Swamp Thing*, starting with the first series by Len Wein and Bernie Wrightson and including some of the episodes written by Moore as late as 1986. These were still colour editions in books of 64 pages, "but the episodes were not published consistently, this is why readers could not receive enough information on the sequence of the story" (Danesi, personal communication).

In 1995, due to problems and costs of distribution, Comic Art stopped most of its productions and relinquished all rights to the Vertigo material, which included series such as *Sandman, Hellblazer* and the *Swamp Thing*. Within a short time Magic Press acquired all copyrights directly from DC. In 1997 Magic Press launched a completely new edition of the *Swamp Thing*, which had nothing to do with the previous Comic Art version. While

---

[13] Comic Art was founded in May 1965 after the first International Exposition of Comics was held in Italy (Bordighera, February 1965). This generated considerable interest in comics in different fields of Italian cultural life, and there was a general feeling that the time had come for a quality editorial experience thanks to which new authors and international productions would start circulating alongside the classics in Italy. During the 35 years of its activity Comic Art was able to present to its Italian readership characters such as Li'L Abner, Tintin, Dick Tracy, Mandrake, Popeye, Mickey Mouse/Topolino, Donald Duck/Paperino, Dylan Dog, Rip Kirby, Flash Gordon and so on in special editions and quality comic books that were sold mainly in bookshops. During the 1990s Comic Art – together with Granata Press – was one of the first comics publishers to start publishing mangas in Italy. Comic Art faced a serious crisis when a branch of Marvel Corporation was established in Italy, and the publishing house had to renounce publishing American superheroes and start republishing quality comics books in editions for amateurs. In December 2000 publisher Rinaldo Traini stopped publishing all series and had to acknowledge the end of this glorious editorial experience. The 35 years of Comic Art activity, however, can help explain many of the Italian habits related to reading comics.

the comic books were still distributed on newsstands, they were published in black and white rather than in colour, except for the last three issues, in which colour was thought to be functional with regard to the narration. In total, Magic Press published eleven new issues (each containing between 96 and 112 pages), printed on quality paper, with brand new translations and critical notes. Most importantly, Magic Press chose to present only those episodes of the *Swamp Thing Saga* written by Alan Moore.

The translator of the *Swamp Thing* was Leonardo Rizzi, who later became recognized as the 'official' translator of all of Alan Moore's works, as well as of other DC comics authors published by Magic Press. This critical edition also received positive feedback from French readers, who appreciated the novelty of the critical apparatus and Rizzi's notes and translation. In a series of interviews reported on different websites dedicated to comics, Rizzi talks about his experience of translating comics in general and of translating the *Swamp Thing* in particular; he foregrounds the importance of the logic and mental processes hidden behind Moore's rich and varied writing style. According to his Italian translator, Moore's writing changes according to the function it has in a given work. In *Swamp Thing*, for instance:

> Alan Moore's prose has the function of creating a dense atmosphere and of setting the horror style, even though he is also able in this same series to bring his readers towards a kind of a more caustic reading ... Moore's prose signals the borderline between function and emotion, and this is what readers appreciate in comics. (Rizzi et al. 2006: online; my translation)

The interviewers stress how in the translation of the *Swamp Thing* Rizzi had to render into Italian different varieties of language, from the language of 'rhyming demons who talk in iambic pentameters' to that of aliens who speak an idiom rich with assonances, from lyrical passages alternating with passages which are more horrific in style to the speech of characters who express themselves in a typical 'Old Southern American' or 'English Bastards' accents. Rizzi stresses how that specific translation was a 'tough job' not only because of the level of difficulty he had to cope with, but also because the translation had extremely tight deadlines, given that the *Swamp Thing* was a bi-monthly publication. In fact, he comments that writing the notes appended to each episode involved a huge amount of work and research, but that it was also extremely rewarding:

> I do realize right now that the difficulties you have been quoting have helped me in refining my way of translating ... My training on *Swamp Thing* has been able to give me incredible energy for my successive works, and I'm particularly glad now because I've had a chance to review my first translation of the series for the new volumes' edition. I have been able to check what could have been translated better and especially to reinsert some balloons that, let's say, 'got lost' in the first edition ((Rizzi et al. 2006: online; my translation)

Rizzi also recalls how badly he wanted to translate *Swamp Thing*, and how he considered it as 'an act of devotion'. In fact, before being a translator of comics, he was a fan of Alan

Moore, and this is something that happens quite often in the field of comics translation. The research work carried out by the translator, together with his 'insider' status, attests to the quality of the translation, which was specifically commissioned by Magic Press to replace the translation which appeared in the edition published by Comic Art.

Another example that illustrates the specificity of the project is the choice of publishing the series in a black and white edition. Danesi explains that after seeing the British edition of the series published by Titan, they liked it so much that they decided to adopt it for the Italian edition (personal communication). This choice may also have been influenced by the specific conventions associated with this particular comics genre in Italy, where it has always been published in black and white. This may be a case in which a tradition which was initiated for economic reasons subsequently reached extraordinary levels of graphic quality.

Another fact which illustrates the editorial accuracy that informed the publication of this product is that once Magic Press ran out of stock, they decided to republish the complete series in graphic novel format, that is, in the same format of the DC/Vertigo volume editions. The volume edition featured new covers with a new graphic look. In addition, the translator was given the chance to revise his previous edition's translation.

The first three of the six volumes published so far (*La saga di Swamp Thing/The Saga of the Swamp Thing; Amore e morte/Love and Death, La maledizione/The Curse*) are already sold out and reprint editions are being produced. According to Danesi, the Italian, Magic Press edition of the *Swamp Thing* is not only better in quality when compared to the previous one by Comic Art, but it is also superior to the original DC/Vertigo series. Danesi explains this as follows:

> Our black and white edition in 1999 was able to give new depth to the artistic quality of Totleben's graphic sign. The American colour edition was printed on bad quality paper and this resulted in a low definition of the colour shades. After having seen the British Titan edition of *Swamp Thing* we opted for a 96 page/17x26 format which cost 6000 Liras at the time.[14] As regards the volumes published since 2000, again we use quality processes at the different steps of production. Our binding systems are stronger than those used by Mondadori for its bestsellers; our paper is the best paper you can find on the market and our graphics system is the same they use in the US, this means we work at our best. Then there is the other aspect which has to do with the quality of the product, that is what is inside the comic book. After 1986, when *Maus* and *Watchmen*[15] were both published, comics changed their face. Nowadays we are used to talk about authors more than about artists, and this is a new attitude in the field of comics, it did not happen before. Still in Italy no big publisher has a series completely dedicated to comics. In comics you would often find what is missing in a novel. And Alan Moore, in particular, writes comics of a certain standard that needs to be treated at a certain level. That was our editorial policy regarding his production: publishing more

---

[14] 6,000 Liras would correpond to 2 Sterling pounds.

[15] *Maus* by Art Spiegelman and *Watchmen* by Alan Moore were both published in 1986. *Maus* was awarded the Pulitzer Prize in 1992 and *Watchmen* has recently been included in a 'best ever' list in *Time Magazine*, as one of the "100 best English-language novels" between 1923 and the present (on *Maus*, see Baccolini and Zanettin, this volume).

works by Moore, publishing all Alan Moore's production in order to treat it/him as you would treat a novel. Good comics are comparable to good literature because they teach a new language. Graphic novel was a definition invented by Will Eisner when he decided not to participate in serial production every month but to start creating books in graphic format. It was a sort of a movement, it gave authors the opportunity to write full stories, and therefore to change reader attitudes. And this is also what we have done. Since the end of the 90s our wide distribution in the Italian territory and the number of issues published has encouraged the outburst of so called *"fumetterie"*, where readers can find their favourite title, and this has allowed us to avoid distribution on newsstands that would have been too expensive. Readers of our *Swamp Thing* series range from 18 to 40 years old, Moore's stories require high intelligence and deep sensibility. Moore would have fun in presenting sex stories targeted also at teenagers. Readers who buy *Swamp Thing* definitely have a passion for a certain kind of literature or for high-brow comics. Comics, and I would add here horror comics, allow artists and readers to experience considerable freedom in the act of writing/drawing and finally reading. (personal communication; my translation)

Whether Danesi's claim about the superiority of Magic Press's edition is justified is finally a matter of the judgement of individual readers. An example of the difference between the two editions is offered in Figures 6.1a and 6.1b (centre fold).

5. Conclusion

The aim of my paper was to explain why Magic Press's editorial policy was able to make the *Swamp Thing* an editorial success both in terms of sales and critical appraisal. While the publication by Comic Art brought the series to wider attention, Magic Press was able to exploit this attention through meticulous editorial care and by promoting the authorial status of Alan Moore. Magic Press is notable for the extremely careful attention they pay to all their production, but one might also say that the special attention Magic Press dedicates to the quality of the production of Alan Moore's series is a sort of "artistic act of love". This is hardly surprising given that all Magic Press's editors and collaborators are, from the outset, admirers of Alan Moore's production.

The first aim of a company is to make profit. However, publishing companies produce not only commercial goods, but also cultural goods, which means that the quality of what is produced might come before immediate profits, thus going counter to ordinary business practices. The opposition between the commercial and non commercial is, in the final analysis, an opposition between ordinary entrepreneurs and cultural entrepreneurs. Bourdieu (1986:139) distinguishes between

> [o]n the one hand, those who dominate the field of production and the market through the economic and symbolic capital they have been able to accumulate in earlier struggles by virtue of a particularly successful combination of the contradictory capacities specifically demanded by the law of the field, and, on the other hand, the newcomers, who have and want no other audience than their competitors – established producers whom their practice tends to discredit

by imposing new products – or other new comers with whom they vie in novelty. … 'Social problems' are thus social relations: they emerge from confrontation between two groups, two systems of antagonistic interests and theses.

And this is apparently what is happening to Magic Press, which only very recently (September 2006) lost all its copyrights of DC/Vertigo material to Planeta DeAgostini, a colossal player in the Italian publishing sector, on the basis of a more substantial commercial agreement. While Planeta DeAgostini recruited all Magic Press staff as an editorial consultant agency, thus confirming its importance and competence, the editorial board and fans fear that new publication policies may subvert most of the work which had been done by Magic Press to create a new readership and a new market, making *fumetterie* burst out all over Italy.

The story of the Italian editions of the *Swamp Thing* may also be of help in understanding how in the complex field of the translation of comics several factors lie behind the final product itself. The comics publication industry is subject to strict rules as regards copyright, production and distribution. Venuti (2000:482) states that through the process of translation a negotiation takes place after which the differences of a foreign text are reduced and substituted by another set of domestic differences that enable the foreign text to be received. In this same article Venuti outlines the utopian dimension of translation which seems to be particularly relevant in the case of my analysis:

> Yet translation is also utopian. The domestic inscription is made with the very intention to communicate the foreign text, and so it is filled with the anticipation that a community will be created around that text – although in translation. In the remainder lies the hope that the translation will establish a domestic readership, an imagined community that shares an interest in the foreign, possibly a market from the publisher's point of view. (2000:498).

The publishing policy of Magic Press seemed to make possible the utopian dimension theorized by Venuti: the imagined community of Italian horror comic books readers that the publisher wished for became a real market. Apparently, Magic Press was able to choose the right moment to propose a foreign text that was "not so much communicated as inscribed with domestic intelligibilities and interests" (Venuti 2000:482) thus responding to the expectations of its readership, or even better, forging those same expectations by ensuring that its readership became accustomed to good quality products.

References

Primary Sources

Moore Alan, Stephen Bissette and John Totleben (1984-1987) *Saga of the Swamp Thing # 21-50*, DC Vertigo.

Moore, Alan and Rick Veitch (1984-1987) *Saga of the Swamp Thing # 51-64*, DC Vertigo.

Moore, Alan, Stephen Bissette and John Totleben (1989) *Saga of the Swamp Thing Vol 1*, DC Vertigo [*La Saga di Swamp Thing, vol 1*, Italian translation by Leonardo Rizzi, Magic Press, 2003].

Moore, Alan, Stephen Bissette, John Totleben and Shawn McManus (1990) *Swamp Thing – Love and Death Vol. 2*, DC Vertigo [*Swamp Thing - Amore e Morte, vol 2*, Italian translation by Leonardo Rizzi, Magic Press2004].

Moore, Alan, Stephen Bissette and John Totleben (2000) *Swamp Thing, The Curse. Vol. 3 DC* Vertigo [*La maledizione*, vol. 3, Italian translation by Leonardo Rizzi, Magic Press, 2006]

Various authors (1952) *The Vault of Horror #27*, EC Comics.

------ (1964) *Creepy #1. Illustrated Tales of Terror and Suspense*, Warren Publishing.

------ (1969) *Mezzanotte con zio Tibia*, Milano: Mondadori.

Secondary Sources

Barker, Martin (1984) *Haunt of Fears. The Strange History of the British Horror Comics Campaign*, London: Pluto Press.

Benton, Mike (1991) *The Illustrated History of Horror Comics*, Dallas: Taylor Publishing.

Bonetti, Fabio (2001) 'Fantastiche convergenze della storia di cinema e fumetto – ulteriori considerazioni', *Fucine mute 24* (online) http://www.fucine.com/archivio/fm24/bonetti. htm(Accessed 30 November 2006).

Bourdieu, Pierre (1986) 'The Production of Belief: Contribution to a Symbolic Economy of Goods', in R. E. Collins, James Curran and Nicholas Garnham (eds) *Media, Culture and Society*, translated by Richard Nice (first published in French in 1977), Newbury Park, CA: Sage, 131-163.

Cantucci, Andrea (n.d.) 'Fantasie gotiche e letteratura disegnata: breve storia dell'orrore letterario a fumetti', *Comics Code* (online) http://www.comicscode.net/approfondimenti/ horror/storia/ (Accessed 30 November 2006).

D'Arcangelo, Adele and Federico Zanettin (2004) 'Dylan Dog Goes to the USA: A North-American Translation of an Italian Comic Book Series', *Across Languages and Cultures* 5(2): 187-210.

Di Liddo, Annalisa (2006) *Fictional Representation in Alan Moore's Production*, unpublished PhD dissertation, Milano: Università di Milano.

Kaindl, Klaus (1999) 'Thump, Whizz, Poom: A Framework for the Study of Comics under Translation', *Target* 11(2): 263-288.

Lorenzon, Luca (2001) 'Swamp Thing', *Fucine Mute* 28 (online) http://www.fucinemute.com/ archivio/fm28/lorenzon.htm (Accessed 30 October 2006).

Morlacchini, Fulvio (n.d.) 'Swampy in Italia' in *Swamp Thing* (online) http://associazioni.monet. modena.it/glamaz/articoli/swamp/sitalia.htm (Accessed 20 October 2006).

Peroni, Claudio and Vincenzo Raucci (1999) 'An Interview with Claudio Peroni', *Ink on line* 12 (online) http://www.inkonline.info/perogatt.htm (Accessed 26 May 2006).

Pilcher, Tim and Brad Brooks (2005) *The Essential Guide to World Comics*, London: Collins & Brown.

Restaino, Franco (2004) *Storia del fumetto. Da Yellow Kid ai Manga* [A History of Comics. From Yellow Kid to Manga], Milano: UTET.

Rizzi, Leonardo, Nadia Rosso and Fabio Maglione (2006) 'Intervista a Leonardo Rizzi', *ComucUS. it* (online) http://www.comicus.it/view.php?section=interviste&id=97 (Accessed 24 May 2006).

Rota, Valerio (2001) *Nuvole migranti. Viaggio nel fumetto tradotto* [Balloons on the move. On translated comic], Mottola (TA): Lilliput.

------ (2003) 'Il fumetto: traduzione e adattamento' [Comics translation and adaptation], *Testo a Fronte* 28: 155-172.

Saltarelli, Giulio (2006) 'Magic Press. Filosofia Editoriale', *Komix.it* (online) http://www.komix. it/modules.php (Accessed 24 May 2006).

Venuti, Lawrence (2000) 'Translation, Community, Utopia', in Lawrence Venuti (ed.) *The Translation Studies Reader*, London: Routledge, 482-502.

7 Disney Comics in the Arab Culture(s)
A Pragmatic Perspective

JEHAN ZITAWI
Abu Dhabi University, United Arab Emirates

This study attempts to examine the applicability of Brown and Levinson's politeness theory to a particularly challenging discourse genre, namely Disney comics, and to extend the model beyond monolingual and monocultural contexts, to look at politeness strategies in translation between two very different cultures. The study argues that Brown and Levinson's politeness theory can be fruitfully applied to Disney comics translated from English into Arabic, provided we can demonstrate that (a) it is possible to identify a composite speaker and composite hearer in Disney comics, and (b) Disney comics can be read as face threatening texts (FTTs). The starting point of the analysis is a conventional application of Brown and Levinson's politeness theory to original and translated Disney comics, looking specifically at three sources of face threat in this context: verbal and/or visual signals that can be considered taboo or at least unpalatable to the reader; the raising of sensitive or divisive topics (e.g., Jewish and Christian imagery and colonial ideologies, stereotyping and ridiculing the target reader); and the use of address terms and other status-marked identifications that may be misidentified in an offensive or embarrassing way, either intentionally or accidentally. Politeness strategies used by Arab publishers and translators in the data examined in this study include all three categories proposed by Brown and Levinson: Don't do the FTA; Do the FTA on record with mitigation; and Do the FTA baldly with no mitigation. The study also reveals a number of weaknesses inherent in the Brown and Levinson model and highlights the need to refine politeness theory in order to make it more applicable to the analysis of complex genres such as comics and complex types of face threat encoded in discourses which are normative in nature but which present themselves as benign.

When in the early 1990s I chanced upon a group of *Aladdin* Disney comics in Arabic translation, I was intrigued by the way Arabs seem to be portrayed in these stories, which are based on the Arabian legends of Aladdin and Ali-Baba and the Forty Thieves as told in the *Arabian Nights*. In these comics, Arabs are clothed in chadors and koffiyahs; they are unshaven; they are unscrupulous, deceitful, and unhelpful. There is the dungeon, the dancing girls, and intrigue in the palace. Outside there are the masses in the marketplace, camels and goats, and tents. This image of Arabs is indeed quite widespread in American comic books (Rifas 1988, Dorfman and Mattelart 1991, Shaheen 1994, Wingfield and Karaman 1995).

However, this article is ultimately not concerned with Arab stereotypes or the misrepresentation of Arabs and Muslims in Disney comics *per se*, but rather with an analysis of Disney comics and their Arabic translations from a pragmatic perspective. In doing so, it aims to test the application of Brown and Levinson's politeness theory (1978, 1987) to the study of Disney comics in the Arab World, trying to establish the various ways in which Disney comics pose a threat to the face of Arab readers, and how Arab translators working under the constraints of Arab publishing houses deal with these threats. In other words, what do Arab translators and publishing houses do to maintain the face of the Arab child-reader (and the Arab adult-reader as well) when they believe that face is being threatened by negative images and stereotypical representations of Arabs, verbal and/or visual signals that may be considered taboo or at least unpalatable to Arab readers, or address terms and other status-marked identifications that may be employed in an offensive or embarrassing way?

This approach will be useful not only in analyzing the ways in which face threatening acts (FTAs) such as mentioning taboo elements or raising dangerously emotional or divisive topics are articulated through Disney comics translated into Arabic, but also in testing the usefulness of applying politeness theory to complex speech acts such as those contained within a translated comic.

After an overview of Disney comics in the context of the Arab World, I will focus on Brown and Levinson's (1987) politeness theory as a framework for analyzing the data in this study. Finally, I will present an application of Brown and Levinson's politeness theory to the analysis of Disney comics translated into Arabic as face threatening texts (FTTs).

1. Disney Comics in the Arab World

Mickey Mouse and Donald Duck are "two of the most ubiquitous images in Arab countries today" (Douglas and Malti-Douglas 1994:3). Arab children have become fond of the charming Disney animals. Despite the contention that Disney comics include issues that do not fit the value system in Arab societies, statistics show the special position Disney magazines occupy in the Arab World. During the 1990s, 70,000 to 80,000 copies of *Mickey* magazine were printed per week in Cairo, with a 70% sell-through rate. At that time, *Mickey* magazine was worth LE 3.8 million (around $660,000/£350,000) to LE 4.4 million (around $765,000/£406,000) a year in copy sales. The magazine's circulation tripled in 2004 when a new Egyptian publishing house took over. The magazine's total readership stands between 240,000 and 350,000 readers a week, with each copy being read by 4-5 people (Salama 2006). Moreover, 70,000 copies of *Minnie* magazine are produced and published in the UAE and distributed around the world – 33,800 copies in the UAE itself.[1]

The first Disney comic translated into Arabic was published by Dar Al-Hilal in Egypt in 1959, and since then, Disney comics have found a flourishing market in a region with a population of more than 280 million, 40 percent of which are under 14 years old.[2]

---

[1] Flora Santos, International Client Services at The Arabian Press and Media (UAE), personal communication on 2 August 2006.
[2] United Nations Development Programme report (2002) available at http://news.bbc.co.uk/2/hi/business/2246226.stm (visited 9 October 2004). "Unlike Western Europe, [the Arab world] is also characterized by high population growth – up to 4.5 [percent] in some countries. No wonder Disney operates in [it]" (de Wolf 2000).

Disney magazines, books, dubbed films, home videos, and the current Disney Chan-nel have gained a popularity in all Arab countries that cannot be disputed. Saudi Arabia represents about 50 percent of the Disney market and is "the biggest consumer of foreign goods between Western Europe and Southeast Asia" (de Wolf 2000). As the second largest economy in the Gulf region, the United Arab Emirates "accounts for 20 [percent] of the Disney business. It is home to Disney's head office in Dubai, where open-door policies and free trade practices prevail" (de Wolf 2000).

Although the region combines many exciting features (a relatively virgin market with very little quality, mass-market children's magazines and books), it presents many interesting challenges to Disney business:

> The publishing industry faces a vast area to cover larger than Western Europe. It is a fragmented market composed of ten countries (Saudi Arabia, United Arab Emirates, Kuwait, Bahrain, Oman, Qatar, Yemen, Egypt, Jordan and Lebanon), each with its own trade practices, and distribution channels are underdeveloped at best. There is no reading habit and therefore a low print media penetration in general. Add to this the common practice of censorship, the scarcity of good pan-Arab publishers, a high rate of piracy and you have one difficult region! (de Wolf 2000: online)

The production of Disney Comics into Arabic is a complex process involving two main organizational structures: firstly, Disney-Jawa and secondly, Arabic publishing houses under which a team of translators, editors and graphic designers undertake the task of translating, producing and publishing Disney comics in the Arab World.

Disney-Jawa is a joint venture between Disney and the Saudi Jawa family established in Jeddah in 1993 to issue licences to local companies who are interested in using Disney characters with their products, and to non-Middle Eastern companies who have Disney-branded products and are interested in selling in the region. The joint venture is "a unique Disney set-up where Publishing, Merchandise, Home Video, Music and Interactive are all handled under one roof" (de Wolf 2000). Around the middle of 1996, Disney-Jawa moved its head office to Dubai, one of the most important free-trade centres in the re-gion. Disney-Jawa offered a unique support framework for Disney's business to develop and refine its applications and services and to demonstrate commercial and industrial viability in the Arab World (Hiel 1995).

Disney-Jawa has issued many licences to various companies and institutions in the following countries: the Gulf area countries – United Arab Emirates, Saudi Arabia, Kuwait, Bahrain, Qatar, and Oman – Egypt, Lebanon, Jordan, Syria, Yemen, Sudan, and Iran.[3] Ac-cording to articles written in 1996 by *News Publication* from Disney Consumer Products, Disney-Jawa has had remarkable success during its first three years of operation:

> Among its notable achievements are the lobbying for copyright laws now be-ing promulgated and enforced; the signing of 150 licensees; the introduction

---

[3] Iraq is not included due to political reasons. Somalia and Djibouti are not included as well because of the finan-cial difficulties the two countries face. Arab countries in North Africa are covered by Disney's office in France.

of quality Arabic dubbing and publishing programs; the establishment of 32 Disney Corners and the organization of eight licensee/distributor seminars. (de Wolf 2000: online)

Disney-Jawa contracted four European publishers to provide its licensed publishers in the Arab World with Disney comics. These are the French Disney Hachette Presse, the Dutch Sanoma Uitgevers, The Walt Disney Company Italy, and Egmont in Denmark. These publishers of Disney comics usually send samples of their new works of Disney stories to the licensed Arabic publishing houses, which in turn order the stories they decide to translate and publish. The original Disney comics are usually sent in English and on CDs (de Wolf 2000).

The publication of Disney books in the Middle East is managed by a Publication Director at Disney-Jawa,[4] whose role includes reviewing the entire issue of each magazine, making sure that editorials and translations comply with Disney's publishing guidelines,[5] ensuring that the translated Disney stories are free from any grammatical or spelling errors, and that the magazine does not include anything that might be deemed religiously or culturally offensive or unacceptable.

Children's comics in general and Disney comics in particular have been a major part of the literature translated and published by three well-established publishing houses in the Arab World, namely Dar Al-Hilal in Cairo, Al-Futtaim/ITP in Dubai, and Al-Qabas Newspaper in Kuwait.[6]

Founded in Cairo (Egypt) in 1892, Dar Al-Hilal is Disney's oldest publisher in the Middle East, and was the first to translate and produce Disney magazines in the Arab world. It signed a contract with Walt Disney himself in 1958 to translate, publish and distribute Disney comics in the Arab World. Dar Al-Hilal then started to publish Disney titles such as *Mickey*, *Super Mickey* and *Mickey Jayb*, and in 1972 it also produced its own Disney stories (Douglas and Malti-Douglas 1994:13-5).[7] When Disney-Jawa issued a licence to another publisher, Al-Futtaim/ITP in Dubai in 1994, it allowed Dar Al-Hilal to continue publishing *Mickey* for the Egyptian market only. A few years later, Disney-Jawa allowed Egypt to

---

[4] When I started my research, the Publications Director of Disney-Jawa was Abdul Majeed Othman. He gracefully provided photocopies of original materials for Al-Qabas and Disney-Jawa stories as well as all the information about Dar Al-Hilal, in two interviews (21 and 22 April 2002) and one telephone conversation (12 October 2003). Othman resigned as Disney-Jawa's Publications Director in September 2003, and was replaced by Hisham Zahed.

[5] Unfortunately, it was not possible to have access to Disney's written publishing guidelines, since they are apparently subject to a strong policy of secrecy. See also on this point Toivonen (2001), quoted in Koponen (2004:31).

[6] Besides these three publishers, de Wolf (2000) identifies two more: Dar Al-Reisha in Jeddah (Saudi Arabia), which is part of the Hazar Media Group (advertising, publishing, TV, etc.) and Motive Publishing, which is based in Dubai. In September 2003, Disney-Jawa licensed Dar Al-Khayrat in Syria to publish three Disney magazines, based on titles active in the UK.

[7] Apparently, Dar Al-Hilal stopped producing them because Disney decided to restrict its licence to translating and publishing Disney comics. One reason behind Disney's decision could also be the poor integration of art and text and the printing quality of the illustrations. Douglas and Malti-Douglas (1994:13) refer to two indigenous comic stories that were published by Dar Al-Hilal. The first is *mughāmarātu ramsīs fī barīs* ('The Adventures of Ramsis in Paris'), which began on 13 January 1972 and ended on 13 April of the same year. The second is *'aḥmus wa-rrimālu-l-khaḍrā'* ('Ahmus and the Green Sands'), which ran from 31 August to 19 October 1972.

distribute in a few Arab African countries, such as Tunisia and Morocco, because it was expensive for Al-Futtaim/ITP (and later Al-Qabas in Kuwait) to distribute Arabic Disney comics in those areas. Although Dar Al-Hilal started to improve the print quality of its Disney magazines in 1997, Disney was not fully satisfied with their production nor with the fact that Dar Al-Hilal did not pay its royalties. Finally, after some legal quarrel, Dar Al-Hilal ceased translating and publishing Disney comics on 31 March 2003. Disney-Jawa contracted Nahdet Misr for Printing and Publishing to start translating and publishing Disney comics starting from 1 January 2004.

The second most important publisher of Disney magazines in the Arab World used to be Al-Futtaim/ITP of Dubai (UAE), a joint venture between Dubai businessman Othman Al Futtaim and a UK-based publisher, ITP. In September 1994, Disney-Jawa gave AF/ITP the licence to translate and publish Disney comic magazines in the Gulf area and the markets of Syria, Jordan, Lebanon, Yemen and Palestine. Their licence was not renewed after March 2000 as a result of financial disagreements with Disney-Jawa.

Al-Qabas is a Kuwaiti publishing house that took over in September 2000 as the sole publisher with legal rights to translate and publish Disney comics in the Arab World. Al-Qabas sends all copies of its Disney Comics to Disney-Jawa for review and approval, as part of their agreement. Al-Qabas used to publish two other Disney magazines for non-Arabic speakers: *Mickey* in English started in April 2001 and stopped in November 2001, and *Mickey* in Urdu started in June 2001 and stopped in October 2001. They simply did not sell. On 30 September 2003, Al-Qabas's licence ended and The Arabian Press and Media (Abu Dhabi – UAE) took over in 2004.

The data used in this article are taken from a corpus consisting of 138 Disney comics stories in Arabic translation published between 1993 and 2003 by Dar Al-Hilal in Egypt (72 stories), Al-Futtaim/ITP in Dubai (24 stories), and Al-Qabas in Kuwait (48 stories) (see Zitawi 2004 for full details).[8]

2.   Disney Comics and Brown and Levinson's Politeness Theory

The vast majority of studies using Brown and Levinson's (1978, 1987) politeness theory as a framework have focused on face-to-face conversation (e.g. Nwoye 1992, Mao 1994, O'Driscoll 1996, De Kadt 1998, Ji 2000). However, Brown and Levinson's theory may also represent a useful conceptual tool to analyze texts such as comics, and provide credible and coherent explanations for the potential of comics in translation to threaten the face of Arab readers, or assist us in more clearly understanding the pragmatic strategies employed to maintain the face of Arab readers.

Brown and Levinson's theory is based on four basic notions: *face, face threatening acts, politeness strategies,* and the *factors* that determine the selection of the strategies and thus influence the production of politeness. The concept of 'face' consists of two basic aspects: the desire to be free to act without being imposed on by others, coined 'negative face', and the desire that others respect, value and appreciate one's wants,

---

[8] The source stories appeared between 1962 and 2000.

coined 'positive face'. Generally speaking, in conversational interaction it is assumed that participants work together to maintain each other's face because they are aware of the "mutual vulnerability" of their faces (1987:61). Such shared assumptions are claimed to be universal though the 'content of the face' varies from one culture to another (1987:61). Certain kinds of acts intrinsically threaten either or both aspects of the speaker's and the hearer's face and are called face threatening acts (FTAs). Depending on whether it is the speaker's face or the hearer's face that is mainly threatened or whether it is the positive face or negative face of the speaker/hearer that is 'at stake', Brown and Levinson divide FTAs into four main types: (1) acts that threaten the negative face of the hearer (such as orders, requests, suggestions, advice, reminders, threats, warnings, etc.), (2) acts that threaten the positive face of the hearer (such as expressions of ridicule, insults, mentioning of taboo and divisive topics, using address terms in an offensive way, etc.), (3) acts that threaten the negative face of the speaker (such as expression of thanks, making excuses, acceptance of offers, etc.), and (4) acts that threaten the positive face of the speaker (such as apologies, accepting a compliment, self-humiliation, etc.). The current study focuses on the potential threats to the positive face of the hearer – or reader in this case.

The term 'politeness' is used in this article to refer to the observance of the requirements of deference and appropriateness in addressing the Arab reader of Disney comics by pursuing certain strategies to achieve a specific communicative goal without sacrificing or threatening fundamental socio-cultural and religious norms valued and sanctified by the Arab reader.

The 'speaker function' of a Disney comic is far more complex than for a particular individual engaged in conventional conversation, as it involves numerous interventions, from storylining and narrative creation to artwork and editorship. As a consequence, in Disney comics the 'speaker' is a composite of voices reflecting a range of individual creative, editorial and commercial inputs, some of which may be more or less self-consciously represented in the final comics output than others. The very idea of a Disney comic and its embeddedness within particular comic book conventions is the unifying element that allows us to speak of the institution of the Disney comics story as a coherent and singular composite speaker.

When a Disney comic is translated into Arabic, the range of interests that constitute the comic's speaker function is further complicated by input from publishers, translators, and editors who will attempt to ensure that their translations are not only linguistically correct but furthermore that the comic's content does not transgress norms acceptable to Arab audiences and does not promote ideologies that would be seen by such consumers as overtly hostile or offensive in content.

Taking into consideration the complex nature of Disney comics as a form of written discourse involving composite Speaker1 (the combination of those who create the Disney comic and affect its creation such as creative teams of artists, writers, etc., publishing houses, Comics Code Authority, Disney in-house guidelines) and composite Speaker2 (the combination of those who recreate Disney comics in the Arab World: the team of translators and graphic designers, publishing houses, Disney-Jawa and Saudi

Censor at the Saudi Ministry of Information), the term politeness denotes the strategies implemented by these composite speakers when addressing the target reader (Arab children and their parents, teachers, librarians, and any professionals interested in the welfare of children). Since the Target Hearer (reader) for Speaker1 is not exclusively Arab children but comprises a much larger group of children, it is primarily the duty of Speaker2 to observe the requirements of politeness by deleting, blocking, altering or hiding inappropriate, ridiculing or offensive material that is considered threatening to the face of the Arab reader. On such basis, Speaker2 enacts politeness by evaluating the communicative language and material of the original source text according to the prevailing social norms and cultural values in Arab societies. As the examples presented in this study show, however, the 'Arab World' is not a monolithic entity, and the Gulf area publishers (Al-Futtaim/ITP and Al-Qabas) have their own standards and policies in translating Disney comics that are different and distinct from those followed in Dar Al-Hilal in Egypt. While Al-Futtaim and Al-Qabas have been selling their translated comics in Saudi Arabia (hence their adherence to the Saudi Ministry's guidelines), Dar Al-Hilal in Egypt does not have to respond to any external authorities. Therefore, it is extremely important to bear in mind not only that what may be deemed suitable for Hearer1 may not necessarily be suitable or palatable for Hearer2, and vice-versa, but also that Hearer2 is not a homogenous but rather a composite category, comprised of many diverse individuals and groups of readers in different Arab countries.

3. Disney Comics as Face Threatening Texts

In their model, Brown and Levinson focus on the nature of FTAs as a factor influencing the speaker's use of certain politeness strategies to avoid or minimize the threat to the addressee's face. Politeness strategies are identified as follows (in order of increasing face threat): Don't do the FTA, Do the FTA *off record*, Do the FTA *on record with mitigation*, and Do the FTA *baldly with no mitigation*.

Conventional application of Brown and Levinson's politeness theory to analyze whether or not a Disney comic translated into Arabic can be viewed as a face threatening text would depend on whether or not one is able to demonstrate that the comic in question threatens the positive face of the Arab reader.

My data includes numerous examples of comics content being modified during the translation process to remove text or images that might threaten the positive face of the Arab reader. I offer a commentary on the ways in which the face of the Arab reader (Hearer2) is threatened by the original comic, outlining steps taken by Speaker2 to attempt to maintain the face of the Arab reader and minimize the relevant threat. The examples are organized under three main headings: cultural and religious taboo topics, divisive topics (including Jewish and Christian imagery and colonial ideologies), and finally, stereotypical address-terms and status-marked identifications in initial encounters that may be misidentified in an offensive or embarrassing way either intentionally or accidentally (Brown and Levinson 1987:66-67). The discussion is structured under the three main politeness strategies employed by Speaker2 in the Gulf and Egypt to minimize the threat to the face of the Arab reader: 'don't do the FTA', 'do the FTA on record with mitigation', and 'do the FTA on record with no mitigation'. 'Do the FTA off record' means that the speaker, who shows ambiguous intent, cannot be held responsible for committing a face threatening act and any inferred meaning from his or her speech act can be denied.[9] Accordingly, this strategy is not applicable and not evident in my data as one of the strategies followed by Speaker2 in the Gulf and Egypt to minimize the threat to the face of the Arab reader.

I will present examples from both the Gulf area (Al-Qabas and Al-Futtaim/ITP) and Egypt in order to explore the different approaches and strategies followed in the different areas. Al-Qabas and Al-Futtaim/ITP translated comics contain more modifications and deletions than those translated by Dar Al-Hilal, largely as a consequence of market forces. Al-Futtaim/ITP and Al-Qabas comics are marketed widely across Arab countries, and sell particularly well in the more conservative Gulf States, with 50% of production being sold in Saudi Arabia. By contrast, Egyptian comics are sold on the less conservative domestic (Egyptian) market and in parts of North Africa, but not in the Gulf.

3.1 *Don't Do the FTA*

'Don't do (translate) the FTA' is the strategy used most extensively by Arab translators of Disney comics, especially by Speaker2 in the Gulf area – represented by Al-Qabas and Al-Futtaim/ITP as the Gulf publishing houses, Disney-Jawa as a general supervisor, and the Saudi Ministry of Information, whose opinion, feedback and approval of Arabic Disney comics is crucial to Disney-Jawa. Censorship regulations in the Gulf area include monitoring content for anything that might not conform to Islamic teachings.

Brown and Levinson's theory suggests that a face threatening act is one which "criticis[es], contempt[s] or ridicule[s]" the reader's "wants, acts, personal characteristics, goods, beliefs or values" (Brown and Levinson 1987:66-67). It is clear that some Disney stories in English as an expression of western value-systems, norms and ideology do include signs, features and visual elements of classical stereotyping of Arabs, and these can clearly offend the Arab reader. Moreover, this ridicule is firmly embedded in colonial ideologies and draws on stereotypes of Arabs which are generated in colonial discourses. So far as I have been able to ascertain, the majority of such stories have not been translated into Arabic because the texts are highly threatening to the face of the target readers.

According to Brown and Levinson, mentioning "taboo topics, including those that are inappropriate" is an FTA that threatens the positive-face wants of the addressee

---

[9] Off-record strategies violate Grice's four conversational maxims: (1) when the speaker presupposes or gives hints or association clues, s/he violates the maxim of Relevance, (2) being ironic, or using metaphors, rhetorical questions, and/or contradictions, the addresser violates the maxim of Quality, (3) the Quantity maxim is violated when the speaker understates, overstates or uses tautologies, and (4) s/he may go off record and violate the Manner maxim by over-generalizing, displacing the hearer, being vague, ambiguous, incomplete, for example through the use of ellipsis.

(Brown and Levinson 1987:67). Disney comics contain many sketches which could be construed as face threatening to Arab readers. Topics which are perceived as religiously or culturally taboo or inappropriate include: romantic and sexual references; magic; God and god-related references; the human body; images of pigs. In the following examples, I will examine how Speaker2, especially in the Gulf area, has employed the 'don't translate the FTA' strategy. On the verbal level, the strategy takes the form of deleting taboo/inappropriate words, replacing them with other words, changing parts of the dialogue between characters, or replacing the whole story with a new one which matches the pictures. On the visual level, parts of the picture are removed, unwanted but irremovable parts are darkened or blackened, and panels are deleted or replaced. When it is difficult to carry out any 'visual manipulation' and/or change the story dialogue or plot, a whole page may be deleted, and even a whole story may be rejected when the text is deemed highly threatening.

Deeply embedded in the American/Western tradition, Disney comics contain verbal and pictorial romantic and/or sexual references, such as kisses, love relationships, dating, etc. which are considered by the vast majority of Arab parents (a component of Hearer2) taboo or potentially an offensive subject for their children, and these are therefore removed by Speaker2 in the Gulf in an attempt to make the target text more suitable for the target readership.

The story *'ḥaflah faḍā'iyyah'*[10] ('Space Party') translated and published by Al-Qabas in 2001, contains an interesting example that combines both visual and verbal manipulation. A panel submitted to the Publication Director shows the two main characters, male and female, looking smilingly into each other's eyes and holding hands, surrounded by hearts. The Arabic translation of the text in the caption which accompanies the image reads: *"'inna ḥubba tūtū li'akhīha jūjū rā'ida-l-faḍā'i lā yuḍāhihi shay'un! ḥubbun lā yu'athiru fīhi 'ayya furāq!"* ("Tutu's love for her brother Juju, the astronaut, surpasses everything! A love that cannot be affected by separation!"). The Publication Director circled the hearts with a line, adding the instruction "please remove these hearts", which were in fact expunged in the published story.[11] During an interview with the Director, he commented on his proposed change, insisting that Arab children reading the story would believe that Tutu and Juju are brother and sister. Whether the removal of any relevant references throughout the story actually meant that a coherent storyline was preserved and the Arab child found the portrayed relationship believable and understandable is a matter of speculation.

According to the Islamic Sharia, magic is condemned as dangerous not only in the sense that it can involve appeals to devilish powers but also because magic as illusion can affect the senses of people in ways that can prove dangerous or even fatal. Consequently,

---

[10] The transliteration system is taken from Barry (1997).
[11] I obtained the Arabic Disney stories from Al-Qabas and Disney-Jawa in photocopy format, and in some cases I was unable to locate the source texts in English. Unfortunately, the images could not be reproduced in this article since Disney denied me permission to use the illustrations for which they hold the copyright for research purposes, in spite of my repeated attempts to secure such permission. See also introduction to this volume.

it is not surprising to find that comics stories revolving around magic (e.g. 'The Quest for Kalevala', *Uncle Scrooge* No. 334, Gladstone 1999) would normally be considered highly face-threatening and, therefore, rejected as 'not suitable for publishing'.[12]

References to 'God' could also be inappropriate and offensive to Hearer2, and as such Speaker2 could view them as face threatening. In Islam, there is only one God, Allah, who created everything. Nothing can be named or called God but Allah, and nothing can be attributed the qualities of Allah. Consequently, stories in which objects or people are referred to as 'god(s)' are unacceptable in Islam.

For example, in the 1997 story 'Riders of the Living Mummy from Outer Space', by Moore and Pujadas, which was published by Al-Futtaim/ITP in 1995 as *'ghuzātun mina-l-faḍā'* ' ('Invaders from the Space'),[13] a panel drawn in an 'old-Egyptian' style shows an infuriated Zoot, a Goofy-looking character who 'utters' lightning and snakes in a balloon, jumping enraged near a sarcophagus in front of a group of men with a spade, all shown in profile view. A caption in the English source text explains: "…When the coffin was disturbed, a god emerged, and expressed anger at being disturbed…". A balloon connected to the gutter (the 'off-screen' voice of one of Zoot's friends, reading the story) comments: "I have to admit, that sounds like Zoot!". The UAE Arabic translation, in which the caption reads: "…*wa 'indama ḥarrakū-ttābūta, zahara minhu makhlūqun ghāḍibun jiddan li'annahum 'az'ajūhu*" ("… and when they moved the coffin, a creature emerged that was very angry because they disturbed him") and the balloon reads: "'*aẓunnu 'anna-l-'awṣāfa tanṭabiqu 'alā zūt!*" ("I think the description fits Zoot!"), averts the threat to religious prescriptions by translating 'god' as 'creature'.

As with all other societies, Arab and Muslim societies have their own taboos and protocols governing the display and covering of the human body. This constitutes a potential source of threat to the face of the Arab reader. Covering parts of women's bodies is one of the most common visual strategies followed in translating Disney comics into Arabic in the Gulf area.

The Kuwaiti story '*riḥlatun muthīrah*' ('An Exciting Journey'), published in *Minnie* in 2001, illustrates the kind of visual manipulation that can be applied to target images. One panel shows a group of men (in bathing suits) and women (dressed in black) swimming in a swimming pool and having fun. Standing by the hedge, Minnie looks on as everyone is enjoying their time. A thought balloon that hangs over her head reads: "*yabdu 'annahum yuqīmūna ḥaflatan li'aṣdiqā'ihim 'alā ḥawḍi-ssibāḥah!*" ("It looks like they are throwing a party for their friends around the swimming pool!"). Careful scrutiny of the target picture reveals that parts of the bodies (thighs, shoulders, arms, bellies, etc.) of the women swimming and relaxing around the pool have been darkened. Arab graphic artists usually use the colour black to cover undesirable or unwanted images in the source

---

[12] See Zitawi (2004) for a detailed discussion of all examples.

[13] 1997 is given as "first publication date" in the I.N.D.U.C.K.S. database (see note 23), when the story appeared in a number of North-European countries. According to I.N.D.U.C.K.S., the story has never been published in English. So, unless a previous and undocumented published edition exists, it appears that the original story was sold to the Arab publisher before being published in Europe.

picture. However, in this instance, the use of black has not succeeded in hiding the two-piece bathing suits worn by some of the women. Covering female bodies conforms to the norms of the Arab culture, but this form of editing and censorship also impacts on the meaning of the image and the story it transmits. In this case, it makes little sense for all the women around a swimming pool to be dressed entirely in black rather than in bathing suits or bikini.

In Islam, eating pigs is prohibited. It is therefore unsurprising to discover that representations of pigs are frequently edited.[14] There are two ways in which the images of pigs are manipulated: either the nostrils are removed (see, for example, *'aththariy II'* ('The Rich II'), published in *Battut* by Al-Qabas in 2001, in which the Duck City Mayor, a pig-like figure with no nostrils, recommends throwing a high-class party to his host Donald), or the nose itself is blackened (see, for example, *'al-hurūb min wādi-rru'b'* ('Escape from Fear Valley'), translated by Al-Futtaim/ITP and published in *Mickey* in 1999, where a pig miner with a black nose feels the ground shaking and warns his fellow miners to flee, for 'something awful gonna happen!'), leaving the target reader with the image of a creature that can still be recognized as a pig.

The "raising of dangerously ... divisive topics, e.g. politics, race, religion" can also put the positive face of the Arab reader at stake (Brown and Levinson 1987:67). Both Jewish (Israeli?) and Christian imagery and colonial ideologies are divisive for the same reason – i.e., colonial subjugation of Arab populations.[15] Most of the countries of the traditional heartlands of Islam in the Middle East and North Africa have enjoyed scarcely more than half a century of freedom from colonial subjugation by the West, while Palestinians continue to suffer major abuses of human rights inflicted by the Jewish state of Israel. Indeed, the continued imperialism that many Arabs and Muslims feel they still suffer from is often directly compared with older forms of colonialism and even with the crusades. This helps to explain why Jewish and Christian imagery is removed from Disney comics and why it is treated here as an example of divisive topics.

For instance, in line with censorship regulations and practices carried out and followed in Egypt at the time, Uncle Scrooge's top hat was removed in one of the Egyptian *Super Mickey*'s 1994 translated stories: *'iḥtaris min-l-wendīju'* ('Beware of the Wendigo').[16] The longstanding association of Orthodox Judaism with the wearing of top hats and

---

[14] For example, Athamneh and Zitawi (1999) note that Arabic translations of dubbed animated pictures sometimes translate the word 'pig' as 'ram', even though the words refer to images that are clearly identifiable as pigs.

[15] The complex relationship between Judaism, Zionism and the State of Israel is beyond the scope of this article. Suffice it to say that the association of Judaism with Israel is very strong worldwide, and not only in the Arab world.

[16] The original story 'War of the Wendigo', written by Don Rosa and published by Gladstone in *Walt Disney's Comics*, shows Donald, Uncle Scrooge, Huey, Dewey and Louie in one panel standing on a rock and looking over a forest. One of the triplets expresses his delight by saying to Uncle Scrooge, "White or green, it was nice of you to bring us on your tour of your Canadian mills Uncle Scrooge". Another twin adds, "We can do some nature studies". In the next panel, the last triplet says, "We might earn our merit badges in learning the squawks of the common Loon". Uncle Scrooge replies, "Seems like you could do that back home living with your Uncle Donald!". The expression on Donald's face shows that he is shaken by Uncle Scrooge's comment and insulted.

prevalent stereotypes of Jewish people being wealthy (Uncle Scrooge is a particularly well-off comics character) may have motivated the removal of Uncle Scrooge's top hat in the translated version.[17]

However, Uncle Scrooge's top hat was retained in a translation produced a few years later ('Time Bandits', *The Adventures of Uncle Scrooge* No. 1, Gladstone 1998, translated as *'lūṣūṣu-zzaman'* – 'Time Bandits', *Super Mickey* Vol. 39, Dar Al-Hilal 1997). This may be due to recognition on the part of the translator and/or publisher that Uncle Scrooge's top hat was intended in the source text as a symbol of America rather than Judaism. Alternatively, it could be a function of changes in a broader political context, related to developing peace negotiations in the Middle East.[18]

Undoubtedly, the removal of Uncle Scrooge's hat by Egyptian translators does cause some problems in understanding translated stories. In 'Trouble Vision', a 1993 Gladstone story by Kenner, Bernstrup and Vicar, Uncle Scrooge follows his customary habit of concealing money in his hat – in this case a million dollars. In the Arabic version: *'naẓārat 'am dahab'* ('Uncle Dahab's Glasses'), Scrooge lacks a hat.. In the source panel, two of the Beagle Boys are dressed as Arabs and are about to rob Uncle Scrooge. This is proven not only by how they appear to be in mid pounce, but also by the speech balloon above one of the Beagle's heads which reads "But we can still snatch the cash McDuck keeps in his hat!". Uncle Scrooge is drawn clutching his hat and the speech bubble above his head reads "Only one gang of crooks knows about that...The Beagle Boys!". In the target panel where Uncle Scrooge's hat is removed, the Beagle Boy says: "lākin yumkinuna 'ikhtiṭāfa-nnuqūdi-l-mawj'dati ma'hu!" ("But we can still snatch the money he has!"). This clearly undermines the story; while the hat is visibly large enough to conceal money in the English version, without the hat it is unclear how or where Uncle Scrooge could hide this fortune about his person, particularly since the artwork does not show him as having a bag or even any pockets. These difficulties are exacerbated when, knowing that Uncle Scrooge hides his money in his hat, the Beagle Boys, who have constituted a continuous threat to his fortune, attack him, causing Uncle Scrooge to tighten his grip on his hat. However, in the Arabic version, the humorous vision of Uncle Scrooge clinging on to his hat to keep his money is lost.

Disney-Jawa and Kuwait/Dubai publishers also make sure Christian imagery is removed or modified in Disney comics translated into Arabic. Crosses and references to

---

[17] This point was reinforced by Fredrik Ekman, a member of Disney Comics Database List, who explained in an email on 24 February 2001 that "many stories are also retouched so that Uncle Scrooge's hat is removed. This is to avoid him being mistaken for a Jew". A more subtle explanation was offered by the Editor-in-Chief of Dar Al-Hilal's *Samir Magazine*, and former Editor-in-Chief of *Mickey Pocho/Jayb*, who noted during an interview conducted with her in early 2002 that "the hat was sometimes removed to minimize the foreign, i.e. American and/or European, elements in Disney stories". Considering the huge range of 'foreign' elements in Disney comics – which, after all, originate in the United States – it seems likely that 'foreign elements' are deployed here as a shorthand reference to Judaism/Israel.

[18] It seems plausible to read the inclusion and omission of Uncle Scrooge's top hat in Egypt within a broader political context. During the 1970s, the peace process between Egypt and Israel was an extremely sensitive and emotive issue, and one which led eventually to President Sadat's assassination. Earlier comics, in which the top hat is removed, reflect these sensitivities. In later comics, it may have been possible to include Uncle Scrooge's top hat because the peace process had become slightly less contentious over time.

the crusades, for instance, were removed in the Arabic version of 'The Golden Sheep' ('*al-khirāfu-dhdhahabiyyah*', *Madinat Al-Batt* No. 23, Al-Qabas 2001). At the same time, the crescent moon and star – an internationally-recognized symbol of Islam – were darkened to remove references to Muslims being defeated and Muslim lands being invaded by crusaders. Finally, rather than the Crusader being depicted as fighting and defeating Muslims, he is shown as being defeated, which at this point does not make sense because in a preceding panel in the Arabic comic he had already been shown killing and defeating his enemy. Why the crusader was portrayed in this way is not clear, particularly since religious imagery associated with Christianity, Islam and the crusades had already been removed from the comic.

A second example that illustrates the 'don't do the FTA' strategy through removing/modifying/visually manipulating Christian imagery and themes carried out in the Gulf area involves obscuring or removing a Santa Claus hat worn by some characters. For example, in a Kuwaiti story, ''*ughniyyatu-l-'īd*' ('Eid's Song', Eid being a Muslim's celebration), a translation of 'Too Many Christmas Carols', a Don Markstein story published in *Mickey Mouse* 2005, part of the hat worn by a concert presenter who is also a musical instrument store owner is removed, so it will no longer be recognizable as a Santa Claus hat. The editing of the hat may have been a rushed afterthought, because in another panel of the same story the hat worn by the same character remains intact and unchanged.

This decision is particularly puzzling since the picture clearly depicts a Christmas scene, rich in typical festive colours of red and green, Christmas decorations, balloons, winter clothing, and so on. Muslims and Arabs are well acquainted with the concept and rituals of Christians – indeed, the birthplace and historical heartlands of Christianity are located in the Middle East. So, why not retain references to Christianity and Christian celebrations as an educational tool, for instance? Certainly, the usefulness of such strategies has been debated in the literature (see Athamneh and Zitawi 1999, for example).

Finally, according to Brown and Levinson, using "address terms and other status-marked identifications ... [that the reader] may misidentify in an offensive or embarrassing way, either intentionally or accidentally" (1987:67) is another act that threatens the positive face of the hearer. Address terms and status-marked identifications are terms used to precede or replace the name of the addressee; they may include (singly or in combination) title, first name, last name, or nickname. Disney comics do use address-terms and status-marked identifications in ways that stereotype Arabs or can be misidentified in an offensive or embarrassing way by Speaker2, e.g. titles and first names such as Sheik, Effendi, Pasha, Abdullah, or Ahmad. Speaker2 in the Gulf and Egypt employs one main strategy, 'Don't do the FTA', and usually deletes or substitutes them with English address-terms in an attempt to soften the face threatening act.

In Hedman and Peinado's 'A Sticky Story', translated in Egypt as '*murabbā x murabbā*' ('Jam x Jam'), a rich Arab character characterized through very essentialized and stereotypical notions of Arab culture (wealth, clothing, arrogance, etc.) had his nonsensical pastiche Arabic name and title replaced in translation with a name and title that played less to stereotyped racism. In one of the source panels, Uncle Scrooge is trying to land a deal with Sheikh Bugali, a potential buyer of his home-made jam. He leads him into a warehouse where Donald is sitting behind a wooden table, adding a special substance to some of the filled-with-jam jars. "As you can see, Sheikh Bugali, we've developed a super-efficient production system that you can start up in your country for minimal cost", Uncle Scrooge explains. The impressed Sheikh agrees with him: "The economical advantages are plain to see Mr. McDuck!". In the next panel, the open jar containing jam that the Sheikh has just tasted is about to explode due to chemical complications caused by Donald's special substance. "Mmm and the product is quite superb", says the Sheikh not noticing what is happening. Uncle Scrooge, in complete shock, exclaims, "What was that?" asking Donald who astoundingly stares at the jar. In the Arabic version, the title "Sheik" was translated as "*sayyid*" ("Mr. "), though we can still see the stereotyping in the way the Arab Sheik is dressed. Moreover, Dar Al-Hilal translated "*bughālī*" ("Bughali"), an offensive name taken from the Arabic word '*baghil*', which means 'mule', into "'*almaẓī* " ("Almathi"), a name taken from the Arabic word "*almās*' ('almas') (or "*almāẓ*' ('almath'), as pronounced by some Egyptians), which means diamonds.

Interestingly, when in 1998 the American publisher Gladstone published the story, originally produced in Europe in 1997, Disney realized that parts of it could be offensive to Arabs: "in that American printing, some lines of dialogue were censored by Disney in Burbank under fear of being offensive to Arabs (Disney objected to a line about dates being a popular food in the Middle East, for example)" (Gerstein 2001).[19] According to the ex-Editor-in-Chief of Al-Qabas in Kuwait, such a comic would not be translated in Kuwait.[20] Moreover, Al-Qabas, whose publishing guidelines are similar to Disney-Jawa and the Saudi Ministry, avoids translating any Disney comic showing Arabs wearing Bedouin outfits.

3.2 Do the FTA on Record with Mitigation

The second main strategy used in the Gulf area and Egypt is 'do the FTA on record with mitigation'. According to Brown and Levinson (1987:73), the use of this strategy affords the speaker the opportunity to "placate" the hearer; "to counteract the potential face damage of the FTA by doing it in such a way, or with such *modifications or additions* to indicate clearly that no such face threat is intended or desired" (1987:69-70; emphasis added). Thus, depending on which aspect of face (positive or negative) is being attended to, this strategy takes one of two forms: positive politeness, which is redress directed at the hearer's positive face – the positive self-image s/he claims for himself/herself, and negative politeness, which is redressive action addressed to the hearer's negative face – his/her basic want to have his/her freedom of action unimpeded.

When this strategy is applied in the Gulf area and Egypt, one main subcategory emerges, revealing a new dimension to the strategy's function and applicability to written texts such as Disney comics translated into Arabic. This mechanism or redressive

---

[19] Personal communication, email of 18 January 2001. David Gerstein is a Disney comics researcher and historian.
[20] Manal Bahnasawi, ex-Editor-in-Chief of Disney Magazines in Al-Qabas, personal communication – interview 10 December 2001.

action is 'the use of euphemism'.

In addition to deleting any romantic and sexual references (realizing the 'don't do the FTA' strategy), Speaker2 in the Gulf area uses euphemistic expressions to translate terms considered inappropriate for an Arab reader. For example, in one panel of *"aṣdiqā"* ('Friends'), a Kuwaiti story published in *Battut* in 2000, Donald is in a daze as he speaks blissfully, *"maraḍun min naw'in khāsin yaj'aluka ḥāliman ṭuwāl-l-waqti wa mushattatu-dhdhihni wa ka'annaka fī ḥālati ḥub!"* ("A special sickness that makes you dream all the time and makes you feel as if you're in love!"). The panel shows the Publication Director's instruction to change the word *"ḥub"* ("love") into *"tawaddud"* ("liking"). Similarly, the Publication Director also requested that the word *"ḥub"* ("love") be changed into *"dhālika-shshay'"* ("that thing") in another panel.

Changing 'in love' into 'in liking', which is an understatement, and 'fall in love' into 'fall in that thing', which is a metonym, results in unnatural dialogue. Indeed, 'in liking' and 'fall in that thing' sound just as ludicrous in Arabic as they do in English. In the same story, the word 'date' or 'rendezvous' was changed into 'errand' because 'date' is often invested with sexualized meaning. By contrast, an errand sounds more innocent, even though it may still be clear from the story that 'errand' is merely a euphemism for 'date'.

The strategy of 'familiarization' is applied in the Gulf and Egypt to minimize the threat of Christian-related references. As seen above, for instance, the story 'Too Many Christmas Carols' was translated as *"ughniyyatu-l-'īd"* ('Eid's Song'). The Christian celebration of Easter is treated in an interesting way in Egypt, by contextualizing the festival within Egyptian culture, and translating 'Easter' as *'shammu-nnasīm'* ('Spring Day') in 'The Easter Beasties from Outer Space', re-titled as *'baydu-l-fulayfil'* ('Al-Fulayfil's Eggs') when translated by Dar Al-Hilal in 1998.[21] The opening target panel shows a caption placed at the top right corner that reads: *"idhā kunta taẓunnu 'anna shamma-nnasīmi bi-nnisbati lil'awlādi wa baṭūt lan yakhtalifu 'an kuli 'am fa-'anta mukhṭi'..."* ("If you think that "Sham El-Nasim" won't be different this year for the kids and "Battut", then you are mistaken..."). Donald announces to the boys who are gathered around a table to paint their Sham El-Nasim eggs: *" maw'idu-nnawmi yā 'awlād! Al-firāshu yunādīnā! ghadan shammu-nnasīm wa nurīdu-l-'iḥtifāla bihi mubakiran wa bi-nashāṭ!"* ("Time for bed, kids! Our beds are calling us! Tomorrow is "Sham El-Nasim" and we want to celebrate it early and with energy!"). Meanwhile, Huey asks Dewey to give him the blue dye for eggs. Dewey in return asks Louie to pass the red paint because he wants to dye the egg with two colours. 'Sham El-Nasim' is a Coptic festival of Pharaonic origin which celebrates the arrival of spring and takes place on Easter Monday.

3.3   Do The FTA on Record with No Mitigation

The third strategy, used mainly in Egypt, is 'do the FTA on record (baldly) with no mitigation'. In the bald-on-record strategy, the face threat is not minimized either because the hearer's face is ignored or is irrelevant (as in cases of great urgency or desperation), or because the speaker minimizes face threats by implication (as in expressing welcome,

---

[21] The proper translation of 'Easter' is *'īdu-l-fiṣḥ'*.

bidding farewell, etc.) (Brown and Levinson 1987:95-101).

As discussed earlier, romantic and sexual references and references to magic, God and horoscope are removed in the Gulf area, and the human body and images of pigs are routinely covered to avoid offending the sensibilities of Arab, largely Muslim, readers. However, it is also important to note that what may be deemed to offend sensibilities in one Arab country may not be perceived as offensive in another. Egypt is a traditionally less conservative country than countries in the Gulf area, and also has a fairly large Christian population. Thus, it is interesting to note that in Egypt most Disney comics are translated with no mitigation, possibly because the weightiness of the FTA is lower, or perceived to be lower.

Nevertheless, many Egyptian experts in literature for children and young people and other allied professionals working with children or interested in the field of writing and translating for children have expressed concern about the content of translated children's comics, especially Disney comics in Egypt, because they reflect western/American beliefs, values and culture. For instance, Sahrif Arafah, a famous Egyptian caricaturist, criticizes the type of relationship depicted between Donald and his three nephews on the one hand, and Donald and Daisy on the other.[22]

In spite of opposition to the content of Disney comics and the kind of relationship Disney characters have, Dar Al-Hilal does not construe love and romantic relations as taboo or inappropriate topics that need to be censored or edited.

Scenes involving kissing (see, for example, '*bunduq wa-nnaḥt*' ('Bondok and Carving'), translated and published in *Mickey* in 1999, in which a couple is kissing and hearts appear all around them) as well as expressions such as 'he fell in love' (e.g. '*al-miṣbāḥu-ssiḥriy*' ('The Magic Lamp'), *Mickey* Vol. 69 (I), Dar Al-Hilal 1994) are retained without change, reflecting different social conventions in Egyptian society, as well as clearly different processes of censorship.[23]

It is also possible to find depictions of women wearing bathing suits in Egyptian comics, as for instance, in '*ḥawādītu minī*' ('Minnie's Stories'), published by Dar Al-Hilal in 1998 in Vol. 41 of *Super Mickey*. One panel shows Minnie, Clarabelle and a blonde lady in a bikini strolling at the beach. Clarabelle comments saying the girl is beautiful, which does

---

[22] The caricaturist Sahrif Arafah notes that the characters of Battut, his three nephews Tutu, Susu, and Lulu, and Zizi in the Arabic translations of *Mickey Magazine*, represent the widespread rupture in American families. The three children live with their uncle (Battut) with no reference to their parents, as if it is completely normal not to have a parent! He adds that the Magazine "presents a suspicious relationship between Battut and Zizi (Battutah) that puzzled the Arab translator. How is the translator to render the word 'boyfriend' (from a Western perspective) for an Arab child who is raised in an Eastern environment that does not acknowledge such a thing?". Although the Arabic magazine has translated the word as 'his fiancée', the confusion remains when the two characters (Battut and Mahthuth) fight over her. She is not engaged to either of them; instead she is a [girl]friend of both! Arafah adds that Arab children should be presented with a normal family that consists of a father, mother and children; not nephews who live with their uncle who is the boyfriend of a girl who dumps him when they fight and goes out with someone else! (*Majallat Al-Mujtama'* (Society Magazine) 4/12/2003); my translation.

[23] This is not to claim that censorship is not widely exercised in Egypt. See e.g. *Al-Adab's* special issue on censorship in Egypt (November 2002), which contains reports and personal accounts of censorship of the press, cinema, art and education.

not sit too well with Minnie since a dark lightening cloud appears above her head.

According to Brown and Levinson, the prime reason for bald-on-record usage lies in the fact that "S[peaker] wants to do the FTA with maximum efficiency *more than* he wants to satisfy H[earer]'s face, even to any degree" (1987:95; emphasis in original). Thus, even if Speaker2 in Egypt perceives women's semi-naked bodies as a threat that needs to be redressed by covering them, images of women in bikini are retained because maximum efficiency is deemed more important in this context. In other words, it is more important for Speaker2 to present a story for Hearer2 that reflects an image of reality (i.e., women in bathing suits or bikinis lying on the beach) than a far-fetched image (i.e., women on the beach dressed entirely in black).

In Egyptian translations there seems to be no problem with printing comics containing Christian imagery and, by contrast to Kuwaiti translations, crosses are retained (see e.g. *'nidā'u-l-māḍī'* – 'Call from the Past', *Mickey* Vol. 77 (II), Dar Al-Hilal 1998 – the source story's title is 'Call of the Past'). While the hat of Santa Claus was removed in Kuwaiti translations, it and even the whole traditional custom of Santa Claus are kept without manipulation in Disney comics translated by Dar Al-Hilal (see e.g. *'khid'atu bābā nawil'* – 'Papa Noel's Trick', *Mickey* Vol. 75 (II), Dar Al-Hilal 1997 – the source story's title is 'The Christmas Eve Caper'). Moreover, "Santa Claus" is translated into its Arabic equivalent *"bābā nawil"* (Baba Nawiyl, from the French *Papa Noel*).

4. Conclusion

This article has shown how Brown and Levinson' politeness theory can be fruitfully applied to written texts, including written texts which are heavily dependant on the interplay between words and images. The few available studies which attempted to apply Brown and Levinson's theory to written texts have focused completely on the verbal aspect and neglected the role of visual material in complex genres such as comics. This study aimed to redress the balance and demonstrate that Brown and Levinson's politeness strategies are realized both verbally and visually.

Although Brown and Levinson's theory does not provide for **complex composite speaker/hearer functions**, it has been shown that the speaker is more than a text writer, and the hearer is more than a text reader. Due to the complexity of the genre itself, the speaker function of a Disney comic is far more complex than for a particular individual engaged in conventional conversation. Speaker1 in Disney comics is a composite of voices reflecting a range of individual creative, editorial and commercial inputs, and codes and conventions of acceptable and responsible comics content. The intended or actual recipient of Disney comics – Hearer1 – is not only the child but also the parents, teachers, librarians and any professionals interested in the welfare of children whom the speaker is keen to gratify when producing and publishing Disney comics. When Disney comics are translated from English into Arabic, a new composite speaker coined as Speaker2 and a new composite hearer coined as Hearer2 are identified and accounted for. Accordingly, there seems to be a need to extend the scope of text speaker/hearer functions in both source texts and their translations.

In addition, Brown and Levinson's theory cannot account for **complex face threatening acts**; it is not sufficiently elaborated to read the nuances of complex discourses that are normative in nature while presenting themselves as benign or harmless. In examining the theory, the most problematic point in this respect is the idea that one of the hallmarks of a face threatening act is criticizing or ridiculing the reader's wants, acts, personal characteristics, goods, beliefs or values. On one level, it is clear that some Disney comics do criticize and ridicule Arabs by portraying them, for example, as bandits, thieves, backward Bedouins, or greedy oil sheiks. It is easy to see how such crude examples of racial stereotyping can be conceptualized within the terms of Brown and Levinson's theory.

Where the theory is more likely to encounter difficulties in its application is in the more subtle expression of Orientalism alongside these crude and overtly offensive examples of stereotyping. This is because Orientalism, as Said (1978) has theorized it, is not simply a collection of overtly offensive statements and acts, but rather has the respectability of being an academic discourse as much as a mode of characterizing and constructing the 'orient' and 'occident' and being implicated in colonial subjugation of the non-western 'other'. As Abdirahman Hussein notes (2002:236-37), "Orientalism, he [Said] tells us, is not "a positive doctrine", but a specific family of ideas – a style of thought, a set of practices, and affiliated institutions – which together constitute a broad, interdisciplinary discourse that evolved in the common cultural consciousness of Europeans for centuries for the purpose of making imaginary and actual purchase on the Orient (especially the "Near East") and its inhabitants".

To recap, politeness theory can be applied to comics through the notion of face threatening acts. However, the notions of positive and negative face that underpin the idea of face threatening acts are a little too binary and Manichean to allow for robust analysis of the ways in which complex institutional discourses (such as Disney comics) encode normative projects often articulated around syncretic ideological formations. It may be that a third category can be fruitfully added to positive and negative face, a category of 'ideal face', which is the face to which normative projects appeal.

References

Primary Sources[24]

Friedmann, Joachim (1998) *Call of the Past*. http://coa.inducks.org/story.php/x/D+96322// [In *Mickey* Vol. 77 (II), Dar Al-Hilal 1998].

Goodall, Scott (1996) *Time Bandits*. http://coa.inducks.org/ story.php?c=D+92551 [In *Super Mickey* Vol. 39, Dar Al-Hilal 1997; In *The Adventures of Uncle Scrooge* No. 1, Gladstone 1998].

Hedman, Per Erik and Francisco Rodriguez Peinado (1997) *A Sticky Story*. http://coa.inducks.

---

[24] For each story, authors, title and original year of publication are provided, as listed in I.N.D.U.C.K.S., an online database containing "a detailed list of more than 160,000 Disney comics stories and more than 50,000 publications" (http://inducks.org). A pointer to the I.N.D.U.C.K.S. address for each title is given together with details of the publications cited in the article.

org/story.php/x/D+95027 [In *Super Mickey* Vol. 39, Dar Al-Hilal 1997; In *Uncle Scrooge* No. 310, Gladstone 1998].

Kenner, Jim, Sven Bernstrup and Vicar (1978) *Trouble Vision*. http://coa.inducks.org/story.php/x/D++3762 [In *Mickey* Vol. 69 (I), Dar Al-Hilal 1994; In *Uncle Scrooge* No. 282, Gladstone 1993].

McGreal, Pat (1996) *The Christmas Eve Caper*. http://coa.inducks.org/story.php/x/D+96097// [In *Mickey* Vol. 75 (II), Dar Al-Hilal 1997].

McGreal, Pat and Vicar (1997) *The Easter Beasties From Outer Space*. http://coa.inducks.org/story.php/x/D+96187//outer+space++_ [In *Mickey* Vol. 76 (II), Dar Al-Hilal 1998].

Markstein, Don (2000) *Too Many Christmas Carols*. http://coa.inducks.org/story.php/x/D+99005//Too%20Many%20Christmas%20Carols [In *Mickey* No. 326, Al-Qabas 2003; In *Mickey Mouse* No. 283, Gladstone 2005].

Moore, John Blair and Antoni Bancells Pujadas (1997) *Riders of the Living Mummy from Outer Space*. http://coa.inducks.org/story.php/x/D+95128//mummy++Mickey+Mouse [In *'Ijazah ma'a Mickey* No. 12 (II), Al-Futtaim/ITP 1995].

Nicolli, Dominique and Carmen Pérez (1996) *Minnie Mouse*. http://coa.inducks.org/story.php/x/F+JM+96624 [In *Super Mickey* Vol. 41, Dar Al-Hilal 1998].

Pihl, Andreas (2000) *The Rise and Fall of Donald Duck*. http://coa.inducks.org/story.php/x/D+99171// [In *Battut* No. 306, Al-Qabas 2001].

Rosa, Don (1991) *The War of the Wendigo*. http://coa.inducks.org/story.php/x/D+91192 [In *Super Mickey* Vol. 32, Dar Al-Hilal 1994; In *Walt Disney's Comics* No. 633, Gladstone 1999].

------ (1999) *The Quest for Kalevala*. http://coa.inducks.org/story.php/x/D+99078// kalevala+++_ [In *Uncle Scrooge* No. 334, Gladstone 1999].

------ (1999) *Escape from Forbidden Valley*. http://coa.inducks.org/story.php/x/D+98346//++_ [In *Mickey* No. 265, Al-Futtaim/ITP 1999].

Sutter, Jack (1998) *The Golden Sheep*. http://coa.inducks.org/story.php/x/D+97048// The%20Golden%20Sheep [In *Madinat Al-Batt* No. 23, Al-Qabas 2001].

ḥaflah faḍā'iyyah (Space Party) [In *Minnie* No. 26, Al-Qabas 2001].

al-miṣbāḥu-ssiḥriy (The Magic Lamp) [In *Mickey* Vol. 69 (I), Dar Al-Hilal 1994].

riḥlatun muthīrah (An Exciting Journey) [In *Minnie* No. 23, Al-Qabas 2001].

bayḍu-l-fulayfil (Al-Fulayfil's Eggs) [In *Mickey* Vol. 76 (II), Dar Al-Hilal 1998].

bunduq wa-nnaḥt (Bondok and Carving) [In *Mickey* Vol. 78 (I), Dar Al-Hilal 1999].

ḥawādītu minī (Minnie's Stories) [In *Super Mickey* Vol. 41, Dar Al-Hilal 1998].

Secondary Sources

Athamneh, Naser and Jehan Zitawi (1999) 'English-Arabic Translation of Dubbed Children's Animated Pictures', *Babel* 45(2): 127-48.

Barry, Randall (ed.) (1997) *ALA-LC Romanization Tables: Transliteration Schemes for Non-Roman Scripts*, Washington: Library of Congress (online) http://lcweb.loc.gov/catdir/cpso/romanization/arabic.pdf (Accessed 31 January 2004).

Brown, Penelope and Stephen Levinson (1978) 'Universals in Language Usage: Politeness Phenomena', in Esther Goody (ed.) *Questions and Politeness*, Cambridge: Cambridge University Press, 56-311.

------ (1987) *Politeness: Some Universals in Language Usage*, Cambridge: Cambridge University Press.

De Kadt, Elizabeth (1998) 'The Concept of Face and its Applicability to the Zulu Language', *Journal of Pragmatics* 29(2): 173-91.

De Wolf, Arthur (2000-03) 'Disney Comics Worldwide' (online) http://www. wolfstad.com/dcw (Accessed 30 December 2005).

Dorfman, Ariel and Armand Mattelart (1991) *How to Read Donald Duck: Imperialist Ideology in the Disney Comic*, translated by David Kunzle, New York: International General.

Douglas, Allen and Fedwa Malti-Douglas (1994) *Arab Comic Strips: Politics of an Emerging Mass Culture*, Indiana: Indiana University Press.

Hiel, Betsy (1995) 'Franchising Opportunities in the UAE: Over 1.4 Billion Served' (online) http://www.arabdatanet.com/news/DocResults.asp?DocId=466 (Accesed 12 July 2003).

Hussein, Abdirahman (2002) *Edward Said: Criticism and Society*, London: Verso Books.

Ji, Shaojun (2000) "Face' and Polite Verbal Behaviors in Chinese Culture', *Journal of Pragmatics* 32(7): 1059-62.

Koponen, Maarit (2004) *Wordplay in Donald Duck Comics and Their Finnish Translations*, Post-graduate thesis, Department of English, University of Helsinki.

Mao, LuMing Robert (1994) 'Beyond Politeness Theory: 'Face' Revisited and Renewed', *Journal of Pragmatics* 21(5): 451-86.

Nwoye, Onuigbo G. (1992) 'Linguistic Politeness and Sociocultrual Variation of the Notion of Face', *Journal of Pragmatics* 18(4): 309-28.

O'Driscoll, Jim (1996) 'About Face: A Defence and Elaboration of Universal Dualism', *Journal of Pragmatics* 25(1): 1-32.

Philippe, Robert (1982) *Political Graphics: Art as a Weapon*, New York: Abbeville.

Rifas, Leonard (1988) 'The Image of Arabs in U.S. Comic Books', *Itchy Planet. Summer* 2: 11.

Said, Edward (1978) *Orientalism*, New York: Pantheon Books.

Salama, Vivian (2006) 'It's a Small World'. BusinessToday.com (online) http://businesstodayegypt. com/article.aspx?ArticleID=4535 (Accessed 2 August 2006).

Shaheen, Jack (1994) 'Arab Images in American Comic Books', *Journal of Popular Culture* 28(1): 123-34.

Toivonen, Pia (2001) *En serietidning på fyra språk*, Acta Wasaensia No. 88, Vaasa: Vaasan yliopisto.

Wingfield, Marvin and Bushra Karaman (1995) 'Arab Stereotypes and American Educators', ADC and Education Official Website (online) http://www.adc. org/index.php?283 (Accessed 7 January 2003).

Zitawi, Jehan (2004) *The Translation of Disney Comics in the Arab World: A Pragmatic Perspective*, Unpublished PhD dissertation, Manchester: University of Manchester.

8   Translating Educational Comics[1]

HEIKE JÜNGST
University of Leipzig, Germany

Educational comics are comics with an informative content. They do not differ from fiction comics where the use of elements of the comics format is concerned and normally use a prototypical comics format with a narrative sequence in panels and dialogue in speech balloons. However, educational comics are produced and distributed in social contexts which differ from those we find with fiction comics. This fact exerts a strong influence on the design of educational comics and on their translation. Very often, educational comics are designed for narrow target groups, e.g. teenagers from a particular social background or farmers in a particular geographical area, and are not meant for translation. On the other hand, we find educational comics that have been designed for use in a plurilingual world and therefore also for translation, for example for intra-country translation into a minority language. Language policies play an important part here. Very often, the design strategies used in these comics are those we find in other texts meant for global usage: the pictures have been globalized to carry meaning for readers with different backgrounds. At the same time, there are educational comics where localization strategies are practised in translation, hoping that the new target group will find the adapted verbal text and pictures particularly appealing. There are educational comics which were not originally meant for translation but were nevertheless translated. Sometimes, the reason for translating them hinges on the use of the comics format for informative content, which is thought to be attractive for a new target group. In other cases, the content of the comic is the determining factor, with the translator wishing to give the new target group access to the specific knowledge found in the comic. This means that the reasons and strategies for translating educational comics vary considerably.

Although educational comics can be found all over the world, few of them are subject to translation.[2] In most cases, educational comics are custom-made for a particular target group, and even those educational comics that are translated are not translated into as many languages as their fiction counterparts. Moreover, their circulation is much smaller.[3]

If educational comics are translated, the translator is faced with several problems. Firstly, there is the problem of the format with its restricted space for verbal text, with

---

[1] Many thanks to Leonard Rifas who provided me with all the information and primary texts about the All-Atomic Comics. Many thanks also to all the institutions, companies and comics producers who generously provided me with material.

[2] The educational comics which form the basis for this article are part of a larger textual corpus, namely the educational comics I collected for my *habilschrift*. I chose mostly those comics where I have versions in several languages.

[3] Educational comics that are published not by organizations but by publishing houses follow the same rules for translation as other non-fiction books. In Germany there was a boom in translated and other hard-cover educational comics in the 1980s, but this trend has since abated and none of the comics published back then is still on the booksellers' backlist.

which all translators of comics are familiar. Secondly, there is the problem of conveying special factual knowledge in a popularized shape, which all translators of specialized texts for non-experts are faced with. And thirdly, the problem of style should not be underestimated. As will be demonstrated later, some translators of educational comics find it difficult to write natural dialogue, a fact which has to do with the kind of people who actually translate educational comics.

There are, however, other translation issues which are particularly interesting in educational comics and which will make up the main part of this article. Firstly, there is the question of choosing educational comics for translation. As stated before, many educational comics are not meant for translation but are custom-made for narrow target groups (see the examples in Packalén and Odoi 2003). However, there are situations where the translation of a specific educational comic seems desirable, and there are also situations where educational comics are designed for translation right from the beginning. It is therefore interesting to see what kinds of educational comics have been translated by whom and with what purpose in mind. The choice of language pairs involved is closely linked to these questions. The target language may be a minority language, which normally leads to intra-country translations. But there are also inter-country translations where the idea behind the translation is to distribute the specific knowledge in the comics format the educational comic provides to a completely new target group.[4]

This article attempts to describe typical situations in which educational comics are or have been translated. Some of these situations are highly specific, for example the translation of educational comics into German by members of the German No-Nukes movement. Others are rather more common, for example the translation of company comics. In each case, the strategies followed are described.

1.   Educational Comics

Basically, educational comics are comics that are specifically written in order to inform, change the readers' behaviour or instruct the readers in how to do something. In *Comics and Sequential Art*, Eisner uses the terms "technical instruction comic" and "attitudinal instruction comic" (2001a:144) for two types of educational comics. Whereas technical instruction comics focus on informing the reader about processes which can be carried out following the instructions in the comic, attitudinal instruction comics try to get the reader to change his or her behaviour. Eisner takes up these points again in *Graphic Storytelling and Visual Narrative* (2001b) in the chapters 'Telling Stories to Instruct' (2001b:24) and 'Telling a How-to Story' (2001b:25). There is, however, a third group of educational comics, that is comics which are meant to teach the readers facts

---

[4] An extremely interesting case of an educational comic which has been translated into a number of languages, the Japanese comic *Hadashi no Gen*, an eyewitness account of the Hiroshima bombing, is discussed in Jüngst (this volume).

from science, history, etc. I use the term 'fact comics' to refer to these comics (Jüngst, forthcoming b). Educational comics can be, and often are, entertaining, but the information transfer is the important factor in an educational comic. Comic book editions of famous works of literature such as the *Classics Illustrated* series may also be counted as educational comics. They are not analyzed here, as the problems they present to translators are different from those presented by comics which deal with facts, instructions or behavioural issues.

Different languages have different preferences in naming educational comics, but the 'educational' can also be found in the French term *bande dessinée pédagogique* and in the Japanese term *gakkushū manga*. In German, the preferred term is *Sachcomic*, which can be translated either as 'non-fiction comic' or as 'information comic'. There are numerous subgroups of educational comics. They are normally classified by topic. Research on educational comics is relatively scarce (Jüngst forthcoming b); most studies of educational comics deal with comics with historical topics. The analysis of translations does not play a role in these studies.

In most cases, educational comics are not experimental in their use of the components of the comics format. Rather, the design chosen is that of a prototypical comic, albeit with cultural variations. The comics format is used in order to grab the reader's attention; it is assumed that the target group will find the comics format attractive. Very often, particularly in the case of behaviour-regulating comics, the educational content consists of facts the reader might not really want to learn. An example would be comics that deal with health issues and that criticize common kinds of unhealthy behaviour the reader partakes in, such as smoking or eating too much fast food.

This also means that educational comics have certain features which are meant to guarantee maximum attention-keeping and optimum reader identification. A very common feature is the **focalizer**, a character the reader is meant to identify with. Focalizers are highly target-group specific. Normally, the focalizer is a character who might be a member of the target group him- or herself. Educational comics for children normally feature a boy and a girl who are approximately the readers' age. Comics for grown-ups are often addressed either at women or at men, which is again reflected in the choice of focalizer (Renaud et al. 1990).

1.1   Donor Genres

Information comics come in a variety of genres, such as cooking recipes, instruction manuals or biographies. Since these genres did not originate in the comics format but are copied from models, I refer to them as donor genres (Jüngst 2000). The donor genre activates everyday ideas of genre convention in the reader's mind and consequently shapes reader expectations, as does the comics format itself. Educational comics normally use everyday genres the reader can recognize readily. Oral donor genres such as lessons or confidential talks appear alongside written donor genres such as biographies and verbal-visual donor genres, often from TV, such as animal documentaries. The reader's genre competence enables him or her to recognize donor genres even if they come in the shape of a comic, and the fact that the readers are familiar with the genre structures used contributes to the popularization of information in the comics format. Many donor genres are used worldwide. In the case of educational comics, the genres that have managed to reach larger audiences and that have been translated into a variety of languages are Joe Sacco's journalistic comics and biographical or autobiographical comics such as Marjane Satrapi's *Persepolis* and Art Spiegelman's *Maus*. It has to be admitted that most educational comics are not as artistically satisfying as these two examples.

Normally, educational comics use a narrative structure for embedding the informative content and for maintaining the readers' attention. Often, the narrative structure is that of the donor genre used. However, some donor genres are descriptive rather than narrative and have to borrow a narrative structure from another genre, often from a typical comics genre such as the superhero comic. There is a tendency to use everyday storylines for behaviour-regulating comics and a variety of more fantastic storylines for fact-based comics that deal with subjects from the natural sciences (Jüngst forthcoming b).

1.2 Design for Plurilingual Information Transfer

Many information comics are not meant to go beyond a specific target group. The focalizers, for example, have been designed to appeal to this target group and may not appeal to another target group at all. The circumstances of life depicted in the picture are often those of the readers, or else they refer to a fantasy donor genre the readers like and recognize. Many of these features are culture-specific (Packalén and Odoi 2003:9):

> If the comics are made by local artists and writers, the visual world is culturally correct and the meanings of the pictures and events in the story make sense to the reader. If comics from other cultures are used, the setting of the story can often confuse the reader, who cannot relate to the various characters and events in it. Therefore, it is important that the comics are thoroughly rooted in the target group's own surroundings and culture. This is best achieved by using local creative talent.

Educational comics that are meant for translation will be designed in a different way. Culture-specific elements in the pictures may be avoided. There is still a need to use focalizers, but there may be a whole group of focalizers now (as in *Tools for Living*, analyzed below) or the focalisers may come from different nations (as in *Les Eaux Blessées*, analysed below). The following guidelines circulate in the world of picture-book publishing and describe in detail how to design globalized pictures in non-fiction books for children. Some authors of information comics seem to follow these guidelines too, whether consciously or unconsciously. Although many authors of children's picture books reject these guidelines, they are actually worth considering when designing a picture book or a comic for an international audience.

Sofern nicht genau dies das Thema ist:

o   Keine Bilder mit Volksbräuchen, Trachten, typischer Kleidung, typischen Ver-
    haltensweisen etc.

o   Keine Bilder mit Briefkästen, Telephonzellen, Taxis, Linienbussen, Polizeiautos
    und Polizisten, Uniformen aller Art, Straßenbahnen, Krankenwagen, Feuer-
    wehr, Verkehrsschildern aller Art (außer international gültigen, z. B. STOP,
    Vorfahrt etc.)

o   Keine Bilder mit Typographie, z. B. Aufschriften, Hinweise, Werbetafeln, Zeitun-
    gen, Zeitschriften, Bücher, Geschäftsnamen, Autokennzeichen etc. Erlaubt sind
    allenfalls international gebräuchliche und verständliche Worte (z. B. Hotel).
    Falls Typographie in Bildern unbedingt notwendig ist, dann nur in Schwarz
    auf einen Decker! (Künnemann 1994 quoted in O'Sullivan 2001)

[Unless the items named in the following list are the main topics of the book, do
not depict them],

o   Avoid pictures that show local customs, national costumes, typical clothes,
    typical behaviour, etc.

o   Avoid pictures that show post boxes, phone boxes, taxis, buses, police cars and
    policemen, uniforms in general, trams, ambulances, fire engines, traffic signs
    (except for traffic signs that are used across national boundaries such as STOP,
    etc.)

o   Avoid pictures that include print, e.g. labels, inscriptions, information boards,
    advertising signs, newspapers, magazines, books, shop signs, number plates
    etc. Exceptions may be made for internationalisms (e.g. hotel). If using print
    within a picture cannot be avoided, it must be in black on a white background.
    (my translation)]

This means that educational comics can be designed in a style we would normally describe as **globalized**. The comics would be as devoid of cultural signals as possible and
therefore suitable for a variety of cultures. These comics can remain in their globalized
form throughout.

However, there is another group of educational comics mentioned earlier which are
highly **localized** and which in turn may be localized in translation (on the translation
of comics as localization see Zanettin, this volume). Localization of educational comics
in translation takes place on different planes. They resemble the techniques used in the
translation of children's books (for these see O'Sullivan 2001) and can be summed up
as follows:

1. Material aspects. These concern the format of the comic and the lettering (on the
    translation of comics formats see Rota, this volume).

    1.1 The size of the books is normally adapted to the formats the target culture
         readily recognizes as typical of comic books. When the *All-Atomic Comics* were
         translated into German, the format changed from the American legal format to
         the standard A4 format used in Germany in one case. In contrast to this practice,

the translation of **manga** brought a new format with it, the **tankōbon**.

1.2   Different cultures prefer different kinds of lettering. Japanese comics use machine lettering as hand lettering would quickly become illegible in smaller print. Most American, Italian, German and Franco-Belgian educational comics use hand lettered capitals-only script. The preference for using lowercase along with uppercase letters in Germany does not exist anymore for fiction comics, but can still be observed with many information comics.

2.   Content.

2.1   Names. Changing the names of the characters is a very common strategy for adapting comics for a new target group.

2.2   Pictures. Pictorial content is hardly ever changed in information comics. However, colours can be changed (e.g. characters' skin or hair) if it is deemed useful for higher identification potential.

2.3   Deletions, replacements and additions (for these categories see Kaindl 1999). Additions in the verbal text are common if the new target group has less prior knowledge than the source text target group or if the comic is localized thoroughly. Deletion is very rare. Replacements are common, e.g. for helpline telephone numbers or addresses of organizations that follow a behavioural instruction comic.

The degree of localization needed in translation depends to a large extent on the topic of the comic. Comics with historical topics, including biographies, may need additions, but nothing else besides. The same is true for other fact-based comics, although it has to be noted that there are preferences for showing native scientists in a particularly good light. Examples of non-localized translations into German are *Storia della filosofia* (Italy 1989) and *Histoire de la musique* (France 1980). Both work well in a broader European context.

Yet the reasons for choosing an educational comic for translation may lie in culture-specific elements that are exotic and attractive for the target group in the target culture. This is the case with educational manga, which have been translated following the general boom in manga.

1.3   Distribution and the Need for Translation

The decision to translate educational comics is to a large extent a social decision. It is often based on the needs and interests of target groups rather than on the qualities of the comic in question. It is also normally not a decision based on marketability as many educational comics are not sold in bookshops but distributed by organizations and authorities. Of course, sometimes the interests of target groups and the quality of the comic both play a role in the translation decision.

As said before, many educational comics are designed for narrow target groups and are not meant for translation. This is true for example of information comics in the developing countries, as in the quotation from Packalén and Odoi above. Such information comics use visuals the readers can recognize: the clothes, the hairstyles, the surroundings, everything shows the reader that he or she is the addressee of this particular comic. Other information comics are distributed by local authorities and set out to draw the reader's attention to facts and figures which pertain to the local area in question only. Examples of this kind of information comics can be found in many countries. They are typical of the comics output of single US states and may refer to historical or environmental topics.

Contrary to common belief, educational comics use verbal text, sometimes extensively so. Often one will read that information comics are a very good information tool for a non-literate audience and that silent strips are a good model for information comics. This claim has to be taken with a grain of salt. Information comics without words are not at all common. They do exist, as do information comics with long stretches of information graphics that are not in the comics format,[5] but they remain the exception. Information brochures that rely on pictures will not normally be termed comics, unless the producer of the brochures wants to reach an audience for whom comics are attractive. However, the fact that there is no verbal text in silent strips does not mean that they could be used everywhere. Translating comics may very well mean changing the pictures along with the words, and it may mean changing the pictures for an audience that cannot readily understand them for cultural reasons.

Sometimes, the authors of information comics are faced with a target group that consists of sub-target groups that do not share the same first language. In the US, many educational comics brochures are translated into Spanish for the Spanish-speaking community very quickly after they appear in English. The EU produces information comics which, following the rules that apply to all EU documents, have to be translated into all the EU languages.

As with all kinds of popular non-fiction text, the relevance of the topic for the target group and their previous knowledge of the topic are very important where translation decisions are concerned. It cannot always be assumed that the source text target group and the target text target group have exactly the same background knowledge. Sometimes, introducing additional visual information may be the best choice in bridging the knowledge gap between the two groups, but then it is difficult and expensive to change the pictures in a comic. To my knowledge, this strategy has so far never been attempted in an educational comic. Instead of extra visual information we may find verbal footnotes.

A new target group from a different culture might need extended verbal information, for example, if the pictures show places or customs the original readers would be familiar with, or if the text relies on previous knowledge common in the source culture but not in the target culture. This can happen even in educational texts where we might assume

---

[5] The comics published by the organization Migrantclinicians are good examples of this type of slightly hybrid information comics.

that special care has been taken to explain everything to the reader.[6] But texts never explain everything, and the question of whether much additional information is needed in order to enable the target group to make the most out of the text is one upon which the decision to translate the text may rest. After all, the space for verbal text in comics is limited, and extra text would in most cases only fit into the gutter, which would destroy the page layout. So far, the translated educational comics I have found were carefully chosen to work well for the new target group.

Very few educational comics which deal with problems that are time- and/or place-specific are chosen for translation. An exception is the boom in manga translation, which includes the translation of educational manga. In most cases, the topics are of a more common kind (general teenage problems, topics from history that might appeal to more than one culture), or else they are of such prime importance that the culture-specific properties of design and content do not matter, as in the case of *Hadashi no Gen*.

I have excluded the translation of information comics where it serves to inform an academic audience about the content of a particular information comic. This type of translation does exist (Packalén and Odoi 2003 offer some examples). However, it is not subject to the same constraints as translations for 'real audiences'.

1.4   Special Language and the Translator

Educational comics are meant for readers who are non-experts. Still, they may contain a large number of special terms, particularly as picture-word combinations where these special terms are explained. Also, educational comics are hardly ever the work of one author. Rather, the organization that commissions a comic will provide experts and expert knowledge and the author and illustrator will act as mediators.

Special knowledge as well as a solid background and competence in special language are acknowledged competences for special translation, e.g. in engineering or economics (for recent discussions see Bergien 2004; Muráth 2004). This competence is also important for the translation of educational comics. However, the special vocabulary needed may well be the kind that has found its way into everyday language, or else it may be new and special to a young target group but not necessarily to the adult translator.

Authors of educational comics can often rely on expert help. The translator may have access to the same resources, particularly if the translations are done in-house, produced in the same place as the comic. Organizations that commission a comic may be prepared to help with advice, and this advice may extend to the translated versions.

In other cases, the translator could work with a different group of specialists. One example is the German version of a French educational comic, *Histoire de la musique en bandes dessinées – Geschichte der Musik in Comics*, where the translator had the support

---

[6] There are educational comics that would need extensive glossing and have therefore never been translated. A good example is the series *Quer-Comics*, which was published in Germany in the early 1980s and which can only be fully understood by a reader who is familiar with the peace movement and the general political situation back in the 1980s, as well as with certain educational ideals which existed in Germany back then (Jüngst 2005a).

of the team of editors from the music department of a schoolbook publisher. In the case of the World Wildlife Fund-comic *Elefanten*, again the German version of a French comic, two 'wissenschaftliche Berater' (experts) helped the translators. In both books, the support of these teams is acknowledged. This means that the translator receives the kind of support the authors themselves enjoyed, and of course this makes perfect sense. As with all kinds of literature that popularizes knowledge, the verbal text has to maintain a balance between offering new, correct information and not giving too much information, making the information palatable and accessible for the reader.

In many cases, however, the translator has to rely on other sources in order to find special vocabulary and special information. In that respect, translating comics is not different from translating other popular texts with a special content. Many educational comics contain either lists of further reading or a bibliography of the sources the author used for factual information about the topic. This is true of Rifas' *All-Atomic Comics* (analyzed below), where the author gives references in order to underline what he is saying. He also provides a list of further reading. The latter idea is taken up by only one of the German versions, where the translator, Ulrike Breitschuh, offers the German readers a list of German books about nuclear power. These books may also be the sources for the special terminology she uses in the translation. As she states in the afterword, she has tried hard to adapt the information in the comic for German readers and the situation in Germany back in the late 1970s.

2.   Educational Comics by Publisher

Educational comics can be classified according to the publishing institution. It makes a difference whether a comic is published by a non-profit organization or by a commercial company. Normally, companies will have the money to produce glossy, stylish comics in full colour, whereas political comics may come from sources which lack the relevant funding (Jüngst forthcoming b). The following sub-sections offer examples of types of educational comics classified by publisher.

2.1   *Institutions and Educational Comics*

The EU has a language policy that demands that EU documents must be available in the languages of all member states. Consequently, comics published by the EU are subject to this policy too.

The EU has published several information comics so far. Most of these comics deal with attitudinal issues or with political problems which at the same time demonstrate the function of the EU. *Les Eaux Blessées* (EU 2002) is an example of the latter. An environmental crime is detected right when the EU is about to pass a bill on pollution bans. The story is quite gripping, and the style is a grown-up **bande dessinée** style. *Les Eaux Blessées* (EU 2002) is also interesting in terms of its translations. The translated versions use different kinds of lettering, and there is a multilingual metapanel which reveals this.

Figure 8.1a: European Parliament, *Troubled Waters*, 2002

The comic is originally in French. Figure 8.1a is from the English version. The text which appears as a caption in the two inserted panels where we see the heroine of the comic is probably not hand lettered but uses print imitating hand lettering. The speech balloon in French right next to the first inserted panel uses the same typeface. All the other speech balloons use a different kind of lettering, probably hand lettering. There is a typo in the German speech balloon ("erebtes Gut" instead of "ererbtes Gut" (heritage)), something which is very rare in hand lettered texts, unless the letterer does not speak the language. This is probably the case here: all speech balloons that are neither in English nor in French are from the original version.

Figure 8.1b: European Parliament, *Trübe Wasser*, 2002

Interestingly, the typeface chosen for the German edition (Figure 8.1b) is different yet again. It is a machine type that uses uppercase as well as lowercase letters. This is not typical of lettering, but German uses uppercase versus lowercase in order to distinguish between various grammatical forms, so that it actually makes sense to use both. The

French text is now where the German text was in the English example. It uses the same typeface the English version uses throughout. Consequently, the attentive German reader is faced with three different types of lettering. However, this mix of hand lettering and typeface only appears in this metapanel, which is used to demonstrate the EU's attempt at multilingualism.[7]

2.2   Political Movements and Educational Comics

As far as information comics are concerned, those with a political content are among the most commonly selected for translation. This is particularly obvious with the Peace Movement and No-Nukes Movement of the 1970s and 1980s. These movements also produced their own comics, and they had comics from various countries translated. These comics were then printed by small presses, which accounts for the poor quality of paper and print.[8]

Among the comics translated were those by Rius (Eduardo del Rio) from Mexico. Rius had and still has a strong influence in the field of educational comics. However, the comics he designed are in highly hybrid formats. They use collage, photographs, copies of texts, and also elements of comics. Rius' comics are far from the comics prototype. The fact that there are often texts in the photographs adds to the difficulty of translating the format.

But there were also translations of more prototypical comics. One of the most interesting examples is the *All-Atomic Comics* by Leonard Rifas (EduComics, San Francisco, 1976). *All-Atomic Comics* is a collection of comics that inform the readers about the dangers of nuclear power. There is an ongoing narrative, combined with informative graphics and fact sheets.

There are no less than three competing German versions of the *All-Atomic Comics*. One is a home-made edition published by a citizens' action group against nuclear power in the north-German town of Lübeck. The second was published by an alternative publishing house (Nexus in Frankfurt am Main), and the third was published by a comics publisher proper (U-Comix), which also published fiction comics. I will refer to them as Lübeck version, Nexus version and U-Comix version. The three translations appeared between 1978 and 1981.

Readers interested in the comic would not necessarily have come across more than one version. The Lübeck version was probably never distributed far from Lübeck. The U-Comix version would have been sold in specialized shops and in train station bookshops.[9] Moreover, it was addressed to a target group that was mainly interested in comics with

---

[7] This analysis first appeared in a more entertaining form in *Lebende Sprachen* 4 (Jüngst 2005b).

[8] Of course, using recycled paper and non-glossy print was also a signal for the in-group that the comic in question was not an industrial product but was rather produced by people like oneself, people the reader could trust.

[9] This seems to be a culture-specific phenomenon. In Germany, bookshops at train stations have always offered quite a good choice of comics from all kinds of comics publishers – not just easy-reading trash for passengers to take on the train.

new and interesting topics, not necessarily to members of the Peace Movement. The Nexus version, however, may have reached a similar target group as the Lübeck version, although probably in a different geographical area.[10] The only one of these versions that does not suffer from poor lettering is the one published by U-Comix, which used a professional letterer. The examples in Figures 8.2a-d demonstrate how substantially the German versions available differ – from each other as well as from the original.

The lettering in this version is admittedly unprofessional but is fairly comfortable and easy to read. The Lübeck version is clearly superior to the other two when it comes to the use of special language. This is particularly interesting as there are some very cumbersome solutions for language structures in everyday German, normally caused by a too strict adherence to the syntax and structures of the English original. This starts with the cover, where the translator simply uses the structure from the original and addresses one of the characters as "Kind". Although this is the German word for "kid", it is a very uncommon term for addressing a child. Also, the word order used in the German version is often based on the word order in the English version. This does not make the resulting text unreadable, as German word order is extremely flexible; however, there are preferred structures even within this flexible system. A sentence such as "Das erste Problem ist, dass es nur ganz wenig Uran gibt auf der Welt" borrows the structure from the English original ("First problem is that there isn't much U-235 in the world"), thus using an uncommon word order, since normally "auf der Welt" should come after "es". Obviously, the person who produced the translation was not a trained translator but had familiarized herself thoroughly with the facts and language of nuclear power. She took great pains to use the correct terms and to inform her readers properly.

The example in Figure 8.2c is from the Nexus version. The use of special language is not as precise as in the Lübeck version, and the visual aspect is poor. Even the edition owned by the Deutsche Bücherei (a copyright library) is a simple photocopy. The lettering is unprofessional and often difficult to read. The speech balloon in the last panel in the second-last row, where the last line seems squeezed in, is typical of this version. It is also sometimes impossible to identify footnotes (the numbers appear in brackets in the speech balloons) and to find them.

The Nexus version is also the only one of the three that uses a different title page: instead of the human character, the three-legged frog appears next to Greedy Killerwatt.

The third version of the *All-Atomic Comics* appeared with a professional comics publisher, U-Comix. Legibility is a positive feature of this version, but the translation itself is often no better than that of the Lübeck version where the use of sentence structure is concerned. The speech balloon in the second panel in Figure 8.2d is an example of the use of an unmotivated uncommon sentence structure (it is not a reflection of the English original) "Es tritt eine Strahlung aus ihnen aus …", where the normal version would be "Aus ihnen tritt Strahlung aus …".

---

[10] Rifas remembers that there was some kind of fight or lawsuit going on between two of the publishers as to who had the rights to the German version, but he no longer remembers which two publishers were involved (personal communication).

Figure 8.2a: Leonard Rifas, *All-Atomic Comics*, 1976

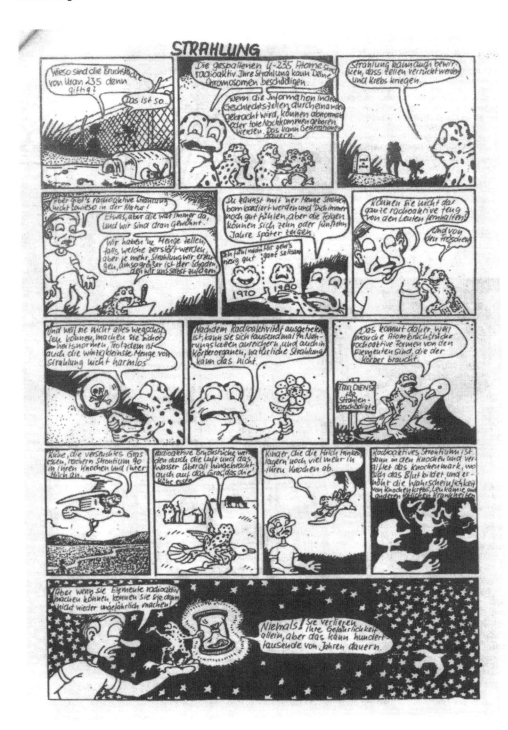

Figure 8.2b: Leonard Rifas, *Atom-Comic*, Lübeck version, 1978

Figure 8.2c: Leonard Rifas, *Atom-Comic*, Nexus version, 1980

Figure 8.2d: Leonard Rifas, *Atom-Comic*, U-Comix version, 1981

The Lübeck version starts with a word-for-word rendering of the title page, which sounds extremely strange in German. Lack of feeling for the German vernacular these characters might speak is typical of this translation. The style is often stilted, whereas the use of the vernacular in the English original seems natural.

However, significant efforts to adapt the contents to German needs are evident throughout the Lübeck version, e.g. "Das erste Problem ist, dass es nur ganz wenig Uran gibt auf der Welt. Die Bundesrepublik hat zum Beispiel gar keins …" (The first problem is, there is very little Uranium in the world. Germany has none at all) versus "Problem Nr. 1: Es gibt nicht viel U235 in [sic!] der Welt. 1989 könnte alles bis jetzt entdeckte Uran aufgebraucht sein" (Problem no. 1: There is not much U235 in the world. By 1989 all Uranium sources we know by now could be used up) in the Nexus version and "Problem Nr. 1: Es gibt nicht viel U-235 auf der Welt. Alles bisher gefundene Uran kann bis 1989 aufgebraucht sein" (Problem no. 1. There is not much U235 in the world. The Uranium found by now could be used up by 1989) in the U-Comix version. This element of localization in the Lübeck version anchors the text for German readers.

The Nexus version and the Lübeck version take the idea of localization for their target groups even further. They both include texts which were not in the American original but which might be interesting for a German readership. In the case of the Nexus version, the text in question is an added protest song. The Lübeck version adds a text by Gerhard Zarbock which deals with safety problems in nuclear power stations in a satirical way; the text had previously been published in the leftist satirical magazine *Pardon*.[11] As *Pardon* had roughly the same target group as the Lübeck version and the Nexus version, the readers might recognize the text and take this choice as a signal of in-group knowledge on the part of the publisher.

Other translation choices where the three versions differ concern the aptronyms[12] of certain characters. For "Greedy Killerwatt" we find "Raffy Killerwatt" (Grabby or Snatchy Killerwatt) in Nexus, "Guido Gierig" (Guido Greedy) in Lübeck, "Nimmersatt Kilowatt" (Cantgetenough Kilowatts) in U-Comix (all three are good and creative choices). Moreover, the three versions make different decisions about whether to use or not to use titles for the pages that are not in the comics format. Lübeck uses "Wahre Atomgeschichten zum Wissen und Weitersagen" for "Fun Facts to Know and Tell About Nuclear Power" (the irony of the original title is lost here, as "fun facts" is replaced by "true facts"; moreover, "zum Wissen" is not natural German); U-Comix has the very good version "Geschichten aus der Atomkiste",[13] which has the ring of giving away insider information to it.

The in-group element of these translations cannot be overestimated. The material appearance of the Lübeck as well as of the Nexus version is poor and unprofessional. However, this marks the translator and the publisher as members of the No-Nukes in-group and the comics as very different from the glossy brochures of the nuclear power

---

[11] The text chosen is Gerhard Zarbock, 'Nur nicht durchknallen! Aus dem Alltag einer Kernkraftwerkssicherung' (*Pardon*, March 1977).

[12] An aptronym (or aptonym) is a name that is well suited to its owner.

[13] Literally: 'Stories from the Atomic Box'; 'aus der Kiste plaudern', 'to tell stories from the box', means to give away secrets, often business secrets.

lobby. The photocopies and the lettering with its poor legibility may therefore actually have been interpreted as a sign of quality by the target group.

2.3   Company Comics

In addition to political organizations and non-profit organizations, we find a third group of comics publishers: companies. Company brochures in the comics format are not particularly popular, but they are common enough to be considered here. Although they serve to advertise the company's products, they are often designed as educational comics. If the company in question operates on an international level, it may very well wish to distribute the comics in question to international customers. This is true of the comics distributed by the French tyre producer Michelin.

The Michelin comics are done in a French **bande dessinée** style, with realistic drawings in colour. The quality of the print is excellent, and the paper is glossy and expensive. The drawings are to a large extent globalized, so that they present no obstacle to translation. There are very few inscriptions or signs, and most of these are in English, although the comics themselves are originally French. Indeed, the comics could be localized, if needed.

The comics themselves have one topic: tyres. The reader learns everything about the proper treatment of tyres (*La juste pression*) or about tyres and recycling (*Der Reifen und die Umwelt*). In both narratives, tourists who are en route with their vehicles visit information booths set up by Michelin. The friendly Michelin specialists explain everything to the non-experts; a process during which they use all kinds of visuals. They are helped by the company's mascot Bibendum, which comes alive in these comics. The most interesting trait of Michelin's comics is not their globalized design or their use of technical drawings, but the fact that no one is ever surprised by the fact that Bibendum can walk and talk.

However, other companies which use information comics normally do not have them translated (examples in Jüngst forthcoming a).

3.   Educational Comics by Language

Educational comics can also be classified according to the languages used. It is particularly interesting to see which language pairs are typical of translated information comics. Often, the use of specific languages has political or social implications. The place of publication and the publisher play an important role in the choice of languages too.

3.1   Minority Languages

In many places in the US, the number of Spanish-speaking citizens is high, and information leaflets are distributed in Spanish as well as in English.[14] This is particularly true for

---

[14] There are also educational comics that are directed exclusively at the Spanish-speaking community. Typical examples can be found at the Northwest Communities Education Center – Novela Health Education website (www.radiokdna.org).

information dealing with health issues. The three examples of information comics in English and Spanish discussed here all fall into this category. *Ojos por el mundo – Eyes for the World*, deals with eye problems; *Tools for Living – Herramientas para vivir* informs young readers about speech and hearing; and *¡Hablemos! – Let's Talk About It!* is directed at teenagers with psychical problems. All three comics were produced by the Custom Comics Company, a company that specializes in the production of information comics and has contracts with several artists whose drawing styles differ considerably. Whereas *Tools for Living* is rendered in a cutish style meant for a primary school target group, *Let's Talk About It!* uses a realistic comic book drawing style that might appeal to the teenage target group the book tries to reach.

Let's Talk About It! – ¡Hablemos! (see Figure 8.3) is about a girl who suffers from depressions and who needs help. As she talks to various people such as a school consultant or her mother, everyone is very understanding and tries to help her. In the end, she takes sessions with a psychiatrist and begins to feel better. The two comics are addressed at two target groups that differ only in terms of language use. Their living circumstances may very well be rather similar, which means that the overall design of the comics need not be changed. Clothes, buildings, everyday actions can remain – although, upon closer scrutiny, some of the gestures in *¡Hablemos!* look Anglo-Saxon rather than Latino. It is difficult to judge whether the target group will be put off by this. The room we see in the two examples reprinted here is almost empty. There are no indications as to what ethnic group lives there – no trinkets which might give away that they are Catholic (e.g. a crucifix upon the wall) or All-American (e.g. a flag of a football team).

Some of the efforts made to adapt the translated comic for better reader identification seem rather pointless. It makes sense that the heroine in *¡Hablemos!* is dark-haired whereas her counterpart in the English version is blonde (the same is true for the girl's mother). Also, the change in the focalizers' names may help reader identification. However, the decision to call a coloured girl – who is Lisa in the English version – Ana in the Spanish version is strange as she is so clearly not Latino. Other decisions to change characters' names are strange and unmotivated too. For some reason, the Latino teacher who is Mr. Rodriguez in the English version is Señor Ramos in the Spanish version (p. 3) – as both names are Spanish, it is not clear why one is given preference over the other in the Spanish version. The counsellor Mrs. May becomes Señora Landa in the Spanish version, which gives the unrealistic impression of an all-Latino school staff (p. 5). Mrs. Mills, a psychiatric consultant, becomes Señora Molina in the Spanish version (p. 9). Thus, the comic seems slightly over-localized into an all-Latino environment.

The strategies used in *Tools for Living – Herramientas para vivir* are different from those used in *Let's Talk About It!*. The comic uses a whole group of characters made up of school children who come from all kinds of ethnic backgrounds. The book features several short episodes during which a child is helped by proper treatment of speaking or hearing problems. In the end, they are much happier and manage to overcome their problem, as in the case of the little girl who can play the piano with the school orchestra now that she has a hearing aid.

Figure 8.3a: Scott Deschaine and Mike Benton, *Let's Talk About It,* 1990

Figure 8.3b: Scott Deschaine and Mike Benton, *¡Hablemos!*, 1990

Many of the children in the group already look Latino, and therefore most names remain the same in the Spanish version. However, the name of the baseball star Pete is changed to David. The character has been designed in a way that defies grouping him ethnically right away. One of the teachers is Mrs. Lopez in the English version and Señora Lopez in the Spanish version (p. 9). The audiologist remains Mr. Moore in both versions (p. 10). In contrast to *Let's Talk About It!*, the strategies used in *Tools for Living* seem pre-designed for addressing two target groups. *Tools for Living* is a more globalized text and does not need extra localization.

A different strategy is used by the *Big ARISE Safety Book* (some examples of which are available online, see bibliographic references), a comic that tries to teach children and young teenagers safe behaviour such as refusing alcohol at a party or, for very young readers, memorizing their address and phone number. The illustrations are not among the best found in educational comics; the children and teenagers depicted smile in a somewhat deranged way in most pictures. The pictures themselves carry bilingual text: either the girl depicted says the necessary phrases in Spanish and the boy in English, or vice versa. The book thus works quite well as a primer for either English or Spanish, although this is not its primary purpose.

School in the Middle – La escuela de por medio (available online) is based on a true story. Therefore, the names and looks of the characters could not be changed; we are faced with a very straightforward kind of translation based on the fact that the content might be interesting to English-speaking youths as well as to Spanish-speaking youths.

In some cases, it makes sense to translate comics into very small minority languages. This is true of comics with a health message which are meant to reach the whole population. There are also educational comics which are designed for an ethnic minority. To be on the safe side, the authors may choose to publish one version in the majority language of the country in question, as minorities do not always consist of prolific speakers of their own language only.

This is the case with *The Adventures of Sananguaqatiit* (Figure 8.4), a comic series which appeared in Canada in the 1990s and which teaches Inuit artists about proper tool maintenance, creator's rights and other issues connected with making and selling art. Every booklet of this series can be read in English from one cover and in Inuktitut from the other cover. The booklets were written in English and translated into Inuktitut. The publisher is a charitable organization, the Inuit Art Foundation.

Some language pairs are more commonly used in the translation of educational comics than others. Moreover, some languages/cultures are more popular as sources for comics chosen for translation than others, and this is evident in the translation of educational comics too. Many translated educational comics come from the traditional comics nations such as the US, France, Belgium, Italy and Japan.

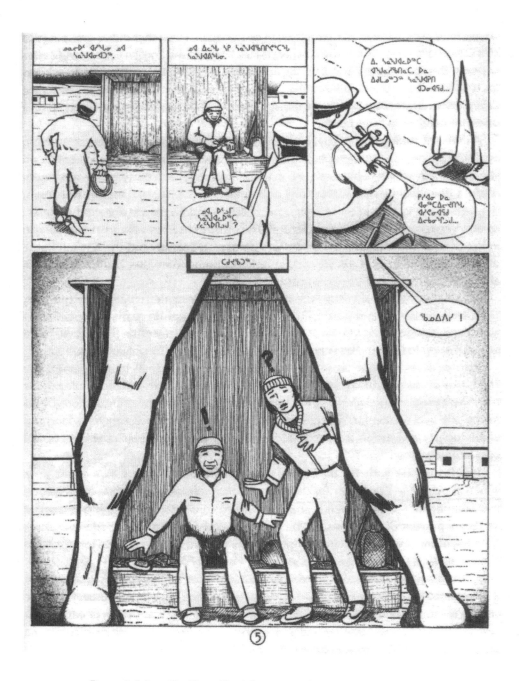

Figure 8.4: Jennifer Ring, *The Adventures of Sananguaqatiit*, 1993
(Inuit translation: Michael Haqpi)

3.2   Educational Manga and the Manga Readership

The first manga ever translated from Japanese into European languages was in fact an educational manga: *Hadashi no Gen*, Keiji Nakazawa's eyewitness account of the Hiroshima bombing. However, its publication and reception history is very specific and is treated more extensively elsewhere (Jüngst, this volume). The same is true for *Nihon Keizai Nyūmon*, a kind of economics primer.

Other educational manga only found their way into European languages after manga had become a firmly established segment of the comics sector. One series chosen for publication in Germany is *Confidential Confessions*. It is addressed at young girls and deals with problems as varied and as depressing as suicide, rape, sexual harassment in schools and drugs. The format is that of the **shōjo manga**, the manga for girls. The caption boxes[15] are used for the story as the heroines tell it to their readers, while the action is acted out in the panels, with dialogue in the balloons.

Before manga came to Germany, girls hardly ever read comics. With manga, the situation changed, and many girls began to read shōjo manga. In fact, these manga have become cash cows for the publishers.

Whereas the educational comics I have mentioned so far were adapted for the target groups, *Confidential Confessions* was only partly adapted. The stories in the manga remained as they were and show Japanese characters in a Japanese setting. Some of the problems are fortunately not pressing in Germany but are associated with some Japanese cities, for example schoolgirl prostitution (*Confidential Confessions 4*). These stories do not work in the same way for German readers as they do for Japanese readers, but given that the readership is not only interested in the confessions themselves but also in Japan, there will be no shortage of interested readers. Other topics, such as bullying in schools, are phenomena that are not culture-specific and that consequently translate well.

In any case, the books are supplemented by address lists of organizations which deal with the problem depicted in the manga and where readers who suffer from the same problem can find help. New lists had to be compiled for the German readers, but this is the only element of localization we find in this series.

3.3   The Case of Latin

Sometimes, comics are translated for an additional educational purpose. Translations of popular texts into Latin are typical of this practice. They are meant to motivate young learners who might not be readily interested in Caesar's and Cicero's writings.[16] Often, the comics chosen are fiction comics, *Astérix* being the favourite choice, but we also find educational comics which have been translated into Latin. The example presented here is *Prisca et Silvanus* (Switzerland 1995-1997). The comic was originally meant as a kind of

---

[15] Complying with manga customs, the text can also appear without borders, somewhere in the panel.
[16] Latin seems to be particularly popular for comics: there are also comics versions of classical Latin texts, e.g. by Plautus.

museum guide for children who visited the excavations at Augusta Raurica, a small place near Basel (Switzerland). The authors tried to make the Roman ruins come alive for their young readers, and at the same time they wanted to tell the complete story of the place as they follow several generations of a family. The original version was in German (Basel is in the German-speaking part of Switzerland), followed by French and Latin versions. The choice of Latin rests on the fact that Augusta Raurica was an important market town founded by the Romans. Children who are interested in the excavations might also be interested in the Latin language.

The translations of the *Prisca et Silvanus* comics are interesting where the question of target groups is concerned. Normally, the translations of educational comics are not addressed at the same target group as the originals. The translations of *Prisca und Silvanus* into Latin, however, are addressed at the same target group as the original German version, with the sole restriction that they are now addressed at that section of the target group who reads Latin or who is taking Latin at school. As far as secondary target groups such as teachers or parents are concerned, *Prisca et Silvanus* in Latin probably appeals to the same kind of person as the original version. Only Latin teachers might show a preference for the Latin version, as it is quite well suited for classroom use.

The question of special vocabulary is different here from the cases listed above. In fact, the special vocabulary needed for the German and French comics is largely Latin. In the Latin version, it ceased to be special vocabulary, as the words were now those the Romans would have used in everyday conversation. At the end of the books, the readers find a glossary with pictures where these special terms are explained for today's readers.

The strategy used for translating the text into Latin is not specific to educational comics but is nevertheless interesting:

> Der Text hält sich grundsätzlich ans klassische Latein. Die Wahl der Wörter und Formulierungen jedoch konnte nicht wie bei einer lebendigen Sprache aus der eigenen Alltagserfahrung … erfolgen. Deshalb haben die Spezialisten in den antiken Textquellen nach möglichst ähnlichen Szenen, Beschreibungen, Stimmungen und Konstellationen gesucht, wie sie in der Geschichte von Prisca und Silvanus vorkommen. Aus nahe liegenden Gründen wurden die Übersetzer, Bruno W. Häuptli … und Markus Clausen …, in erster Linie bei den römischen Komödiendichtern Plautus und Terenz, bei Fachschriftstellern wie dem älteren Plinius und nicht zuletzt in vielen inschriftlichen Texten fündig und haben so eine lateinische Sprachform für unsere erfundene Geschichte ausgesucht, die dem sprachlichen Ausdruck in römischer Zeit möglichst nahe kommt. (*Augusta Raurica*: online)

> [The text uses classical Latin. However, the translators could not rely on their everyday knowledge for choosing appropriate expressions as is possible with a living language. Therefore, the specialists searched historical sources for scenes, descriptions, atmosphere and constellations which correspond to those in *Prisca et Silvanus*. Using the comedies by Plautus and Terence suggested itself, as did the writings by Pliny the Elder and, last but not least, many inscriptions. The translators thus managed to find a form of Latin which is as close as possible to the Latin spoken in Roman times. (my translation)]

The comic is quite successful, which again shows that there are many different ways of choosing a target group and a comic for translation.

4. Conclusion

As is evident from the above discussion, there is no single way to translate educational comics. Translation decisions, beginning with the decision of whether or not to translate the comic at all, are based on a variety of factors, many of them social and political. Since very few educational comics are published by mainstream or comics publishers, very few educational comics are translated for the comics market. Rather, the decision of whether to translate a comic rests with the authority or organization which publishes the comic and with their idea of which target groups to reach.

Several standard techniques and strategies could be observed in those cases where comics were translated. Firstly, there are comics which are designed for translation, and these comics tend to be designed in a globalized style. Where this was not the case, the translated comic was often localized in verbal text and pictures. Strategies of localization could also be seen in comics which were not originally meant for translation but where the decision to translate rested with translators who were themselves members of the target group and who wanted to underline the importance of the comic's content for readers of the translation.

A rare case is the translation of educational comics into Latin. The target group for these translations would probably find it easier to read the original in a modern language, but the translation is meant to give the readers the extra benefit of language training.

The motto of the 2006 CIUTI spring forum, 'Languages in a changing world – between linguistic human rights and the economic needs of international communication', mirrors the situation of the translated educational comic exactly.

References

Primary Sources

Big ARISE Safety Book/El Gran Libro de la Seguridad ARISE. Sample pages "Alcohol/Alcohol", "Addresses and Phone Numbers/Direcciones y Números de Telefóno" and "Air Pollution/Polución del Aire" (online) http://www.ARISElife-skills.org (Accessed 13 May 2004).

Brown, Delia M. and Ricardo Garcia O'Meany (2004) *School in the Middle: Teens Take On Toxics* (*La escuela de por medio: Las adolescentes enfrentan tóxicos*, Spanish translation by Sonia Alas, Los Angeles: UCLA – Labor Occupational Safety and Health (LOSH) Program (online) http://www.gseis.ucla.edu/rights/features/5/pdf/ucla_losh.sp.pdf (Accessed 5 July 2004).

Casamassima, Domenico, Eugenio Fiorentini and Pino Casamassima (1989) *Storia della filosofia* [*The History of Philosophy in Comics*], [*Geschichte der Philosophie in Comics. Das griechische Denken. Von den Anfängen bis zur Spätantike*, German translation by Helmut Schareika, Stuttgart etc.: Klett, 1994].

Concerto Brussels, Cristina Cuadra, Rudi Miel, Dominique David and Etienne Simon (2002) *Troubled Waters / Trübe Wasser / Les Eaux Blessées*, European Parliament, Luxembourg:

Office for Official Publications of the European Community.

Concerto Brussels, Sergio Salma and Mauricet (1998) *What? Me? A Racist?* European Commission, Luxembourg: Office for Official Publications of the European Communities.

del Rio, Eduardo [Rius] (1979) *Marx para Principantes* [*Marx for Beginners*], [*Marx für Anfänger*, translated from English into German by Ludwig Moos, Reinbek: rororo].

Deschaine, Scott and Mike Benton (1990) *Let's Talk About It / ¡Hablemos!*, Glenside, PA: Custom Comic Services, sponsored and distributed by the American Psychiatric Association.

Deschaine, Scott and Vic Lockman (1998) *Tools for Living: Hearing, Speech and Language / Herramientas para vivir*, Doylestown, PA: Discovery Comics, sponsored and distributed by the American Speech-Language-Hearing Association.

Deschaine, Scott, Mike Benton, Mike Roy and Chris Bonno (1995) *Ojos Por El Mundo – Eyes for the World*, Austin, TX: Custom Comic Services, distributed by the American Optometric Association.

Deyriès, Bernard, Denis Lemery and Michael Sadler (1985) *Histoire de la musique en bandes dessinées* [*The History of Music in Comics*], [*Geschichte der Musik in Comics*, German translation by Rainer Redies], Stuttgart: Thienemann [also: Stuttgart: Klett, 1980].

Momochi, Reiko (2005) *Confidential Confessions*, Vol. 1-5, Hamburg: Tokyopop.

Nakazawa, Keiji (1972/73) *Hadashi no Gen 1* [*Barefoot Gen*], [*Barfuß durch Hiroshima*, German translation from English and Japanese by Hans Kirchmann and Kumiko Yasui, Reinbek: Rowohlt, 1982].

------ (1972/73) *Hadashi no Gen 2* [*Barefoot Gen: The Day After*], [*Barfuß durch Hiroshima: Der Tag danach*, Geman translation by Nina Olligschläger, Hamburg: Carlsen, 2005].

------ (1982) *Ore wa mita – I Saw It*, [English translation by Project *Gen*], San Francisco: Edu-Comics.

Paccalet, Yves and Gabriel Paccalet (1995) *Elefanten – Kinder der Savanne* [*Elephants – Children of the Savannah*] [German translation by Elfie Riegler], Bern: Zytglogge.

Rifas, Leonard (1976, 1980 [rev. ed.]) *All-Atomic Comics*, San Francisco: EduComics [*Atom-Comic*, German translation by Ulrike Breitschuh, Lübeck: Bürgerinitiative Lübeck gegen Kernenergiegefahren, 1978; *Atom-Comic*, Frankfurt/Main: NEXUS Verlag, 1980; *Atom Comics*, U-Comix Extra. No. 11, German translation by Robert Lug, lettering by Marianne Nuß, Linden: Volksverlag, 1981].

Ring, Jennifer (1993) *The Adventures of Sananguaqatiit*, Vol. 1, No. 3 [English and Inuktitut. Translated by Michael Haqpi, Nepean, Ontario: Inuit Art Foundation].

------ (1993?) *The Adventures of Sananguaqatiit*, Vol. 1, No. 1 [English and Inuktitut. Translated by Michael Haqpi, Nepean, Ontario: Inuit Art Foundation].

------ (1994) *The Adventures of Sananguaqatiit*, Vol. 2, No. 2 [English and Inuktitut. Translated by Simeonie Kunnuk, Nepean, Ontario: Inuit Art Foundation].

------ (1994?) *The Adventures of Sananguaqatii: Close Call in the Quarry*, Vol. 2, No. 3 [English and Inuktitut. Translated by Simeonie Kunnuk, Nepean, Ontario: Inuit Art Foundation]

Ripp, Matthias and Atelier Wilinsky (1998) *Der Krieg ums Himbeereis / La Guerre de la glace à la framboise / The Raspberry Ice Cream War*, European Commission, Luxembourg: Office for Official Publications of the European Community; Wiesbaden: Universum Verlagsanstalt.

Sacco, Joe (2003) *Palestine*, London: Jonathan Cape.

Satrapi, Marjane (2000/03) *Persepolis*, Paris: L'Association.

Šimko, Dorothee and Roloff [Rolf Meier] (1995) *Prisca und Silvanus 1: Unruhige Zeiten in Augusta Raurica* [Prisca and Silvanus: Troubled Times in Augusta Raurica], Augster Museumshefte 15, Augst, CH: Römermuseum Augst.

------ (1995) *Prisca und Silvanus 2*: *Die Zerstörung von Augusta Raurica* [Prisca and Silvanus: Augusta Raurica Destroyed], Augster Museumshefte 18, Augst, CH: Römermuseum Augst.

------ (1996) *Prisca et Silvanus 1. Turbida Tempora Augustae Rauricae* [Prisca and Silvanus: Troubled Times in Augusta Raurica], (Latin translation by Bruno W. Häuptli and Marcus Clausen), Augster Museumshefte 17, Augst, CH: Römermuseum Augst.

------ (1997) *Prisca et Silvanus 2. Augusta Raurica Deleta* [Prisca and Silvanus: Augusta Raurica Destroyed], (Latin translation by Bruno W. Häuptli), Augster Museumshefte 20, Augst, CH: Römermuseum Augst.

Secondary Sources

Augusta Raurica – Publikationen: Zusammenfassungen ... (online) http://www.bl.ch/docs/kultur/augustaraurica/publ/sum_hefte3.htm#d (Accessed 15 December 2005).

Bergien, Angelika (2004) 'Sprach- und Sachkompetenz beim Übersetzen von Informatiktexten – ein Übersetzungsvergleich', in Eberhard Fleischmann, Peter A. Schmitt and Gert Wotjak (eds) *Translationskompetenz*, Tübingen: Stauffenburg, 471-479.

Eisner, Will (2001a [1985]) *Comics and Sequential Art*, Tamarac, FL: Poorhouse Press.

------ (2001b [1996]) *Graphic Storytelling and Visual Narrative*, Tamarac, FL: Poorhouse Press.

Fleischmann, Eberhard, Peter A. Schmitt and Gerd Wotjak (eds) (2004) *Translationskompetenz*, Tübingen: Stauffenburg.

Frahm, Ole and Michael Hein (1993) 'Maus' *Lexikon der Comics*, Vol. 3, Part 1, September 1993.

Jüngst, Heike (2000) 'Educational Comics: Text-type or text-types in a format?', *Image [&] Narrative: Online Magazine of the Visual Narrative* No. 1 (online) http://www.imageandnarrative.be (Accessed 20 December 2000).

------ (2004) 'Die Oberflächengestaltung von Comics als Problem der Wissensvermittlung im Sachcomic', in Susanne Göpferich and Jan Engberg (eds) *Qualität fachsprachlicher Kommunikation*, Tübingen: Narr, 69-80.

------ (2005a) 'Quer-Comics', *Lexikon der Comics*, September [Encyclopedia published in quarterly installments].

------ (2005b) 'Das Dolmetschen übersetzen: Ein ganz kurzer Zwischenruf', *Lebende Sprachen* 4: 1-6.

------ (forthcoming a) 'Broschüren im Comics-Format als massenmediale Kommunikation', in Kersten Sven Roth and Jürgen Spitzmüller (eds) *Textdesign und Textwirkung in der massenmedialen Kommunikation*.

------ (forthcoming b) *Information Comics: Knowledge Transfer in a Popular Format*, Leipzig: Universität Leipzig.

Kaindl, Klaus (1999) 'Thump, Whizz, Poom: A Framework for the Study of Comics under Translation', *Target* 11(2): 263-288.

Muráth, Judith (2004) 'Sprachliches und enzyklopädisches Wissen beim Übersetzen von Wirtschaftstexten', in Eberhard Fleischmann, Peter A. Schmitt and Gert Wotjak (eds) *Translationskompetenz*, Tübingen: Stauffenburg, 525-532.

O'Sullivan, Emer (2001) *Kinderliterarische Komparatistik*, Heidelberg: Winter.

Packalén, Leif and Frank Odoi (2003) *Comics with an Attitude*, Helsinki: Ministry for Foreign Affairs of Finland, Department for Development Policy.

Renaud, Lise, Monique Caron-Bouchard and Gloria Sacks-Silver (1990) 'Oui, j'arrête: un instrument scripto-visuel sur l'anti-tabagisme pour les femmes analphabètes fonctionelles. Problématique et recherche formative' [Designing a non-smoking comic for women with reading problems], *Hygie* 9(1): 16-21.

9 The Translation of Comics as Localization

On Three Italian Translations of La piste des Navajos

FEDERICO ZANETTIN
University of Perugia, Italy

While the translation of comic books and strips obviously differs in many ways from localization, as the term is generally understood, certain aspects which characterize the 'translation' of computer programmes and web sites can help explain how comics published in translation become different products from what they were when originally published in another language. These aspects concern processes of internationalization, localization and upgrading of both verbal and visual signs, which involve teamwork and different agents and stages. This paper looks at the translation of comics as a localization process, in which the translation of the verbal components of translated comics is only part of the adaptation of the product to the target locale. A number of internationalization/localization practices are exemplified, notably using the production of Disney comics in different countries, and the upgrading practices involved in the republication of some Italian comics, which have been "updated" to respond to social changes, are illustrated. The second part of the paper deals more specifically with the re-translations, or rather, re-localizations of a French western comic series, Charlier and Giraud's Blueberry, *first published in the magazine* Pilote *in the 1960s and republished in Italy a number of times since then. The analysis shows how the Italian 'translations' are part of larger localization processes which have led to the publication of target products designed for markedly different audiences.*

According to the Localization Industry Standards Association (LISA), localization "involves taking a product and making it linguistically, technically, and culturally appropriate to the target locale where it will be used and sold" (quoted in Esselink 2003:67). This general definition of localization could arguably cover much of what has traditionally simply been labelled 'translation'. However, although not explicitly mentioned in this definition, localization usually refers to the 'translation' of electronic products like software programmes, web sites and videogames (see e.g. Esselink 2000, Yunker 2003, Scholand 2002), and as such it differs from translation in a more traditional sense in that 'interlingual translation' is seen as only one part of the process. In other words, the scope of localization is larger than that of translation, as it does not only refer to the replacement of natural language strings (e.g. software documentation, help texts, error messages, etc.) but also to the re-writing of programming code to alter the length of screen dialog boxes, adapt the size, shape and colours of icons and other objects (especially in multimedia applications), or to account for languages with different character sets (e.g. English vs. Chinese and Japanese) or reading direction (e.g. English vs. Arabic and Hebrew).

While the term 'translation' has traditionally been used as a shorthand for 'interlingual translation' and applied to the republication in a different language of written, usually printed, texts, with particular reference to works of literature, the term 'localization' is gaining currency in the literature on translation studies to refer to the adaptation of signs that are not strictly linguistic, such as the transposition of currency rates, measures, icons, and all aspects of translation which do not primarily involve language.[1]

In this article, I suggest that translated comics can be usefully analyzed within a localization framework. The translation of comics is not quite as large an industry as localization 'proper', and the analogy can, of course, be pursued only up to a certain point. The practice of software translation relies to a large extent on computer technologies such as translation memory (TM) and terminology management tools, whereas the practice of translating comics predates the advent of computers. Comics are usually printed products, even though many authors currently create comics using a computer and the Internet has become a publication outlet for many comics genres and authors (McCloud 2006). Indeed, the practice of 'scanlation', i.e. Japanese manga that are scanned, translated and distributed on the Internet by fan groups (Jünsgt, this volume) involves many technical aspects typical of 'localization proper'.[2] I would like to argue that, while most translated comics are works of fiction (but see Jüngst, this volume, on educational comics), and may be approached with concerns which are more typical of literary translation research, a number of aspects involved in the localization industry can help explain how comics published in translation are different from what they were when originally published in another language.

In LISA's definition, two keywords appear which are not usually found in traditional definitions of translation, namely 'product' and 'locale'. The word 'product' emphasizes the commercial aspect of localization, while 'locale' underlines the physical location of the end users. The definition highlights the commercial nature of localization, which is primarily concerned with material objects rather than with languages, and with products rather than with texts.

The localization of a product is the result of a 'global product development cycle'. This begins with an analysis of market and user needs, continues with an internationalization process (design, development, testing and quality assurance) and ends with the product being finally localized (comprising the stages of product testing and quality assurance, and marketing support) (Fry and Lommel 2003). While the tools, technologies and practices of software and web site localization are quite different from those involved in the translation of comics, an internationalization stage at the source end and a localization stage at the target end can often be clearly distinguished in the process leading to the production of translated comics. The publication of a foreign comic can also be seen as an instance of localization in that it involves not only linguistic translation but also the adaptation of visual/cultural information, as well as technical constraints.

A prominent feature of localized products is often their short life-cycle, exemplified, for instance, by the subsequent translations of subsequent versions of software programmes and web site updates. In software localization, when version 1 of a product is updated to

---

[1] Indeed, as Pym (2004) suggests, the notion of 'locale' in localization could be a great terminological contribution to translation studies, possibly to replace items such as 'linguaculture' and 'linguistic and cultural factors'.
[2] See for instance 'Manga editing FAQ' at http://www.questie.com/manga/ScanEditGuide/editing.htm.

include new features, it is renamed version 2, and it is on this new version that the new localized version is based. In a similar way, comics are updated with new features when they are republished, and re-translations are in turn based on these updated versions. The widespread practice of 'product update' in the comics industry, i.e. the re-publication of stories for different, same-target-language readerships over time, can thus also be appreciated within a localization framework. A large percentage of all published comics is in fact made up of reprints and republications, and like original comics, translated comics are constantly updated and re-localized. This localization process involves teamwork and different agents and stages. The 'translator' is not simply one person, but different people successively acting on source and target texts, a 'collective translator' collaborating with other professional figures in order to create an end product. Other work profiles associated with the production of translated comics include, for instance, the letterer, i.e. the person responsible for writing the translated text in the balloons and caption boxes; the person(s) responsible for graphic modifications to the pictures; and the series or magazine editor, who oversees the entire process.

This paper focuses on how these two aspects of the localization process, internationalization/localization and product update, can be applied to the study of translated comics. With regard to the first aspect, the discussion focuses mainly on Disney comics production, but also considers the translation of three popular Italian comic series into American English and the translation of an American comic strip into Italian. To illustrate the second aspect, I first describe 'monolingual' upgrading practices in the republication of native Italian comics, then I discuss in some detail the re-translations, or rather, re-localizations of a French western comic series, *Blueberry*, which has been republished in Italy a number of times since the 1960s.

1. Internationalization and Localization Processes in Comics

The production of comics in translation is often a complex process involving the work of a number of people – revolving around two main actors, the original producer and the target publisher. Along the production line, at least two stages can often be detected, an internationalization stage in which the product as originally published is modified at the source end in preparation for one or more foreign version(s), and a localization phase in which the product is adapted to local norms, as concerns target readership culture and comics reading habits.

The first example comes from Disney comics. As is well known, the Walt Disney Company is one of the major multinational corporations in the entertainment industry. Its publishing division, Disney Publishing Worldwide, which manages the licensing of Disney materials as well as direct publishing, and is responsible for brand retention initiatives, is the biggest publisher of children's literature in the world. Comics are just one minor branch of the Disney empire, and one which is not now primarily located within the United States. In fact, since 1984 Disney comics have only been published in the US in minor imprints, and even then with long pauses between publications. Right from their launch, the 1930s Disney comics have always been an international affair. The first Disney comics were published in translation almost simultaneously in European countries, and all the 'golden age' stories (from the 1930s to the 1950s) by authors such as Floyd Gottfredson and Carl Barks are still republished all over the world. The quality and quantity of Disney comics produced in the US declined from the second half of the 1950s, and in European countries, such as Italy and France, the demand for Disney comics was increasingly filled by native stories produced under license. Today, most Disney comics are produced by European and South American corporate and licensed publishers and studios. Authors (script writers and artists) are Italian, French, Brazilian, Danish, Dutch, Spanish as well as American and British. Currently the three most active groups in comics production are Disney Italia, which produces more than half of all Disney comics, Egmont in Denmark, and an international 'studio' in Barcelona (Botto 2004).[3] The comics created in these countries are produced not only for internal consumption, but also for the international market. Scripts are usually written in the authors' native languages, but dialogues and captions are then translated into English, which is used as a *lingua franca* before stories are translated for publication in different languages and countries.

For instance, the story 'A door opens … and closes', starring Donald Duck's nephews Huey, Dewey and Louie, was created by Giorgio Cavazzano (pencils), Sandro Zemolin (inks) and Byron Erickson (story and script). It was published in Italy and Germany (2003), Finland (2004), Brazil, Norway, Sweden and the US (2005). Giorgio Cavazzano and Sandro Zemolin are Italian, whereas Byron Erikson is American (working in Denmark for Egmont). The story 'Mickey et les douceurs de Noël' was written, scripted and pencilled by Romano Scarpa and inked by Lucio Michieli in Italy. It was first published in France (1998), then in Germany, Denmark, Norway, Finland and Sweden (2001), and then in Italy (2002), the Netherlands (2004) and the US (2005). These authors (and many others) have had their stories published in more than 50 countries.

When a Disney story is produced in foreign translation the source text is first 'internationalized' by providing the final publisher with a provisional English translation which is then 'localized' according to a set of guidelines that are often explicitly stated. Koponen (2004:31-33) describes how the material for the Finnish magazine *Aku Ankka* (Donald Duck) is sent by the Danish publisher Egmont together with "a set of instructions concerning translations to all the publishers of Disney comics in different countries", called "Translation – Guidelines for translator".[4] The texts are first translated by freelance translators, and then revised by in-house editors, who are responsible for implementing the guidelines according to the values and attitudes promoted by the company. Dialogues are often freely re-written, using the translation provided as a script.

A second example of an internationalization process for comics, i.e. the preparation of comics at the source end before localization at the target end, is the American publication of a number of Bonelli series. In the late 1990s three mini-series (*Dylan Dog*, *Martin*

---

[3] See the online database I.N.D.U.C.K.S. (at http://inducks.org), which "contains a detailed list of more than 160,000 Disney comics stories and more than 50,000 publications" for extensive information.

[4] Unfortunately, Disney's guidelines are not publicly available. See Koponen (2004:31), Zitawi, (this volume).

Mystery, *Nathan Never*, each consisting of 6 comic books) starring three Italian popular heroes were produced for the American market and published by Dark Horse Press (see D'Arcangelo and Zanettin 2004 for a detailed analysis of the *Dylan Dog* series). The American publisher took over the localization process only after the Italian publisher had selected a number of stories from those most successful in Italy and retouched them for the international market, for instance, by removing references to episodes not included in the translated series and by removing any potentially controversial material, such as copyrighted images. A preliminary translation of the comic books was also provided by the staff translators of Strip Art Features, Bonelli's agent for distribution abroad. Finally, the localization process was completed at the American end, where dialogues were further 'adapted', and the comic books were lettered, further retouched and repackaged (new covers, paratextual materials, etc.) for the new target market.

When looking at the North-American translations of Tiziano Sclavi's *Dylan Dog* series vis-à-vis the Italian originals, one notices immediately that the dialogues in the American *Dylan Dog* are generally much shorter than in the Italian comic books, so the balloons appear almost 'oversized' in relation to the text inside them. This can be explained in terms of the different cultural expectations of the American and Italian readerships. The average reading time for an Italian popular Bonelli comic book is longer than that of an average American one, where action prevails over dialogues and written texts are generally less dense.

This visual impression is reversed when considering the Italian version of *Casey Ruggles* by Warren Tufts, originally published as syndicated daily strips in American newspapers (1949-54) and translated into Italian by Gian Luigi Bonelli, the creator of the popular Italian western series *Tex* (see below). In the 1950s, when the Italian magazine *L'Audace* published the stories of Casey Ruggles, not only was the main character renamed Red Carson, a much more recognizable name for Italian readers, but the Italian edition also introduced a number of changes regarding dialogues and captions. The English dialogues are rather bare, terse and graphically uniform. Balloons are often absent from panels. The Italian translation recreated the texts almost completely. In *Red Carson* the text occupies a much larger surface than in *Casey Ruggles*, even to the point where additional balloons had to be inserted and existing ones enlarged, at the expense of the drawings. Not only were the dialogues longer, thus filling up more space in the panels, but captions and inscriptions were added to explain even unnecessary details. As a result, the Italian translation takes longer to read, and the rhythm of the narration becomes more fluent and less syncopated. The loss of drama is balanced by the use of multiple, linked balloons in the same panel, exclamations and the introduction of highlighting devices such as bold lettering and underlining (Iori 2002:25).[5]

These last examples show how translated comics are often modified to suit local comics conventions, and not only the text either, but sometimes even the illustrations. Practices such as these have always been common in the translation of comics.

---

[5] The language was similar to that used in *Tex*. When the original *Casey Ruggles* stories began to thin out, Bonelli started to write new ones from scratch. The same happened with *Buffalo Bill* by F. Meagher.

For instance, when the first American comics were published in Italy, as elsewhere in Europe, they were redrawn. Balloons were removed, and dialogues were replaced by rhymed narration using a written linguistic register (see introduction to this volume). In the 1930s, American adventure comics like *Flash Gordon* were often heavily retouched when printed in Italian magazines (Zanettin 2005:94). Notable examples of localization involving changes to the pictures include the translations of Disney comics in Arab countries (Zitawi 2004, this volume), and translations of Hergé's story *Tintin in Congo*, where a whole page was redrawn when the comic was published in foreign editions (Zanettin 2007). Finally, when Japanese comics were first introduced into Western countries, they were usually re-coloured and printed as mirror images, in order to reverse the reading direction (left-to-right rather than right-to-left) (see e.g. Rifas 2004, Jüngst 2004, this volume, Rota, this volume).

2. Updating Comics

A major percentage of comics publishing consists of re-publications. Comic strips originally published in newspapers and stories published in installments in magazines are often republished in comic book form. Comic books are republished as reprints with no alterations except for covers and paratextual information, but they are also re-published as new versions with changes to both text and pictures. One example of these product-updates is retranslation.

The updating of comics takes place intralingually, i.e. popular comic book stories and series are often reprinted and sometimes the dialogues are rewritten and pictures retouched or redrawn.

In the Italian context, two examples that illustrate this process well are the 'reprints' of stories featuring two very popular characters: *Tex*, published by Sergio Bonelli Editore, and *Paperinik*, published by Disney Italia (previously by Mondadori under licence from Disney), possibly the two main Italian publishers of comics, specialized in adolescent/adult and children comics, respectively.

Tex (Tex Willer) is one of the most long-lasting and successful of Italian comics characters, and is largely responsible for the introduction and success of the Western genre in Italian comics (Paglieri 2003, Busatta 1998, Detti 1984). Created by Gian Luigi Bonelli (scripts) and Aurelio Galeppini (drawings) shortly after WW II (1948), *Tex* is still the best selling title of the publishing house named after Gian Luigi's son Sergio. The first stories were originally published in weekly strip format booklets (12 pages, 6x12 cm) in the 1940s and 1950s, then republished in monthly notebook format (96 pages, 17x24 cm) from 1959, and then again from 1964 as first installments of a series which still continues today. *Tex* has been translated in many European and Latin American countries, and past issues are periodically reprinted in Italy, so that at least three different issues of the series can be found each month in the newsstands. Between the first and later publications a number of changes have been made, affecting both the texts and the drawings of some panels (Detti 1984:79-109). All instances of 'crude language', e.g. interjections such as 'bastardo!' ('bastard!'), 'sangue del diavolo!' (lit. 'by the blood of the devil!') have been replaced by milder expressions, and references to the hero's 'illegal' or 'immoral' behaviour (Tex was originally an outlaw, but later became a Texas ranger) have also disappeared. Images have been retouched to remove realistic representations of violence (e.g. blood spots deleted from corpses), cover women's previously naked legs and shoulders, and tone down scenes where women played too active a role. Figure 9.1 (reproduced from Detti 1984:83) shows how such changes were sometimes made even at the expense of coherent narration. In this post 1948 republication, Tex is made to shoot the villain, instead of the now more demurely dressed female character, even if he was previously said to be unarmed.

Figure 9.1a: Gianluigi Bonelli and Aurelio Galeppini, *Tex*, 1948

Figure 9.1b: Gianluigi Bonelli and Aurelio Galeppini, *Tex*, later editions

As can be seen from Figure 9.1, not only has the woman's dress been retouched to cover her shoulders, but the upper part of her face has been (badly) drawn to fill up the space left by the caption in the second panel. A dramatic narration of her passionate intervention in defence of Tex[6] is replaced by a balloon in which she is made to shout out "*Attento!*" (Watch out!), followed by a short caption in which Tex is said to turn around "as quick as lightning". Self-censorship of this type was adopted by many other similar publications in this period, as a result of changes in the cultural climate. The 'updating process' responded to moralistic and ideological intents which in the 1950s strongly influenced comics production both in Europe and in the US.[7]

A second example of 'comics updating' can be seen in Paperinik. Paperinik is one of the most successful creations of Italian Disney comics authors (most notably Guido Martina for the scripts and Giovan Battista Carpi, Romano Scarpa and Massimo de Vita for the drawings). The first story featuring Paperinik (*Paperinik il diabolico vendicatore*, 'Paperinik the avenger from hell'), Donald Duck's secret identity when he goes out at night wearing a dark costume, a cape and yellow boots, was published in 1969 and was followed by a number of new stories in the 1970s. The character, whose name is a combination of Paperino (Donald Duck) and Diabolik, is a parody of the latter, the most famous of Italian 1960s 'black' comics, i.e. adult pocketbook sized comics starring criminal anti-heroes,[8] but there are also clear references to American superhero comics characters such as Superman (Paperinik flies and is super-strong). In his detailed study of the 'reprints' (or rather, updated versions) of three Paperinik stories in Italy, Castagno (2003) lists all the instances where the dialogues have undergone changes. From the first to the last publication, the changes were mostly minor, and included corrected spelling mistakes or, more puzzlingly, changes in onomatopoeia (e.g. from 'Berk' to 'Uack'). More consistently, it seems that all instances of possibly controversial language have been 'sanitized' over time. Uncle Scrooge shouting at his nephew Donald Duck "questo pelandrone non è nemmeno capace di derubare un sordomuto cieco e paralitico" (this loafer cannot even steal from someone who is deaf-mute, blind and paralytic) becomes in later editions "questo pelandrone non è nemmeno capace di derubare un cane randagio del suo osso" (this loafer cannot even steal a bone from a stray dog) and later still a more politically correct (and less dangerous) "questo pelandrone non è nemmeno capace di rubare una noce a uno scoiattolo" (this loafer cannot even steal a nut from a squirrel). A young boy who said that for a dollar he would "set fire to the school" in the original edition, says in later editions that he would "take a letter to Timbuktu". Donald Duck with a sandwich and a bubbling glass in his hands was eating ham and bread and drinking beer in the 1970s but only a nondescript sandwich and cola in later editions.

The general impression may be that these are just two specific cases, the norm being that comics are simply reprinted with just a few changes in the 'packaging' (covers and paratext). However, these examples do point to a widespread practice among comics

---

[6] A literal translation of the text in the caption of the 1948 edition would read "But Marie Gold, driven by an irresistible urge, seeing that Tex was about to be shot in the back, grabs a tiny revolver she keeps inside her ribbon corset and …".

[7] Perhaps the most known publication which embodies the new moral and ideological agenda was Fredric Wertham's *Seduction of the Innocent*, which spearheaded the anti-comics crusade in the 1950s in the US (see e.g. Restaino 2004:147-152).

[8] On Italian 'black' comics see Restaino (2004) and Raffaelli (1994).

publishers, to 'upgrade' each 'new' publication of a comic, either in the same or in a different language, and adapt/localize the old product for a new audience (chronologically or/and geographically).

3.   Blueberry

In this section I will look in some detail at three subsequent Italian translations of a Blueberry story, in order to highlight how republication practices and translation strategies concur in the localization of comics. I will first discuss the source text(s) and then the Italian translations.

Blueberry, created by Jean-Michel Charlier and Jean Giraud, is probably the most famous French western comic series. It first appeared on the pages of the magazine *Pilote* in 1963, and new episodes are still being issued (the last album, *Dust*, was published in 2005). Jean-Michel Charlier (1924-1989) is one of the most highly respected authors and script writers in the history of Franco-Belgian comics. In 1959, he co-founded with Goscinny and Uderzo (the authors of Astérix) *Pilote*, the most popular and innovative French comic magazine of the 1960s. His very successful characters include Buck Danny (an American Air Force pilot, drawn by Victor Hubinon and later by Francis Bergèse), Tanguy et Laverdure (two French Air Force pilots, drawn by Albert Uderzo and others), and Lieutenant Blueberry. Jean Giraud is one of the most famous contemporary French authors. Born in 1938, he has drawn comics since the 1950s, and in 1963 he began working with Charlier drawing Blueberry's adventures. His international reputation, however, is largely due to his work under the pseudonym of Moebius. In the 1970s, with a group of comics authors he co-founded the magazine *Metal Hurlant*, which saw a new generation of comics artists (e.g. Philippe Druillet, Enki Bilal), writing often as full authors of stories for an educated/intellectual readership, with a predilection for science-fiction/fantastic contents. His stories and illustrations under the name of Moebius are surreal and loosely structured, and his dramatic settings and drawing style (which are often quite different from the realistic style used in the Blueberry stories) have influenced not only many contemporary comics artists but also visual imagery in general. For instance, the settings of Hollywood science-fiction films such as *Blade Runner* and *The Fifth Element* are inspired by his drawings.

3.1   Fort Navajo

The first Blueberry story, *Fort Navajo*, consisted of five episodes, each later published in the classic French album format of 48 to 64 pages, in full colour. At the time of *Fort Navajo*, Mike Steve Donovan, alias Blueberry, was just one of the characters, even if without doubt the main one. He resembled French actor Jean-Paul Belmondo, but this likeness disappeared after the first episodes as the character developed.

Given the success of the story, new ones were produced, this time with Blueberry as the title bearer. Apart from the main series, consisting of 28 albums (8 cycles, each subdivided into 2 or more albums, and 2 'one-shot' stories), two spin-off series have also been published, *La jueness de Blueberry* (Blueberry's Youth, from 1975), now counting 14 albums, and *Marshall Blueberry* (3 albums, from 1991). After Charlier's death in 1989, new script writers (Corteggiani) and artists (Wilson, Blanc-Dumont, Vance and Rouge) joined Giraud, who continued as the sole author of the last cycle of the main series (*Mister Blueberry*) and as scriptwriter for the *Marshall Blueberry* series.

Blueberry has thus grown into a complex western saga, which spans the years from the American Civil War (1861-1865, the years in which the series 'Blueberry's Youth' is set) to 1881, the year of the legendary gunfight at the OK Corral (described in the cycle *Mister Blueberry*). The adventures of Blueberry are set against a carefully documented historical and geographical background, where real characters (US presidents, gunfighters like the Earp brothers, Indian chiefs like Cochise) meet fictional ones. The drawings are inspired by classical Hollywood western movies (by directors such as John Ford and Sam Peckinpah) as well as by Italian 'spaghetti-western' movies by Sergio Leone. The *Fort Navajo* cycle, set in the years 1867/68, is in fact a classic western story whose plot is loosely based on that of *Fort Apache*, the film directed by John Ford and starring John Wayne and Henry Fonda. Blueberry, a US army Lieutenant, is described as a bit of a disrespectful troublemaker who likes to gamble and drink, but who is also a brave and loyal soldier. As the series progressed and Giraud/Moebius became more involved in its thematic and visual development (Groth and Fiore 1988:282), it changed from "a straightforward adventure" into "a much darker tale incorporating anti-militarist and anarchist themes" (Sabin 1993:188). Over the years Blueberry became more and more of an anti-hero, who takes the side of dispossessed Indians and fights against white villains such as army generals and bounty hunters. At the same time, the background for this development was provided by the prequel *Blueberry's Youth*.[9]

This study focuses on the first cycle and in particular on its fifth and last episode, *La piste des Navajos*, which was first published in *Pilote* in 1965 (issues 313-335, see figure 9.2), as a comic book in 1969, and has been reprinted various times since. In 1996, the French publisher Dargaud issued a new edition, "remaquettés et agrémentés de nouvelles couleurs" (Dargaud website). This new edition was recoloured by Claudine Blanc-Dumont, who has also drawn the latest episodes in the Blueberry's Youth series.

The plot is, in short, as follows: Lieutenant Mike Blueberry has been given the assignment by the president of the United States to bring a peace proposal to the Indian tribes, whose leaders, having been deceived and almost killed by the US army in the first episodes of the cycle, are now distrustful and are waiting for a group of Mexican arm dealers to supply them with guns and ammunition before fighting back. Blueberry and his aid, the old miner and drunkard Jimmy Mac Clure, manage to destroy the weapon supplies, kill the Mexican arm dealers and reach the Indian camp where the Navajo chief Cochise is finally persuaded to agree to a peace treaty. They are helped by Crowe, a 'mixed-blood' scout, an old Mexican miner (they both die in the process) and a group of 'jayhawkers' (former Southern Army troops during the Civil War and now pro-slavery guerrillas). Finally, Blueberry faces the main Indian villain in a duel and wins.

---

[9] On the evolution of the Blueberry series, see e.g. Marín (2001).

Figure 9.2: *Pilote* No. 313, 1965, Cover

3.2   The Italian Translations

The Blueberry albums have been translated in many languages, including German, Danish, English, Italian, Greek, Turkish, etc. In Italy, all the episodes of the series have been published over the years, usually first as installments in comic magazines and then in single volumes/albums. Most episodes have also been variously republished or reprinted by different Italian publishers.

La piste des Navajos (The trail of the Navajos) has so far been published in Italy 6 times (Giordano 2000:31). Under the title *La pista dei Navajos*, it was first published in January 1971 in the *Albi Ardimento* comic book series (by Crespi, a small comic book publisher), following the 1969 French album edition by Darguad, in which some pages had been modified from the original installments published in *Pilote* to account for the change in publication format. This edition will be from here on referred to as AA71.

Crespi, who published the monthly series *Albi Ardimento* from July 1969 to December 1971, was a publisher closely associated with the weekly magazine *Il Corriere dei Piccoli* (The Children's Post), a Sunday supplement of the main Italian newspaper *Il Corriere della Sera*. For over sixty years since its first publication in 1908, *Il Corriere dei Piccoli* was the most prestigious illustrated periodical for children in Italy. It was aimed at the children of the educated middle class readers of the newspaper, and until the 1950s its policy with regard to foreign, mostly American, comics was to convert them into 'illustrated stories', i.e. in the traditional Italian format without balloons and with a narrative commentary on the illustrations placed under each panel. From 1961 onwards, the magazine began to introduce French comics into Italy (balloons included) and to address an older readership (ages 10-15 rather than 5-10). While the magazine eventually changed its name to *Il Corriere dei Ragazzi* (The Boys Post) in December 1971, it was always very considerate of its younger readership (and of their parents).[10] The age of the projected target readership can also be deduced from the products advertised in the *Albi Ardimento* edition, namely, a plastic rifle, pens, crayons and board games. To make room for advertisements, the Blueberry episode was actually shortened by merging two pages into one. This was done by cutting out 3 short narrative sequences (each composed of a couple of panels), and while the first two gaps go unnoticed in the Italian translation, the third creates a certain narrative incoherence (see Figure 9.3, centre fold). The last deleted panel contained Blueberry's 'off-screen voice', a balloon connected to the gutter, thus coming from outside the panel. The following panel, in which Cochise says *"Chi osa interrompere il consiglio di guerra?"* (Who dares to interrupt the war council?), originally meant as a reply to Blueberry's utterance (*"Chi parla di morire?.. Gli uomini bianchi sono pronti a fare la pace!..."*, lit. Who's talking about dying?.. The white men are ready to make peace!..; see Figure 9.3b, centre fold), becomes less comprehensible here because it reads only as a comment on Blueberry's unannounced entrance to the tent (Figure 9.3a, centre fold).

La pista dei Navajos was then published in four installments in the weekly comic magazine *Skorpio* in 1980 (issues 18-21).[11] Two years later it was published again in soft cover album format by *Edizioni Nuova Frontiera,* as part of a Blueberry series which presented all the stories from the main French Blueberry series. The same publisher later reprinted it in a pocket book edition in black and white (1986) and in a hard cover album format in 1990. This edition will be referred to as NF82.

The 1982 translation targets an older readership, one which has grown up with the French, Argentinian, Italian etc. comics '*d'auteur*' published in magazines in the 1970s and 1980s, as well as with Italian popular Western adventure stories from the 1950s, such as Bonelli's *Tex*. Readers of Italian western comics would for example be familiar with the name Kociss, an alternative Italian spelling and pronunciation for Cochise, the historical native-American leader popularized in Italy by western movies and comics.[12] This spelling only appears in NF82, whereas both the 1971 and 2005 publications keep

[10] 'Children', i.e. up to 10 years olds, have been estimated to make up about one third or the readers, while the remaining were 'boys', mostly aged between 10 to 14 years (Scillitani 2004).

[11] As it was not possible to find these publications, the analysis will be restricted here to the three album editions. However, even a summary analysis of a different episode serialized in the *Skorpio* magazine (issue 33, 1980) reveals striking characteristics. First of all, the magazine (which contains mostly stories by South-American authors) is targeted to an adult readership, one which would appreciate the pictures of semi-naked women on the covers. Blueberry's stories are in a shorter format than the original, in black and white. Balloons and captions have been enlarged to accommodate long translations, which are typewritten rather than manually lettered.

[12] Kociss was for instance the name of a character and monthly series created in 1957 by Gian Luigi Bonelli (script) and Emilio Umberti (drawings) (see http://www.sergiobonellieditore.it/editore/cinquanta.html).

the original French (and English) spelling, i.e. Cochise.

This reading public is also presumed to be familiar with both the *Fort Navajo* cycle (all intertextual references to previous episodes are kept), and the way in which the series develops. In fact, a short critical note by Javier Coma, prefacing each of the 22 episodes of the saga published by Nuova Frontiera between 1982 and 1987, provides this sort of background information, including a comment on Giraud's other artistic identity, Moebius. The later episodes of Blueberry had been published in France on the pages of the magazine *Metal Hurlant*, which, like its Italian edition (published by Nuova Frontiera), was targeted at a more sophisticated and older readership. These episodes, where Blueberry evolves into an anti-hero, had also already been published in Italy in comic magazines for adults.

Finally, Blueberry was published in 2005 by Alessandro Editore as a hard cover, luxury edition, following the 1996 French edition by Dargaud. This edition will be referred to as AD05.

Translators as such are not acknowledged in either of these editions. However, the production of AA71 is attributed to Enrico Bagnoli and to Gianfranco Ravasi (for graphic adaptation).

Comparing a sample panel from the three editions under examination reveals striking differences, as can be seen in Figure 9.4 (centre fold): both the text and the colours are different. The panel in AA71 is dominated by basic colours (green, red, blue, yellow) and is divided into well-defined, colour-contrasted areas. The caption has a yellow background in which the narrator informs the reader that "Crowe è su di un sentiero senza uscita" (lit. Crowe is on a path with no exit). A black arrow pointing downwards can be seen in the white space separating the panel from the one above. This indicates that the panel should be read after the one immediately above, rather than after the one at the end of the row above, to avoid the potential ambiguity deriving from the layout of this particular page. This graphic reading sequence facilitator is not present in NF82, nor in AD05.

In both NF82 and AD05 the colours are in softer shades and the objects are less sharply contrasted than in AA71. However, it can be clearly seen that the colours in AD05 are more vivid than those in NF82, while NF82 reproduces the original colours used by Giraud in the 1969 French edition (which were changed considerably in AA71), AD05 is based on the colour-enhanced, glossy paper French edition of 1996, which 'updates' for the second time the original *Pilote* publication of 1965. The lettering is written manually in AA71 and NF82, whereas in AD05 it is computerized.

In both these editions, the captions are on a white background and the text is longer than the AA71 version (13, 14 and 8 word, respectively). The text in the caption in NF82 reads as follows: "Infatti, Crowe non si è accorto di essersi cacciato in un vicolo cieco" (lit. Indeed, Crowe did not realize he had gotten himself into a blind alley), while in AD05 it reads: "Infatti, Crowe non si è accorto che si stava dirigendo verso un vicolo cieco" (lit. Indeed, Crowe did not notice that he was heading towards a blind alley). In NF82, on the other hand, *vicolo cieco* (blind alley) is part of a larger idiomatic chunk ("cacciarsi in un vicolo cieco", lit. to throw oneself in a blind alley), in AD05 it collocates with the verb *dirigersi* (to head towards/to direct oneself), which is a higher register synonym for *andare* (to go). This characterizes the language in NF82 as belonging to a spoken, informal register, whereas in AD05 it belongs to a more literary, written variety.

A closer comparison of the dialogues in these three Italian translations reveals other such differences, which form a consistent pattern of 'localization' choices. In AA71 captions and dialogues are shorter, simpler and do not contain any 'bad language'. For instance, in one panel (p. 13) one of the Indians pursuing Crowe shouts:[13] "ATTENTION! Ce rat doit se terrer quelque part dans …", which is rendered in AA71 as "Quel topo deve essersi rintanato da qualche parte" (lit. That rat/mouse must have holed himself up somewhere), in NF82 as "Attenzione! Quel bastardo deve essersi nascosto da qualche parte…" (lit. Watch out! That bastard must have hidden himself somewhere), and in AD05 as "Attenzione! quel cane deve essersi rintanato da qualche parte…" (lit. Watch out! That dog must have holed himself up somewhere). As compared to the French source 'rat', the *topo* in AA71 mitigates the force of the interjection, since Italian *topo* ('mouse' rather than 'rat') is less offensive than French 'rat', whereas *cane* (AD05) is perhaps a closer pragmatic equivalent. *Bastardo* (NF82) is, like its English cognate term, a rather stronger expression.[14] Even more extreme examples of how the 1980s edition replaces mild French expletives with much stronger and coarser insults can be found in the first episode of the Fort Navajo cycle, where expressions such as "face de rat" (lit. rat's face) and "mêle-toi de tes oignons" (lit. mind your own onions, meaning mind your own business) are translated as *faccia da culo* (pragmatically similar to fuckface/shitface) and *fatti i cazzi tuoi* (pragmatically similar to mind you own fucking business), respectively.

In AA71 (p. 16) Blueberry calls out "EHI … guarda!" (HEY, look!), in NF82 the same balloon has "!??! Dannazione!... per tutti i fulmini, guarda!.." (!??! Damn, by all lightnings, look!) and in AD05 "Hell!.. per mille tuoni!.. guarda!.." (Hell! .. by a thousand thunders, look!..). Again, the text in AA71 is much shorter than that of the other translations (including the original text) and avoids using any swear words. NF82 uses an interjection which is typical of Italian western comics such as *Tex* (see above) and is therefore recognizable by many Italian readers. AD05 is a rendition which is closer to the French utterance ("!??! Hell!.. tonnerre de dieu!... regarde!..") as it mentions thunder rather than lightning, but is also more idiosyncratic and uncommon as an Italian expression. Dialogues in AA71 are not only shorter, but some words – usually interjections like *vite!/presto!* (quick!), *quoi?/che?* (what?), *gasp!/gasp!* (gasp!) – are graphically highlighted through the use of bold type and character enlargement.

The other major difference between the translations in AA82 and AD05, which are otherwise much more similar to each other than the translation in AA71 is with either of them, is most apparent when comparing the translations with the original French. In the example above, for instance, the French dialogue contains the English word *hell*, which is omitted in AA71, translated with *dannazione* in NF82 and left untranslated in AD05. As stated above, the Blueberry series carefully recreates a western setting, and

---

[13] Words in capital letters stand for some typographic highlighting (bold type or larger size) in the text in the balloons.
[14] I would like to thank Elio Ballardini for his valuable help in the analysis of the French original texts.

this is done not only through reference to real historical events and characters and by showing territorial maps, but also through the dialogues. The characters often intersperse their normal language (French) with words in English or Spanish, usually interjections like "hell!", "damn!", "shut up!" and "good lord", or "carai!" and "por la virgen", but also terms referring to the western setting, such as "sierra", "mexicanos", "hoogans", "pow-pow". Often these foreign words or phrases are accompanied by a note in a caption inside or below the panel which provides a French translation. Other notes provide intertextual references to events and people from previous episodes. Most of these notes were simply deleted in AA71: those referring to previous episodes of the story probably because this was the first Blueberry story issued by the publisher, since the four previous episodes had been serialized in the magazine *Corriere dei Piccoli* and had been published in volumes by Mondadori. The notes providing a translation for foreign words were deleted because non-Italian words are generally not present in this translation. Figure 9.5 (centre fold) shows how the panel was retouched to remove the note. The original Spanish – "Aqui vienen!", translated in the note as "Il viennent ici!" (They are coming here! – is rendered instead with the Italian "Che succede?" (What's happening?). A few foreign words are retained in AA71, for examples in comments by Mexican characters who are, however, made to speak a much more restricted range of Spanish words (*señor, caramba*). If compared to both later translations and to the French original, AA71 portrays a fictional world in which not only colours but also characters are sharper and more basic (see e.g. Figure 9.6, centre fold).

Intertextual references were retained in NF82 (Nuova Frontiera published all the cycles in the main series which had since been published in French), as were the notes providing translations of foreign words. When foreign words are not given a translation in the French original (usually with short interjections like Blueberry's "hell!" or the Mexicans' "carai!") they were given an Italian translation within the dialogue instead, for instance Blueberry often says "dannazione!" (damn!). In AD05, both the notes and foreign words are consistently retained.

Generally speaking both NF82 and AD05 adhere to the syntax and wording of the French original. Differences in lexico-grammatical choices may certainly be due to different (anonymous) translators' styles, and from the point of view of readers different solutions may appear to appeal to individual preferences. However, as already noted, the register in which NF82 is written seems to be more idiomatic and 'slangish' than that in AD05. For instance, Figure 9.7 (centre fold) contains a caption with the narrator's voice commenting on the adjacent picture. In the first sentence, whereas AA71 simply has *Ecco i tre uomini* (Here are the three men), NF82 has *Tre uomini soli avanzano guardinghi, all'ombra compiacente degli alti speroni rocciosi* (Three men proceed alone wearily, in the pleasing shade of the high rocky cliffs) and AD05 has *Tre cavalieri isolati, prestando la massima attenzione, si nascondono nell'ombra protettrice delle alte falesie* (Three isolated horsemen, paying the maximum attention, hide in the protecting shade of the high falaises). The Italian *falesie* corresponds to the French *falaises*, and the whole sentence in AD05 is a rather literal rendition of the original French ("Trois cavaliers isolés, l'oeil aux aguets, se glissent dans l'ombre protectrice des hautes falaises"). However, while the French word is part of general French language and is rather common and widespread, its Italian prima face equivalent is a rather more learned and specialized term. In NF82, the phrase *speroni rocciosi* (rocky cliffs) belongs instead to general language and to a more colloquial register. In the same panel, the leading horseman, Crowe, says that the Apache camp is *Dietro quella catena di montagne* (Behind that mountain range) in NF82, and *Dietro a questa sierra* (Behind this sierra) in AD05. Jimmy Mac Clure exclaims *Ma che allegria* (How jolly) in NF82 and *Che posticino sinistro* (What a nice sinister place) in AD05. Again, NF82 is more colloquial, while AD05 is closer to the wording of the French original (*derriere cette chaines de sierras* and *quel patelin sinistre*).

A second example which illustrates the differences between NF82 and AD05 is provided in Figure 9.8 (centre fold). When Crowe is shot in the thigh by his pursuers he says: *Le coyotte!... il ... il m'a brisé la ... la cuisse!... impossible d... de me maintenir en selle!.. cette fois c'est la fin!..* (lit. The coyote! He broke my thigh! It's impossible to ride/remain on the saddle! This time it's the end). NF82 translates *Quel coyote!... ma ha beccato a una coscia! non ... ce la faccio a restare in sella ... ormai è proprio la fine!...* (lit. That coyote! He got me in a thigh! I can't ride, it's really the end now!..), which is fluent colloquial, even 'slangish', Italian. AD05 translates instead with *Il coyote! Mi ... mi ha sfondato la ... la coscia!.. Impossibile mantenersi in sella! Stavolta è la fine!..* (lit. The coyote! He broke down my thigh! It's impossible to ride! This time it's the end), which is again a very close rendition of the original French and belongs to a slightly more formal register.[15]

3.3 Summing Up

The examples in the previous section illustrate how each of the three successive Italian album editions of "La pista dei Navajo" designs its own particular audience. Each product is the result of a localization process in which different 'translations' in the strictly linguistic sense of the term are only part of a wider transformation involving the modification of other visual sign systems, both at the source and at the target end. The Italian editions were not only based on different source texts (subsequent French publications), but they were also designed for different receiving audiences, in terms of age group and cultural background.

The *Il Corriere dei Piccoli* readership, for which the Italian editions of the Blueberry series were designed in the 1960s and early 1970s, was somewhat younger than the *Pilote* readership targeted by the original French editions. The Italian edition was therefore simplified and rendered more basic both at a visual and a verbal level, and there was a sharper distinction between the 'good guys' and the 'bad guys'. Dialogues were not only shortened but also 'sanitized' to eliminate any expressions that might offend the ears of the young readers' parents: *ACC...*, short for *ACCIDENTI*, a very mild interjection which could be translated with something like good golly/my goodness/dash, is the strongest remark we hear from Blueberry.

---

[15] In AA71 the whole sentence is translated as *Questa volta ... è la fine ...*, lit. This time ... it's the end.

On the other hand, the 1982 Italian edition of 'La pista dei Navajo' targets an older audience than that of the original French edition, one that is familiar with the Italian tradition of western comics as well as with 'revisionist' American western movies of the 1970s (e.g. *Soldier Blue* by Ralph Nelson and *Jeremiah Johnson* by Sydney Pollack). These same readers, who had possibly grown accustomed to later, more 'adult' developments of the Blueberry character and stories, were also thought to be more responsive to a language that was much coarser than that used in both *Pilote* and *Il Corriere dei Piccoli*.

The two reprints published by Nuova Frontiera in 1988 and 1990, while keeping the same translation, nevertheless seem to address more specific segments than the 1982 edition. The 1988 publication is, in fact, smaller in format and printed in black and white, thus resembling the Bonelli notebook format and appealing to readers of popular comics. On the other hand, the 1990 publication is a hard bound and otherwise unchanged version of the 1982 one, and is thus targeted at collectors and more educated (and wealthier) readers.

The latest edition published by by Alessandro Editore in 2005 goes even further in this direction. It is a hard bound and rather expensive volume, distributed in regular bookshops and specialized comic bookshops. It is based on the 'updated' French edition and contains a translation which is extremely 'respectful' of the original. In functional terms, this latest translation could be said to be 'documentary' (Nord 1997:47-50), in the sense that the French text can almost be reconstructed working back from the translation. Being almost literal and very close to the original French syntax, it is as a result both more 'literary' and more 'overtly' a translation (House 1981/1997).

The general translation strategy of the 2005 edition could be characterized as 'foreignizing' (Venuti 1995), in as much as it brings the reader closer to the original text, replicating French linguistic structures and lexis, as well as other features of the original such as an 'exotic' characterization through code-switching between the readers' and the characters' native language (French or Italian and English, Spanish and Native American languages). On the other hand both the 1971 and the 1982 editions respond to 'domesticating' strategies, in as much as they are adapted to the linguistic (and graphical) expectations of two diverging readerships, children in the case of the 1971 edition and adults in the case of the 1982 edition, in both cases a different age group from that of the original French general readership.

4. Conclusion

Comics translation has often been described as an instance of constrained translation (e.g. Mayoral et al. 1988, Rabadán 1991, Zanettin 1998, Valero Garcés 2000). This term, initially applied by Titford (1982) to subtitling, is now usually understood to include the translation of comics, songs, advertising and any type of audiovisual and multimedia translation, the latter including film subtitling and dubbing, as well as software and website localization (Hernández-Bartolomé and Mendiluce-Cabrera 2004). In a 'constrained translation approach', the focus of analysis is on the linguistic features of comics, while the non-verbal components are only seen as constraints that the translator must take into account. Such an approach may be useful, for example, to investigate how the verbal components of comics can or have been translated given the constraints posed by the size of balloons and the visual components.[16]

However, localization can be seen not only as a subcategory of constrained translation, that dealing with the 'translation' of electronic products, but also as a different perspective from which to approach translated products – i.e. an approach which deals with the production and distribution of material objects for/in different locales (Pym 2004). In a 'localization approach', the focus is on a production process in which different actors are involved in addition to the translator proper, and the work of the 'translator' is related to the general context and workflow, which leads to the creation of a target product that is different from the source, not only in terms of its verbal components. In this broader sense, which is indeed that of the LISA definition quoted in the opening section of this article, a localization approach may usefully be applied not only to the 'translation' (in its broader sense) of software, websites and videogames, but also to all types of products, especially those in which non-verbal elements play a major part in shaping the information offer available to the end user/viewer (comics, marketing material, films, TV programmes, etc.). Such an approach may of course also be applicable to written, printed products such as books. However, while translated comics are commercial products and textual artefacts in which 'translation', understood as the 'replacement of strings of natural language', is only a component of the process, in the book publishing industry 'translation proper' may arguably be seen as coinciding to a large extent with the localization process as a whole.

I would like to suggest that a localization approach to the translation of comics may provide some useful insights into this practice. The adaptation of both verbal and visual signs to the target locale can be better understood by relating these changes to the wider context of production and reception of comics, and by looking at the internationalization/localization and updating practices which characterize the publication of a foreign comic in translation. Thus the Italian translations of *La piste des Navajos* can be seen as successive product adaptations, responding each time to changing target users. Together with the reprints and republications of local, native comics they can be considered as product updates, localized for diachronically as well as for geographically different readerships.

References

Primary Sources
Bonelli, Gianluigi and Aurelio Galeppini (1948 -) *Tex*, Milano: Sergio Bonelli Editore.
Charlier, Jean-Michel and Jean Giraud (1965/1996) *La piste des Navajos*, Dargaud [*La pista dei Navajos*, Crespi Editore 1971; Edizioni Nuova Frontiera 1982; Alessandro Editore 2005].

---

[16] See for example Koponen's suggestion that space limitations may restrict the translator's use of strategies like explicitation (2004:18).

Martina, Guido and Giovan Battista Carpi (1969) *Paperinik*, Walt Disney.

Sclavi, Tiziano (1986 -) *Dylan Dog*, Milano: Sergio Bonelli Editore.

Tufts, Warren (1949-1954) *Casey Ruggles*, Mountain Home, Tennessee: Manuscript Press.

Secondary Sources

Botto, Armando (2004) 'Le pubblicazioni Disney in Italia' [Disney publications in Italy], *Gli articoli di Papersera* 2(3) (online) http://www.papersera.net/articoli/alln3.pdf (Accessed 30 February 2006).

Busatta, Franco (1998) *Come Tex non c' è nessuno. Storia di un eroe e del suo editore* [There's no one like Tex. The history of a hero and his publisher], Milano: Punto Zero.

Castagno, Paolo (2003) 'Paperinik e il diabolico censore' [Paperinik and the censor from hell], *Gli articoli di Papersera* 1(4) (online) http://www.papersera.net/articoli/aln4.pdf (Accessed 30 February 2006).

D'Arcangelo, Adele and Federico Zanettin (2004) 'Dylan Dog Goes to the USA: A North-American Translation of an Italian Comic Book Series', *Across Languages and Cultures* 5(2): 187-210.

Detti, Ermanno (1984) *Il fumetto fra scuola e cultura* [Comics between school and culture], Firenze: La Nuova Italia.

Esselink, Bert (2000) *A Practical Guide to Localization*, Amsterdam & Philadelphia: John Benjamins.

------ (2003) 'Localisation and Translation', in Harold Somers (ed.) *Computers and Translation. A Translator's Guide*, Amsterdam and Philadelphia: John Benjamins, 67-104.

Fry, Deborah and Arle Lommel (2003) *Lisa. The Localization Primer. Second Revised Edition*, SMTP Marketing & LISA (online) http://www.cit.gu.edu.au/~davidt/cit3611/LISAprimer.pdf (Accessed 30 February 2006).

Giordani, Mauro (2000) *Alla scoperta della Bande Dessinèe. Cento anni di fumetto franco belga. Tutti i personaggi e gli autori del fumetto franco belga in Italia fino all'anno 2000* [Discovering the Bande Dessinée. One hundred years of Franco-Belgian comics. All the characters and authors of Franco-Belgian comics in Italy up until the year 2000], Bologna: Alessandro Editore.

Groth, Gary and Robert Fiore (1988) *The New Comics*, New York: Berkley Books.

Hernández-Bartolomé, Ana Isabel and Gustavo Mendiluce-Cabrera (2004) 'Audesc: Translating Images into Words for Spanish Visually Impaired People', *META* 49(2):264-277.

House, Juliane (1981) *A Model for Translation Quality Assessment*, Tübingen: Gunter Narr.

------ (1997) *Translation Quality Assessment: A Model Revisited*, Tübingen: Gunter Narr.

Iori, Walter (2002) 'Quando tradurre vuol dire creare. In ricordo di Gian Luigi Bonelli' [When translation means creation. Remembering Gian Luigi Bonelli]', *Il fumetto* 11(44):25.

Jüngst, Heike Elisabeth (2004) 'Japanese Comics in Germany', *Perspectives: Studies in Translatology* 12(2):83-105.

Khepri Comics Online (n.d.) 'Interview with Alfredo Castelli' (online) http://www.khepri.com/i-bvzm.htm (Accessed 30 February 2006).

Koponen, Maarit (2004) *Wordplay in Donald Duck Comics and their Finnish Translations*, Postgraduate thesis, Helsinki: Department of English, University of Helsinki.

Marín, Rafael (2001) 'Blueberry: la odisea de un desclasado', *Yellow Kid* 1:49-53 (online) http://www.gigamesh.com/historico.html (Accessed 30 February 2006).

McCloud, Scott (2006) *Making Comics*, New York, London, Toronto & Sydney: Harper.

Mayoral Asensio, Roberto, Dorothy Kelly and Natividad Gallardo (1988) 'The Concept of Constrained Translation. Non-Linguistic Perspectives on Translation', *Meta* 33(3):356-367.

Nord, Christiane (1997) *Translating as a Purposeful Activity*, Manchester: St Jerome.

Paglieri, Claudio (2003) *Non son degno di Tex. Vita, morte e miracoli del mitico ranger* [I don't deserve Tex. Life and adventures of the famous Texas ranger], Milano: Marsilio.

Pym, Anthony (2004) *The Moving Text: Localization, Translation and Distribution*, Amsterdam & Philadelphia: John Benjamins.

Rabadán, Rosa (1991) *Equivalencia y Traducción. Problemática de la equivalencia translémica inglés-español* [Translation and Equivalence. Questioning English-Spanish Translemic Equivalente], León: Universidad de León.

Raffaelli, Luca (1997) *Il fumetto* [The comics], Milano: Il saggiatore.

Restaino, Franco (2004) *Storia del fumetto. Da Yellow Kid ai Manga* [A History of Comics. From Yellow Kid to Manga], Milano: UTET.

Rifas, Leonard (2004) 'Globalizing Comic Books from Below: How Manga Came to America', *International Journal of Comic Art* 6(2):138-171.

Sabin, Roger (1993) *Adult Comics*, London & New York: Routledge.

Scillitani, Giovanni (2004) 'Il Corriere dei Piccoli. Fumetti anni 70', *P70 News* (online) http://www.pagine70.com/vmnews/wmview.php?ArtID=527 (Accessed 30 February 2006).

Scholand, Michael (2002) 'Localización de videojuegos' [Videogames localization], *Tradumàtica* 1 (online) http://www.fti.uab.es/tradumatica/revista/articles/mscholand/art.htm (Accessed 30 February 2006).

Titford, Christopher (1982) 'Subtitling – Constrained Translation', *Lebende Sprachen* 27(3):113-116.

Valero Garcés, Carmen (2000) 'La traducción del cómic: retos, estrategias y resultados' [The Translation of Comics: Challenges, Strategies and Results], *Trans: Revista de traductología* 4:75-88.

Venuti, Lawrence (1995) *The Translator's Invisibility: A History of Translation*, London & New York: Routledge.

Yunker, John (ed.) (2003) *Beyond Borders: Web Globalization Strategies,* Indianapolis, IN: New Riders Publishing.

Zanettin, Federico (1998) 'Fumetti e traduzione multimediale' [Comics and multimedia translation], *inTRAlinea* 1 (online) http://www.intralinea.it/volumes/eng_open.php?id=P156 (Accessed 30 February 2006).

------ (2005) 'Comics in Translation Studies. An Overview and Suggestions for Research', in *Tradução e Interculturalismo. VII Seminário de Tradução Científica e Técnica em Língua Portuguesa – 2004*, Lisboa: União Latina, 93-98.

------ (2007) 'La traduzione dei fumetti. Approcci linguistici, semiotici e storico-culturali', in Vittoria Intonti, Graziella Todisco and Maristella Gatto (eds) *La traduzione. Lo stato dell'arte/ Translation. The State of the Art,* Ravenna: Longo, 137-150.

Zitawi, Jehan (2004) *The Translation of Disney Comics in the Arab World: A Pragmatic Perspective*, Unpublished PhD Thesis, Manchester: CTIS, University of Manchester.

10 *The Winx* as a Challenge to Globalization
Translations from Italy to the Rest of the World

ELENA DI GIOVANNI
University of Macerata, Italy

Children and teenagers throughout the world might not realize it, but major TV chan-nels in 130 countries are showing, for the first time ever, a cartoon series which started out in Italy and is accompanied by comic magazines in one-third of these countries. The Winx *Club cartoons and comics, produced in Italy as a response to the growing passion for all things magical and supernatural and translated into approximately thirty languages, runs counter to the usual cultural traffic which sees translation trans-ferring entertainment – and the cultural implications embedded in it – mainly from the US to the rest of the world. As translation seems to be ideally placed to observe the effects of this reversed flow of texts for young audiences, as well as to reveal traces of an unusual source language/culture within the target English versions, this paper sets out to explore translation strategies at a macro and micro-level, from cartoons to comics. Introduced by an analysis of the hegemonic practices often hidden behind the production, distribution and reception of texts addressed to mass audiences, making reference to film studies, sociology and translation studies, the examples provided aim to highlight the small-scale, but nonetheless somewhat revolutionary role which cartoons and comics can play within the globalized media market. Limited as the perception of an unusual source can be through the English translations of the* Winx, *it can still be positively interpreted as a step towards a redefinition of what has so far been an almost unidirectional, unquestioned flow of media productions.*

Trapped in a vortex of multimedia products, captured by the entrancing power of printed and animated heroes, young and teenage viewers and readers in all corners of the world grow up amidst a huge variety of texts[1] which often reveal common features and are constructed so as to produce similar stimuli.

The ever-increasing pace of globalization of multimedia products, especially those which are addressed to large audiences, allow for an unprecedented, rapid and thorough diffusion of texts to be read, listened to or watched on the big or small screen.

However, globalization is only apparently egalitarian: on the whole, it has been for a long time – and still is today – a Western-driven phenomenon, and when it comes to the media the overall flow of technologies and texts, of the media and the messages (McLuhan and Fiore 1967), is mainly controlled by the US. America has, over time, set the standards for the production as well as reception of multimedia texts, and it still plays a major role in orienting the creation, translation, distribution and success of products.

---

[1] The term 'text' is here to be interpreted as a multimodal unit comprising elements from at least the verbal and visual code. Such features, common to cartoons and comics, are of the utmost importance for the creation and reception of the texts themselves, and their interaction has to be the starting point for all translational processes (Gambier and Gottlieb 2001).

Resistance to an unavoidably biased circulation of texts is often advocated, at times overtly by means of theoretical or politically-inspired protests against power asymmetries, but also covertly, through practices which somehow indirectly attack the predominance of standards imposed by the main drivers of globalization.

The media are undoubtedly major purveyors of communication and cultural orientation, as well as the main vehicles through which biased globalizing trends travel. This paper will focus on cartoons and comics for young and teenage audiences, putting in the spotlight an interesting case of resistance to standardized production and reception with a view to examining its limited but nonetheless significant anti-globalizing impact.

The corpus of texts analyzed here is part of the *Winx Club*. Made famous by a cartoon series featuring five young fairies from the planet of Magix, the trademark has been developed through a number of other products, from gadgets and clothes to computer games and a successful series of comics. Taking into account only the Winx cartoons and comics, we shall see that the worldwide success of these Italian-made products can be analyzed by relying almost entirely upon translational solutions. As an act of communication in itself, and a determining factor in the shaping of taste, reception and also cultural identities, translation here becomes an essential parameter to measure the effects of the anti-globalizing nature of such texts. As Michael Cronin states in *Translation and Globalization*, translation can make an important contribution to "genuine biocultural diversity in the contemporary world" (2003:73), especially when it is able to bring to the fore minor languages and cultures which become the source for translation into the most common language of the world and the most powerful vehicle of media products: English.

In the following sections, the success story of the Winx cartoons and comics will be discussed, first by taking into account their overall distribution and the role played by English within it, and subsequently by commenting on translation strategies and choices, with a view to highlighting those little traces of resistance to globalization which are, as we shall see, often involuntarily left to surface in the passage from Italian to English.

1.   Mass Production, Translation and the Media

Before analyzing the Winx cartoons and comics, it may be useful to reflect upon certain broader concepts whose weight can also be felt on these texts and their distribution. In this section, I will attempt to consider such huge and somehow mercurial issues as mass audience, consumption, hegemony and resistance, to conclude by relating all of my remarks to the translation of multimedia texts and to the case of the *Winx Club*. Throughout this section, reference will be made to media studies, the social sciences and translation studies, in an attempt to clarify the current impact of media products and their worldwide distribution, as well as the possibilities offered to products and producers which, to a varying extent, go against the tide.

A much-cited popular comment by Marshall McLuhan (see e.g. McLuhan and Fiore 1967), "the medium is the message", suggests that mass media carry 'mass messages': these messages are profoundly influenced by the media themselves and can generally be identified and classified thanks to recurring patterns of narrative, filmic and ideological construction. As McLuhan predicted in the nineteen sixties, when worldwide homogenization of cultures and tastes through the media was just beginning to be evident, the media are not only containers but generators of messages. In the decades that followed, the ever-increasing control of the media's potential and power by a limited number of agents has fostered the canonization of specific narrative structures and strategies, which have been endlessly exploited, often without considering their ideological implications. These practices have been marked by the development of a large number of Hollywood genres, and in terms of cartoon production they can be related to the production of major companies such as Disney or Warner Brothers.

But how did this 'massification' of the media – and of the societies which they influence and shape – come to be? A response to this question may be partially found in the words of the American sociologist James Lull (2004:114), who states that

> as Western societies became industrialized and modernized over the past two
> centuries, observers realized that the pace and scale of all social life were expand-
> ing rapidly. In the process, modern societies were creating not only mass media
> and mass communication, but also mass industrial production, mass education,
> mass health care, mass marketing, mass taste, mass everything, And who lives in
> the midst of such massification? The masses, of course.

As a result of ever-increasing modernization and technological developments, the worldwide dissemination of products, tastes and trends has brought about a sort of wholesale massification, whereby everything can potentially be made available to everybody. With the advent of globalization –a word which has been used and abused in books, news reports, newspapers and TV shows over the past few decades – the possibility of spreading any message to every corner of the world through the media has given way to a relentless dissemination of texts, firstly through the press and then increasingly through audiovisual channels, bringing along with it the illusion of equal sharing of media and messages. While technology has made it possible for people around the globe, including children and teenagers with their specially-designed products, to have access to TV, cinemas and the news, major producers and distributors have progressively imposed their control on the media, their own standards for production and, most of all, for audience reception.

Hegemony, as "a process of convergence, consent and subordination" (Lull 2000:54), has come to be a reality within mass media production and consumption. Consent and subordination here stand for (passive) acceptance of choices and viewpoints, whereas convergence points to a more interesting tendency, especially with regard to texts conceived for young audiences. Convergence suggests an increasing uniformity in terms of the creation of media products; it implies movement towards internationally-acknowledged and accepted ideologies, ultimately opting for assimilation rather than distinction to achieve 'mass-success'. Thus, all minor – or simply non-American – subjects, be they directors or creators of multimedia texts, generally tend to conform to the standards set and maintained by major distributors and producers to achieve success, suffocating plurality of expression while still trying to claim originality and difference.

At this point, it may be worth taking a rapid look at the history of the American film and TV industry, as James Monaco does in *How to Read a Film. Movies, Media, Multimedia* (2000), and see as he does how movies and, subsequently, television have provided the cultural format for the discovery and description of national identity, "whether they simply reflected the national culture that already existed or produced a fantasy of their own that eventually came to be accepted as real" (2000:262). Alongside audiovisual media, American culture has certainly come to define its own identity through the press, with daily newspapers and other publications such as comics shaping the perception of young audiences from an early age. It is no secret, for instance, that Disney's cartoons have embodied the American myth and supported a strong national identity since their very early days. As for comics, after the crash of the Stock Market in 1929 America went through the Golden Age of printed stories, whose most glorious period spanned over a decade and was welcomed as a positive reaction to the hardships of a financial breakdown which touched every American citizen. The Golden Age of comics saw the birth and success of a host of new, two-dimensional myths, spearheaded by the much beloved, brave and politically-correct national superhero Superman.

If the growth and development of the media in the US, throughout the first half of the last century, were spurred by a will to strengthen national identity (Belton 1999:2), major distributors as well as policy makers soon realized the economic, political and ideological potential of worldwide dissemination and control of the ever more successful media. Thus, throughout the second half of the century the American media industry has strived to maintain overall control of its international influence, leaving a very limited space for the appearance of other agents on the global media marketplace. All of this has been necessarily accompanied by language policies which have helped to reinforce the international diffusion of English and have relegated other languages and cultures to minor positions.

However, over the past decade or so there seems to have been a surge of texts from countries other than the US, or rather an increase in visibility and acceptance of difference which has come mainly as a result of commitment, investments and often a good dose of courage on the part of new agents. This can be felt particularly within the domain of printed and audiovisual products addressed to young audiences. Let us consider, for instance, the great success achieved by Japanese comics and cartoons, which have imposed their own conventions and style while also instigating a review of the most widespread canons of audience reception. In terms of television cartoons, public and private TV networks across Europe nowadays feature productions from a host of different countries, from France to Croatia, from Spain to Italy.[2]

---

[2] By observing, for instance, the daily programming of two major TV channels in Italy (the national channel Raidue and the privately-owned Italia Uno), it becomes evident that young viewers are currently exposed to a plurality of products, reflecting specific cultures and languages. While Raidue favours products addressed to very young viewers, material mainly produced in European countries and often containing strong educational messages, privately-owned Italia Uno tends to privilege Asian cartoons for the not-too-young, coming from Japan but also from other countries such as Korea and Taiwan.

In translational terms, although the American overflow of printed and audiovisual texts for the young is still predominant, in Europe and especially in the rest of the world, the appearance of alternative 'voices' implies the reversal of the most typical linguistic and cultural traffic where English is the only source aimed at countless target cultures. Although this is far from being a regular phenomenon, whenever English becomes the target culture it allows for the filtering of certain linguistic and social specificities belonging to other realities which are normally expressed only within their own linguistic boundaries. Translation, as Spivak says, leaves "traces of the other in the self" (2004:379), scattering through the printed and audiovisual media traces of 'uncommon' selves and making small but meaningful moves towards a greater variety and away from centralization and assimilation (Cronin 2003:42-75). Therefore, beyond the dynamics of mass media productions for the young, the major role played by translation, as well as its great potential, become more evident.

When the production, distribution and, of course, translation of multimedia texts imply overturning the usual linguistic, cultural and, in the case of products addressed to the young, educational traffic, they deserve special attention and, to this purpose, translation strategies and solutions can prove especially illuminating. In the next sections, the keys to the success of the *Winx Club* cartoons and comics, as well as their dynamics of resistance to globalizing trends, will be observed through translation.

2.   *The Winx* Cartoons and Comics: Assimilation and Resistance

In order to proceed with an adequate evaluation of the scope of translation and world-wide distribution of the *Winx*, let us first of all introduce some important facts and figures. The *Winx Club* is a trademark created and owned by Rainbow S.r.l., an Italian company unusually located in Macerata, in a provincial area of central Italy, far from the usual routes of production and distribution of media products. The cartoon series, launched in Italy in 2003, has been translated and broadcast in over 130 countries, covering the whole of Europe and reaching as far as the Philippines, New Zealand and India. Already distributed in part of the US and in Canada, from May 2005 the *Winx* have been regularly appearing on Cartoon Network, thus reaching all of the United States as well as most satellite broadcasters worldwide.

After the huge success of the first cartoon series the Winx magazine was launched, first in Italy and subsequently in an impressive number of countries: from Norway to Turkey, from Israel to Malaysia, and by late spring 2005 reaching several countries in North and South America.[3]

---

[3] "La prima serie è stata venduta in 130 Paesi tra cui la Francia, la Germania, l'Australia e anche la Scandinavia, uno degli Stati mai toccati finora dall'animazione italiana. E in più le magiche Winx sono riuscite a espugnare anche il difficile mercato americano. Negli Stati Uniti infatti, è prevista per la prima volta la messa in onda di un prodotto d'animazione italiano" (Salerno 2005: online); [lit.: The first series has been sold to over 130 countries including France, Germany, Australia and also the Scandinavian peninsula, with countries which had never before been reached by Italian cartoons. Moreover, the magic Winx have incredibly managed to conquer even the difficult American market. As a matter of fact, the *Winx Club* is the first Italian series to be broadcast within the US].

It goes without saying that the role played by translation in the successful distribution and continuous development of the *Winx Club* has been of the utmost importance. As for the cartoons, the majority of episodes are written in Italian, to be subsequently translated into English and a few other languages directly. The English translation has, in turn, worked as a pilot version for the adaptation into a number of world languages, but the imprint provided by the Italian language and by a rather exclusive cartoon-making style have helped preserve the special flavour of the *Winx*.

On the other hand, the creation of different versions of the magazine has followed a twofold strategy: while the comics featured in each number have been written in Italian, translated into English and other languages according to the scheme illustrated for the cartoons, the rest of the contents (interviews, music and fashion reviews, games, etc.) have been designed locally according to the trends and tastes of the teenage public. Once again, English has played the role of pilot version for the translation of the comics into a number of languages, but we shall see how the influence of Italian can be felt even through the words and expressions used in the English translation.

Throughout the year 2005, the *Winx Club* was adapted for the stage, and the five fairies appeared on all possible gadgets, from clothes to mobile phones, from decorated cakes to bicycles. All of these by-products have helped spread the popularity of the trademark even further, while also fuelling competition with the rival Disney series W.I.T.C.H. This competition has so far proved fruitful for the *Winx Club*, although the latter was created after the launch of the W.I.T.C.H. comics and are, according to some critics, inspired by this American-brand series which was itself created in Italy. Whether this is true or false, the success of the *Winx* remains undeniable, and it leads us to wonder what sort of secret formula lies behind it.

Undoubtedly, the recipe for worldwide success entails a certain neutralization of culture-specific elements, a strategy which is normally seen as being against the enhancement of diversity and 'locality'. However, this tendency is inherent in the very nature of the *Winx Club* and their adventures, which require a fictional, magical, glittering and unearthly world.

As to the choice of the domain of magic for the *Winx* adventures, it has clearly not been made in a vacuum, but rather on the wave of an international frenzy for all-things-magic, spurred by the success of Harry Potter and similar heroes. In this sense, the *Winx* can perhaps be said to reveal a somewhat assimilative tendency, which has oriented the general choice of an extremely popular topic but is also original. The critics generally agree that the five animated teenage fairies make up an original set of characters whose physical traits have been inspired by such young, popular stars as Britney Spears and Jennifer Lopez and whose personalities, movements and attitudes have been the object of long and detailed studies:

> Le hanno disegnate pensando a star come Jennifer Lopez e Britney Spears; le hanno vestite come tutte le ragazzine di 16-17 anni adorerebbero vestirsi, top variopinti, stivaloni aggressivi, tutine scintillanti; le hanno dotate di caratteri

diversi, ma complementari; le hanno messe tutte insieme, un po' femministe e un po' modaiole, in una squadra dal fascino imbattibile che ha raccolto tifosi in tutto il mondo. (*La Stampa*, 22 April 2005)

[Lit. They have been drawn with stars such as Jennifer Lopez and Britney Spears in mind; they have been dressed in clothes all 16-17-year-olds would love to wear (multi-coloured mini-tops, aggressive thigh-boots, sparkling and skimpy outfits); they have been endowed with different but complementary characters; they have been put together, with a hint of feminism and a passion for fashion, to form a glamorous team of unbeatable appeal which has captured fans all over the world].

Even though they are made to move against a fancy background, with the planet of Magix being defined as "a parallel world, not too far from the Earth",[4] the young fairies' attitudes as well as some of their expressions mark a departure from the conventionalized characters imposed by major cartoon producers such as Disney. This 'distance' from the widespread American standards can be first observed in the traits used to draw the five fairies (Figure 10.1, centre fold), whose features bring them closer to Japanese animation than to the Disney-style, positive female characters, typically drawn with wide, dreamlike eyes and romantic, fuzzy outlines.

Before moving on to analyze translation choices and effects, it is essential to stress that, on the whole, the *Winx Club*'s resistance to standardization in multimedia products for the young can be ascribed to their creation and production process, which are meticulously carried out in Italy and are subject to precise technical, distributional and promotional strategies imposed by the creators. However, these issues will not be the object of detailed investigation in this paper, whose main interest lies in identifying hints at an unusual narrating voice, hints which are allowed to surface in the English versions, often involuntarily but never without a meaning. As a matter of fact, slight as these glimpses of the narrating voice may be, they should still be appreciated for supporting plurality of expression and, hopefully, diversity in media production and reception.

3.   Translations against the Tide: *The Winx* from Italian into English

To quote James Lull again, "we learn who 'we' are and who 'they' are largely through language" (2000:139). And if language undoubtedly guides our experiences in life, participates in and determines the growth and acknowledgement of our encyclopaedia (Eco 1994:143-151), so does translation, even though at varying degrees for different countries and through different media.

Translation of mass media products, as already stated, has been and still is generally dominated by the unidirectional flow of texts translated from English (mainly American English) into the languages of the world, with the ensuing influence of the source culture

---

[4] From the introductory page of each issue of the *Winx Magazine*.

and its media policies which are, of course, reflected through language use. As Henrik Gottlieb declares in an article on the language-political implications of audiovisual translation (2004:90),

> Hollywood reigns supreme, and the American media industry is still unchallenged when it comes to export figures and influence worldwide.

However, the case which is to be discussed here seems to somehow deny this unchallenged supremacy and, as was pointed out earlier, it seems to be more than a mere drop in the ocean of multimedia production for young viewers and readers.

Analyzing what he defines as "the (all too rare) situation where foreign-language productions are screened or broadcast in English-speaking countries" (2004:92), Gottlieb states that, when they reach a foreign country and its audience, these productions seem to be vainly in search of an audience, and their translation amounts to a mutilation or, at best, a domestication to conform to anglophone norms and tastes. In this sense, the *Winx Club* translations into English stand out as a twofold instance of resistance to multimedia globalization: they imply a reversal of the usual flow of media products and, more importantly, the producers' management and supervision of all English versions of the *Winx* printed and audiovisual products ensures an overall Italian control of the translation process.

Looking at instances of translation from Italian into English for these rather unique products will mainly involve finding a few traces of a new 'self' within the language of an uncommon 'other',[5] and identifying them as traces of resistance, as part of a positive, creative, beneficial diversity, for a plurality of voices and strategies which is especially important when it comes to products addressed to young audiences.

Even though talking of anti-globalization with reference to this very special case may seem too strong, as the term often evokes ideologically-loaded reflections, I will only take anti-globalization here to mean silent, small-scale but nonetheless successful resistance to the mainstream, American-dominated traffic of multimedia texts for the young.

Anti-globalization, then, constitutes the expression of a different voice and viewpoint, which are reflected through translation and scattered worldwide by means of successful audiovisual and printed texts. These phenomena will be observed, in the following paragraphs, in terms of micro-level and macro-level solutions, first of all with reference to the *Winx* cartoons and their journey from Italian to English and subsequently to the comics.

---

[5] The whole issue of cultural representation, where the often unbalanced relationships between the 'self' and the 'other' are taken into consideration, has been – and still is – widely discussed within the framework of postcolonial studies. Over the past decade, after the so-called 'cultural turn' in translation studies, issues of postcolonialism and cultural representation have permeated the study of translation, thanks to the contributions of outstanding scholars from the West as well as the non-West. For further reference see, for instance, Bassnett and Trivedi (1999).

3.1   Cartoons

Upon watching one or two episodes of the *Winx* first cartoon series, many international viewers may not be struck by huge differences from other cartoons addressed to four-to-thirteen year olds.[6] However, even non-experts in the field of audiovisual productions and translations, after being exposed to these cartoons, will be struck by a somewhat original flavour which belongs to these texts and which can be felt in terms of narrative and character development (see previous paragraph), educational purpose, and also in terms of language.

Focusing on this last element we can say that, in general terms, having been conceived for worldwide distribution, the original Italian versions of the *Winx* cartoons are generally characterized by the use of standard language, which is enriched by variations in register but, on the whole, rarely appears to be too culture-specific. Such an overall description of the Italian language used for the original versions, however, should not be misleading: scripts are filled with puns, clever gags, informal expressions, catchy tunes and a number of other elements which play a vital role in ensuring success for the series but unavoidably lead to some instances of neutralization in the target versions.

Therefore, before moving on to consider some examples from the scripts it is important to stress that the source language – and inevitably the culture to which it belongs – is in some cases made to surface directly but, even more often, its importance is felt *in absentia* throughout the target English versions of the *Winx* cartoons. In other words, by taking into account the tangible traces of the source language which emerge from the English versions, as well as by comparing the richness of the original Italian scripts with more neutral solutions for the translations, the uncommonly overwhelming role of Italian as a source language will be highlighted.

To this end, let us start by considering an excerpt from the first series episode entitled 'La Palude di Melmamora', which becomes 'Blackmud Swamp' in the English version. The following lines are uttered towards the beginning of the episode by two of the specialists, the young and smart guys who are trained to become warriors and skilful users of magic powers in a school not too far from the fairies' college of Althea. After Techna, one of the five Winx, accuses the self-confident and ambitious specialist Riven of having too easily lost track of a troll, he provides the following explanation in Italian while his friend Timmy makes a joke about the mishap:

> Techna: Un troll? Trasportavate un troll e l'avete lasciato fuggire?
> Riven: Ehi, noi non abbiamo lasciato fuggire nessuno! C'è stato un incidente…
>   la navetta ha perso quota e…
> Timmy: … e il troll ha tolto il disturbo!
> [lit. Techna: A troll? You were transporting a troll and you let him escape?

---

[6] Information about the age group to which the *Winx* cartoons are addressed, along with other data provided in this paper, were supplied by the managing team at Rainbow S.r.l. during two interviews carried out in March and December 2005.

Riven:	Hey, we didn't let anyone escape! There was an accident, we lost altitude…
Timmy:	…and the troll waved us goodbye!]

The English translation of this very brief exchange reveals one instance of neutralization, which of course does no harm to the success of the cartoon but, in fact, leads to a rather awkward exchange. The words uttered by Timmy in English do not contain any ironic remark, as this is replaced by a mere restatement of the facts which have occurred.

Official translation	Literal translation
Techna: You were transporting a troll and you guys let him escape? *Riven:* We didn't let anyone escape! There was an accident…we lost altitude… *Timmy:* Mechanical failure.	*Techna:* A troll? You were transporting a troll and you let him escape? *Riven:* Hey, we didn't let anyone escape! There was an accident, we lost altitude… *Timmy:* …and the troll waved us goodbye!

On the whole, even though a number of instances of neutralization can be found in the English translations of the *Winx* cartoons, they reveal few cases of awkward translation and generally prove to be both adequate and acceptable (Toury 1995), as is demonstrated by the great success achieved by the *Winx* cartoons in countries where English is the official language (UK, US and Singapore). Nonetheless, a number of difficulties arose in the translation process, in the attempt to maintain the original flavour of the series while striving to adapt it to a different language, the culture(s) connected to it and the habits/expectations of viewers accustomed to the more widely accepted American standards. In most cases, difficulties have been cleverly overcome before the cartoons have reached the English-speaking audience, but let us consider one interesting example of literal translation from the Italian version which has caused a number of problems[7] and has led to further revision.

The theme song which introduces each episode, originally written in Italian, was first translated literally into English and recorded in Italy to accompany the first English episodes of the *Winx* cartoons. However, while the Italian tune turned out to be extremely catchy and worked very well, in the English version only the catchy rhythm was left, with the lyrics proving awkward in terms of meaning as well as pronunciation, as the English song was recorded in Italy by an Italian singer.

The following transcript of the first refrain for the two versions[8] will clarify the case in point:

---

[7] Information obtained through interviews with the managing team at Rainbow S.r.l., carried out in March and December 2005.

[8] The transcript for the English song results from the comparison of several unofficial versions. There seems to be no official record of this English song available, either accompanying DVDs or on the Internet.

Se tu lo vuoi, tu lo sarai, una di noi...
Winx, la tua mano nella mia,
più forza ci darà, uno sguardo e vinceremo insieme...
Winx, un sorriso è una magia, che luce ci darà,
solo un gesto e voleremo ancora...
Winx![9]

If you desire, you can become, one of our bunch...
Winx, if your hand is warm in mine,
it will give us greater power, with a feeling we'll be sure five winners...
Winx, with a smile you can't enchant, and then lighting up our work,
with a feeling we can take off, watch us...
Winx!!

When the first series was successfully broadcast in several East Asian countries – including English-speaking Singapore – with the awkward-sounding English song, fans of the cartoons expressed their doubts about the theme song in discussion forums on the Internet as well as by means of letters to the national distributors. When the producers decided to tackle the American and British market, they submitted the cartoons to one of the most important distributors worldwide and the latter immediately saw the potential damage to the success of the *Winx* cartoons deriving from a lack of coherence and fluency in the theme song. Therefore, the producing company had a new tune specifically written and recorded for the series to be distributed in the United Kingdom and the US, with lyrics and rhythm that are totally different from the original Italian song. The first, Italian-made, literal English version is nonetheless still used for the cartoons distributed in other English-speaking countries, and is still the object of long discussions amongst the thousands of fans who visit the more or less officially acknowledged websites dedicated to the five Italian-born fairies.

After considering translation strategies on a micro-level, let us now focus on some interesting micro-level choices. One of the main difficulties in translating the *Winx* cartoons arose when having to adapt names of places and characters which had been cleverly invented by Italian scriptwriters. Among the countless examples let us quote, for instance, "palude di Melmamora" [lit. swamp of dark mud] and "bosco di Selvafosca" [lit. dark and gloomy forest], where a number of adventures involving the five fairies take place, or the specialists' trainer "Professor Codatorta" [lit. Professor twisted tail], the cook at the fairies' college of Althea called "Signor Mastrosfoglia" [lit. Master 'layer of pasta'[10]] and the young boys' training institute named "scuola di Fonterossa" [lit. Red Fountain School]. The two place names have been replaced by "Blackmud Swamp" and "Gloomy Woodforest", with

---

[9] [lit. If you wish so, you can become one of us...
Winx, your hand in mine will give us greater power,
just one look and we will win together...
Winx, one smile is like magic, it will enlighten us,
just one sign and we will fly again...
Winx!]

[10] 'Sfoglia' is an Italian word used to designate the layers of fresh pasta used to make lasagne.

an undoubted loss of effect due to the necessary substitution of the creative juxtaposition of old-fashioned and standard Italian words, whereas for the third, fourth and fifth examples two different solutions have been envisaged. While "Professor Codatorta" and "Mastrosfoglia" have been left unchanged in the English version, thus leaving traces of the Italian flavour of the *Winx* cartoons, the school name, clearly inspired by the area of Fonterossa where the producers' headquarters are located, has been literally rendered as "Redfountain School". The local flavour, in the latter case, cannot be perceived by non-Italian viewers, but it proves that the *Winx* cartoons do carry a number of little references of their original context. These little cultural traces have in fact mainly been used by the creators of the series as a source of inspiration for the *Winx* magic universe rather than as deliberate references, but their presence somehow stands witness to their origin.

3.2   *Comics*

Leaving the cartoons behind to take a look at the almost equally successful *Winx* magazines, a slightly different approach needs to be taken. First of all, it is important to point out that translation takes numerous guises in the adaptation of the *Winx* magazines in English: the comics are the common core which somehow unifies all national editions, while the contents of the magazine as well as its internal structure are made to vary in each country according to its young readers' tastes and expectations. As a matter of fact, while the comics are subject to an 'ordinary' process of interlingual transfer from Italian into English (or other languages) and are featured in every edition, all the other elements are designed anew, including the gadgets which are added to each number. Thus, for instance, the English versions of the magazine which are distributed in Singapore, Hong Kong, the United Kingdom and the US will only have the translated comics in common, while the contents will be inspired by the 'essence' of the Winx universe and their adventures but subject to a process of cultural translation[11] whereby the interviews, games, music charts, fashion suggestions and the overall structural organization are rewritten according to local preferences.

By comparing the English-language versions published in different countries (i.e. Singapore and the US), one can easily identify various degrees of rewriting, or 'indigenization' of the magazine contents, with an ever-changing distance taken from the original Italian version which, nonetheless, always acts as a reference point. The concept of indigenization seems to be particularly interesting and relevant in our case. James Lull, for instance, suggests that processes such as indigenization "involve considerable cultural creativity" (2000:249). It is undeniable that the process of cultural translation which the Winx world undergoes in the rewriting of the magazine contents entails a good amount

---

[11] The expression 'cultural translation' is used here to refer to a process of adaptation which goes well beyond linguistic transfer to encompass all possible transformations performed on a text and its context in order to make it 'locally' acceptable and reflect the target audience's tastes. For further reference, see Johnston and Kelly (forthcoming).

of cultural creativity, projecting a magic universe that reflects the experiences and desires of young girls the world over.

By contrast, no cultural creativity can be detected in the interlingual translation of the comics from Italian into English, and the literal approach which has generally been adopted, at least for the first series, seems to give up all pretence at cultural adaptation while leaving a number of traces of the self in the language of the receiving other. Due to the supernatural nature of the *Winx* world, the comics in fact require no particular effort in terms of cultural adaptation, but the above-mentioned literal translation occasionally brings to light some elements which will at best be perceived as strident by native speakers of English.

Undoubtedly, translating comics implies coping with a number of important constraints. The space limit, for instance, is a determining factor for translational choices, but finding the right expressions and giving subtle, effective nuances to each character's way of speaking is equally essential to ensuring smooth and pleasant reception by readers.

In general, a literal approach to translation tends to stem from the erroneous assumption that by translating each word and sentence as faithfully as possible, the meaning as well as the effect of the original will be somehow automatically reproduced, thus remaining unchanged. However, translating literally often implies overlooking the need to create some sort of idiolect for each character and, with reference to spatial constraints, a literal translation does not ensure that the length of original lines will be maintained but occasionally leads to longer, paraphrased sentences.

In the *Winx* comics English translations, undoubtedly performed by native speakers of the target language who were, nonetheless, not necessarily skilful translators of comics, the above-mentioned problems sometimes come to the surface. These seem to leave more evident traces of the original, its unique character and structure, and occasionally give rise to inadequate, awkward translations. Therefore, the translated comics more than the cartoons will reveal a certain lack of coherence within the texts themselves as well as with the overall, specifically designed contents of the magazine.

A few examples are offered below from 'I ragazzi di Fonterossa', the comics published both in Italian and in English with the third issue of the magazine and translated into English as 'The Boys from Red Fountain'. The following English excerpts are taken from the version of the *Winx* magazine distributed in Singapore, but the comics translation, as mentioned earlier, is exactly the same for the versions published in the United Kingdom and the US.

Towards the beginning of the comics adventures, the young specialist Brandon expresses his fears for Prince Sky, who has just left on a small spaceship with Stella and hopes to capture a huge and evil troll. Brandon fears that the prince may not be able to do it by himself and rejects Bloom's suggestion that Stella might be able to help him:

> *Bloom:*   Beh, non è proprio da solo, c'è Stella con lui!
> *Brandon:*   Figuriamoci! Ci vuole altro che una ragazza per tener buoni quei bestioni!
> *Bloom:*   Cosa? Come sarebbe?

In the English version, which shows the first signs of a literal translation approach, the very common and informal exclamation uttered by Bloom ("come sarebbe") is replaced by a less common English question, which seems to call into play an unjustified, higher register and produces a rather different effect on the readers. Compare a literal translation with the official one:

Official translation	Literal translation
Bloom: Well, he's not exactly alone, Stella is with him, isn't she? *Brandon:* Oh, come on! It takes more than a girl to handle those beasts! *Bloom:* What are you implying, Brandon?	*Bloom:* Well, he's not exactly alone, Stella is with him! *Brandon:* Come on! It takes more than a girl to keep those big beasts quiet! *Bloom:* What? What do you mean?

Going on in the adventure, Brandon and Prince Sky, finally reunited, find out through the words of one of their college masters that someone has probably been trying to kill them:

Brandon: Qualcuno è arrivato fin qui dal nostro regno e ha cercato di ucciderci!
Insegnante: E' probabile! Evidentemente avete laggiù degli amici molto pericolosi!

Despite some slight variation from the wording of the original lines, the English version proves to be faithful to the source text, especially when it comes to rendering the short exclamation uttered by the college master. As a matter of fact, the solution adopted for "è probabile" reveals a choice which clearly does not correspond to the most common expressions which would be used in English:

Official translation	Literal translation
Brandon: So you're saying that someone came all the way to the college to try and kill us? *Master:* It's probable! It seems like you have some very dangerous enemies around!	*Brandon:* Somebody came all the way from our kingdom to try and kill us! *Master:* I'd say so. You must have a number of dangerous enemies down there!

Finally, let us focus on a brief exchange between the two Winx Musa and Flora, part of which is shown in Figure 10.2 (centre fold).

Musa: Oh, mamma mia! Pensate che ci abbiano visto?
Flora: Non credo…
Flora: …ma anche Brandon farebbe meglio a non stare qui! Bloom, perché non lo porti a fare una passeggiata nel bosco?

The English translation of these three lines reveals several awkward choices: first of all, the exclamation uttered by Musa ("Oh, good grief!") at the beginning of the exchange sounds rather uncommon for a young, modern teenager. Moreover, in Flora's last line the use of the verb 'to stay' seems to be a calque from Italian the verb 'stare', which is more likely to be translated with the English 'to be' when referring to a fixed position. Finally, the choice of the word 'even' in the same line by Flora, probably determined by what at times becomes an excessively literal translation approach, leads to a certain ambiguity and could have been omitted:

Official translation	Literal translation
Musa: Oh, good grief! Do you think anyone heard us? *Flora:* I hope not… *Flora:* …and even Brandon shouldn`t stay here! Bloom, why don`t you take him for a walk in the forest?	*Musa*: Oh, mother! Do you think they saw us? *Flora:* I don't think so… *Flora*: …but Brandon shouldn't be here, either! Bloom, why don't you take him for a walk in the forest?

According to Gideon Toury's popular definition of acceptability in translation referred to above, whereby a translated text is deemed acceptable when it fulfils all the requirements of the target language and culture, the translation of the *Winx* comics seems to reveal, as illustrated by the examples, a number of small but meaningful elements which contrast with this very principle. Even though English-speaking readers will be able to smoothly go through all the translated comics without any particular difficulty, they might be left with the feeling that some words and, most of all, a number of exclamations uttered by the protagonists evoke a vague sense of strangeness. Unaccustomed as English readers – and viewers – are to the perception of linguistic and cultural inadequacies in mass-media texts,[12] they might either reject the texts in question or, as seems to be more likely, they may tend to overlook such occasional awkward elements and, in the case of the *Winx* comics, simply enjoy the five fairies' adventures, perhaps unconsciously retaining some of those awkward-sounding expressions.

On the whole, whether or not the traces of the original language which are reflected through the translation are perceived as dissonant notes by young readers, they can be attributed a certain meaning. Bearing in mind their small-scale relevance, but also considering their value in terms of anti-globalizing translation trends, they could also be seen as positive, somehow revolutionary. If instances of translation into English from the languages of the world were able to become more frequent, especially through captivating and successful texts, the English language and culture could – should – be drawn to acknowledge linguistic and cultural difference more adequately and overtly.

---

[12] For a definition of mass-media texts, among which texts appealing to large portions of young audiences can easily be classified, see Eco (1981).

4.   Conclusion

As Cronin (2003) points out, giving a definition of 'globalization' is anything but simple, and each theoretical stance taken to observe globalizing trends and phenomena implies a slightly different viewpoint, often not deprived of ideological and cultural implications. However, among the few definitions Cronin takes into account, the words of Jonathan Friedman sound particularly relevant for the examples discussed above. Friedman, as Cronin reports, states that globalization is connected to "the attribution of meaning of a globalized nature through globalized institutions", and that, in a global context, it implies "the formation of centre/periphery structures, their expansion, contraction, fragmentation and re-establishment throughout cycles of shifting hegemony" (Friedman 1995, quoted in Cronin 2003:77). Mass media have a large share in shaping centre/periphery structures or, perhaps much more frequently, in reinforcing leading positions within them and, ultimately, in orienting audience tastes as well as expectations.

It goes without saying that translation is involved in virtually all processes of globalization as well as acts of resistance to it, and also that, as Cronin repeatedly advocates, translation can play a crucial role in countering linguistic and cultural hegemony.

In this respect, we could say that translation can either be a weapon or a vehicle: when used to deliberately try and counteract hegemonic powers, in the media but also in literature and other forms of communication, translation is a weapon which can be skilfully used to change power asymmetries. Translation, more commonly, can be indirectly responsible for the transmission of cultural specificities, being a vehicle for linguistic and cultural habits which come from the periphery and are encoded in the texts adapted into the language of the centre.

The *Winx* cartoons and comics, widely discussed with reference to the various translation strategies and choices as well as to their adequacy/acceptability, seem to reveal a common core: notwithstanding the great care taken in the translation process and in the effectiveness of its products, the English language still remains a target for a partially visible, never totally alienable source. Therefore, translation from Italian into English of the *Winx* cartoons and comics acts, albeit involuntarily and perhaps unconsciously, as a vehicle for traces of a language and culture which are often erased in the most common flow of media productions, but whose surfacing through successful stories can positively affect the redefinition of media-generated cultural traffic.

References

Primary Sources
CARTOONS
'Benvenuti a Magix', *The Winx Club*, Series 1, Episode 2, 2004 ['Welcome to Magix', *The Winx Club*, Series 1 (English version), Episode 2, 2004].
'La Palude di Melmamora', *The Winx Club*, Series 1, Episode 4, 2004 ['Blackmud Swamp', The Winx Club, Series 1 (English version), Episode 4, 2004].

Comics
Pezzin, Giorgio, Michele Lilli, Juliette and Luca dell'Annunziata, 'I Ragazzi di Fonterossa', in *The Winx Club Magazine*, Edizioni Play Press, n.3, 2004 ['The Boys from Red Fountain', in *The Winx Club Magazine* (English Edition distributed in Singapore, Hong Kong, Singapore and Malaysia), Chuang Yi, n.3, 2005].

Secondary Sources
Bassnett, Susan and Harish Trivedi (eds) (1999) *Post-Colonial Translation. Theory and Practice*, London & New York: Routledge.

Belton, John (ed.) (1999) *Movies and Mass Culture*, London: Athlone.

Caprara, Fulvia (2005) 'Winx e Witch, la Sfida è Aperta', *La Stampa*, 22 April.

Cronin, Michael (2003) *Translation and Globalization*, London & New York: Routledge.

Eco, Umberto (1981) *The Role of the Reader*, London: Hutchinson.

------ (1994) *Trattato di Semiotica Generale*, Milano: Bompiani.

Friedman, Jonathan (1995) 'Global System, Globalization and the Parameters of Modernity', in Mike Featherstone, Scott Lash and Roland Robertson (eds) *Global Modernities*, London: Sage, 69-90.

Gambier, Yves and Henrik Gottlieb (eds) (2001) *(Multi)media Translation. Concepts, Practices and Research*, Amsterdam & Philadelphia: John Benjamins.

Gottlieb, Henrik (2004) 'Language-political Implications of Subtitling', in Pilar Orero (ed.) *Topics in Audiovisual Translation*, Amsterdam: John Benjamins, 83-100.

Johnston, David and Stephen Kelly (eds) (forthcoming) *Betwixt and Between. Place and Cultural Translation*, Cambridge: Cambridge Scholars Press.

Lull, James (2000) *Media, Communication, Culture*, New York: Columbia University Press.

McLuhan, Marshall and Quentin Fiore (1967) *The Medium Is the Message*, New York: Random House.

Monaco, James (2000) *How to Read a Film. Movies, Media, Multimedia*, New York & Oxford: Oxford University Press.

Orero, Pilar (ed.) (2004) *Topics in Audiovisual Translation*, Amsterdam and Philadelphia: John Benjamins.

Salerno, Katia (2005) 'The Winx Club', *Cinecittà News*, 18 April (online) http://news.cinecitta.com/kids/articolo.asp?id=5411 (Accessed March 15 2006).

Spivak, Gayatri Chakravorty (2004) 'The Politics of Translation', in Lawrence Venuti (ed.) *The Translation Studies Reader*, Second Edition, London & New York: Routledge, 369-388.

Toury, Gideon (1995) *Descriptive Translation Studies and Beyond*, Amsterdam & Philadelphia: John Benjamins.

11 Onomatopoeia and Unarticulated Language in the Translation and Production of Comic Books
A Case Study: Comic Books in Spanish

CARMEN VALERO GARCÉS
University of Alcalá, Spain

The study of unarticulated and onomatopoeic forms has not traditionally received much attention, although this field has sparked interest and curiosity, especially among researchers interested in comic books and those with a particular sensitivity for the problems of language. The number of published works related to this elusive topic is growing, and this article aims to offer a contribution to the study of onomatopoeia in comic books. The author investigates the use of onomatopoeia in comic books in Spanish in recent decades and compares translated with original production. To achieve this end, attention is paid to two different aspects, namely the strategies used by Spanish translators when translating onomatopoeia in source American comics, and the use and creation of onomatopoeic forms in original Spanish comics. Data comes from three sources: American comic books translated into Spanish, comic books originally written in Spanish, and results from a questionnaire on the use of onomatopoeia distributed to Spanish cartoonists and comics writers. The conclusions point to the fact that, since onomatopoeia show the same patterns and similar distribution in original Spanish comics as in those translated from English, it is difficult to ascertain to what extent onomatopoeia in American comics translated into Spanish are 'translated' or simply 'copied'. When English onomatopoeia are retained in translated comics, this may simply mean that they are not perceived as 'foreign'.

According to the *Oxford Dictionary*, an 'onomatopoeia' is a combination of sounds in a word that imitates or suggests what the word refers to; and an 'onomatopoeic word' is a word which imitates, reproduces or represents a natural sound. The study of these forms has often been neglected within linguistic and literary circles; when the topic has been studied, it has usually been as a secondary aspect of broader endeavours, for example as a section in the general study of comics or as the stylistic characteristics of a particular writer (Gubern 1979:153-160, Santoyo 1985:169-172, Rabadán 1991:154-155).

Schnetzer (2004) points out some of the reasons for this neglect. First of all, onomatopoeia is difficult to classify. Secondly, onomatopoeic words are forms whose expressive force is customarily aided by other elements, such as punctuation, typographical and graphical signs. Thirdly, onomatopoeia does not have a clear and conventional graphic representation and may even involve new creations. Finally, the use of onomatopoeia is associated with genres (e.g. comic books, cartoons, children's literature) that are still considered by a large sector of the general public as not 'serious' enough to be the subject of academic research.

In comics, onomatopoeia may appear inside or outside the balloons. In both cases, "the iconic framework imposes specific limits on the translation of the linguistic message" (Rabadán 1991:154; my translation)[1] because of physical constraints related to the use of space, fonts and typography. When used outside the balloons the constraints might be greater as the onomatopoeia is then part of the picture, and "the way handwriting is used as part of the iconic message makes it very difficult, and sometimes impossible, to render the message in Spanish, even in situations where this would be possible from a linguistic point of view" (Rabadán 1991:155; my translation).[2]

Moreover, as is commonly known, the representation of sounds does not always coincide across languages. So, for example, a dog can say 'guau-guau' in Spanish and 'woof-woof' in English. Onomatopoeia might be iconic and culturally related as, for example, in the representation of censured expression of insults or imprecations (e.g. combinations of consonants such as '¡grftjx!' in Spanish), and in these cases the meaning might be only familiar to the source language readership but unknown to the target language readership.

There are other cases where onomatopoeia might reflect conventions accepted (or known) by most readers, as for example the representations of some metallic sounds, an area in which English is highly productive and in which its creations are systematically reproduced unchanged in Spanish comics.

The main objective of this paper is to illustrate and discuss the use of onomatopoeia in translated comics in Spain in recent decades. To this end I will not only analyze the treatment of onomatopoeia in translated comic books, but also the use of onomatopoeia in comic books originally written in Spanish, and will compare my findings with the results of a questionnaire distributed among Spanish comics writers and cartoonists.

1.   Onomatopoeia in Translated Spanish Comics

According to Román Gubern (1979:153), one of the first cartoonists to introduce onomatopoeia was Tom Browne in his comic strip *Weary Willie and Tired Tim* in 1896. It was a resource that carried a lot of expressivity and took up little space in the strip, which made onomatopoeia very popular and widely used by comics authors and cartoonists. Subsequently, the importance of onomatopoeic expressions in comics grew to such a degree that they started to appear even outside the balloons, becoming a new component of the drawing. Replacing the onomatopoeia in comic books sold by American press syndicates to almost all western European countries with target language equivalents would have implied high costs and technical difficulties, so that most publishers chose not to consider this an option.

The 1950s and mid 1960s saw the first period of mass diffusion of comic books in Spain (for more information see Altarriba 2001, Guiral 2004, Lladó 2002), and authors and translators were finding it difficult to create onomatopoeia or sound representations

---

[1] "el soporte icónico impone límites específicos a la traducción del mensaje lingüístico".
[2] "la incrustación de la grafía en el mensaje icónico dificulta (y en ocasiones impide) su transferencia al castellano, caso que esa sea posible desde el punto de vista lingüístico".

in Spanish at such a rapid pace. Even in those cases in which Spanish had a traditional onomatopoeic form ('pam', 'blam', 'rin'), on many occasions there was a rivalry with the English forms ('bang', 'slam', 'ring') for reasons of snobbery or because of the need for exoticism or local colour. In other instances, maintenance of the English forms was attributable to the translator's lack of expertise and to technical problems raised by translation when these forms were located outside of the balloon. In still other cases, no Spanish equivalent existed, as with the expression 'oink' (for a pig), now commonly used in Spanish cartoons.

In the decades that followed (1960s, 1970s), Spanish translations still showed a tendency to retain English onomatopoeia. American comics fulfilled a double function: on the one hand, they served to export models of the American way of life, and on the other hand, they carried beyond national borders those English nouns and verbs converted into onomatopoeia, along with other foreign sounds (e.g., -sh, -ck, and -ng) that nonetheless were accepted by readers because of the acoustic eloquence of the particular action (for example, 'boom' as the graphic representation of 'bum', which would more closely correspond to a Spanish pronunciation). As Gubern rightly states, "the linguistic colonialism of the United States executed through the channels of its syndicates is obvious here as in other fields of mass communication (songs, film, etc.)" (1979:155). In the 1980s, comic books continued to be greatly influenced by English, and as a consequence the permanence of the borrowed forms was ensured.

The phenomenon of retaining English onomatopoeia is not limited to Spanish. For instance, upon establishing his lists of onomatopoeia in comic books written in French, Benayoun (1968, quoted in Gubern 1979:155) counted 103 onomatopoeia of English origin, and only 58 in French. Schnetzer (2005) stresses that German speaking countries belong to the importing group of nations on the international comic books market as they have practically no domestic production, and that they show a tendency to retain English onomatopoeia.

Relevant information about the translation of onomatopoeia in Spanish comic books is provided by Santoyo (1985), Mayoral (1984, 1992), Valero Garcés (1995a, 1995b, 1997, 2000) and Martinez Fuentes (2003). Santoyo (1985:70) analyzes the Spanish translations of some *Freak Brothers* stories by Gilbert Shelton, published in 1977 by Producciones Editoriales (Barcelona) as *Las Famosas Aventuras de los Freak Brothers*. In this translation, by Luis Vigil, all original onomatopoeia were retained ('jab', 'crunch', 'blink', 'tweet', 'bounce', 'burp', etc.) and many lexical elements vital to each panel were not translated. Santoyo concluded his study by stressing that English was a more dynamic language than Spanish in the invention of onomatopoeic forms and the representation of sounds. He stressed that the Spanish language lacked the facility that English enjoys for grammaticalizing these representations and converting them into verbs or nouns without the addition of endings or some other type of modification. Consequently, there was an extensive use of English onomatopoeic verbs and nouns integrated into the panel, which included 'creek', 'bump', 'smash,' 'zip', 'crash', 'snap', 'click' and 'boommm', to name but a few.

Santoyo (1985) and Martínez Fuentes (2003) also point out that it is more difficult to represent sounds graphically in Spanish (and Romance languages in general) than it is in English. The more synthetic character of English as opposed to the more analytic quality of Spanish influences this feature, as does the great American tradition of comics production. Given that Americans are unquestionably the creators of comics, it is no surprise that the contact between English and other languages in this field of sound and onomatopoeic representation occurs predominantly in the direction of English to Romance language and, in particular, through comics and cartoons.

The strategy of retaining English onomatopoeia is largely used when these are found outside the balloon, as seen in Figure 11.1. This may be due to technical constraints, since intervening in the picture would involve greater expense and require a high standard of graphic skills.

Figure 11.1a: Robert Crumb,
My Troubles with Women II, 1986, p. 52

Figure 11.1b: Robert Crumb,
Mis problemas con las mujeres II, 1987, p. 55
(Spanish Translation: Narcís Fradera)

Another technical constraint may relate to the use of colour. Eva Martinez Fuentes (2003) analyzed a corpus of American *Calvin and Hobbes* comic strips and their translations into Spanish and found that more than three-quarters of onomatopoeia produced in colour were retained in their original English form, whereas only 50% of onomatopoeia produced in black and white strips were treated in this fashion. Martinez Fuentes also analyzed a German black and white comic and its translation into Spanish and found that only approximately 40% of the onomatopoeia used were translated. According to Martinez Fuentes these figures illustrate that the translation of onomatopoeia depends heavily on the prestige of the source language in the field of comic books as well as on the use of colour. She also adds that onomatopoeic expressions produced in colour are sometimes translated in black and white because of the technical and financial difficulties involved. Figure 11.2 reproduces her example of the word 'Hooray!', which was originally coloured, and was translated as '¡Hurra!' but in black and white (see Figure 11.2, centre fold).

Preserving the source language form in the target text is not uncommon either, as in 'ouch', 'splash', or 'wow!' instead of the Spanish '¡guau!' to show surprise, or 'blam', 'knot', 'mug', 'mut' to signal all sorts of blows (see Figure 11.3, a translated panel, centre fold). According to Martinez Fuentes (2003:online),

> [d]ue to the technical difficulties that graphic changes entail, coloured onomatopoeic words tend to remain the same in the target text, provided that the meaning can be easily understood through the context. If the meaning of the source onomatopoeia cannot be understood or if no further explanations exist in the same comic strip, translation is likely to occur. However, these are only exceptions to the rule, because the norm appears to be to translate only those onomatopoeic expressions that do not require excessive expenses.

I do not completely agree with this conclusion since research shows that there are other elements that influence the translation of this type of text (Gubern 1979, Valero Garcés 1995a, 1995b). These include the translator's experience, type of publication, intended readership, as well as a long tradition of copying directly from English, which still persists in spite of the growth of an important national market since the 1950s.

The colouring of comic books might also depend on the prevailing taste in the respective countries. For instance, Schnetzer (2005) calls attention to the fact that most manga (Japanese comics) are in black and white, while in the first translations made for an American readership colours were added because Americans generally prefer coloured comic books (Jüngst and Rota, this volume). Furthermore, technological advances have now made it possible to separate drawings from the dialogue and the narrative text, as well as from the rest of the elements that combine together to make a comic book.

Studies focusing broadly on the period 1950s-1980s (Santoyo 1985, Mayoral 1984, 1992, Valero Garcés 1995a, 1995b, 2000) identify two main translation strategies applied in Spain regarding the translation of onomatopoeia. Either English onomatopoeia are replaced with Spanish equivalents, or they remain unchanged in the translated comics. The choice between the two seems to rest largely on the type of sound which is represented. English onomatopoeia are usually replaced by Spanish equivalents in the case of sounds produced by animals, unarticulated sounds produced by humans, and sounds used to show feelings or attitude, whereas they are usually retained when representing 'mechanical' sounds.

In the case of sounds produced by animals (a donkey, a cow, a dog), whereas English shows a great variety of forms, the range of Spanish equivalents seems to be more limited. So, for example, in English a dog can 'say' 'bow-wow', 'woof-woof', 'roof-roof', 'yap', 'yelp', 'yip', and 'grr' – translated in Spanish as 'guau-guau', 'grr', 'grñ', or 'auuu-auuuu'. In English cats 'meow', 'yoewl', 'screech', 'purr', or 'rrr', while in Spanish the possibilities are 'miau-miau', 'marramiau', or 'rrr'. In English a little bird can say 'tweet-tweet', 'cheep-cheep', 'schreech-screech', 'fwee', 'zip', 'swee', 'caw-caw', or 'twitter-twitter', while in Spanish the same bird usually just says 'pío-pío'.

When onomatopoeic expressions are used to represent unarticulated sounds produced by humans, they are usually translated by a Spanish equivalent, where one exists. For example, a 'slapping' sound may appear in English as 'smack' and in Spanish as 'plaf'. The sound of clearing one's throat might be 'ahem' in English and 'ejem' in Spanish. A sneeze could be represented as 'atchoo' or 'a-tissue' in English, and as 'aatchis' in Spanish. A crying sound might be 'boo-hoo' in English and 'buaa' in Spanish. The action of 'bubbling' is represented in English as 'glub', 'slub' or 'bubble', and in Spanish as 'glu-glu'. Sometimes 'creative' English onomatopoeia such as 'baw blubber' (Figure 11.4a) are translated by means of other, more recognizable onomatopoeia in English, which have become part of the Spanish language of comic books ('sob! sniff!' in Figure 11.4b).

Figure 11.4a: Robert Crumb, *My Troubles with Women I*, 1986, p. 62

Figure 11.4b: Robert Crumb, *Mis problemas con las mujeres II*, 1992, p. 64 (Spanish translation: Narcís Fradera)

Sounds used to show feelings or attitudes are usually adapted in spelling when they are 'heard' similarly, and translated by their Spanish equivalent where one exists (Valero Garcés 1997a, 1997b). Narcís Fradera's translation of Robert Crumb's underground comic books is a good example. In this case the translator tends to adapt the spelling for onomatopoeia 'heard' in the same form in both languages. Thus 'heh, heh' is translated as 'je, je', the English common expression for relief 'phew' is translated most often as 'uf'; the common expression for a good meal 'yummy-yummy' is translated as 'ñam, ñam'; the expression of fear 'aargh' is translated as 'uy'. Common English expressions for happiness or satisfaction such as 'wow', 'hm' and 'yip-pee' are translated as 'yupi'; the typical 'owwoow!' is translated as '¡oh,ohoh!'; and 'kissy, kissy' is translated as 'mua, mua'.

The second strategy, which consists of retaining English onomatopoeia in translated Spanish comics, is instead more noticeable in the case of onomatopoeia representing artificial sounds or sounds produced by objects, actions, or the result of actions. Thus, for the action of closing a door, both languages are likely to coincide in the use of 'blam', 'slam', or 'bang'. To refer to the action of hitting, Spanish has the forms 'pam', 'pum', 'clac', or 'toc', but in comic books original English lexical forms such as 'crack', 'bump', 'punch', 'knock', 'bang', 'beat', 'tap' and 'pound' are more frequently seen. For the action of honking a car horn, a purely Spanish representation is 'pii-pii' or 'po-po', but the English forms 'bleep', 'beep', 'honk', 'moc- moc' and 'peep-peep' are also common, as seen in Figure 11.2. The comic books published by Marvel Comics (see primary sources), which show a preference for action, have entire panels containing no other text besides the onomatopoeic representation of a punch, a gunshot, an explosion, or the disintegration of the villain, and the translated text is often identical to the original text without any intervention on the part of the translator. Even in those comic books where feelings are more important than action, the representation of metallic sounds is systematically retained from English. Thus 'smack', 'click', 'squirt', 'clamp' all commonly feature in Spanish comics.

Results from a more recent survey of onomatopoeia in comic books translated from English and published in the last 15 years reveal that the prevailing norm is to retain English onomatopoeia. The corpus used (see primary sources) consists of two different genres: underground comics, or comix, and superhero comic books, both of which have been very popular since the 1980s and include a wide range of onomatopoeia. An analysis of this corpus showed that 75% of all onomatopoeia (60 out of 80 examples) retain the English form.

However, my survey also reveals that some comic book writers, such as Narcís Fradera, strongly prefer to replace English onomatopoeia with traditional Spanish forms. Fradera used Spanish equivalents for more than 80% of the onomatopoeia found in his translations (28 out of 37). This impetus for using the Spanish forms may be due to the technological advances that make it easier than before to modify pictures, but also to a particular reaction in defence of Spanish, which has led to the creation of new forms along with the revitalization of purely Spanish forms such as 'pimba', 'ploff', 'taclanc' and 'cronch' found in the Spanish comic book (called *tebeo*) *Mortadelo y Filemón* – instead of 'crash', 'crack', or 'smash'.

2.   Onomatopoeia in Comics Originally Written in Spanish

In order to analyze the treatment of onomatopoeia in comics translated into Spanish, I compared my data with the use of onomatopoeia in comic books originally written in Spanish. Data for this come from two main sources: an analysis of comic books written by Spanish authors in Spain, and results from a questionnaire about the use of onomatopoeia distributed to Spanish cartoonists and comics writers.

2.1   *Analysis of Comic Books*

A direct consequence of the open attitude towards 'borrowed' forms is the fact that Spanish artists composing their own vignettes mimetically introduce foreign onomatopoeia into them, as a quick look at a humour magazine such as *El Jueves, la revista que sale los miércoles*[3] will show. Nowadays it is easy to find onomatopoeia of English origin which have been incorporated into Spanish through different processes such as borrowing (e.g. 'boom', 'click', 'crash', 'clap'), adaptation (e.g. 'coff' from the English 'cough'), and creation of new forms (e.g. 'krak', 'kronk').

My analysis is based on a corpus of humorous comic books (*tebeos*) originally published in Spain from the late 1980s and until the present (see primary sources). Not only do humorous comics contain a lot of onomatopoeia, but they are arguably the most distinctive genre of comics in the history of Spain's comics market (Altarriba 2001). The total number of onomatopoeia in the current corpus is 130.

An analysis of the data on the representation of onomatopoeia in comic books originally written in Spanish shows that there are three main types of onomatopoeia used by Spanish comic book writers. These are English forms that are now seen as part of the Spanish language in comic books, traditional Spanish forms, and new creations which are a combination of English sounds and Spanish spellings. When dealing with the representation of natural sounds (sounds produced by animals, or humans, or the expression of feeling and/or attitude, 53 instances out of 130), more than 50% of the examples are originally Spanish onomatopoeia. When dealing with artificial sounds (e.g. metallic sounds, 65 instances out of 130) more than 50% of the examples are representations of sounds directly copied from English, although they are not necessarily perceived as foreign words by the readers. New creations represent 9% of all onomatopoeia (12 out of 130).

The following examples are taken from some of the most popular Spanish comic book writers.

Ibáñez uses English or English looking onomatopoeic forms such as 'snif', 'crac', 'crunch', 'boom', 'clap', 'plaff', and 'borrobom' in *Rompetechos* and in *Mortadelo y Filemón*, but he also uses typical Spanish forms such as '¡ñaca! ¡ñaca!' when eating; 'gluc' when swallowing; '¡ñieck ñieck!' for a spring, '¡ñiaoiiik!' to indicate that something is breaking, or '¡tronch!' and '¡cronch!' to hit.

---

[3] Lit.: *Thursday, the magazine released on Wednesday.*

While using onomatopoeia in *Zipi y Zape* much less frequently than Ibáñez, Escobar prefers to avoid foreign onomatopoeia and instead uses Spanish adaptations such as 'plas', 'plop', 'clinc', or 'bum'. Other artists, such as Raf in *Sir Tim O'Theo* and Vazquez in *Angelito*, prefer a mixture of Spanish and English representations of sounds: 'ay', 'zaas', 'sniff', 'plaff', or 'crash'. Comics recently published (2005-2006) in magazines such as *El Pequeño País*, *El País Dominical* and *El Jueves* follow the same patterns found in translated comics for the representation of human sounds: 'je, je', 'ja, ja', 'ji, ji', when laughing; 'atchiiis' when sneezing; 'buaaaahhhhh' when crying; or '¡aaayyy!', '¡uuyyyy!', '¡aaay!' when being hurt.

Following a tendency that is also common in the graffiti seen on the street and tube station walls, with a predominance of some letters and/or special combinations that were not common 10 years ago, new creations and spellings are also found in the data. For example, the non-Spanish letter 'k' is found in 'krak', 'klonk', 'krask', 'kronk' and in all kinds of bangs. One panel in the comic strip by Sanvi and Vergara (2005, p. 9) depicts the feet of a so called 'Invincible Man' breaking through a wall. The sound made by the impact is expressed through the onomatopoeia 'krak' and 'broom'. The prototypical Spanish letter 'ñ' is found in 'ñaaoooo, ñaaaooooooo' when driving fast, or in 'ñññññiiiiiiiiiiii' when stepping on the brakes; and the 'ch' in 'chof, chef' when walking in mud, or 'choffff' when hit on the head with something soft.

2.2 *Analysis of the Results from the Questionnaire*

The third source of data comes from an empirical study on perceptions about the use of onomatopoeia by Spanish cartoonists and comics writers, and is based on results from a questionnaire which was distributed to the caricaturists and cartoonists registered in the graphic-humour database of the *Cátedra de Humor- FGUA* at the University of Alcalá. The database includes 300 entries. Only 10 answers had been received at the time this article was completed; however, we need to bear in mind that caricaturists and cartoonists, at least in my experience, are among those professionals who usually like reading and doing some research on comics and humour, even if they do not use (many) onomatopoeia themselves. This fact, together with their experience and contact with other cartoonists and humour writers, makes their opinion worthy of attention.

The questionnaire consisted of 10 questions. Questions 1-5 were about the caricaturists and cartoonists' use of onomatopoeia (how they created them, whether they had a catalogue, whether they updated it, and how they collected it). Questions 6 to 9 were about their perception of the use of onomatopoeia (whether they had seen any changes or evolution in the last decades or if they still felt the strong influence of English and the repetition of English onomatopoeia in Spanish comic books). Question 10 was about translation. Most of the respondents were comics writers and readers too, so we asked them what they would do if they were asked to translate comics containing onomatopoeia.

In their replies to the first question, about how comic book writers usually represent onomatopoeia, 7 authors out of 10 replied that they re-use existing onomatopoeia, 2 said that they do not use them, while 1 informant did not answer. All respondents also said they make use of other features such as symbols, iconic elements and motion lines.

The next three questions (Questions 2, 3, 4) were about the use of documentation: whether they have a catalogue, whether they use it, and whether they upgraded it. Six respondents answered that they do not have a specific catalogue although they liked to keep a note of some onomatopoeia, while 4 answered that they have one.

When asked whether they used a catalogue – that is, if they try to use the same onomatopoeia for the representation of the same sound every time they use it, 4 out of 10 said they tried, 2 said they didn't really care even though they had sometimes tried, and the rest didn't even try.

As for the way they developed a catalogue, the options given by the 6 who answered that they had one were that they collected it by reading comic books, by observing the way people express emotions, and by paying attention to noises and drawing their representation in their notebook at that moment. Only 4 said that they sometimes upgraded it, which may mean that this is not an element they considered relevant.

When asked about how and when they create onomatopoeia (Question 5), 7 said that they sometimes use their own catalogue; but 3 said that they just invented a new onomatopoeia when they needed it and couldn't find or didn't remember any. This may mean that they prefer to use existing onomatopoeia, even if they don't keep a catalogue. Three respondents didn't answer.

Respondents also pointed out that their main sources (Question 6) were American comic books and authors such as Steinberg, Larson or Eisner and some Spanish comic book writers such as Ibáñez, Vázquez, Dodot, Calpurnio or Carlos Giménez.

The next questions (Questions 7, 8, 9) were about the change in the use of onomatopoeia in Spanish over the last 30 years. Seven respondents saw some evolution, but 5 said this evolution had been really small. Only 2 saw a significant evolution while 1 said there had not been any evolution. Two respondents did not answer.

The last question (Question 10) was about how the respondents would treat onomatopoeia from other languages if they had to translate them in comic books. In this case and considering the technical restrictions already mentioned, there were two parts to the question. The first one dealt with onomatopoeia inside the balloon and the second with onomatopoeia outside the balloon. In each case there were three options, namely retaining the English form, translating it into Spanish, or adapting the spelling into Spanish.

As regards onomatopoeia inside the balloons, the answers were as follows: 4 said they would copy the English onomatopoeia, 3 said they would replace it with a Spanish equivalent, and 3 did not answer.

In the case of onomatopoeia outside the balloon, 6 said they would retain the English representation of sound. This answer might be connected with the technical problems this type of onomatopoeia poses. Only 2 said they would sometimes translate it and 2 did not answer.

In short, these answers suggest that most of the respondents use existing ono-matopoeia when creating their vignettes; most of them also admitted the influence of English, but when asked about this influence today, 5 out of 7 (the other 3 respondents did not answer) said that this influence was felt more strongly before, and is not so significant today.

When asked about the evolution of Spanish in terms of the use and reproduction of onomatopoeia, 7 said that it had changed very little in the last 30 years or so. This answer may again indicate that the respondents perceive the use of English onomatopoeia or spellings in comic books as common since some of the English forms have already been accepted in Spanish, are recognized by their readers, and are used by writers and translators.

When asked about translating comic books, the respondents did not feel they had to translate onomatopoeia, especially if they were outside the balloons; as a consequence the tendency is to simply reproduce the English form. At this point I should specify that most of the respondents were comics artists and cartoonists, but not translators.

3. Conclusion

The translation of onomatopoeia in American comics into Spanish evidences some of the typical problems in translating comics, which result from technical, linguistic and cultural constraints.

Data from my own research as well as from previous studies show that two main strategies are used. On the one hand, English onomatopoeia are replaced by Spanish equivalents, especially when dealing with the representation of animal sounds, inarticu-late human sounds, and the expression of feelings and attitudes. On the other hand, onomatopoeic expressions representing artificial, mechanical sounds or those denoting action are retained in their English form, even when there may be an equivalent form in Spanish. This tendency to consider some English borrowings as part of the Spanish language of onomatopoeia is confirmed by the use of well-known English onomatopoeia to translate lesser-known ones, for example 'sob! snif' to translate 'baw blubber'.

Original Spanish onomatopoeia show the same tendencies and similar percentages as those translated from English. Furthermore, the results of my empirical study based on a questionnaire show that for Spanish writers in the 1990s and onwards, English continues to be the indisputable source for the representations of sounds and onomatopoeia, and many onomatopoeic expressions now feel as though they are part of the Spanish lan-guage in spite of the fact that they were originally borrowings from English. In addition, some new creations and spellings – following a tendency that is also seen in graffiti – are also found in the latest Spanish comic books. It seems thus that onomatopoeia in Span-ish comics are a language of their own, a mix of original English forms, original Spanish forms and intermediate forms, i.e. English 'sounds' but with Spanish spelling.

It is difficult to ascertain to what extent onomatopoeia in American comics trans-lated into Spanish are 'translated' or simply 'copied', since when English onomatopoeia are retained this may simply mean that they are not perceived as 'foreign'. On the one hand, the fact that English onomatopoeia are retained – either because of technical or economic constraints, and/or because they are understandable in context, and/or because there is no clear inventory of such forms – has helped to create a tradition of 'Spanish' onomatopoeia in 'English'. On the other hand, the fact that onomatopoeia in original Spanish comics include English or forms that look like English may explain why only a minority of onomatopoeia in American comics are translated with Spanish equivalents.

Paradoxically, it may be the case that some original Spanish comics contain, in addition to original Spanish creations, a larger percentage of 'English' onomatopoeia than is usually found in American comics translated into Spanish. It is hoped that this paper may serve as a basis for future research on onomatopoeia in Spanish comic books, translated and originally written in Spanish, to be carried out with more extensive corpora, including comics translated into Spanish from other languages.

References

Primary Sources

Crumb, Robert (1987) *My Trouble with Women I, II* San Francisco: Last Gasp [Spanish translation by Narcís Fradera, *Mis problemas con las mujeres* [I and II] Barcelona: Ediciones La Cúpula, Collection *El Víbora*].

El País Dominical (2005) Madrid: El País.

El Pequeño País (2005-6) from November 2005 till June 2006. 32 issues. Madrid: El País.

Escobar, Josep (2005) *Zipi and Zape*, in *Las mejores historias del comic español*, Biblioteca del Mundo, 2.

Ibáñez, Francisco (2005) *Mortadelo y Filemón*, in *Las mejores historias del comic español*, Biblioteca del Mundo, 4.

Ibáñez, Francisco (2005) *Rompetechos*, in *Las mejores historias del comic español*, Biblioteca del Mundo, 6.

Jones, Gerard, Jeff Johnson and Dan Panosian (1992) *Wonder Man* no. 12, ' Espejo' [Spanish translation by Madelón Trumpi], Barcelona: Planeta Agostini [original title: *Wonder Man*, 'Shadow of the Infinite', no. 15, Marvel Comics].

Kaminki, Len et al. (1993) *¿Y si los vengadores?*, part 2 of 2, no. 64 [Spanish translation by Xavi Marturet], Barcelona: Planeta Agostini [Original text: *What if . . .?*, vol. 2, no. 56, Marvel Comics].

Kaminski, Len and Kev Hopgood (1992) *El origen de la máquina de guerra*, no. 1 of 6 [Spanish translation by E. Braun], Barcelona: Planeta Agostini [Original title: *Iron Man*, no. 280 and 281, Marvel Comics].

Midam (2006) *Kid Paddle*, in *El Pequeño País*, January 22, 2006.

Mills, Pat, Tony Skinner, Tom Morgan, Jim Palmiotti and Ian Laughlin (1993) *Punisher 2099* no. 5 of 12 [Spanish translation by Madelón Trumpi], Barcelona: Planeta Agostini. [Original title: *Punisher 2099*, 'Punishment Hotel', vol. 1, no. 5, Marvel Comics)].

Potts, Carl, Tom Lyle, Al Milgrom and Josef Rubinstein (1993) *Veneno* no. 2 of 3 [Spanish translation by Celia Filipetto], Barcelona: Planeta Agostini [Original title: *USA Venom: Funeral Pyre*, no. 2, Marvel Comics].

Sanvi & Vergara (2005) *Multiman*, in *El Jueves, la revista de humor que sale los miércoles*, Nov. 2005.

Shelton, Gilbert (1977) *Las Famosas Aventuras de los Freak Brothers* [Spanish translation by Luis Vigil, Barcelona: Producciones Editoriales].

Valentino, Jim (1991) *Guardianes de las Galaxias* no. 12 [Spanish translation by Xavi Marturet], Barcelona: Planeta Agostini [Original title *The Guardians of the Galaxy*, vol. 1, no. 12, Marvel Comics].

Watterson, William (1994) *Calvin y Hobbes* [Spanish translation by Gabriel Roura], Barcelona: Norma Editorial.

Secondary Sources

Alatarriba, Antonio (2001) *La España del tebeo* [Comic books in Spain], Madrid: Espasa Calpe.

Benayoun, Robert (1968) *Le Ballon dans la bande dessinée, vroom, tchac, zowie*, Paris: A. Balland.

Gubern, Román (1979) *El lenguaje de los comic books* [The language of comic books], Barcelona: Península.

Guiral, Antonio (2004) *Cuando los cómics se llamaban tebeos. La Escuela Bruguera (1945-1963)* [When the comic books were called 'tebeos'. The Bruguera School (1945- 1963], Barcelona: El Jueves.

Lladó, Fernando (2002) *Los cómics de la transición (el boom del cómic adulto 1975-1984)* [The comic books of the transition period. The boom of the comic books for adults 1975-1984]), Barcelona: Glénat.

Martínez Fuentes, Eva (2003) *Onomatopoeia Translation in Comic books* (online) http://www.fut.es/~apym/students/eva/eva.html (Accessed 10 January 2006).

Mayoral, Roberto (1984) 'Los cómics: de la reproducción gráfica de sonidos a los verbos dibujados en inglés. Más sobre problemas de traducción' [Comic books: from the graphic reproduction of sounds to verbs which are drawn in English. More on problems of translation], *Babel: Revista de los estudiantes de la EUTI* 2: 120-30.

------ (1992) 'Formas inarticuladas y formas onomatopéyicas en inglés y español. Problemas de traducción' [Unarticulated and onomatopoeic forms in English and Spanish. Translation problems], *Sendebar* 3: 107-39.

Rabadán, Rosa (1991) *Equivalencia y Traducción. Problemática de la equivalencia translémica inglés-español* [Translation and Equivalence. Questioning English-Spanish Translemic Equivalente], León: Universidad de León.

Santoyo, Julio César (1985) *El delito de traducir* [The crime of translating], León: Universidad de León, 169-172.

Schnetzer, Michaela (2004) *Problems in the Translation of Comic books and Cartoons* (online) http://www-unix.oit.umass.edu/~michaela/Writing/comicbooks%20translation.pdf (Accessed 10 January 2006).

Valero Garcés, Carmen (1995a) 'Un subgénero literario en traducción: los cómics y tebeos' [A literary subgenre in translation: the comics], in Carmen Valero Garcés (ed.) *Apuntes sobre traducción literaria y análisis contrastivo de textos literarios traducidos*, Alcalá de Henares: Universidad de Alcalá de Henares, 93-106.

------ (1995b) 'Uso y traducción de formas inarticuladas y formas onomatopéyicas en comic books y tebeos' [The use and transation of partially articulated forms and onomatopoeia in comic books], in Carmen Valero Garcés (ed.) *Apuntes sobre traducción literaria y análisis contrastivo de textos literarios traducidos*, Alcalá de Henares: Universidad de Alcalá de Henares, 107-126.

------ (1997) 'Humor and Translation. American Comic Books in Spanish. A Case Study: R. Crumb', in Ricardo J. Sola, Luis A. Lázaro and José A. Gurpegui (eds) *Proceedings of the XVIII Congreso de AEDEAN*, Alcalá de Henares: Universidad de Alcalá de Henares, 351-358.

------ (2000) 'La traducción del cómic: retos, estrategias y resultados' [Translation of Comic books: Challenges, Strategies and Results], *Trans: Revista de traductología* 4: 75-88.

12 Proper Names, Onomastic Puns and Spoonerisms

Some Aspects of the Translation of the Astérix *and* Tintin *Comic Series, with Special Reference to English*

CATHERINE DELESSE
University of Artois, France

This article deals with the English translations of two famous comic series, Tintin *(by Hergé, Belgium) and* Astérix *(by Goscinny and Uderzo, France), both of which aim to amuse the reader and are based to a large extent on verbal humour. After introducing the two series and their translators, this study examines the specificity of the language of the original texts. Given that the large number of books in the series makes an exhaustive analysis impossible in the space of a single article, only the translation of some proper names, onomastic puns and spoonerisms is examined. The selected examples are analyzed in some detail: first the author discusses the linguistic devices used by the authors of the French original texts, and second, the choices made by the translators, which depend both on the nature of the target language (English) and on the relationship between image and text, and which lie between formal equivalence and total adaptation. The British editions are the result of the work of a single set of translators for each of the two series, and often show greater coherence than their original counterparts. The translators, especially those of the* Astérix *series, used different types of compensation strategies and successfully achieved 'generalized compensation' throughout the text.*

Astérix *and* Tintin are two of the most famous comics characters in the world, and their stories have been translated into more than 50 languages. While the aim of the authors of both series was first and foremost to entertain the reader, the plots, characters and language used in the two series are different.

Hergé's production of *Tintin* spans the years 1929 to 1976. Humour in the *Tintin* series depends not only on puns but also on slapstick and visual gags. Hergé, who is famous for his style and artwork – called *la ligne claire* (lit.: 'clear line'), restricts the use of wordplay to a few emblematic characters. Whereas Tintin speaks like the man in the street would, the other major characters display a number of idiosyncrasies. The two detectives, Dupont and Dupond, specialize in blunders of all kinds, which result in their constant use of spoonerisms. The Italian opera singer, Bianca Castafiore, behaves like a diva, uses Italian expressions and spends her time getting people's names wrong. Captain Haddock is famous for his use of sailors' phrases and his creativity in the field of insults, whereas Professor Tournesol's deafness results in constant misunderstandings. Thus it can be said that each character has his or her own idiolect.

Astérix was created in 1959 by Goscinny (the writer) and Uderzo (who did the artwork). After Goscinny's death in 1977, Uderzo continued the work on his own. The whole *Astérix* series is largely based on humour. The style of drawing is caricatural, with some characters being based on real-life people. Verbal humour relies extensively on wordplay, and is mostly based on cultural allusions and clichés distorted for comic purposes (Delesse 2001), with many jokes depending on the interplay of verbal and visual elements. Unlike *Tintin*, which is more or less set in the modern world, the adventures of *Astérix* are supposed to take place in the Gaul of 50 BC while really describing French society in the 50s and 60s; as a result, *Astérix* is full of anachronisms.

Astérix's and *Tintin*'s adventures are probably the most researched comics in translation studies literature (see the annotated bibliography at the end of this volume). Aspects investigated include the translation of humour, citations, cultural allusions and stereotypes, and the interplay between verbal and non-verbal elements, while target languages include Arabic, Spanish, English, Polish, Italian, German, Finnish and Croatian. In this article I discuss how English language translators have met the challenge of translating humorous language in the *Astérix* and *Tintin* series, focusing on the translation of proper names, onomastic puns and spoonerisms.

Both *Tintin* and *Astérix* have their own set of translators who have translated the series in its entirety. All *Tintin*'s adventures were translated by Leslie Lonsdale-Cooper and Michael Turner, and Anthea Bell and Derek Hockridge have likewise translated the whole *Astérix* series into British English.[1] While both series are read by both adults and children in France, in the United Kingdom they are mainly viewed as child-oriented. Leslie Lonsdale-Cooper has stressed this fact in one of her letters: "As we [Lonsdale-Cooper and Turner] see it Tintin is an entertainment, aimed first at children, to be taken from one culture – French – and made an entertainment for those in another culture – the English. So we aimed, like Hergé, to entertain".[2]

The large number of books in the series – 23 in the case of *Tintin* and 33 in the case of *Astérix* – makes an exhaustive analysis impossible in the space of a single article. Translating humour sometimes involves dealing with cultural references for which there is no equivalent in the target language, and the translators have to take into account not only the text but also the drawings, which may help or hinder them in their translation. The visual component partly reveals what the language hides: we find at work in comics two strategies acting together, one aiming at concealing and another at revealing what is hidden – which makes the task of translating difficult. As far as wordplay is concerned, special attention is required for those systemic features of language on which puns are based, such as polysemy, homophony and paronymy. I focus here on examples from a few albums to see how the translators solved the problems they faced.

I first explain the meaning of proper names in French and the methods used by the authors to construct them, providing a literal gloss for all examples. Then I discuss how they have been translated into English as well as into other languages. In the following sections I discuss the published translations of onomastic or 'naming' puns and of spoonerisms or *contrepèteries*.

---

[1] It is to be noted that a few *Astérix* stories – five in all – have been translated into American English, but this study will be mainly concerned with the British translations.

[2] Personal letter from Leslie Lonsdale-Cooper, 9/9/1992. For Anthea Bell's comments on her translations, see Bell (1996, n.d.).

1. Proper Names

Proper names created by the authors of both series were translated in the majority of cases. However, in each series the names of the main characters remained identical in English, either because the meaning was the same, or the sounds could be pronounced easily in the target language. In *The Adventures of Astérix*, we also encounter real historical characters whose names have been kept in English with the appropriate spelling: Cléopâtre → Cleopatra, Jules César → Julius Caesar, to give but two examples. In *Tintin*, there are no real historical characters as such, so all the names have been invented, but since the adventures take place in the twentieth century, the names in the series sound more familiar than do Goscinny's, which are often elaborate creations with the sole purpose of producing humorous effects.

1.1 *Proper Names in* Tintin

The name of the hero Tintin is pronounced /tɛ̃tɛ̃/ in French and /tɪntɪn/ in English, with a similar effect in both cases due to the repetition of two identical syllables. In French, the word is either onomatopoeic, evoking the chinking of glasses, or an exclamation meaning 'nothing doing' or 'no way'. In English the repetition of the word 'tin' makes it easy to pronounce for children and may evoke the sound made by a metal container. The name was maintained in Italian and Spanish but was changed into *Tim* in German and became *Tantan* in Russian – perhaps because the word *tina* in Russian means 'silt' or 'mud', something too unpleasant to be associated with a pure, positive hero like Tintin. The two detectives or policemen in the series, Dupont and Dupond, were the first characters created after Tintin and his dog. Their name is very common in French: it is said to be the most common surname after Martin. The choice of a banal name reveals their general mediocrity and stupidity, but it is also a reflection of their physical appearance, since, just as their names differ in only one consonant (both are pronounced /dypɔ̃/), so they look like identical twins except for the shape of their moustache. The choice made by the translators fills the requirements: the names Thomson and Thompson have an identical pronunciation (/tɒmsn/), they differ by one mute consonant only, have two syllables just like the original and are commonplace English names. As the two characters use this slight spelling difference as a mode of identification, especially when on the phone, it was very important to keep it: *Ici Dupond avec d et Dupont avec t…* (lit.: This is Dupond with 'd' and Dupont with 't')(*Les bijoux de la Castafiore / The Castafiore Emerald* (from now on *Castafiore*),[3] p. 28) translated as "This is Thompson and Thomson with a 'p' and without…".

Table 12.1 shows how for the names of the detectives most translators worked along the same lines as the English translators. The idea of keeping names that look almost identical and differ in one phoneme is faithfully respected by all translators, although we

---

[3] After the first mention each album is referred to throughout the article by using one word from the title. See the bibliographical section for full references.

note that the Russian translator chose to keep the original names, using a vocalic sound as a variant, and that the Italian translator was the only one who chose not to translate.[4]

French	English	German	Italian	Russian	Spanish
Tintin (reporter)	Tintin	Tim	Tintin	Tantan	Tintin
Milou (dog)	Snowy	Struppi	Milù	Melok	Milú
Dupont (detective)	Thomson	Schulze	Dupont	Djupon	Hernández
Dupond (detective)	Thompson	Schultze	Dupond	Djupan	Fernández
Haddock (Navy captain)	Haddock	Haddock	Haddock	Xaddok	Haddock
Tryphon Tournesol (professor)	Cuthbert Calculus	Balduin Bienlein	Trifone Girasole	Trjufon Lakmus	Silvestre Tornasol

Table 12.1: The names of the main characters in *Tintin* in six languages

Captain Haddock, Tintin's faithful friend in all the stories from *Le crabe aux pinces d'or / The Crab with the Golden Claws* to the last album *Tintin et les Picaros / Tintin and the Picaros*, has an English name to begin with (an English loan word in French), so perhaps the question of translating it never arose. It seems Hergé encountered an international success with this, since the captain keeps his name in all the languages into which the series was translated. Being a navy man, it is fitting that he should be named after a fish. Moreover, the fact that the sounds of the word can be found in most languages probably explains its popularity. Fresnault-Deruelle noted the fact, stating that the name was composed of two vowels, <a> and <o>, which are quite distinct (1972:151). I would suggest that the articulation of these two open vowels is quite evocative of the mouth of the captain, usually wide open for shouts and insults. These two vowels are so characteristic that when Haddock meets the Italian opera singer, Bianca Castafiore, the vocalic sounds are always retained even though she constantly misquotes his name. For example, in the French version of *Castafiore*, she calls him Bartock, Kappock, Koddack, Mastock, Kosack, Hammock, Kolback, Karbock, Kornack, Hablock, Maggock, and Kapstock, thus keeping both vowels, doubling the <o> as in Hoclock or the <a> as in Karnack and Balzack, and only once changing one vowel to <e> as in Medock. The sound /k/, a voiceless plosive, appears in each variant, and as is the case in the original name with /d/ a voiced consonant is added, and the new names created always end with the written form <ck>. As far as the meaning of the words is concerned, we find a famous musician, a well-known

---

[4] It would probably have been possible to find two similar names in Italian, but my Italian colleagues suggested that the pleasure of a French-looking and sounding name was important for an Italian audience.

French writer, an Egyptian archeological site, a photographic firm, a Bordeaux wine and common words like *cornac* ('mahout'), *colback* (familiar for 'neck'), the adjective *mastoc* ('hefty'), an idiomatic expression *à bloc* ('as tight as possible'), to name but a few. The English translations, given in the same order as the French names above, are: Bartok, Fatstock, Drydocks, Hopscotch, Stopcock, Hammock, Paddock, Hassock, Bootblack, Bedsock, Padlock, Stockpot, Maggot, Havoc, Balzac and Hatbox. As can be seen from the list, the translators have respected the original in the sense that they have made variations around the same vowels <a,o>, with one exception concerning the <y> in Drydocks, and kept the same sound /k/ in all the words. But they did not keep the idea of combining voiced and voiceless consonants, since words like Hopscotch, Stockpot, Hassock and Stopcock only contain voiceless ones. The written form <ck> at the end of the words is not regularly used either, but that is not surprising for names like Bartok and Balzac, since, compared to French, English always remains closer to the original spelling of foreign words. Only three of the original sixteen words were kept in English (Karnak and Cossack would have been understood by an English reader, whereas others obviously had to be changed), which means the translators clearly looked for words which would amuse the reader rather than cling to the original for fidelity's sake.

The name of the Professor is also an interesting creation because it uses devices Hergé favoured for a certain number of characters: the use of a very old-fashioned first name (Haddock's is Archibald, as we find out in the very last book *Picaros*) and two words starting with the same initial, T in this case. The word *tournesol* has two meanings in French: 'sunflower', or the chemical called 'litmus' in English. All translators have looked for an equally old-fashioned and ridiculous first name, either creating a new one from scratch or adapting the original one to target language conventions, as in Italian and Russian. However, only the English and German ones have respected the alliteration. The term 'calculus' is in keeping with the character's knowledge of physics and his invention of the moon rocket. The German translation evokes the bee with the word *Biene* + the diminutive suffix *-lein*, thus referring to the Professor's hyperactivity as an inventor. The Italian and Spanish words are exact translations of 'sunflower', whereas the Russian word means 'litmus', the other – and first – meaning of the French word. Table 1 seems to me a perfect illustration of what Dirk Delabastita says about translators who "permanently have to make choices which involve weighing 'loss' against 'gain' and pondering the pros and cons of some 'sacrifice' or other, so that there are good reasons for viewing *any* translations as the outcome of a delicate balancing act" (Delabastita 1997:11). The Italian, Russian, and to a certain extent, Spanish translators rendered most of the names with almost literal translations, possibly because of specific target readership conventions and norms and publisher's demands, while the words chosen by English and German translators are not faithful to the French in meaning. However, I would argue that the latter are closer to the original in spirit, because they kept features such as alliteration, retained the same number of syllables and often created names based on words bearing a relationship to the characters' activity.

Let us now turn to proper names which are based on combinations of words and need to be deciphered. For instance, in the book *America*, a character named Tom

Hawake works for a firm called Slift, which produces canned corned beef: his name reads as 'tomahawk' when pronounced in French, but could be read as 'awake' in English,[5] so the translators changed it into Maurice Oyle, corresponding phonetically to 'Morris Oil'. There does not seem to be any specific meaning for Slift, so it might have been chosen because it sounded English, unless Hergé used a word from the Brussels dialect as a basis for this name, which he often did (Delesse 2006). This name was translated as Grynde, a reference to the activity of the factory and to the fact that Tintin himself was intended to be ground into corned beef during the visit. The name of the firm in English bears a direct relationship with the events described in the illustrations, whereas the French name of the character corresponds more to his actions: after all, Tom Hawake tries to kill Tintin and a tomahawk is a weapon.

Two other examples of a combination of names can be found in *Cigars*, where a man named Philémon Siclone possesses a manuscript leading to a pharaoh's tomb. The pharaoh's name is Kih-Oskh. If we read these names aloud in French, we get *Filez mon cyclone* for the first name and *kiosque* for the second one. The latter can be easily deciphered by an English reader despite the difference in spelling (*kiosk*), while the former is a simple sentence composed of a verb in the imperative form followed by a possessive determiner and a noun which can be glossed as follows: 'rush / speed off, my cyclone'. The name of the pharaoh was kept unaltered in the translation, probably because the same word exists in English and can be easily deciphered when read aloud. The translators rendered the name of the Egyptologist as Sophocles Sarcophagus. Philémon is a real first name in French, and as it is the name of a character in Ovid's *Metamorphoses*, it probably inspired the translators who chose the name of a great figure of Ancient Greece – Sophocles – in order to keep some kind of cultural equivalence. The reason for the English surname is to be found in the drawing (Figure 12.1).

When the Egyptologist disappears, Tintin follows him into a tomb where he finds a row of sarcophagi, among which there are three empty ones, bearing the following inscriptions: *PH. SICLONE égyptologue, MILOU chien, TINTIN journaliste* (S. SARCOPHAGUS Egyptologist, SNOWY Dog, TINTIN Journalist). The drawing must have triggered the translation, but the English name is also in keeping with Hergé's use of identical initials for his characters, as seen in Figure 12.1. In this example humour is present in both cases but hinges on different mechanisms, since the French name is based on a linear reading of the text, whereas the English one is situational. This is also true of the names Tom Hawake and Grynde.

This device is used on a further occasion, again in *Cigars*, where one of the sarcophagi (a full one, this time) bears the name of another Egyptologist, I.E. Roghliff, which reads *hiéroglyphe* (hieroglyph). It was probably difficult to get the same effect in English since the <h> is not mute as it is in French, so the translators decided to transform the name into P. Schwartz, pronounced /piːʃwɔːts/, which is close to 'peach warts'. Another sarcophagus contains a certain E. P. Jacobini,[6] who is none other than E. P. Jacobs, a close collaborator of Hergé's at the time, who later produced his own comic series entitled *Les aventures de Blake et Mortimer* (*The adventures of Blake and Mortimer*).

---

[5] Actually, Tom Awake was the name given in the first French version of 1931.
[6] This name is kept in English of course, as it is a coded allusion.

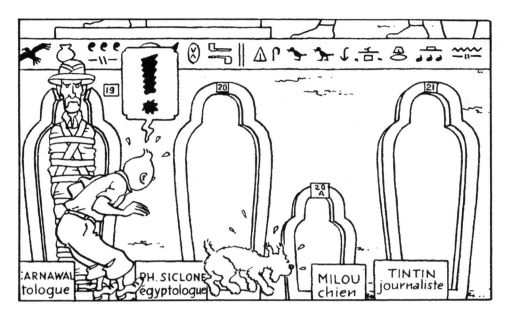

Figure 12.1: Hergé, *Les cigares du Pharaon*, 1955, p. 8

In *Cigars* the same device is repeated a number of times: we meet the tribe of the *Bouaras* (*boiras* = 'will drink') translated as the Djelababi tribe ('jelly baby' or 'jellaba' + 'baby'); Tintin enlists as a soldier giving an Arabic-sounding name *Beh-Behr* (*Bébert*, a French diminutive for Albert) which will become Ali-Bhai in English, thus using a real Muslim name 'Ali' as well as producing a name that reads 'alibi' and is particularly adapted to the circumstances, since Tintin is a deserter. In the last cases, the translators adopt Hergé's device of juxtaposing words. In this respect one of the best names in Hergé's work is unquestionably that of the butcher of the village where Haddock lives: *Sanzot* (*sans os* = 'without bones'), splendidly translated as Cutts the butcher.

Of course, it would be necessary to examine all the names created by Hergé to draw a definite conclusion, but it is clear that the translators used the illustrations as an aid to translating when it became difficult to follow the French in the way words are juxtaposed or amalgamated – although they do it when then can (alibi, jelly baby). The French uses phonemic combinations and syntactic combinations, whereas the English transposes from the visual component into a syllabic or word combination.

1.2   Names and Nationalities in Astérix

Even more challenging in the *Astérix* series, since Goscinny used the device systematic-ally, is the question of translating complicated portmanteau names. A general policy of adaptation was followed by the translators of *Astérix*. According to Anthea Bell (personal communication) the translators decided that, if they could not keep to the letter and the spirit of the original, then clearly the spirit had to come first. The translators adapted the texts especially, but not exclusively, when the names or puns were based on systemic features of the source language (see Embleton 1991 for a cross-language comparison of translated names in the *Astérix* series).

One of the challenges the translators had to face in *Astérix* is the way the patronymics (and toponyms) are built around a radical to which a suffix of nationality is added: *-ix* for the Gauls, *-ic* for the Goths, *-us* for the Romans, *-um* for Roman place names, *-af* for the Normans, *-ax* for the Britons and so on. This implies that the translators had to find words to which the suffixes could be added in a natural way. Another problem is the construction of the names themselves because, if the two heroes' names are based upon a single noun, most of the time the authors have used two words or more, combining them so that their meaning stands out only when read aloud. This was also done to some extent by Hergé in *Tintin* (see section 1.1), but not as systematically as by Goscinny, who even created names by using whole sentences (including at least one complex sentence) or subordinate clauses. The following example may serve as an illustration: in *Astérix gladiateur/Asterix the Gladiator*, a Gaulish restaurant owner is called Plaintcontrix in French which, when read aloud, gives *plainte contre X* – a legal term meaning 'complaint against person or persons unknown'. A literal translation would have implied using an exceedingly long English phrase as well as attaching the required suffix *-ix*. The translators decided to change the name altogether and called him Instantmix, a name which bears a strong relationship with his profession. The result in English is a name which amuses the reader, is related to cooking and to what is shown in the panels, but is an anachronism – thus keeping in tune with the series in which anachronisms abound – and can be pronounced easily. Last but not least, the word 'mix' already has the required ending. Obviously the translators could not always find words which already ended with the desired suffix, but in each case (there are over 440 invented names in the *Astérix* series) they managed to find words whose endings fit the suffix requirement quite naturally. Where the Gaulish and Gothic endings are concerned, the translators have used adjectives and nouns ending in *-ic(s)*, a very productive suffix in English which is of Latin origin, via French – Lat. *-icus* > Fr. *-ique* > E. *-ic*. The French authors have also used the same suffix for the names of the Gauls and Goths. A few examples of names which are identical can be given, i.e. Satiric (Fr. *satirique*), Prefix (Fr. *préfixe*), and the Roman Tullius Octopus.

For the Roman suffixes the translators used many words borrowed from Latin, such as 'status', 'bonus' or 'album', and for the most part they picked adjective and noun suffixes such as *-ous*, *-ious*, *-uous*, *-ium*, *-ius*, etc. which are common in English. By doing so, they managed to create proper names which are easily recognizable (with only minor spelling alterations: *-ous* > *-us*) and pronounced identically, since these endings are always pronounced /əs/. The translators seem to have been very careful to respect the English language; in general they have avoided adding a syllable when adding the suffix, but when on occasion they have done so, the word is easily recognizable, as is the case with Marcus Ginantonicus, who appears in *Astérix le Gaulois / Asterix the Gaul*, in spite of the added suffix. One can see that the added suffix does not hamper the pronunciation in any way. This name is also a case of total adaptation: in French he was called Marcus Sacapus, or *sac à puces* (lit.: 'bag of fleas'), which used to refer to a bed but nowadays refers to a dog. The way the words are combined conceals the original spelling, but reading the word aloud brings back the hidden meaning. This almost systematic use of word-combination was a problem for the translators, as was the different word order between the two languages. In French the adjective is usually placed after the noun, whereas the reverse is true in English (one of the reasons why *Astérix chez les Bretons / Asterix in Britain* is so hilarious in French is that Goscinny copied the structure of English in French). This of course led to various strategies of compensation.

Table 12.2 shows the names of the main characters in *Astérix* in the translations by Anthea Bell and Derek Hockridge for the British market. By way of comparison, the translation for the American editions by Steven Caron is also listed, as well as the translations in three other languages.

French	British English	American English	German	Italian	Spanish
Astérix	Asterix	Asterix	Asterix	Asterix	Asterix
Obélix	Obelix	Obelix	Obelix	Obelix	Obelix
Idéfix (dog)	Dogmatix	Dogmatix	Idefix	Idefix	Idefix
Panoramix (druid)	Getafix	Magigimmix	Miraculix	Panoramix	Panoramix
Abraracourcix (chief)	Vitalstatistics	Macroeconomix	Majestix	Abraracourcix	Abraracurcix
Assurancetourix (bard)	Cacofonix	Malacoustix	Troubadix	Assurancetourix	Asuranceturix
Ordralfabétix (fishmonger)	Unhygienix	Epidemix	Verleihnix	Ordinalfabetix	Ordenalfabetix

Table 12.2: The names of the main characters in *Astérix* in six languages

As stated above, the two heroes of *Astérix* kept their names in English as well as in other languages. The only difference between the French original and the translations is the accent on the <e> in French, which naturally disappears in English. The meanings of the names are obvious in both languages (*astérisque / asterisk, obélisque / obelisk*). Asterix is the hero of the adventures, the 'star' which is the etymological basis of the name. Obelix is quite fat and the beginning of his name in both languages rhymes with 'obese'; the name also fits his profession since he cuts and delivers menhirs.

All the other names are the result of word-combinations: Obelix's dog is called Idéfix in French, with the Noun-Adjective order, *idée fixe* ('fixed idea' or 'obsession'). Translating it literally would have meant combining words so as to produce 'Fixedidea*ix*' which would have been difficult both to pronounce and to decipher visually. Another option would have been to keep the French name, thus violating the rules of English syntax. Anthea Bell stated (personal communication) that she regretted "jettisoning the name 'Idéfix' for the dog," but that she realized "that the accent would have made it a little difficult for children in the English-speaking world".[7] In fact the English name, Dogmatix, is excellent (so much so that the American translator chose the same), for although the word 'dogmatic' is not the exact equivalent of the French *idée fixe*, it is nevertheless not far from the idea it conveys, and it has the advantage of containing the word 'dog'. As can be seen in Table 2, the name is left as in the original in all the other translations.

To give another example of a name based on the Noun-Adjective order, I will analyze the name of the fishmonger, whose English name appears more meaningful than the French. Ordralfabétix (*ordre alphabétique* or 'alphabetical order'), although amusing, does not tell us anything about the character himself. Here again the constraint of putting the adjective first in English prevented the translators from resorting to a calque. In the village he is famous for selling rotten fish, which causes many fights. This led the British translators to adopt Unhygienix, a strategy imitated by the American translator who called him Epidemix. The idea of the lack of hygiene was extended to his wife, whose name in French is Iélosubmarine – a clear reference to the title of a Beatles song – and to his father, whose French name Oftalmologix (*ophtalmologiste* = ophtalmologist) is linked to the medical field, a favourite source of the authors. However, since the translators had decided to lay the stress on the poor quality of the fish, they called the fisherman's wife Bacteria and his father Unhealthix. This has a very important consequence, since in English the patronymic has a connotation the French original name does not have and, as often happens in the English translation, is thus perfectly tuned to the content of the books.

The German translator drew her inspiration from the first appearance of the fishmonger in the Spanish adventure. As the little Spanish boy refuses to eat boar and wants fish instead, Obélix borrows a fish from Ordralfabétix and, pretending he had rented it, he brings it back later. This episode led to the translation as Verleihnix: *verleihen* means 'rent' and the name reads as *verleih(e) nix* (lit.: 'do not rent'). However, whereas the German translation is inspired by a specific episode in a particular book, with the risk that it will not be understood by all readers, the English name refers to a situation recurring in all the adventures and is thus more consistent with the general context of the series.

In the case of the fishmonger's name, connotation is greater in English than in French, while in other cases it is the denotation which is greater: in French the two bandits in *Le tour de Gaule / Asterix and the Banquet* bear the names Plexus and Radius, which refer to parts of the human body (bones are among the authors' favourite naming sources), whereas the translation points to their trade with the names Villanus and Unscrupulus. Contrary to what happens in French, the English names give them away immediately, as often happens with negative characters. This may be due to the fact that in England comics are targeted primarily at children. However, it does not really

---

[7] Personal e-mail, November 2005.

impede the suspense, because we generally see very quickly what a character is up to. The plot is never very intricate in the *Astérix* stories so that it can be understood easily by children, although adults read them at a different level in order to enjoy all the jokes, cultural references and double entendres.

One of the techniques extensively used by the translators of *Astérix* in order to make up for the impossibility of keeping the Noun-Adjective order in English was to use an Adjective-Noun order for the Romans, the adjective becoming a first name and the noun a surname. In French, the Romans almost always have a real Roman Christian name (Caius, Gaius, Lucius, etc) followed by a family name which is a combination of words. A good example is the name Encoreutilfaluquejelesus (lit.: I might have if I had known) in *Banquet*. This is the most complicated French name in the series, composed of a main clause [*encore eût-il fallu*] and a subordinate clause [*que je le susse*]. What makes the name possible in French is the fact that the past subjunctive of the verb *savoir* (know) ends in *-usse*, easily transformed into the Roman ending *-us*. The French language can make great use of the conjugation system and the fact that adjectives are not invariable (often used as adjectives, past participles ending in *-u* give *-us* in the plural and have been used extensively by the authors), whereas English has a limited amount of declensions. This is a clear case of compensation linked with "a systemic mismatch between source and target languages" (Harvey 1995:69). The character mentioned above is called Poisonus Fungus in English; the translators, being unable to make such a complicated compound as in French, chose to simplify the name, using the adjective 'poisonous' as the first name and 'fungus' as the surname. They did this quite often, producing such combinations in English as Dubius Status or Odius Asparagus. This is a clever way of using the language in order to create patronymics which are as amusing as the original ones, even if they are not a faithful translation, and it enables the translators to generalize compensation throughout the text. The term "stylistic-systemic compensation" coined by Harvey (1995:78) can be used here, since the use of patronymics both has a stylistic effect and draws upon the systemic features of the language.

Yet another way of compensating for the combinations was to create series of names with a semantic relationship, such as the list of the clan chiefs in *Astérix en Corse / Asterix in Corsica*. The French names bear no relation to each other and form a rather heterogeneous list: Violonccellix (cellist), Tropolix (too polite), Hérettix (heretic), Mineralogix ('mineralogical', or refers to car number plates), Appatix (apathetic), Sinfonix (symphonic), Plaindetix (full of tics / ticks), Osterlix (Austerlitz), Paléontologix (paleontological) and Squinotix (water skiing). The English translations are Potatognocchix, Semolinagnocchix, Spaghettix, Raviolix, Tagliatellix, Cannellonix, Lasagnix, MacAronix, Fettucinix and Rigatonix. In English we are given a list of the different kinds of Italian pasta, which makes a consistent meaningful whole. The proximity between Corsica and Italy undoubtedly inspired the translators, but they may also have got the idea from the authors themselves, who used the names of Italian and Corsican sausages for two characters in the story, Salamix and Figatellix, and even Chipolata for one female character. Again the translations are in keeping with the general tendency of the series, since Goscinny and Uderzo used many words from the semantic field of food and drink (their other favourites are the fields of health and medicine, arts and literature, and plants, which we find in similar proportions in the English translations).

The translation quite often improves on the original, not in the sense that the patronymics are funnier than in French (although sometimes they are) but, as the translators could not always follow the authors in their word-combinations or in keeping the same meaning, they tried to make up for this loss by creating a stronger link between the names and the characters' professions, personalities or physical aspects. An alternative strategy was to make lists of names (as seen above) with words from a specific semantic field, thus applying different strategies of compensation, whether analogical, contiguous or parallel according to Harvey's terminology (1995:81-82).

2.   Onomastic Puns

Many puns are linked with proper names, especially in the *Astérix* books, and here again I will be selective in illustrating the way the translators tackled the problems. I shall start with one pun which could not be translated as such, and had to be changed entirely. The pun in question comes out of a dialogue between two Norman warriors (see Figure 12.2a, centre fold), designated by letters A and B.

> (1) PLAF ! (Splash)
> A: Présent ! (Here)
> B: Mais non ! (No one called you) (*Normans*, p. 21)

The gloss between brackets gives an idea of the problem involved. One of the warriors throws water at a Gaul who has been clubbed. The onomatopoeia in French for this sound is *Plaf*, and as the Norman names all end in *-af*, another warrior, thinking he has been called, answers 'here', then a third one corrects the mistake. The problem for the translators was that the natural onomatopoeia in English in this case is 'splash', which is the one they have used, but it cannot work as a Norman name because it does not have the required nationality suffix. The translators had to get round the difficulty but had no other solution for the onomatopoeia, so they changed the rest of the exchange as follows (see Figure 12.2b, centre fold):

> (1') SPLASH!
> A: Hasting's the word…
> B: Surely it's not 1066 yet? (*Normans*, p. 21)

This pun is based on a historical allusion, inspired by the fact that we are dealing with Normans, but nevertheless, it is far from the original text and cannot be explained without looking at what the Norman chief says in the preceding frame: "Right. Bring him round. Come here, all! Make haste!". In the French original text, the rapidity is not mentioned and the word 'haste' has clearly been added in order to make the pun on Hastings possible because of the paronymy / heɪst / versus / heɪstɪŋz /. The translation here again plays with the anachronisms for which the series is famous, using the same kind of wordplay based on phonetic similarities that the authors themselves often use. The translators displaced the pun slightly as regards the original text, but managed to maintain a kind of wordplay based on phonemic features, adding a cultural reference into the bargain.

In the following example they kept a similar idea, but with a change of words due to a difference of connotation between French and English. On the first page of *Astérix aux jeux olympiques / Asterix and the Olympic Games*, one legionary wonders what all the noise he hears is about. Another one explains that they are celebrating the selection of one member of the garrison for the Olympic Games (the athlete's name is *Claudius Cornedurus* in French, *Gluteus Maximus* in English), which triggers the following exchange (*Olympic*, p. 5):

> (2) A: Cornedurus ? Qui est-ce ?
> *Gluteus Maximus? Who's he?*
> B: On voit bien que tu es un **bleu, Deprus** !
> *You're pretty **green**, aren't you, **Bilius** ?*

The published translation, in italics, immediately follows the French text, and the words under scrutiny are highlighted in bold. There is a change of colour from blue to green, which led to a change of patronymic for A. Legionary A does not know the champion, so B mocks him, referring to his inexperience, *un bleu* meaning a 'beginner', or rather in this context a 'rookie'. His name *Deprus* enables the French to read the words as *bleu de Prusse* (Prussian blue), thus making a horizontal pun. In English the colour green suggests youth and inexperience, so naturally the translators used this colour, which implied by way of consequence a change of name. The word 'bilious' refers to green and enables the translators to have a two-syllable name as in French, keeping a pun based on the same idea.

I will give a third example from *Asterix* before turning to Hergé's work. In *Le combat des chefs / Asterix and the Big Fight*, *Langélus*, the centurion of Totorum,[8] is angry because the Gauls keep ridiculing the Roman army, so his aide-de-camp says to him:

> (3) Il faut trouver une solution, ô **Langélus**… sinon **Rome va te sonner les cloches** !
> *We have to find a solution, o **Nebulus Nimbus**… if they get to hear of this in Rome,* **you'll be under a cloud.** (*Fight*, p. 6)

In the French version, the humour comes from the association of the patronymic *Langélus*, which refers both to the Catholic rite and to the ringing of the bell calling people

---

[8] This is another clever translation, since the French name of the Roman camp is Babaorum, that is to say *baba au rhum*, a French pastry. Here food is turned into drink but the reference to rum is kept with the same kind of compounding as in French.

to this prayer. *Sonner les cloches* literally means 'ring the bells' but, figuratively, it means 'give a telling-off'. The English translation keeps the general idea but changes the way the meaning is communicated to the reader. Since the Angelus is perhaps unfamiliar to those who do not know Catholic rituals, and there is no figurative meaning that could possibly be attributed to bell-ringing in English, the translators transferred the meaning by using the expression 'to be under a cloud', linking it with a technical word referring to a type of cloud in order to form the patronymic. They carried the pun further by adding the adjective 'nebulous' as a first name, which makes the whole a very cloudy metaphor indeed. The intended effect is conveyed to the reader through what Andrejs Veisberg (1997:155) refers to as "a contextual change of idioms".

We will now analyze one example of onomastic pun from a *Tintin* story, *Coke en stock / The Red Sea Sharks*. Tintin and Haddock are on a raft, having just rescued a pilot from the plane they have shot down. As before, the words under analysis are highlighted in bold both in the original text and in the translation.

> (4) Haddock: (…) Et d'abord, qui êtes-vous ?… Votre nom ?
> *Who are you anyway? What's your name?*
> Pilot: **Szut**.
>   **Skut**.
> (*Sharks*, p. 35)

> (5) Haddock: Comment, **Zut** ?!!… M'en vais vous apprendre la politesse, moi, **espèce de Bibendum** !… Vous dégonflerai, moi, ectoplasme !…
> *What do you mean, **scoot**? I'll teach you manners, you **blithering bombardier**. I'll soon deflate you! Ectoplasm!*
> Pilot: Mais…mais…Szut, ça mon nom… Piotr Szut… Moi estonien…
> But…but…my name Skut…Piotr Skut…Me Esthonian (sic)…
> Tintin: Prenez garde !… Votre canif !
> *Look out!… Mind your knife!*
> (*Sharks*, p. 35)

First let us examine the play on the name of the pilot, again based on homophony: *zut* in French is a familiar – and impolite – exclamation. As an answer to a question it could be the equivalent of 'heck' ('damn' or 'shut up' are some of the equivalents given by bilingual dictionaries). This explains the sudden anger of the captain when he hears the name of the pilot. The spelling of the word makes it sound exactly like the exclamative word, so Haddock thinks he has been insulted. 'Scoot' is informal but not too familiar and may well have been chosen as being right for the intended readers (in French, the word *zut* is less offensive now than at the time Hergé was writing). The effect conveyed seems to be equivalent in both languages. In (5) there is also a cultural allusion which disappeared in the translation: the pictures show the pilot wearing an inflated life-jacket, which explains why Haddock compares him to Bibendum, a familiar figure made of white tyres used to advertise the French Michelin factory and known as the Michelin Man in

English. The word has entered the French language and designates someone huge or obviously overweight. However, since the allusion would be lost on English children, the translators decided to translate *espèce de Bibendum* ('you Bibendum') by 'blistering bombardier', thus relating both to the immediate context – 'bombardier' alludes to the fact that the pilot shot at the two heroes earlier, and to the general context of the series, as 'blistering barnacles' is the captain's favourite swear-word. The translators kept the /b/ alliteration which echoes the French term.

3. Spoonerisms or *Contrepèteries*

Having dealt with puns mainly based on sound, homophony or paronymy, this study will now turn to spoonerisms, which are based on a specific way of transposing sounds, namely metathesis. They abound in *Tintin* and usually arise from the speech of the two policemen or from Professor Tournesol's deafness. Spoonerisms are generally thought to be untranslatable, since they are indissolubly linked with the phonetic features of a given language (Toury 1997). However, Toury reminds us that phonological features are not the only ones to be considered, since spoonerisms "also have a lexico-semantic and syntactic dimension. This manifests itself most clearly in the marked preference for **legitimate words** in both the input and the output, i.e. words which are at least possible in the language, if not actually existing lexical items." (Toury 1997:276).

> (6) Dupond : Nos meilleurs **boeux** de…euh…nos **beilleurs mœux** de… Enfin, en un mot, toutes nos félicitations capitaine. (*Castafiore*, p. 28)
> *Thompson: Our* **west bishes**…*er*…*our* **wet dishes**…*I mean, many congratulations, Captain.*

Here the spoonerism is based upon the same words in French and in English: the policemen congratulate Haddock, whose marriage to Bianca Castafiore has just been announced in the papers. *Meilleurs vœux* is the exact equivalent of 'best wishes'. In French the first sequence substitutes *bœufs* (oxen) to the expected *vœux*, then the author proceeds with the spoonerism. *Beilleurs mœux* does not mean anything in French, although it does not violate the rules of the language, and as the onomatopoeia for 'moo' is *meuh*, pronounced exactly like *mœux*, it creates a visual and phonetic link with the animal *bœufs* used in the first part of the sentence. The translators could not change the text but managed to achieve a similar effect, changing the sequence of syllables as follows: (/best wɪʃɪz/) l /west bɪʃɪz/ l / wet dɪʃɪz̃ /, whereas the original text operates in the following way: (/mɛjœr vø/) l / mɛjœr bø/ l /bɛjœr mø/. As is the case in French, one word is meaningless – bishes – but it makes the transition towards 'dishes' possible.

A different strategy was adopted by the translators when dealing with spoonerisms in a later page of the same *Tintin* story (examples 7, 8, 9 and 10 below). Here they resorted to what Harvey calls "contiguous compensation", that is, a type of compensation which "occurs in the target text within a short distance from the lost effect of the source text" (Harvey 1995:82).

(7) Tintin : Justement non !... Le courant n'a pas été coupé : ce sont les fusibles qui ont fondu...
Dupont : Fusibles **coupés** ou courant **fondu**, jeune homme, pour moi, c'est la même chose : l'obscurité s'est faite, et c'est exactement ce que **volait le vouleur** ! (*Castafiore*, p. 37)
(7') *Tintin: Out of the question...The current wasn't cut off: the fuses went.*
Thomson: A fuse, a power failure, it's all the same to me, young man. It was dark, and that's what the thief wanted.

In this case the translation is very close to the meaning of the original French text. My analysis is centred on the lexical items highlighted in bold, where the difficulty lies. In the first part of this sentence, Dupont mixes up two words. In French you 'cut' the electric current – hence the word *coupés*, and the fuses 'melt' – hence *fondu*. Dupont inverts the verbs which have just been employed correctly by Tintin. Then he makes a spoonerism between *voulait* (wanted) and *voleur* (thief) which is possible because of the graphic and phonetic proximity between the verb and the noun. No such proximity between the corresponding terms exists in English, making it impossible to imitate the French.

(8) Dupont : Vous dites que ce sont les *fl*ombs qui ont *p*ondu... Soit !... Mais, l'avez-vous constaté vous-même ?... (*Castafiore*, p. 38)
Thomson: You say the fuses blew... All right... But did you discover that for yourself ?...

In example (8), it was perhaps possible to create a spoonerism in English, although inverting the initials of 'fuses' and 'blew' would not be very satisfactory, since 'few' is not a verb, but the translators decided against this, compensating elsewhere instead:

(9) Dupont : C'est vous la chanteuse, madame ? Enchanté ! (lit.: You are the singer, madam? Delighted!)
*Thomson: Ah, Signora **Nightingale**, the Milanese **Castafiore**...* (*Castafiore*, p. 38)

(10) Dupont : Madame, nous sommes ici pour faire la lumière, toute la lumière sur le vol dont vous venez d'être la victime... (lit.: Madam, we are here to throw light, all the light about the theft you've just been the victim of)
*Thomson: Madam, we are here to **set** light to... er, to **throw** light on the circumstances surrounding your terrible loss...* (*Castafiore*, p. 38)

Bianca Castafiore is usually nicknamed 'the Milanese Nightingale', so in (9) Dupont / Thomson inverts the singer's last name and the noun 'nightingale'. This is not a proper spoonerism, since they invert two lexical items instead of sounds, but their language is characterized by lexical inversion as well as metathesis and the translator's choice echoes the paronymy between *chanteuse* and *enchanté*. In example (10) they use the improper verb 'set', and then replace it with the correct form. Here the translators follow the author's technique of word inversion seen in (7), but they also imitate Hergé, who makes the policemen resort to constant self-correction:

(11) Dupond : Pour plus de clarté, madame, voulez-vous me dire où se trouvaient vos **bougies**... euh... pardon !... vos **bijoux** ?... (lit.: For more clarity, madam, can you tell me where were your candles...er...sorry!...your jewels?...)
*Thomson: Just to clear up one point, madam: where were the jewels usually **h**ocked...*
*I mean **l**ocked? (Castafiore*, p. 38)

Here Dupond / Thompson corrects himself, and the translators follow suit. The difference lies in the words chosen, in French the word *bougies* (candles) is substituted for *bijoux* (jewels), the metathesis hinging on the vowels: /buʒi/ versus /biʒu/. The four phonemes are identical, which makes the spoonerism easy. The translators chose to make the same kind of variation on one phoneme, this time an initial consonant, by using the words 'hocked' and 'locked', /hɒkt/ versus /lɒkt/; the joke is even greater because jewels can indeed be hocked. Many other examples of this kind could be added but one can see that the translators usually try to translate the spoonerism, which often implies a change of lexical items, and that they resort to a form of compensation when the nature of the target language makes it difficult or impossible.

4. Conclusion

Recent work undertaken with a colleague on all the aspects of the English translation of the whole *Astérix* series (Delesse and Richet forthcoming) has convinced me that, while being relevant to the translation of all text types, compensation strategies are particularly crucial to the translation of humour in comics, for the reason that humorous features often cannot be translated literally from one language to another. Harvey's (1995) typology could be applied very effectively to the translation of humour in these two series, although a systematic classification would mean an enormous amount of work, especially considering the number of wordplays in the *Astérix* series. The translators of *Astérix* were faced with texts in which everything was a pretext for wordplay, whether it be onomastic puns or the twisting of existing idioms, songs or clichés in order to make a joke related to the theme of the story or the scene depicted in the drawings (see e.g. Delesse 2001). The consequence of this, of course, is that compensation is used by Bell and Hockridge on a larger scale than by Lonsdale-Cooper and Turner in *Tintin*.

The translations of both *Astérix* and *Tintin* are primarily aimed at amusing the reader, and while there are dissimilarities linked to the themes of the adventures, the language and general tone of the series, I have deliberately focused on the features both series have in common. The translators had to deal not only with the systemic features of the two languages, but also with different connotations and perceptions of humour. It seems to me that they did their utmost to translate the various puns and spoonerisms, managing to convey the overall effect intended by the authors.

Since the translations of both series are the result of the work of a single set of translators for each, they have strong unifying features, making them stand out as works in their own right. As I have shown, coherence is often greater in English, because the translators looked for solutions to specific problems in the drawings, or motivated their translations through a closer relationship to the characters in the stories. To do so they used the different types of compensation defined by Harvey, and successfully achieved "generalized compensation" throughout the text. As Kathleen Davis quite rightly reminds us, "the appropriate unit of translation is the entire text, rather than its individual words or sentences, since the system of relationships comprising the text informs any understanding of its elements" (Davis 1997:25).

References

Primary Sources
Goscinny, René and Uderzo Albert (1961) *Astérix le Gaulois*, Paris: Dargaud [*Asterix the Gaul*, English translation by Anthea Bell and Derek Hockridge, London: Hodder Dargaud, 1969].
------ (1963) *Astérix et les Goths*, Paris: Dargaud [*Asterix and the Goths*, English translation by Anthea Bell and Derek Hockridge, London: Hodder Dargaud, 1974].
------ (1963) *Le tour de Gaule d'Astérix*, Paris: Dargaud [*Asterix and the Banquet*, English translation by Anthea Bell and Derek Hockridge, London: Hodder Dargaud, 1979].
------ (1964) *Astérix gladiateur*, Paris: Dargaud [*Asterix the Gladiator*, English translation by Anthea Bell and Derek Hockridge, London: Hodder Dargaud, 1969].
------ (1965) *Astérix et Cléopâtre*, Paris: Dargaud [*Asterix and Cleopatra*, English translation by Anthea Bell and Derek Hockridge, London: Hodder Dargaud, 1969].
------ (1966) *Le combat des chefs*, Paris: Dargaud [*Asterix and the Big Fight*, English translation by Anthea Bell and Derek Hockridge, London: Hodder Dargaud, 1971].
------ (1966) *Astérix chez les Bretons*, Paris: Dargaud. Trans [*Asterix in Britain*, English translation by Anthea Bell and Derek Hockridge, London: Hodder Dargaud, 1970].
------ (1966) *Astérix et les Normands*, Paris: Dargaud [*Asterix and the Normans*, English translation by Anthea Bell and Derek Hockridge, London: Hodder Dargaud, 1978].
------ (1968) *Astérix aux jeux olympiques*, Paris: Dargaud [*Asterix and the Olympic Games*, English translation by Anthea Bell and Derek Hockridge, London: Hodder Dargaud, 1972].
------ (1973) *Astérix en Corse*, Paris: Dargaud [*Asterix in Corsica*, English translation by Anthea Bell and Derek Hockridge, London: Hodder Dargaud, 1980].
------ (2003) *Astérix et la rentrée gauloise*, Paris: Les Éditions Albert René [*Asterix and the Class Act*, English translation by Anthea Bell and Derek Hockridge, London: Orion Books Ltd., 2003].
Hergé (1945) *Tintin en Amérique*, Tournai: Casterman [*Tintin in America*, English translation by Leslie Lonsdale-Cooper and Michael Turner, London: Egmont Books Ltd., 1978].
------ (1955) *Les cigares du pharaon*, Tournai: Casterman [*Cigars of the Pharaoh*, English translation by Leslie Lonsdale-Cooper and Michael Turner, London: Egmont Books Ltd., 1971].
------ (1958) *Coke en stock*, Tournai: Casterman [*The Red Sea Sharks*, English translation by Leslie Lonsdale-Cooper and Michael Turner, Tournai: Casterman / Methuen, 1980].
------ (1963) *Les bijoux de la Castafiore*, Tournai: Casterman [*The Castafiore Emerald*, English translation by Leslie Lonsdale-Cooper and Michael Turner, Tournai: Casterman / Methuen, 1963].
------ (1976) *Tintin et les Picaros*, Tournai: Casterman [*Tintin and the Picaros*, English translation by Leslie Lonsdale-Cooper and Michael Turner, Tournai: Casterman / Methuen, 1976].

Secondary Sources
Bell, Anthea (n.d.) 'Astérix – What's in a name', *LiteraryTranslation.com, The British Council Arts* (online) http://www.literarytranslation.com/usr/downloads/workshops/asterix.pdf (Accessed 15 January 2007).

------ (1996) 'Translating Astérix', in Jane Taylor, Edith McMorran, and Guy Leclercq (eds) *Translation. Here and There. Now and Then*, Exeter: Elm Bank, 125-138.

Davis, Kathleen (1997) 'Signature in translation', in Dirk Delabastita (ed.) *Traductio: Essays on Punning and Translation*, Manchester & Namur: St Jerome Publishing / Presses Universitaires de Namur, 24-40.

Delabastita, Dirk (1997) 'Introduction', in Dirk Delabastita (ed.) *Traductio: Essays on Punning and Translation*, Manchester & Namur: St Jerome Publishing / Presses Universitaires de Namur, 1-22.

Delesse, Catherine (2001) 'Le cliché par la bande : le détournement créatif du cliché dans la BD', in Paul Bensimon (ed.) *Le cliché en traduction*, *Palimpsestes* 13, Paris: Presses de la Sorbonne Nouvelle, 167-182.

------ (2006) 'Hergé et les langues étrangères', in Michel Ballard (ed.) *La traduction, contact de langues et de cultures* (2), Arras: Artois Presses Université, 33-45.

Delesse, Catherine and Bertrand Richet (forthcoming) *Le coq gaulois à l'heure anglaise*, Artois: Artois Presses Université.

Embleton, Sheila (1991) 'Names and Their Substitutes: Onomastic Observations on Astérix ad Its Translations', *Target* 3(2): 175-206.

Fresnault-Deruelle, Pierre (1972) *La bande dessinée. Essai d'analyse sémiotique*, Paris: Hachette.

Harvey, Keith (1995) 'A Descriptive Framework for Compensation', *The Translator* 1(1): 65-86.

Toury, Gideon (1997) 'What Is It That Renders a Spoonerism (Un)translatable?', in Dirk Delabastita (ed.) *Traductio: Essays on Punning and Translation*, Manchester & Namur: St Jerome Publishing / Presses Universitaires de Namur, 271-291.

Veisbergs Andrejs (1997) 'The Contextual Use of Idioms, Wordplay, and Translation', in Dirk Delabastita (ed.) *Traductio: Essays on Punning and Translation*, Manchester & Namur: St Jerome Publishing / Presses Universitaires de Namur, 155-176.

13 Comics in Translation: An Annotated Bibliography

FEDERICO ZANETTIN
University of Perugia, Italy

The works listed in this bibliography, while not exhaustive of the literature on comics translation in its wider sense, do extensively document this area of interest. The publications range over almost forty years, the oldest being a 1970 study of the English, Italian and Dutch translations of *Astérix* by Jacqmain and Cole. Interest in the study of translated comics has increased over the years, and about half of the articles listed have been published in the last decade or so. About one third of them deal with foreign translations of *Astérix* and/or *Tintin* (from French into English, Italian, German, Spanish, Arabic, Polish, Croatian, etc.), and usually either focus on aspects of intercultural communication, or matters such as the translation of names, onomatopoeia and wordplay, all issues that while often found in comics are not limited to this genre. All in all, the articles and books (although only a couple of full length volumes seem to have been written on the subject) offer a variety of approaches, ranging from strictly linguistic, to semiotic, to cultural. Some articles only mention the translations of comics within a wider theoretical framework (e.g. Mayoral et al. on constrained translation), whereas many take the works discussed as representative of comics translation in general. Most of the articles appeared in translation studies publications (journals, conference proceedings, other collected volumes), while others appeared in publications devoted to different academic disciplines (e.g. semiotics, cultural studies, comics scholarship), often in languages other than English. Translation matters are also debated among comics fans, who often express their views through fan magazines (fanzines), online community sites and communication tools such as webzines, chatlines, forums and blogs. Such material (see e.g. the articles filed under 'Lost in Translation' at http://www.sequentialtart.com/), however, is not recorded here.

While focusing on comics in translation, this bibliography also includes some items on intersemiotic translation (i.e. from comics to other semiotic systems and vice versa) and articles dealing with the translation of animated cartoons, although not in a systematic way. A number of Internet publications and dissertations are also included. Each entry offers full bibliographic information, with the title translated into English if the article is written in a different language, and a number of keywords identifying the geographical origin of the comic(s) discussed, the languages involved (ST and TT), and the main focus(es) of the article (e.g. the translation of humour). Most titles are also accompanied by an abstract in English, compiled either by myself, the author of the article, or an independent abstractor.[1]

---

[1] I would like to thank the following for their help: Maria Bagoly Grun, Elio Ballardini, Maria Carreras, Nadine Celotti, Catherine Delesse, John Kearns, Giovanni Nadiani, Minako O'Hagan, Maeve Olohan, Gabriela Saldanha, Jürgen Schopp, Carmen Valero Garcés, José Yuste Frías and Jehan Zitawi.

1. **Keywords: Franco-Belgian comics; Translation of Humour; French/Arabic; Astérix**

   Arias Torres, Juan Pablo (1997) 'Adiós a los jabalíes y la cerveza: la versión árabe de Astérix y Cleopatra' [Good-bye to boars and beer: the Arabic version of 'Astérix and Cleopatra'], in Miguel Ángel Vega (ed.) *La palabra vertida: investigaciones en torno a la traducción: actas de los VI Encuentros Complutenses en torno a la Traducción*, Madrid: Universidad Complutense, 371-378.

2. **Keywords: Comics translation**

   Artuñedo Guillén, Belén (1991) 'Problemas específicos de la traducción del cómic' [Specific problems in the translation of comics], in Brigitte Lepinette, María Amparo Olivares Pardo and Amalia Emma Sopeña Balordi (eds) *Actas del primer coloquio internacional de traductología (2 - 4 mayo, 1989)*, Valencia: Universidad de Valencia, 57-58.

   This short paper offers an overview of the main difficulties of comics translation. The main problem is represented by the dichotomous aspect of this genre (text/images).

3. **Keywords: Film dubbing; English/Arabic; Animated cartoons; Children**

   Athamneh, Naser and Jehan Zitawi (1999) 'English-Arabic Translation of Dubbed Children's Animated Pictures, *Babel* 45(2): 127-148.

   This study aims at evaluating the translation of dubbed children's animated pictures shown on Jordan Television and other Arab televisions in terms of accuracy and faithfulness to the original text. In an attempt to achieve this goal, the researchers have studied the translations of 56 episodes of Arabic versions of five children's animated pictures. Upon close examination of the translated material, it has been found that most of the translators have given erroneous renderings of some portions of the original texts, thus distorting the message conveyed in the target language text and, consequently, affecting, in a direct way, the educational level of the children. The researchers analyze and categorize some erroneously translated words, phrases and sentences observed in the corpus of the study. They also try to attribute the errors to their possible causes. Finally, the researchers suggest alternative, supposedly more appropriate translations of the source language utterances. The study concludes with some recommendations which would hopefully enhance the process of translating dubbed children's animated pictures in general and improve the performance of Arab translators working in the field of English-Arabic dubbing.

4. **Keywords: Franco-Belgian comics; Tintin**

   Baetens, Jan (2001) 'Tintin, the untranslatable', *SITES* 2: 236-271.

5. **Keywords: Franco-Belgian comics; French/Catalan; Astérix**

   Barbera, Núria and Miracle Freixes (1991) 'D'Astérix en Corse' à 'Astérix a Córsega" [From 'Astérix en Corse' to 'Astérix a Córsega'], in Brigitte Lepinette, María Amparo Olivares Pardo and Amalia Emma Sopeña Balordi (eds) *Actas del primer coloquio internacional de traductología (2 – 4 mayo, 1989)*, Valencia: Universidad de Valencia, 61-62.

6. **Keywords: Japanese comics; Japanese and Western publication practices; Reading direction; Written vs. visual language**

   Barbieri, Daniele (2004) 'Samurai allo specchio' [Samurai in the mirror], *Golem – L'indispensabile*, n.8, novembre 2004 (online) http://www.golemindispensabile. it/Puntata43/articolo.asp?id=1688&num=43&sez=511&tipo=&mpp=&ed=&as=

   Barbieri discusses the adaptation practices of the Western comics industry when publishing Japanese comics in translation. A first, more traditional approach consists in reversing the original reading direction, while a second, more 'philological' approach consists in printing the comic book in the original left to right reading direction. The author argues that when translated Japanese comics are printed from left to right, the reading direction of the images contrasts with that of the written text, from right to left. So, while by reversing the reading direction of the images we simply end up with a lot of left-handed samurai, by adopting a 'philological' approach we are faced with two conflicting streams of information, in which the words may contradict the images. Images are not symmetrical and their interpretation depends on the direction in which they are read. In the Western figurative tradition a movement which is represented as going from left to right is seen as fluent and effortless, while it is perceived as difficult when in the opposite direction. The reverse is true in the Japanese figurative tradition, so that we perceive tired samurai as vigorous and vice versa. Thus, when printed from right to left Japanese comics are translated in their integrity, whereas when printed left to right the translated verbal language runs contrary to the rhythm of the original visual language.

7. **Keywords: Japanese comics; Cultural hybridization**
    Barbieri, Daniele (2006) 'Il fascino discreto del fumetto giapponese' [The discreet charm of Japanese comics], *Golem – L'indispensabile*, n. 4, giugno 2006 (online) http://www.golemindispensabile.
    it/Puntata58/articolo.asp?id=2049&num=58&sez=656&tipo=&mpp=&ed=&as=
    Western writers and readers have always been fascinated by stories with an Oriental setting. Perhaps less comprehensible may seem the success of comics written by Japanese authors in Europe and America, where they have achieved mass distribution. Mass consumption in fact implies familiarity. Japanese manga (comics) and anime (cartoons) are not produced with a Western audience in mind, since the internal comics market is so vast as to preclude an interest in the West. The reason for their success is to be found in the fact that in manga the Japanese tradition of graphic storytelling merges with that of the American comics form. In this sense, Japanese comics are as much familiar as they are foreign to a Western audience, and testify to globalization as well as to the basic similarity of all human beings.

8. **Keywords: Franco-Belgian comics; French/Spanish; Tintin**
    Barrera y Vidal, Alberto (1995) 'Traducción e interculturalidad: la versión española del mundo de Tintín' [Translation and interculturality: the Spanish version of Tintin's world], in Rafael Martín-Gaitero (ed.) *V Encuentros complutenses entorno a la traducción*, Madrid: Universidad Complutense, 483-498.

9. **Keywords: Franco-Belgian comics; Astérix**
    Bell, Anthea (1996) 'Translating Astérix', in Jane Taylor, Edith McMorran and Guy Leclercq (eds) *Translation. Here and There. Now and Then*, Exeter: Elm Bank, 125-138.

10. **Keywords: Franco-Belgian comics; Translation practice; Literary translation; Astérix**
    Bell, Anthea, (n.d.) 'Astérix - What's in a name'. LiteraryTranslation.com, The British Council Arts (online) http://www.literarytranslation.com/usr/downloads/workshops/asterix.pdf
    This short article first provides a brief presentation of the Astérix *series, its characters and the settings of the adventures, as well as some information about its creators. It then focuses on the English translations, which the author of the article, a professional translator, carried out together with Derek Hockridge, a lecturer in French. Bell first addresses the issue of making the text fit to the artwork, including the special pictorial constraints posed by the size of speech bubbles. The discussion of the translation of a panel from an* Astérix *album serves as an illuminating example. Then in the rest of the paper some of the main issues concerning the translation of names, songs, puns and accents are exemplified. Bell explains how the names of the characters – comic spoofs on names made up out of French words in the original – were all changed into similar made-up names in English. Wordplays based on dated cultural allusions also pose the problem of the obsolescence of translations.*

11. **Keywords: American comics; South Asia; Sanskit**
Bhatia, Tej K. (2006) 'Superheroes to super languages: American popular culture through South Asian language comics', *World Englishes* 25(2): 279-298.
Although under immense pressure from television, movies, and video games, comics are a very effective and nonintrusive means of introducing American popular culture in South Asia in the age of globalization. The introduction of American comic books in South Asian languages, although a recent phenomenon, has already stimulated the South Asian/Indian appetite for American superheroes and comics and has added various new cognitive and (psycho) linguistic dimensions to traditional Indian comics. The paper attempts to account for the creative linguistic strategies employed in the representation of superheroes through super languages (Sanskrit and English) in South Asian language comics and to explain the highly diverse appeal and positive perception of comics in South Asia.

12. **Keywords: Animated cartoons; Intersemiotic translation; Shakespeare**
Bottoms, Janet (2001) 'Speech, Image, Action: Animating Tales from Shakespeare', *Children's Literature in Education* 32(1): 3-15.
Two assumptions are challenged in this article: that children are naturally disposed toward the animated cartoon, and that translating Shakespeare's plays into this medium automatically simplifies them and gives them child appeal. It examines the confusions and cross-purposes that surrounded the making of the Animated Tales videos, and argues that there are dangers in their uncritical use in schools. It concludes with suggestions as to how they may, nevertheless, be effectively employed with children of all ages.

13. **Keywords: Japanese comics; Japanese/French; Globalization**
Bouissou, Jean-Marie (1998) 'Manga Goes Global. With special reference to Ōtomo Katsuhiro's *Akira*' (online) http://www.ceri-sciences-po.org/archive/avril00/artjmb.pdf
Ōtomo Katsuhiro's eleven volumes series Akira *was published in Japan from 1982 to 1993 and translated into French from 1991 to 1995. Its French publisher targeted well-educated high-income urbanites at a time when manga were still considered cheap stuff for children or semi-illiterate teenagers, and* Akira *became a cult series in France as well as in the USA.* Akira's *echo in the West epitomizes the fact that contemporary manga, whose aesthetical and ethical standards are worlds apart from those of American mainstream comics, is the vehicle of a culture which appeals to audiences all around the world and a major element of Japan's soft power.* Akira *is an empty structure for every reader to fill with his or her own experiences, dreams and desires. This is quite the opposite of Disney's way to reach "global" audience - but nevertheless an efficient one. Ōtomo also "globalized"* Akira *by using innumerable images and clichés drawn form Western culture, while at the same time making the best of the movies-like narrative technique of the manga to produce a cultural object deliberately intended for the world market. Thus,* Akira *is a striking example of successful globalization.*

14. **Keywords: Franco-Belgian comics; Translation of names; French/Spanish; Tintin**
Brito de la Nuez, Immaculada (1994) 'Análisis y traducción de las variants paronímicas de Haddock en *Le Bijoux de la castafiore* (Tintín)' [Analysis and translation of paronimic variants of Haddock in *Le Bijoux de la castafiore* (Tintín)], in Juan Bravo Castillo (ed.) *Actas del Segundo Coloquio sobre los Estudios de Filología Francesa en la Universidad Española*, Cuenca: Universidad de Castilla-La Mancha, Servicío de Publicaciones, 95-111.

15. **Keywords: Spanish comics; Spanish/German**
Cáceres Würsig, I. (1995) 'Un ejemplo perfecto de traducción intercultural: la historieta gráfica (español-alemán)' [A perfect example of intercultural translation: The comics (Spanish-German)], in R. Martín-Gaitero (ed.) *V Encuentros Complutenses en torno*

a la Traducción. 22-26 de febrero de 1994, Madrid: Editorial Complutense, 527-538. *On the basis of the German version of the comics stories of* Mortadelo y Filemón *by Ibáñez, the author of this article attempts to exemplify the specific problems of the translation of comics. To this end, it seems necessary to analyse the defining features of comics as well as the differences from other genres, and to discuss the main problems they pose for tranlation.*

16.   **Keywords: Franco-Belgian comics; Translation of Humour; French/Spanish; Astérix**

Campos Pardillos, Miguel Angel (1992) 'Las dificultades de traducir el humor: Astérix le Gaulois – Asterix the Gaul – Asterix el Galo' [The difficulties in translating humour: 'Astérix le Gaulois' - 'Asterix the Gaul' – 'Asterix el Galo'], *Babel A.F.I.A.L.* 1: 103-123.

The process of translating humour, if already far from easy, verges on the sophisticated when such humour is based on cultural on linguistic allusion; in the case of the Astérix series, the worldwide success of versions in various languages is due to the personal craft of the translators in conveying translatable aspects and even creating new jokes. This essay reviews the difficulties encountered and the techniques used in the Spanish and English versions of Astérix chez les Bretons *and* Astérix chez les Belges; *the author attempts to prove the superiority of the English translation compared to the Spanish one, and lists a number of fragments which, due to an extensive usage of puns, could be considered as an improvement on the French original.*

17.   **Keywords: Franco-Belgian comics; Constrained translation; French/Spanish; Astérix**

Carrasco Criado, Ana María (1997) 'La traducción subordinada del cómic: análisis de la traducción al español de *Astérix en Hispanie*' [Subordinate translation in comics: An analysis of the Spanish translation of *Astérix en Hispanie*], in L. Félix Fernández and Emilio Ortega Arjonilla (eds) *Estudios sobre traducción e interpretación, Actas de las Primeras Jornadas Internacionales de la Universidad de Málaga*, Universidad de Málaga, 385-395.

18.   **Keywords: Constrained translation; Text/image; Translation of proper names; Translation of onomatopoeia**

Castillo Cañellas, Daniel (2002) 'El discurso de los tebeos y su traducción' [The discourse of comics and their translation], *Tebeosfera* 020430 (online) http://www.tebeosfera. com/Documento/Articulo/Academico/01/tebeostraduccion.pdf

The author first discusses the various terms used in Spain to refer to 'sequential art' (cómics, historietas, tebeos), and the position of comics as a type of paraliterature. He then proceeds to illustrate how words and images in comics are not simply juxtaposed but rather interplay in the creation of meaning and how the language in comics, especially those of North-American origin, belongs to a colloquial register, and the consequences of this for Spanish translation. Theoretical and technical factors are involved in the translation of comics, which can be seen as a type of constrained translation. The constraints are primarily posed by space limitations and by pictures. Since the size of balloons and captions is limited, translators use a number of devices to keep down the number of letters used in a translation. Images are difficult to modify because of ethical, technical and economical reasons. There follows a discussion of the translation of onomatopoeia and proper names, with examples from Astérix *and superhero comics. The author concludes with a brief assessment of and some recommendations for the translation of comics in Spain.*

19.   **Keywords: Constrained translation; Text/image; Translation of proper names; Translation of onomatopoeia**

Castillo Cañellas, Daniel (1997) 'Limitaciones en la traducción de tebeos' [Limitations in

the translation of comics], in L. Félix Fernández and Emilio Ortega Arjonilla (eds) *Estudios sobre traducción e interpretación*, Universidad de Málaga, 397-403.
This is a former version of Castillo Cañellas (2002), another version of which was also published in 1998 in Apuntes, #1, vol. 6, New York Circle of Translators.

20. **Keywords: Word/image**
Celotti, Nadine (1997) 'Langue et images en présence: des espaces langagiers pluriels comme moment de réflexion pour la traductologie contemporaine' [The language-image combination: multilanguage spaces and Translation Studies], in *L'histoire et les théories de la traduction*, Berne et Genève: ASTTI et ETI, 487-503.
Following Roland Barthes's analysis of images as meaning-making signs, this article discusses how images, especially because of their cultural meaning, can give a contribution to the discussion about foreignization vs domestication in Translation Studies. The article focusses on the translation of comics to stress that an image is neither universal nor a constraint for the translator. The paper is based on some examples from French comics translated into Italian.

21. **Keywords: Research review; Semiological approach; Text/image; French/Italian**
Celotti, Nadine (2000) 'Méditer sur la traduction des bandes dessinées: une perspective de sémiologie parallèle' [Reflections on the Translation of Comics: A Parallel Semiology Perspective], *Rivista internazionale di tecnica della traduzione* 5: 41-61.
In the first part the author provides a review of the existing research on the translation of this particular textual genre and finds that, for a long time, comics have been ignored by Translation Studies as an object of investigation in their own right. Sometimes used as mere examples to illustrate the technique of 'compensation' or a 'reader-centred' translation approach, comics have been recently included in a new type of translation called 'constrained translation', where the illustration is seen as a constraint for the translator. In contrast to such an approach, the second part of the article proposes that the linguistic and the semiological approaches have a parallel status. Translators need therefore to develop their semiotic competence in order to be able to consider the illustration as a fundamental semantic feature of the linguistic message in the creation of the story.

22. **Keywords: Franco-Belgian comics; French/Polish; French/English; Astérix; Stereotypes**
Chantry, Xavier (2002) 'Stereotypy i ich przekład w komiksie: Astérix chez les Bretons i jego wersja polska' [Stereotypes and Their Translation in Comics: *Astérix chez les Bretons* and its Polish Version], in Skibińska, Elżbieta and Marcin Cieński *Język Stereotyp Przekład*, Wrocław: Dolnośląskie Wydawnictwo Edukacyjne, 45-55.
In this article the author compares the treatment of stereotypes of England and the English in the original French version of Astérix chez les Bretons *and in Jolanta Sztuczyńska's 1992 Polish translation* Astęriks u Brytów. *The translator is obliged to present the Polish reader with French stereotypical visions of the English and is further constrained by the limits imposed by the images. While the visual stereotypes of the English are comparable in terms of both French and Polish readerships, the linguistic stereotypes are more marked in the French than in the Polish version (with the lexical proximity of French and English assisting greater cross-semantic transfer than is possible with Polish). The article discusses a range of English idioms in terms of their equivalents in French and Polish.*

23. **Keywords: Animated cartoons; Verbally Expressed Humour; English/Italian**
Chiaro, Delia (2004) 'Investigating the perception of translated Verbally Expressed Humour on Italian TV', *ESP Across Cultures* 1: 35-52.
Verbally Expressed Humour (VEH) is a specific variety of language which has been largely

ignored by scholars despite its widespread use in numerous text types. Apart from the use of VEH for purely entertainment purposes, numerous mediatic genres such as advertisements, newspaper articles, headlines and even political discourse are also renowned for their frequent use of VEH. Despite the existence of a global village in which the same text is often presented in a variety of languages, the issue of how VEH is mediated across cultures and languages has received little attention. This paper sets out to explore the sphere of VEH and how it is perceived when it is mediated linguistically, in other words when it is interlingually translated in one way or another. In order to do this, a small corpus of situation comedies and cartoons dubbed into Italian was extracted from a larger corpus of television programmes. A web-based self-reporting questionnaire aimed at exploring people's reactions to translated humour was prepared based on instances of VEH contained in the corpus. The questionnaire was administered to a random sample of Italians and the qualitative data which emerged provides insight not only on how audiences actually perceive VEH on screen, but also on the quality of the translations themselves.

24. **Keywords: Comics terminology; French/English**
Coupal, Michel (1978) 'Terminologie de la bande dessinée' [The terminology of comics], *Meta* 23:4 (online) http://www.erudit.org/revue/meta/1978/v23/n4/002417ar.pdf
An essential guide to the terminology of comics, within a short but detailed discursive description of comics production processes. The article is in French, but for each term an English equivalent is provided.

25. **Keywords: Italian comics; Italian/English**
D'Arcangelo, Adele and Federico Zanettin (2004) 'Dylan Dog Goes to the Usa: A North-American Translation of an Italian Comic Book Series', *Across Languages and Cultures* 5(2): 187-211.
This paper is about the translation of comic books from an 'importing' country like Italy to an 'exporting' country, the USA. It focuses on the publication by an American 'independent' comic books publisher of a 'mini-series' featuring Dylan Dog, the main character and title bearer of a monthly series of considerable success in Italy. After a description of the Italian comics market and readership, and of the Dylan Dog *series, there follows a discussion of the general publishing strategies which characterize the North American edition. Using the 'anatomy of comics' proposed by Kaindl (1999), a comparative analysis of original and translated elements is carried out, with a description of the changes which have taken place during the translation process.*

26. **Keywords: Franco-Belgian comics; French/English; Astérix**
Delesse, Catherine (1998) 'Astérix d'un bord à l'autre de l'Atlantique, ou 'La Grande traversée" [Asterix from one side to the other of the Atlantic Ocean, or 'La Grande traversée'], *Palimpsestes* 11: 173-186.
This article compares the British and American English translations of the Astérix *album* La grande traversée *(Astérix and the Great Crossing), focusing on the translation of proper names and cultural references.*

27. **Keywords: Franco-Belgian comics; French/English; Astérix**
Delesse, Catherine (1998) 'La culture européenne telle qu'elle est représentée dans *Les Aventures d'Astérix* et la traduction anglaise de cette bande dessinée' [European culture as it is represented in 'Les Adventures d'Astérix' and the English translation of this comic], in Michel Ballard (ed.) *Europe et traduction*, Arras and Ottawa: Artois Presses Université and Université d'Ottawa, 273-282.
Contemporary Europe in general and France more specifically are the setting of Astérix's *adventures. Through pictures, dialogues and explicatory notes which give pseudo-historical*

precision, clichés and stereotypes of the 1960s and 1970s are parodied. This article first provides an overview of the ways the authors of the French comic series succeed in transmitting cultural references about people from different European countries to a large reading public, at different levels. It then focuses on the episode Astérix chez les Bretons, *and on its English translation. The translators have often resorted to British linguistically connotated expressions and cultural references. The result is a transpostion in the target language which is balanced by fidelity to the source language because pictures remain unchanged.*

28. **Keywords: Franco-Belgian comics; Astérix; Tintin; Spoken language**
Delesse, Catherine (2000) 'Les dialogues de BD: une traduction de l'oral?' [Dialogues in Strip Cartoons: A Translation from the Oral?], in Michel Ballard (ed.) *Oralité et Traduction*, Arras: Artois Presses Université, 321-340.
This paper explores the representations of verbal sounds in strip cartoons and comics using examples from originals and classics of the genre (Tintin, Astérix). The range of effects studied is wide: from variations in the intensity of voices, through the connotations of proper names, to onomatopoeia, accents and insults. It is noted that translators (in a variety of European languages) employ a wide range of strategies to cope with these aspects of orality, often using target-language specific effects to recreate the effects of the original.

29. **Keywords: Franco-Belgian comics; Humour; French/English; Astérix; Tintin**
Delesse, Catherine (2001) 'Le cliché par la bande: le détournement créatif du cliché dans la BD' [Clichés in comics], *Palimpsestes 13, Le cliché en traduction*: 167-182.
The aim of this article is to analyse the way clichés are used in comic strips (mainly Astérix *and* Tintin*) and how they are translated into English. The authors use the clichés in a humorous way, thus modifying their content according to their needs and the necessities of the context, including the drawing. Translators are thus faced with a difficult challenge. The solutions they have chosen are analysed through a number of significant examples which prove that they can be as creative as the authors.*

30. **Keywords: Franco-Belgian comics; French/English; Astérix; Tintin**
Delesse, Catherine (2004) 'Accents étrangers et régionaux : Le cas des séries Astérix et Tintin et leurs traductions anglaises' [Foreign and Regional Accents: The case of Asterix and Tintin and their translation in English], in Fabrice Antoine (ed.) *Argots, langue familière et accents en traduction* (Ateliers 31/2004), Lille: Université Charles-de-Gaulle, 113-126.
The different accents and their visual transcriptions in francophone comic strips Astérix and Tintin are examined in turn with examples. They include regional accents from Marseilles, Auvergne and Belgium, as well as foreign ones, e.g. Italian, Spanish, African, Russian, and German. Graphical, phonetic, lexical and syntactical aspects in French are covered The English translations of these accents are then discussed, especially regarding the various strategies employed for the regional accents and the differences in the marking of foreignness. Finally there is a short discussion of the translation of the Italian accent in one Tintin comic strip, into four languages, English, German, Italian, and Spanish, where a contrastive study of the translation strategies are briefly broached.

31. **Keywords: Franco-Belgian comics; French/English; Tintin**
Delesse, Catherine (2006) 'Hergé et les langues étrangères' [Hergé and foreign languages], in Michel Ballard (ed.) *La traduction, contact de langues et de cultures* (2), Arras: Artois Presses Université, 33-45.
In his albums Hergé used two invented languages, the Arumbaya and the Syldavian languages. These correspond to imaginary countries, which can nevertheless be situated in

South America and the Balkans. In order to create these languages, Hergé used a Brussels dialect spoken by his grandmother as a substrate language. The article studies the way he constructed these languages and how the translators adapted his creations.

32.   **Keywords: Franco-Belgian comics; French/English; Astérix**
       Delesse, Catherine and Bertrand Richet (forthcoming) *Le coq gaulois à l'heure anglaise* [The French cockerel going English], Artois: Artois Presses Université.

33.   **Keywords: Japanese comics; Japanese/English; Scanlation**
       Deppey, Dirk (2005) 'Scanlation Nation: Amateur Manga Translators Tell Their Stories', *The Comics Journal*, 269 (online) http://www.tcj.com/269/n_scan.html
       In the late 1990s, the Internet offered new possibilities for fans of Japanese culture to congregate and share materials. Amateur groups of Japanophiles began to gather into online groups to produce and distribute translated manga. Thus were scanlations born. This article in based on the accounts of five scanlators who were contacted via e-mail and asked to describe who they are, how they came to the scanlation hobby, and what their world is like.

34.   **Keywords: Animated cartoons; Fansubs**
       Díaz Cintas, Jorge and Pablo Muñoz Sánchez (2006) 'Fansubs: Audiovisual Translation in an Amateur Environment', *JoSTrans – The Journal of Specialised Translation* 06 (online) http://www.jostrans.org/issue06/art_diaz_munoz.php
       The purpose of this paper is to describe the so-called fansubs, a different type of subtitling carried out by amateur translators. The first part of this study covers both the people and phases involved in the fansubbing process from beginning to end. The second section focuses on the legality and ethics of fansubs. The third part pays attention to the actual translation of fansubs and their unique features, such as the use of translator's notes or special karaoke effects. The paper concludes with a reflection on the work done by fansubbers and the possibilities opened by this mainly Internet phenomenon.

35.   **Keywords: Franco-Belgian comics; French/Italian; Astérix; Translation of names; Translation of wordplays**
       D'Oria, Domenico and Mirella Conenna (1979) 'Sémiologie d'une traduction: Astérix en italien' [Semiology of a translation: Astérix in Italian], *Equivalences: Revue de l'Ecole Supérieure de Traducteurs et d'Interprètes de Bruxelles* 10(1): 19-38.
       The authors analyse the Italian translations of Astérix, *focussing their investigation on linguistic aspects of the text, and discussing the translation of plays on words, Latin quotations, dialects, names and proverbs.*

36.   **Keywords: Translation of humour; Arabic/English; Cartoons**
       El-Arousy, Nahwat Amin (2007) 'Towards a functional approach to the translation of Egyptian cartoons', *Humor. International Journal of Humor Research* 20(3): 297-321.
       This paper focuses on the dilemma facing a translator if (s)he attempts to translate cartoons in general, with special reference to the translation of Egyptian cartoons into English. The dilemma is perceived to be threefold: the translator has to cope with the cultural distinctiveness of the cartoons; to interpret the double scripts expressed in the linguistic component; and finally to resolve the nonverbal and/or semiotic cues of the drawings and relate them to the incongruity expressed in the two scripts. The objective of this study is, thus, to propose a model that is based on Attardo and Raskin's General Theory of Verbal Humor (GTVH 1991); and theories of functional translation, such as Nord's (1991 [1988] and 1997), Reiss's (2000 [1971]), Baker's (1992) and others. The GTVH model, in other words, is adapted to be applicable to the semiotic interpretation and translation of cartoons. In the end, the study

implicates using the translation of cartoons as an application of contrastive methodology in the AFL (Teaching Arabic as a Foreign language), the EFL/ESL, and in the Translation and Pragmatics classes.

37. **Keywords: Franco-Belgian comics; Translation of names; Astérix**

Embleton, Sheila (1991) 'Names and Their Substitutes. Onomastic Observations on 'Astérix' and Its Translations', *Target* 3(2): 175-206.

The Astérix comic-book series, originally in French, is well-known and widely translated. Each book relates an adventurous apisode in which the principal character is Astérix, a small, witty warrior from a fictional Gaulish village, the only village to have successfully resisted the Roman occupation. The series relies on many humorous techniques, but word-play and puns form an integral part. Much humour derives from the names used, combining various comic effects, particularly puns and double entendres. Thus the translator faces not only the usual problems in translating literary names, but also the problem of retaining comic effects. The author examines how these problems were solved in complete collection of name data from all 30 books in 4 languages (French original; English, German, Finnish translations), with numerous references to translations into other languages.

38. **Keywords: Franco-Belgian comics; French/German; Astérix**

Emsel, Martina (2004) 'Textfunktionen von Übersetzungseinheiten als Kriterien für Lösungsstrategien und Bewertungen (am Beispiel von Namen und Zitaten in *Astérix* und *La traviata*)'[Textual functions of translation units as criteria for strategies of solution and evaluation (on the basis of names and citations from *Astérix* and *La traviata*)], in Eberhard Fleischmann, Peter A. Schmitt and Gerd Wotjak (eds) *Translations-kompetenz: Tagungsberichte der LICTRA (Leipzig International Conference on Translation Studies) 4.-6.10.2001*, Tübingen: Stauffenburg , 311-322.

39. **Keywords: Japanese comics; Scanlation; Fansubs**

Ferrer Simó, María Rosario (2005) 'Fansubs y scanlations: la influencia del aficionado en los criterios profesionales' [Fansubs and scanlations: the influence of the amateur on professional criteria], *Puentes* 6: 27-43.

Fansubs are non-official editions of anime, or Japanese animation, subtitled by fans and usually distributed through the Internet, which do not meet professional, translational and technical criteria. They are used to promote new series among fans prior to their commercial distribution. The dimension of this phenomenon is such that fansubtitling can even influence some decisions in professional translations, such as the coining of terms within the series, the names of the main characters or the imposition of a given translation solution by the client.

40. **Keywords: Franco-Belgian comics; Translation of Humour; French/Spanish; Astérix**

Fernández, Mercedes and Françoise Gaspin (1991) 'Astérix en español y/o la opacidad de la traducción de un código cultural' [Astérix in Spanish and/or the opacity of the translation of a cultural code], in María Luisa Donaire and Francisco Lafarga Maduel (eds) *Traducción y adaptación cultural: España-Francia*, Oviedo: Universidad de Oviedo, 93-107.

41. **Keywords: Franco-Belgian comics; French/Spanish; Astérix**

Fernández, Mercedes and María Alice Pereira (1989) 'La traducción de los nombres propios en el ámbito del cómic: estudio de la serie de Astérix' [The translation of names in comics: a study into the Asterix series], in Julio César Santoyo Mediavilla, Rosa Rabadán, Trinidad Guzmán and José Luis Chamosa (eds) *Fidus interpres: Actas I Jornadas Nacionales de Historia de la traducción*, León: Universidad de León, 189-193.

42. **Keywords: Franco-Belgian comics; French/Spanish; Astérix; Translation of Humour**

Gaspar Galán, Antonio (1993) '*Astérix en Hispania* o la difícil empresa de traducir el humor' [*Astérix en Hispania*, or the difficult task of translating humour], in Fidel Corcuera Manos and Antonio Domínguez Domínguez (eds) *La lengua francesa Y española aplicadas al mundo de la impresa: actas del encuentro internacional*, Zaragoza: Universidad, Dpto. de Filología Francesa, 171-185.

43. **Keywords: Franco-Belgian comics; Translation of humour; Astérix**

Grassegger, Hans (1985) *Sprachspiel und Übersetzung: eine Studie anhand der Comics-Serie 'Asterix'* [Puns and translation: A study on the comics series 'Asterix'], Tübingen: Stauffenburg.

Acknowledging the importance of pictorial elements in the generation of meaning, the author attempts to introduce a systematic classification of plays on words and the ways in which they can be translated. Given the author's view that translation is "a special case of linguistic activity", linguistic factors are emphasized. Grassegger notes that the interplay between verbal and non verbal elements is useful in interpreting the linguistic component of the text. However, the predetermined size of speech bubbles limits the space available in the target language, and the visual context narrows the translator's choice of equivalents. Plays on words are subdivided into two main groups, plays on sense and plays on sound. Only this latter group, which includes onomatopoeia, is specific to comics.

44. **Keywords: American comics; English/Danish; Translation of humour; Comic strips**

Grun, Maria and Cay Dollerup (2003) 'Loss' and 'gain' in comics', *Perspectives: Studies in Translatology* 11(3): 197-216.

This article discusses the translation of comics with specific reference to 'loss' and 'gain'. It is suggested that – for the purpose of a cogent discussion – we may distinguish between 'gain with loss' and 'gain without loss'. Translations of comics represent a special challenge in that, in order to be successful, they have to actively interplay with illustrations as well as genre elements, i.e. 'humour'. The article discusses some of these elements and then focuses on successful renditions into Danish of the American daily strip Calvin and Hobbes *and a* Donald Duck *ten-page comic narrative. The latter, in particular, reveals that subtle forces influence the translation of a comic. This opens for a discussion of the ways comics allow – or make it hard for – a translator to wend her way between 'gain' and 'loss'. These forces involve an interplay not only between pictures and text, but also the people who do lettering, add colours, and the like.*

45. **Keywords: Constrained translation; Astérix**

Gutíerrez, Ruiz M. del C. and J. R. Diza Penalva (1997) 'La traducción subordinada de Cómics: Astérix en traductolandia' [The constrained translation of comics: Astérix in translationland], in *Estudios sobre traducción e interpretación*, Málaga, Centro de Ediciones de la Disputación de Málaga, 429-437.

46. **Keywords: Franco-Belgian comics; French/Arabic; Astérix; Stereotypes**

Hartmann, Regina (1982) 'Betrachtungen zur arabischen Version von 'Asterix'. Ein Übersetzungsvergleich' [Reflections on the Arabic version of 'Asterix'. A comparison of translations], *Linguistische Berichte* 81: 1-31.

This study investigates the Arabic translations of Astérix le Gaulois *and* Astérix et Cléopatre. *According to the author, the translation of cultural specific elements into Arabic is dependent on the assumed cultural knowledge of the potential readers. While working from a largely linguistic perspective, the author identifies three cultural specific-factors which influence the translation. First, the specific linguistic situation in the Arab world, which explains why*

Astérix was translated in Standard written Arabic to ensure distribution throughout Arabic-speaking areas. Second, religious factors, which explain why, for example, the names of the gods in the original texts are completely omitted in the Arabic translations. Third, Arab national feelings are an important cultural-specific factor in determining the strategies used to translate humour based on prejudices, clichés and stereotypes.

47. **Keywords: Translation of humour; Astérix; Compensation**
    Harvey, Keith (1995) 'A Descriptive Framework for Compensation', *The Translator* 1(1): 65-86.
    The author sets out to provide a description of compensation as a translation strategy. The paper starts with an overview of the various treatments of the concept in the literature before proceeding to elaborate a new descriptive framework for compensation along three axes: typological, linguistic correspondence, and topographical. The discussion is illustrated throughout by examples taken from authentic translations, including examples from the series Asterix.

48. **Keywords: Finnish**
    Heiskanen, Jukka (1990) 'Sarjakuvien kääntämisen vaikeus ja helppous' [The Difficulty and the Easiness of Translating Comics], in Maijaliisa Jääskeläinen (ed.) *Kuva – sana – musiikki. Käännös kuvan ja musiikin kontekstissa.* Jyväskylä: Jyväskylän yliopisto, 38-41.

49. **Keywords: American comics; Translation of humour; English/Chinese; Comic strips**
    Hopkins, Drew (2000) 'The Dilberting of Taiwan', *Connect* Fall 2000: 151-160.
    This paper discusses Chinese renderings of the American corporate humour series named for its protagonist, Dilbert. The first of this translated series, Daibote faze, *from the English* The Dilbert Principle, *entered the Taiwan market in 1998 to become an immediate and enduring best-seller. It has since been followed by the publication of a dozen more translated volumes from the US series, nine of which are exclusively collections of comic strips, while the three remaining, like* Daibote faze, *combine textual commentary and reader contributions with the comic. The publication of* Diabote faze *installed a new idiom in popular discourse in Taiwan. Some illustration of this is given, together with a short discussion of equivalence and disjuncture.*

50. **Keywords: Animated cartoons; Japanese comics**
    Howell, Peter (2005) *Textual procedures and strategies in the translation of Manga and Anime dialogue*, Doctoral dissertation, University of Edinburgh.

51. **Keywords: Character voice; Animated cartoons; Anime subtitles; Compensatory procedures; Japanese/English**
    Howell, Peter (2006) 'Character Voice in Anime Subtitles', *Perspectives: Studies in Translatology* 14(4): 292-305.
    One of the main functions of dialogue in film narrative is the construction of character voice, which is partly realized through the skillful use of the sociolinguistic and pragmatic resources of language. In the English subtitling of Japanese animation, there are however two barriers to recreating this function. The first barrier is the major pragmatic and sociolinguistic difference between Japanese and English, and the second consists of the technical constraints of subtitling as a mode of translation. The article describes from a textual point of view how subtitlers have addressed the stylistic problem of character voice, focusing on the work of Neil Nadelman in the film Grave of the Fireflies *("Hotaru no Haka") and in single episodes from two TV series,* Revolutionary Girl Utena *("Shōjo Kakumei Utena") and* Slayers Try *("Sureiyāzu Torai"), and on the work of David Fleming in the film* Akira *("Akira"). For all*

four works, another commercially available subtitled version, either in English or French, is considered for purposes of comparison. Comparison suggests that strategies vary with regard to character voice, but that the decimation of stylistic function is not inevitable in subtitling as a mode of translation.

52. **Keywords: Franco-Belgian comics; Translation of humour; French/German; Astérix**
Jackson, Margret (1980) 'When is a Text Comic?' 'Astérix chez les Belges' and its German Translation', *Information Communication* 11: 55-70.

53. **Keywords: Franco-Belgian comics; Translation of humour; French/English; French/ Italian; French/Dutch; Astérix**
Jacqmain, Monique and Herman Cole (1970) 'Astérix à la conquête de l'Europe' [Asterix conquers Europe], *Babel* 16(1): 4-12.
A study of English, Italian and Dutch translations of Astérix. *The authors differentiate between a range of linguistic features commonly associated with comics (names, plays on words, etc.). While the article acknowledges the importance of cultural context and its impact on components of comics such as song lyrics, rhymes, historical figures, etc., it does not attempt to provide a systematic approach to conceptualizing linguistic or cultural problems.*

54. **Keywords: American comics; Intersemiotic translation; Animated cartoons; Comic strips**
Jones, Matthew T. (2006) 'Fined on Film: Edwin S. Porter's Adaptation of Dreams of a Rarebit Fiend', *International Journal of Comic Art* 8(1): 388-411.
This article is an investigation of a case of intersemiotic translation, namely film adaptation of comic art forms. It begins with a historical overview of the very first film adaptations of comic art which were made between 1898 and 1922, during the era of the silent film. There follows a discussion and synthesis of various theories that have been applied to adaptations of literary texts so that these may be commandeered for the study of comic adaptation. Subsequently a content analysis is reported, comparing the themes and devices in Edwin S. Porter's The Dream of a Rarebit Fiend *(1906) to the themes and devices in* Dreams of the Rarebit Fiend *(fist published in the New York Evening Telegram in 1905), the Winsor McCay comic strip on which it is based.*

55. **Keywords: Japanese comics; Japanese/German**
Jüngst, Heike Elisabeth (2004) 'Japanese comics in Germany', *Perspectives: Studies in Translatology* 12(2): 83-105.
Translating manga, Japanese comics, into a European language, in this case German, involves even more complex translation decisions than translating comics from one European language into another. These decisions concern words as well as pictures. Manga are written back to front; the text in the speech balloons must be read top to bottom (in a vertical direction) and right to left, in contrast to European or American comics, manga are black and white. Over the years, certain translation standards have developed for translating manga into German. Many of these standards have more to do with the demands of fan groups or with publishers' decisions than they do with translators' decisions. They influence the style of the translations and shape translation standards. Twenty years ago, manga were 'Europeanised' in translation. Today, feigned authenticity corresponds to the expectations of the readers.

56. **Keywords: German comics; Pseudo-translation; Comics styles**
Jüngst, Heike (2006) 'Manga in Germany – From Translation to Simulacrum', *Perspectives: Studies in Translatology* 14(4): 248-259.

This article does not focus on translation per se but on cultural exchange and intercultural influences as precipitated and mediated by translation. Manga is a prime example for this kind of exchange. With the translation of manga into German and the ensuing popularity, German artists started producing manga of their own. Some of these manga were (and some still are) an amalgam of elements of European comics and Japanese manga and tried to find new ways of expression within the format. Others, however, have all the characteristics of a simulacrum: They look like manga translated from Japanese into German. However, as with every simulacrum, there is no original. In the case of these manga, there is no original Japanese version.

57. **Keywords: Franco-Belgian comics; French/Croatian; Ideology; Ethics; Astérix**

Kadric, Mira and Klaus Kaindl (1997) 'Astérix – Vom Gallier zum Tschettnikjäger: Zur Problematik von Massenkommunikation und Übersetzerischer Ethik' [Astérix – From the Gaul to the Tschettnik hunter: on the problem of mass communication and translational ethics], in Mary Snell-Hornby, Zuzana Jettmarová and Klaus Kaindl (eds) *Translation as Intercultural Communication*. Amsterdam: John Benjamins, 135-146.

Noting that in the 1990s nationalistic ideologies in many European areas responded to economical and political problems by blaming foreign elements of whatever nature (ethnicity, religion, etc.) the authors argue that widespread mass literature forms such as comics can be used (or abused) by nationalistic ideologies to reinforce national identities. Only a few specialized studies have dealt with these issues, even though comics – especially in translation – are very popular and always a challenge to the translator because of the semiotic complexity of the medium. The authors review the different competences which must be available to translators of comics, namely translation competence, linguistic competence with reference to this specific textual typology, semiotic competence and ethical competence, on which the authors focus, in comics stereotypical contents and characters allow for affective identification on part of the readers. Since comics are mass media, this may affect not only aesthetic values but also ideological, religious and political ones. Ethical issues, which have not so far been discussed systematically, thus come to the fore. While translators may have to bear the ethical responsibility for the effects of their work, current ethics of translation are so that translators are ultimately responsible only to their conscience. The necessity to discuss ethics in Translation Studies is demonstrated by the Croatian translation of Astérix, which manipulates for political purposes the satirical representation of the French ideological system in the original publications in the 1960s. While Yugoslavia still existed, there was only one version on Astérix for both Serbia and Croatia. After the declaration of independence of Croatia, a new Croatian Astérix was launched with extensive media coverage. On the basis of many examples of the transfiguration of cultural and linguistic elements and the use of allusions, the authors show how it was possible to influence the readers to have negative feelings towards the Serbs. Finally, the authors underline that Skopostheorie, according to which the end justify the means, can hide dangers if it is not guided by ethical principles, even admitting that translators are often not responsible for choices made by the commissioners.

58. **Keywords: Culture; Semiotics; History; Social practices; Translation Studies; German; Word/image; Translation-relevant elements; Astérix**

Kaindl, Klaus (1999) *Übersetzungswissenschaft im interdisziplinären Dialog. Am Beispiel der comicuebersetzung* [Translation Studies in interdisciplinary dialogue. Examples from the translation of comics], Doctoral Dissertation, University of Vienna.

This work describes and explains the evolution of Translation Studies through various disciplinary matrices and its struggle for the status of an independent discipline, and taps the research potential of the neglected field of comics for Translation Studies. Chapter 1 discusses the theoretical and sociological implications of the development of Translation Studies from a branch of linguistics and literary studies to a discipline in its own right. Drawing on concepts from the philosophy of science, the author identifies the fuzzy integration of translation into the system of linguistics as well as the narrow linguistic definition of the term 'translation' as the main factors which motivated the establishment of a new disciplinary matrix. Chapter 2 profiles the present state and future perspectives of this still rather young discipline, and discusses and defines the often used concepts of 'the new paradigm of Translation Studies', 'empiricism' and 'interdisciplinarity'. Based on the premises of a functional, theory-based, empirical and interdisciplinary approach, chapter 3 starts with an analysis of the notion of 'triviality', with which comics have traditionally been branded. After a translation-relevant definition of comics as a narrative genre, the chapter reviews the existing literature on comics translation in various fields, such as linguistics, literary studies and semiotics, and points out the main deficiencies in the existing approaches. Chapter 4 outlines a sociological framework for the study of comics in translation based on the concepts of field, habitus and capital as developed by Pierre Bourdieu. The sociological dimension of the translation of comics is then exemplified by an overview of the history of comics translation in German-speaking countries. The chapter concludes with an empirical analysis of the comics translation market at the turn of the millennium. In chapters 5 and 6, the author develops analytical instruments for the analysis of the pictorial, typographical and verbal elements of comics. The culture specific dimension of pictures, the communicative functions of visual elements, the interrelation between verbal and nonverbal signs, the various linguistic components and various problems typical of comics translation (e.g. wordplay, quotations, dialects) are discussed and illustrated with many examples. Chapter 7 represents a case study and serves as a test for the validity of the analytical instruments developed in this work. It deals with the first - politically motivated - German translation of Astérix *and its visual and linguistic manipulations which are analysed as results of sociological and publishing constellations in Germany in the 1960ties.*

59. **Keywords: Semiotics; Linguistics; Word/image; Taxonomy; Translation-relevant elements; Translation strategies**

    Kaindl, Klaus (1999) 'Thump, Whizz, Poom: A Framework for the Study of Comics under Translation', *Target* 11(2): 263-288.

    Notwithstanding the importance of comics as a segment of high-volume translation, the few works that have been published on their translation tend to be limited to comic series which are regarded as linguistically demanding and thus worthy of closer investigation. To date, there has been no systematic attempt at providing a comprehensive account of comics translation. Against this background, this paper sketches a research approach which can serve as the foundation for a systematic account of dealing with comics in translation. Comics are first analyzed as a social phenomenon with the help of Bourdieu's theory of the cultural field. The translation-relevant elements of comics are then identified on the linguistic, typographic and pictorial levels, and concepts of rhetoric are used to establish a classification of translation strategies which applies to both verbal and nonverbal textual material. A number of examples are discussed to highlight the diversity of translation strategies for the various elements of comics.

60. **Keywords: Japanese comics; Japanese/German; Reading direction**

    Kaindl, Klaus (1999) 'Warum sind alle Japaner Linkshänder? Zum Transfer von Bildern in der Übersetzung von Comics' [Why are all Japanese Left-handed? About the Transfer of Images in Translations of Comics], *TEXTconTEXT* 13(3): 1-24.

Translation Studies must depart from its language-only bias and must also take into consideration non-verbal communicative elements. A functional analysis of non-verbal means is necessary in order to determine which aspects of a story are changed by changing images in translations. The study tries to present such a functional analysis, investigating the function of individual pictorial elements as well as the relations between the alterations of certain parts of images. It also considers editorial, technical and political conditions which influence the translation of images.

61. **Keywords: Culture; Semiotics; History; Social practices; Translation Studies; German; Word/image; Taxonomy; Translation-relevant elements; Translation strategies**

Kaindl, Klaus (2004) *Übersetzungswissenschaft im interdisziplinären Dialog* [Translation Studies in interdisciplinary dialogue], Tübingen: Stauffenburg.

Translation *Studies is an interdisciplinary subject. On this basis, the sociological, cultural and semiotic complexity of comics is analyzed. The present book, based on a PhD dissertation (Kaindl 1999), gives a historical overview of comics translation in the German-speaking countries and provides a methodology for analyzing the linguistic, visual and typographic elements of comics. Numerous examples illustrate how diverse the – often manipulative – translation process of comics is in practice.*

62. **Keywords: Translation of humour; Verbal and nonverbal signs;**

Kaindl, Klaus (2004) 'Multimodality in the translation of humour in comics', in Eija Ventola, Cassily Charles and Martin Kaltenbacher (eds) *Perspectives on Multimodality*, Amsterdam and Philadephia: John Benjamins, 173–192.

In the few works on the translation of comics the issues related to the humorous dimension tend to be limited to verbal humour, i.e. playing with names and puns. The examples are almost always taken from 'linguistically demanding' comics such as Astérix *or* Tintin*. This contribution sketches an approach which encompasses not only the verbal but also the non verbal dimension of humour in comics. After a short discussion of the various multimodal forms of humour in comics and possible translation strategies the article focuses on the semiotic complexity of plays on verbal and nonverbal signs, in order to provide a comprehensive account of humour the article also explores visual comic techniques e.g. pictorial intertextuality and visual allusions and discusses briefly the comic potentials of typography and onomatopoeia.*

63. **Keywords: Finnish**

Kankaanpää, Ulla-Maija (1990) 'Sarjakuvien kustannustoiminta Suomessa' [The Publishing of Comics in Finland], in Maijaliisa Jääskeläinen (ed.) *Kuva – sana – musiikki. Käännös kuvan ja musiikin kontekstissa*, Jyväskylä: Jyväskylän yliopisto, 25-33.

64. **Keywords: American comics; Translation of humour; English/Finnish; General Theory of Verbal Humour (GRVH); Text/image**

Kaponen, Maarit (2004) *Wordplay in Donald Duck comics and their Finnish translations*, Master's Dissertation, University of Helsinki (online) http://ethesis.helsinki.fi/julkaisut/hum/engla/pg/koponen/

This study aims to explore one aspect of translating comics, namely translating wordplay, espcially the kind of wordplay that arises from the interaction of words and images. This study assumes that translated wordplays will almost necessarily differ to some extent, and compares how wordplays are created and used in source and target texts. Examples of wordplay come from Donald Duck *comics translated into Finnish during different periods, from the early 1950s up to the late 1990s, covering a time span of nearly 50 years. The General*

Theory of Verbal Humour (GTVH) developed by Salvatore Attardo (1994) is used in compar-ing humour in source and target texts. This study also explores whether evidence can be found to support the hypothesis that the older translations would contain less wordplay than the newer ones.

65. **Keywords: Constrained translation; Onomatopoeia**

Kelly, Dorothy and Roberto Mayoral Asensio (1984) 'Notas sobre la traducción de cómics' [Some notes on the translation of comics], *Babel: Revista de los estudiantes de la EUTI de Granada* 1: 92-101.

The paper discusses the process of comics translation. The translator must conform to two specific constraints of this genre. Firstly, s/he must provide for the same reading time and level of difficulty in the decodification of the message. Secondly, s/he must deal with space limitations when writing the translated text. This second aspect is especially important when translating into languages in which texts come out longer. The most frequent problems in translating this type of texts are onomatopoeia and cultural references.

66. **Keywords: Bible translation; Intersemiotic translation**

Koops, Robert (2004) 'When Moses Meets Dilbert: Similarity and Difference in Print, Audio and Comic-strip Versions of the Bible', in Stefano Arduini and Robert Hodgson (eds) *Similarity and Difference in Translation*, Rimini: Guaraldi, 169-199.

This essay looks at some aspects of audio and comic strip Scriptures in terms of similarity and dissimilarity with their print counterparts. In doing so, it suggests that a scale of 'ac-curacy' or 'fidelity' in illustrated and non-print Scriptures could be established in terms of the acceptability of 're-write rules' analogous to those which are already followed by print translators. Cross-media definitions of 'faithfulness' would need to recognize (near-) equiva-lences between texts on a number of parameters: degree of adherence to print text, amount of conversion of indirect to direct speech, resolution (related to selectivity), and amount of information from immediate context included. The paper proposes that comic strips and audio Scriptures force us beyond the printed text to the world of the original writer and to base many of our translational choices on the mental images in the minds of the writers as well as on elements of the context itself.

67. **Keywords: American comics; Franco-Belgian comics; English/Polish; French/Polish; Word/image**

Kucała, Danuta (2005) 'Tekst a obraz w percepcji tłumaczenia komiksów' [Text and Image in the Perception of Translation of Comics], in Urszula Kropiwiec, Maria Filipow-icz-Rudek and Jadwiga Konieczna-Twardzikowa (eds) *Między oryginałem a przekładem XI – Między tekstem a obrazem: Przekład a telewizja, reklama, teatr, komiks, internet* [Between the Original and Translation XI – Between the Text and the Image: Translation and Television, Advertising, Theatre, Film, Comics, and the Internet], Kraków: Księgarnia Akademicka, 105-111.

The author discusses aspects of the translation of comics. Following an historical introduction on the trends in the development of comics in America and Europe and for both children's and adult markets, she traces some research currents on the subject. She criticises the failure to examine the very important relationship in comics between words and images, a problem which afflicts adult readers to a greater extent than it does children. What are the implica-tions of the simultaneous contextual empowerment and impoverishment of the written word by the imagery in a comic for the decisions a translator must make in rendering it into another language? Often the marginalisation of the text leads to a further marginalisation of the translator, who often remains anonymous. There follow brief analyses of the role of the translator in rendering works such as Cliff Sterrett's Polly and her Pals, *Moebius'* Le garage hermetique de Jerry Cornelius, *Neil Gaiman and Dave McKean's* Violent Cases, *Gaiman's* Sandman, *and others, with particular attention devoted to the complex nature of word/image synergy.*

68. **Keywords: Japanese comics; Japanese/Malaysian**

Lee, Wood-hung and Yomei Shaw (2006) 'A textual comparison of Japanese and Chinese editions of Manga: Translation as cultural hybridization', *International Journal of Comic Art* 8(2): 34-55.

The Japanese ACG (animation-comic-game) industry and culture have exerted a tremendous impact on the creative industry and youth consumer culture in Asia. This paper investigates the domestication of Japanese manga by Hong-Kong publishers through textual comparison of the original Japanese edition with the Chinese edition(s), challenging the the theory of cultural imperialism and showing the active role played by Hong-Kong publishers and readers in altering and adapting Japanese manga to suit their own language and culture. The Hong-Kong Chinese version of Japanese manga is often a highly hybridized cultural product, influenced not only by Hong-Kong publishers' editing, but also by Taiwanese translations.

69. **Keywords: Animated cartoons; Japanese comics; Japanese/English**

Levi, Antonia (2006) 'The Americanization of Anime and Manga: Negotiating Popular Culture', in S.T. Brown (ed.) *Cinema Anime*, New York: Palvrave MacMillan, 43-63.

70. **Keywords: Japanese comics; Malaysian comics; Japanese/Malaysian**

Mahamood, Muliyadi (2003) 'Japanese Style in Malaysian Comics and Cartoons', *International Journal of Comic Art* 5(2): 194-204.

This article deals with the theme of the influence of the Japanese visual language on Malaysian comics and cartoons from an art historical perspective. Its main objectives are to provide an overview of the influence of the Japanese style, as well as to form a basis for future research on the topic by focussing on the history and style of Malaysian comics and cartoons. The author discusses the factors that have brought about the Japanese influence on works by Malaysian contemporary cartoonists and comic artists. Apart from indicating the shift from the Western to the Japanese style as a new source of reference and inspiration, this phenomenon illustrates a continuous effort by Malaysian cartoonists and comic artists in searching for a new style and identity, as well as a new avenue for marketing their products.

71. **Keywords: Word/image; French**

Margarito, Maria Grazia (2005) 'En accompagnement d'images... d'autres images parfois (notes sur des apartés de la BD)' [Next to images ... other images, sometimes (notes on some asides in comics)], *Ela* 138, avril-juin: 243-255.

72. **Keywords: Spoken language**

Martín Martín, Pedro A. (1998) 'Análisis contrastivo de la traducción del discurso hablado en el cómic' [A contrastive analysis of spoken discourse in comics], in Jaime Ramírez and Ana Sofía (eds), *Actas de las I Jornadas de jovenes traductores (1997. Las Palmas)*, Las Palmas de Gran Canaria: Universidad de Las Palmas, 115-124.

73. **Keywords: American comics; English/Spanish; Translation of Onomatopoeia**

Martínez Fuentes, Eva (1999) *Onomatopoeia Translation in Comics* (online) http://www.fut.es/~apym/students/eva/eva.html, Research Paper.

Little has been written on the translation of comics, specifically on the translation of onomatopoeia. English and German comics and their translations into Spanish, as well as some pseudotranslations form the core of this paper. The hypothesis is that the degree of translation or non-translation of onomatopoeia in comics correlates with whether their print is integrated into a coloured drawing or a black–and–white one. The degree to which these onomatopoeic words are translated when they appear in a black-and-white comic will be analyzed, as will a second hypothesis: once the colour factor disappears, the translation of onomatopoeia correlates with the prestige of the source language.

74. **Keywords: Translation of humour; Animated cartoons; Film dubbing; English/ Spanish**

Martínez-Sierra, Juan José (2005) 'Translating Audiovisual Humour. A Case Study', *Perspectives: Studies in Translatology* 13(4): 289-290.

This article presents a descriptive and discursive analysis of how elements in humorous extracts from an animated American television show (The Simpsons) fared in overcoming linguistic and intercultural barriers in dubbing (English-Spanish). The analysis is based on several Translation Studies and Pragmatics methods and on a taxonomy of humorous elements in audiovisual texts. These were used to (1) quantify and (2) analyse the humorous elements in the source and target texts, (3) calculate the percentage of humour in the source texts that had been realised in the target versions, (4) make observations on humour translation in animated serials; and, finally, (5) create a list of translational tendencies – potential norms – in humour translation in audiovisual texts.

75. **Keywords: Japanese/Catalan; Animated cartoons; Translation of humour**

Mas López, Jordi (2004) 'From Tokyo to Barcelona. Translating Japanese Anime into Catalan', *The Globalization Insider*, 3.5 (online) http://www.lisa.org/ globalizationinsider/2004/09/from_tokyo_to_b.html

What is common between Japanese and Catalan – how can Japanese humor be expressed within the context of Catalan culture? This is the equation that the Catalan translators have to figure out in order for Japanese anime and manga to be enjoyed by Catalan viewers. The Japan portrayed in the anime dubbed into Catalan may not be a faithful rendition of the real Japan, but rather like a postcard sent from an exotic location.

76. **Keywords: Japonese comics; Animated cartoons; Language teaching**

Mas López, Jordi (2006) '*La Màgica Doremi* com a eina per a reflexionar a l'aula sobre la traducció del gènere del japonès' [*Oja-maho Doremi* as a classroom tool for reflecting on gender issues in translation from Japanese], *Quaderns: revista de traducció* 13: 55-66.

The Japanese cartoon series Oja-maho Doremi *contains a great amount of oral material which can be used in the classroom when considering the difficulties which arise in translation as a result of the differences between the masculine – feminine language of Japanese speakers. The article describes these differences, considers how they should be dealt with in translation and also suggests teaching activities that can be used in the classroom when translating from Japanese.*

77. **Keywords: Onomatopoeia; English/Spanish; American comics; English/Spanish**

Mayoral Asensio, Roberto (1984) 'Los cómics: de la reproducción gráfica de sonidos a los verbos dibujados en inglés. Más sobre problemas de traducción' [Comics: from the graphic reproduction of sounds to verbs which are drawn in English. More on problems of translation], *Babel: Revista de los estudiantes de la EUTI de Granada* 2: 120-130.

This paper discusses the translation of onomatopoeia and graphic reproductions of sounds in comics. To this purpose, some stories and panels from the series Freak Brothers *were selected, among others. Some techniques of translating unarticulated forms are recognized, such as omission, compensation, calques, equivalence and lexical borrowing, even though this last one is not much recommended.*

78. **Keywords: English/Spanish; Constrained translation; Word/image; Communication theory**

Mayoral Asensio, Roberto, Dorothy Kelly and Natividad Gallardo (1986) 'Concepto de 'traducción subordinada'(cómic, cine, canción, publicidad). Perspectivas no lingüísticas de la traducción'[The notion of'constrained translation'(comic, film, song, advertising). Non-linguistic perspectives on translation], in F. Fernández (ed.) *Pasado, presente y futuro de la lingüística aplicada: Actas del tercer congreso nacional de lingüística aplicada.Valencia, 16-20 abril 1985*, Valencia: a.e.s.l.a. (Asociación española de Lingüística Aplicada) y Universidad de Valencia, 95-105.

The procedures involved in the translation of texts have been widely studied from a linguistic point of view. However, when translation is required not only of written texts alone, but of texts in association with other communication media (image, music, oral sources, etc.), the translator's task is complicated and at the same time constrained by the latter. The authors introduce the concept of constrained translation from the point of view of communication theory (as defined by the terminology of Nida 'dynamic translation'); they also deal with the existence of more than one communication channel, the factors of source culture, target culture, 'noise', and the role of the translator in this complex process.

79. **Keywords: English/Spanish; Constrained translation; Word/image; Communication theory**

Mayoral Asensio, Roberto, Dorothy Kelly and Natividad Gallardo (1988) 'The Concept of Constrained Translation. Non-Linguistic Perspectives of Translation', *Meta* 33(3): 356-367.
An English version of the 1986 paper in Spanish.

80. **Keywords: Translation of onomatopoeia; Translation procedures**

Mayoral Asensio, Roberto (1992) 'Formas inarticuladas y formas onomatopéicas en ingles y español. Problemas de traducción'[Unarticulated and onomatopoeic forms in English and Spanish. Problems of translation], *Sendebar* 3: 107-139.

The objective of this work is to make a comparison of onomatopoeic forms and unarticulated sounds in English and Spanish in order to solve translation problems. The corpus used consists mainly of oral sources. The author discusses various translation procedures of these forms. Part of this article appeared in Mayoral 1984 and in Mayoral and Kelly 1984.

81. **Keywords: American comics; Italian comics; Translation teaching**

Mazzoleni, Marco (2000) 'Per una didattica della traduzione come mediazione linguistica e culturale'[A pedagogical approach to translation as linguistic and cultural mediation], *Annali dell'Università per Stranieri di Perugia, Nuova serie* 8(27): 219-245.

Drawing on Tudor's 'framework for the translational analysis of texts' (1987), Mazzoleni sketches out a three-phase model of the translation process, consisting in the analysis of the source text, the assessment of translation strategies called for, and the application of relevant strategies. The first stage, the analysis of the global meaning and of the communicative force of the source text, is articulated in four levels: a) general textual profile, b) stylistic profile, c) socio-professional profile of the source text writer, and d) profile of the background knowledge. Mazzoleni focuses on this latter level, and discusses cultural allusions, intertextual references and specialized knowledge through examples taken from humorous comic strips (Schultz's Peanuts, Silver's Lupo Alberto, Kelly's Pogo).

82. **Keywords: American comics; Italian comics; Translation teaching**

Mazzoleni, Marco (2001) 'Per una teoria non solo linguistica della traduzione. Il caso dei fumetti di Walt Disney e Lupo Alberto' [Beyond a purely linguistic approach to translation. The case of Walt Disney and Lupo Alberto comics], in M. Lamberti and F. Bizzoni (eds) *La Italia del siglo XX, Actas de las IV Jornadas Internacionales de Estudios Italianos*

(México, D.F., 23-27 agosto 1999), México, D.F.: Facultad de Filosofía y Letras – Universidad Nacional Autónoma de México, 403-427.
A shorter version of Mazzoleni (2000), with slightly different examples.

83.   **Keywords: French**
Merger, M-F. (1994) Une incursion dans le monde traduit des bandes dessinées ou… Faire des bulles dans une autre langue' [Notes on the translated world of comics, or … balloons in another language], *Studi Italiani di linguistica teorica e applicata* 3: 196-211.

84.   **Keywords: Franco-Belgian comics; French/Italian; Astérix**
Merger, M-F. (1998) 'Dialogues culturels dans la traduction italienne de la série 'Astérix leGaulois'' [Cultural dialogues in the Italian translation of the series 'Astérix le Gaulois'], in F. Cabasino (ed.) *Du dialogue au polylogue*, Roma: CISU, 112-122.

85.   **Keywords: American comics; English/Italian; Word/image; Translation of humour**
Monti, Alessandro (1992) 'Il senso nascosto: tradurre la lingua dei fumetti' [Hidden meaning: Translating the language of comics], *Quaderni di Libri e Riviste D'Italia* 28: 153-167.
The author comments on a number of American comics and cartoons, and explains how humour is produced as a result of the interaction of language and pictures. Some possible translations, which preserve the sense of a pun present in the original texts, are offered in the second part of this short article, extracts from graphic novels by Will Eisner and stories featuring Disney characters are used to exemplify the importance of understanding variations of register in dialogues when translating comics.

86.   **Keywords: Franco-Belgian comics; French/English; French/Italian; Stereotypes; Tintin**
Munat, Judith (2004) 'A case study in cross-cultural translation: *Tintin* in English and Italian', *Contrastive and Applied Linguistics* XII: 101-120.
This article discusses the translation of two volumes in Hergé's Tintin *series (from the original French into English and into Italian) from a cross-cultural perspective. The two volumes,* Tintin en Amérique *(set in the USA) and* L'Ile Noire *(set largely in Great Britain) represent intrinsically cross-cultural contexts in that the author (of Belgian origin) inevitably reflects his own (possibly stereotypical) perspective of two different English-speaking cultures, and the translators will presumably have been influenced by their own cultural backgrounds (British and Italian respectively). A comparison of original texts and translated versions provides the basis for a series of reflections: firstly, those regarding the representation of British and American culture in the source texts, in contrast with the British translators' attempts to adapt cultural biases in the target texts, biases that might be offensive to English-speaking audiences. Secondly, the different strategies adopted by the British and Italian translators, including observations regarding less specifically cultural approaches to translation, such as linguistic choices which can not be attributed to cultural stances. Lastly, the author attempts to identify those textual and linguistic features which are culture specific, as distinct from those which might be seen as (cross-cultural) universals.*

87.   **Keywords: Japanese comics; Japanese pop culture; Japanese/Chinese; Southeast Asia; East Asia**
Ng, Wai-ming (2000) 'A comparative study of Japanese comics in Southwest Asia and East Asia', *International Journal of Comic Art*, 2(1): 44-56.
Japan is not only a global economic power but also a growing cultural power. Following the penetration of Japanese products in the Asian market, Japan has become a major force in shaping popular, youth, material, and consumer culture in Asia. This can be seen from the increasing popularity of Japanese video games, comics, animation, cuisine, fashion,

merchandise, TV dramas, pop music, karaoke, photo-stickers, and movies in Southeast Asia in the 1990s. The popularity of these forms of Japanese popular culture varies. Some (such as video games, comics, animation, karaoke, and merchandise) are very popular among a large portion of the population in the region, while others (such as pop music, TV dramas and movies) are only a subculture among some groups of young people. Japanese comics (manga in Japanese) have become extremely popular in many Asian nations in the 1990s. They are translated into different Asian languages. Taiwan and Hong Kong are the major exporters and consumers of Chinese editions of Japanese comics. Malaysia, China, and Singapore also produce some Chinese editions of Japanese comics, but they are mainly for local sales and distribution. This study uses Singapore and Malaysia, the two centres of Japanese comic culture in Southeast Asia, as the main examples to demonstrate the popularization and characteristics of Japanese comics in Southeast Asia from a comparative perspective. The two centres of Japanese comic culture in East Asia, Hong Kong and Taiwan, are used for comparison. This article consists of two parts: part one outlines the development of Japanese comics in Singapore and Southeast Asia in the 1980s and 1990s, and the second part pinpoints some characteristics of Japanese comics in Singapore and Southeast Asia, focusing on the issues in popularization, localization, and their implications.

88.   **Keywords: Japanese comics; Animated cartoons; Japanese pop culture; Asia**
      Ng, Wai-ming (2002) 'The impact of Japanese comics and animation in Asia', *Journal of Japanese Trade and Industry* 21(4): 30-33.
      Japan has replaced the United States as the world's largest exporter of comics and animation. In Asia, Japanese comics and animation have been very popular and influential from the 1980s to the present, and nowadays almost all Asian nations have their own editions of Japanese comics and their televisions show Japanese animated series on a daily basis. Different forms of Japanese comic and animation culture, such as comic café (manga kissha), comic rental, dojinshi (amateurish manga) and cosplay (costume play), have penetrated the consumer culture in major Asian cities. Most Asian comic and animation artists are under very strong Japanese influence in terms of drawing, format, atmosphere, perspective, story and plot, and the production system. The author argues that, while Asia is learning from Japan, Japan should also know more about comic traditions in Asia and work with Asian artists as partners in making comics and animation.

89.   **Keywords: Japanese comics; Japanese/Chinese; Honk-Kong comics;**
      Ng, Wai-ming (2003) 'Japanese elements in Hong Kong comics: History, Art and Industry', *International Journal of Comic Art* 5(2): 184-193.
      Japanese comics (manga) are extremely popular and influential in Asia. Asian editions of manga *have dominated the market and many Asian comics artists draw in the Japanese fashion. Hong Kong is one of the places in Asia that has developed its own comics tradition, in particular, its kung-fu (Chinese martial arts) comics are very popular among Chinese readers in Asia. Although Hong Kong comics are quite different from their Japanese counterparts, they have long used* manga *as main references in terms of story and plot, character design as well as drawing, and in the making of their own Hong Kong-style comics, Hong Kong artists have incorporated Japanese elements in their works. Japanese comics also have an impact on the production and consumption of Hong Kong comics. This article investigates the impact of* manga *on the art and history of Hong Kong comics from historical and cultural perspectives.*

90.   **Keywords: Franco-Belgian comics; Astérix**
      Nye, Russell B. (1982) 'Asterix Revisited', *The Comics Journal* 72: 59-65.

91. **Keywords: Children's literature; Animated cartoons; Film dubbing**
     O'Connell, Eithne (2003) 'What Dubbers of Children's Television Programmes Can Learn from Translators of Children's Books?', *Meta* 48(1-2): 222-232 (http://www.erudit.org/revue/meta/2003/v48/n1/006969ar.html).
     Technical difficulties associated with dubbing, together with the collaborative nature of the dubbing process, explain why traditionally the linguistic challenges of dubbing translation for specific audiences such as children have not been studied very closely. As new developments in sound recording improve the technical quality of dubbing, it is time for the remaining textual translation issues to be addressed in more detail. Due to the many common characteristics of different text types aimed at children, dubbers of children's audiovisual material can learn a considerable amount from the translators of other texts, such as books and comics aimed at children, about the particular challenges posed by this target audience.

92. **Keywords: Animated cartoons; Fansubs; Japanese comics**
     O'Hagan, Minako (2003) 'Middle Earth Poses Challenges to Japanese Subtitling', *LISA Newsletter (Global Insider)* 1.5 (online) http://www.lisa.org/globalinsider/2003/03/middle_earth_po.html.

93. **Keywords: Scanlation; Japanese comics**
     O'Hagan, Minako (forthcoming) 'Fan Translation Networks: An Accidental Translator Training Environment?', in John Kearns (ed.) *Translator and Interpreter Training: Issues, Methods and Debates,* London: Continuum.
     Fan-based translation, which has gained particular attention with regard to animation, comics and videogames of Japanese origin, is a phenomenon that appears to be going from strength to strength despite its dubious legal status and the lack of formal translator training on the part of those involved. If seen as a training ground for translators, fan translation practices bound by a common translational goal fit into the context of a kind of social constructivist framework where the level of learner autonomy is highly driven by love of the subject or genre. This article introduces the phenomenon of fan translation in light of translator training and argues that it forms a potentially highly effective learning / training environment, using Kiraly's work (2000, 2005) as a framework for a social constructivist approach in translator training. Implicit in this argument is the far reaching impact of technological environments on the translation profession in general.

94. **Keywords: Japanese comics; Japanese/English**
     Ono, Kosei (2003) 'How Tsuge Yoshiharu's *Neji-Shiki* was Published in English', in *Manga Studies* 4, 149-169.

95. **Keywords: Semiotics; Word/image; Picture books**
     Oittinen, Riitta (2001) 'Verbaalisen ja Visuaalisen Dialogia' [Dialogue of the Verbal and the Visual], in Pirjo Kukkonen and Ritva Hartama-Heinonen (eds) *Mission, Vision, Strategies, and Values: A Celebration of Translator Training and Translation Studies in Kouvola*, Helsinki: Helsinki University Press, 161-170.
     This article discusses the verbal and the visual in translation, especially in the translation of iconotexts such as picture books. Hermeneutics (especially Mikhail Bakhtin's views of dialogics) is used as the theoretical frame; in addition, inspiration is drawn from semiotics (especially views by Charles S. Peirce). Picture theories, especially research on reading comics, are also used. The main thesis is that a translator's text consists of both the verbal and the visual and that translators need the ability to read both 'languages'. The examples are taken mainly from the author's own translations.

96. **Keywords: Subtitling; Fansubbing; Japanese animation; Visual language; Japenese/English**

Ortabasi, Melek (2006) 'Indexing the Past: Visual Language and Translatability in Kon Satoshi's *Milennium Actress*', *Perspectives: Studies in Translatology* 14(4): 278-291.

This paper re-examines current audio-visual translation practices from a film studies perspective through director Kon Satoshi's full-length animated feature Sennen joyû *(Millennium Actress, 2001), a film that employs, and expects, a fairly deep and broad knowledge of Japanese history and culture. In this film, where the protagonist recounts her life in movies in a realistic historical setting, cinematic imagery becomes the primary medium of communication. Narrative action and dialogue, considered the main components of cinema by many viewers, take a back seat. The real "story" is the history of one of Japan's proudest cultural products: live action cinema, particularly that of the "golden age" of the 1950s and 60s. The aim of this paper is not simply to "translate" for the uninitiated viewer the many components of* Millennium Actress *that cannot be efficiently communicated through standard subtitles. Instead, this film is an ideal vehicle for demonstrating the shortcomings of current audio-visual translation, which is primarily text-based. As recent studies show, technology-savvy "fansubbers" are using methods that challenge not only how we think about subtitling, but the process of audio-visual translation itself, a practice usually defined by its tendency to truncate and delete. By examining the English subtitled version of* Millennium Actress *in the context of emerging translation strategies and technologies, this paper proposes a concept of audio-visual translation that rejects this discourse, and more fully incorporates non-verbal methods of exchange and communication.*

97. **Keywords: Animated cartoons; Japanese animation**
Otsuka, E. and N. Ohsawa (2005) '「ジャパニメーション」はなぜ敗れるか' [*Why Japanimation will Lose Out*], Tokyo: Kadokawa One Theme21.

98. **Kewyords: Japanese comics; Animated cartoons; Japanese/Italian; Hybridization**
Pellitteri, Marco (2006) 'Manga in Italy. History of a Powerful Cultural Hybridization', *International Journal of Comic Art* 8(2): 56-76.

After providing an historical overview of the penetration of Japanese animation (anime) and comics (manga) in Italy, the article deals with Italian "manga-style" comics. The new generations of Italian comic artists which were born after the 1970s grew up being deeply influenced by Japanese graphic and narrative styles. The absorption of the expressive codes of Japanese comics and cartoons has become apparent not only in children's and teenagers' drawings, but also in semi-professional and professional production. Since the mid 1990s a growing Manga fan subculture has influenced both mainstream and experimental comics production. Many Italian popular series now mix Japanese imagery and themes with more traditional Italian and American ones, and hybrid forms characterize low-quality "spaghetti-manga" as well as elite comics, bearing witness to the all-encompassing cultural reception of popular Japanese forms in Italy.

99. **Keywords: Franco-Belgian comics; Word/image; Astérix**
Penndorf, Gudrun (2001) 'Asterix übersetzen ? oder das Wechselspiel in Bild und Sprache' [Translating Astérix? Or alternating between image and language], in Kay Brodersen (ed.) *Asterix und seine Zeit. Die grosse Welt des kleinen Galliers*. München: C.H. Beck.

100. **Keywords: Fansubbing; Japanese animation; Globalisation; Chaos theory; Subtitling**
Pérez González, Luis (2006) 'Fansubbing anime: Insights into the 'Butterfly Effect' of Globalisation on Audiovisual Translation', *Perspectives: Studies in Translatology* 14(4): 260-277.

This article revolves around fansubbing, a subtitling-based mediation phenomenon whose emergence and consolidation in recent years has gone hand in hand with the globalisation

of Japanese animated cinema. The paper begins with an overview of the origins and ration-
ale for the popularity of anime in Japan and beyond. Then it considers the first attempts to
localise anime into other languages and the contribution of fansubbing to the expansion
of anime fandom worldwide. The article then proceeds to delve into the organisation of the
fansubbing process and outline its most distinctive practices. The final section appraises the
potential for propagation of fansubbing practices within a fast-changing cultural land-
scape, drawing on the theoretical models that media sociology has developed to account
for similar developments in the audiovisual marketplace.

101. **Keywords: Japanese comics; Word/image; Hybridization**
     Peterson, Robert S. (2007) 'The Acoustics of Manga: Narrative Erotics and the Visual
     Presence of Sound', *International Journal of Comic Art* 9(1): 578-590.
     Sound in comics is not a stylistic trait or a feature of a particular genre of comics, but is
     endemic to all comics due to the multimodal way words and pictures are formed and
     combined. Comics are read as if aloud, and the speech of the characters and the noise of
     the action is an essential component of the aesthetic experience. Whereas books are read
     at the speed of sight, comics are read at the speed of sound. Japanese manga are perhaps
     the comics that most effectively exploit the dimension of sound. This is partly due to the
     features of Japanese language and script that make it ideally suited to explore the aesthetic
     possibilities of sound in comics, and partly to the cultural history of storytelling in Japan,
     which has long explored the rich possibilities of sound and visual spectacle. Perhaps most
     importantly, however, it is due to manga artists themselves, who through intense competi-
     tion have labored to make full creative use of the intrinsic dynamics of sound in comics. By
     examining the use of sound in Japanese comics, the author identifies some of the range of
     possibilities that sounds can have in comics and discusses why sounds in manga defy easy
     translation.

102. **Keywords: Translation of humour**
     Pina Medina, Víctor M. (1998) 'Sintoonizando con la onda lingüística toon' [Tooned in to
     Toon Language Wave], in Carmen Valero Garcés and Isabel de la Cruz Cabanillas (eds)
     Nuevas tendencias y aplicaciones de la traducción, Alcalá de Henares, Madrid: Servicio
     de Publicaciones de la Universidad, 103-111.
     This study explores the richness and variety of wordplay found in cartoons. Aspects such as
     synonymy, polysemy, and ambiguity, among others, are found not only in dialogues but also
     in characters' names or the titles of the stories, combining phonetic and semantic resources
     to create stylistic effects of different sorts. The study of the possibilities and difficulties of
     translating all this material into other languages further contributes to the knowledge of
     the functioning of wordplay in different linguistic contexts.

103. **Keywords; Argentinean comics; Spanish/Polish; Comic strips**
     Pindel, Tomasz (2005) 'Tłumacz scenarzystą – *Mafalda* po polsku. Kilka uwag o
     przekładzie komiksu' [The Translator as Scriptwriter – *Mafalda* in Polish: Some Remarks
     on the Translation of Comics], in Urszula Kropiwiec, Maria Filipowicz-Rudek and Jadwiga
     Konieczna-Twardzikowa (eds) *Między oryginałem a przekładem XI – Między tekstem a*
     obrazem: Przekład a telewizja, reklama, teatr, komiks, internet [Between the Original and
     Translation XI – Between the Text and the Image: Translation and Television, Advertising,
     Theatre, Film, Comics, and the Internet], Kraków: Księgarnia Akademicka, 114-119.
     The author begins by contrasting the problems posed by comic books with those posed
     by comic strips in translation. Quoting the example of a Spanish comic Goomer. El gordo
     mutante del espacio exterior, *he shows how the specificities of a reference to a traditional*
     Spanish custom in a comic can pose bigger problems to a translator than they would in a

prose text, given the constraints imposed by the image and other aspects of the comic form. He proceeds to examine in detail a Polish translation of Quino's (a.k.a. Joaquín Salvador Lavado's) extremely popular Mafalda comic strips, which owe much to Charles M. Schulz's Peanuts in their style. The selection translated by Carlos Marrodán Casas and published in Poland 1985, is more overtly directed to children than is the ST, though there are also many other kinds of differences between his translations and the originals. The socio-political climate of Poland in the mid-1980s is proposed as having influenced certain translation decisions. More generally, however, the Polish Mafalda has a very different feel to that of the original, and one which relates to translation ethics, with certain radical translation choices having been made.

104. **Keywords: Franco-Belgian comics; French/Italian; Astérix**
Poli, S. (1989) 'Comunicazioni di massa e traduzione: Astérix en Italie' [Mass communication and translation: Astérix en Italie], *Quaderni del Dipartimento di Lingue e Letterature Straniere Moderne 3, Università di Genova*, Bari: Schena, 119-161.

105. **Keywords: American comics; English/Italian; Translation practice**
Previtali, Cristina (2000) *MAUS di Art Spiegelman. Una traduzione in Italiano* [*Maus by Art Spiegelman. An Italian translation*], Unpublished Dissertation, Università di Bologna.
The subject of this thesis is a new translation of MAUS, the story of Vladek Spiegelman, a survivor of the Holocaust and the death camps of Nazi Germany, as told by his son, Art, by means of a graphic novel. A previous Italian translation did not succeed in rendering the nuances and subtleties of Vladek's broken English effectively in Italian, and it is mainly for this reason that this new translation was proposed to the author. The thesis, which acts as a commentary to the translation published by Einaudi in 2000, provides an overview of comics and their development into graphic novels, as well as of the specific problems of comics translation. It then describes the solution adopted for rendering Vladek's ethnolect as effectively as possible, by basing it on the language spoken by Polish immigrants in Italy as well as on the work of Moni Ovadia, a playwriter, author and musician who first introduced an Eastern European ethnolect in Italy. The thesis also includes an interview to Art Spiegelman by the author, reviews of the new Italian translation published in major Italian newspapers, and some iconographic materials.

106. **Keywords: Constrained translation**
Rabadán, Rosa (1991) *Equivalencia y traducción*, León: Universidad del León.
Deals specifically with the translation of comics in one chapter.

107. **Keywords: Franco-Belgian comics; French/Spanish; Temporal information**
Raskin, Lydia (2004) 'La traduction à l'espagnol de la bande dessinée *XXe ciel.com* d'Yslaire: influence sur le temporel' [The translation into Spanish of the comic book XXe ciel.com by Yslaire: effects on temporal information], *Trans: Revista de traductología* 8: 89-104.
This essay analyses the effects of temporal components in translation from French into Spanish, particularly in an avant-garde comic. If the translator modifies temporal information, he or she will alter or undermine the philosophical aspect of the source text. The analysis demonstrates the consequences of the first interpretation and of the variation in translation unit in the Spanish version.

108. **Keywords: Franco-Belgian comics; French/Spanish; Translation of humour; Translation Studies**
Raskin, Lydia (2004) 'Interférences dans la traduction français-espagnol de la bande dessinée humoristique' [Interferences in the French-Spanish translation of comics], in Emilio Ortega Arjonilla (ed.) *Panorama actual de la investigación en traducción e interpretación*, Granada: Atrio (CDROM, Vol. 3), 411-419.

Comics deserve to be analyzed for many reasons. Fist of all, because of their ambiguous status, since they are sometimes defined as 'the Ninth Art' and sometimes as 'paraliterature'. The author argues that it is important to use a scientific approach to the study of this medium which brings together two creative processes especially valued in Western society, visual and verbal. This especially at a time when comics are leaving the dimension of pedagogic and entertainment literature for children and are focussing progressively more on an adult readership. There are many commentaries or summaries, guides, catalogues and encyclopaedias, histories and even works on the creative process of comics, but only a few scientific articles on and only sparse references to comics in serious linguistic works. The semiotic approach used by Román Gubern is notable. While the overview of critical texts on comics has not been completed, the author regrets the lack of a treatise on the translation of comics, even though their international expansion often leads to qualify them as mass culture.

109. **Keywords: Franco-Belgian comics; French/Italian; Tintin**
     Reggiani, Licia (1994) 'Tintin italien' [The Italian Tintin], in Anna Soncini Fratta (ed.) *Tintin, Hergé et la 'Belgité'*, Bologna: CLUEB, 111-123.

110. **Keywords: Franco-Belgian comics; French/English; Literary quotations; Astérix**
     Richet, Bertrand (1993) 'Quelques réflexions sur la traduction des références culturelles – Les citations littéraires dans 'Astérix'' [Some reflections on the translation of cultural items – Literary quotations in 'Astérix'], in Michel Ballard (ed.) *La traduction à l'université: Recherches et propositions didactiques*. Lille: Université de Lille, 199-222.
     The article is based on the English translations of Astérix, and discusses the quality and subtlety of language use in Astérix, stressing its literary and cultural richness. The analysis largely focuses on literary quotations.

111. **Keywords: Japanese comics; Japanese/English; Educational comics**
     Rifas, Leonard (2004) 'Globalizing Comic Books from Below: How Manga Came to America', *International Journal of Comic Art* 6(2):138-171.
     The author is the publisher of the first manga -Japanese comics- published in America (1980 and 1982), the translations of Keiji Nakazawa's stories about the bombing of Hiroshima. In this paper, he describes the failure of his republication not primarily as a result of the supposed limits of Western tastes or of Nakazawa's supposed failing as an artist, but in relation to his situation as a publisher on the fringes of the American comics industry and to the generally cool response of the American peace movement to Nakazawa's work, in explaining how Nakazawa's stories came to be the first manga to be republished in English, the author illuminates a contrast between 'globalized media' and media 'globalized from below'. The republication of Nakazawa's comics was one piece of a paradigmatic project of 'globalizing comic books from below,' and thus may yield lessons and warnings, not only for American comic books and Japanese manga, but about the broader potential of comics as tools for raising social awareness.

112. **Keywords: American comics; Franco-Belgian comics; English/Italian; French/ Italian**
     Rota, Valerio (2001) *Nuvole migranti. Viaggio nel fumetto tradotto* [Balloons on the move. On translated comic], Mottola (TA): Lilliput.
     The author discusses comics translation as the process of adaptation and transformation foreign comics undergo when presented to a target culture. The author stresses that translating comics does not only mean translating a foreign product, but also translating a different way of conceiving comics, of producing them, and above all, of reading them. This short volume starts with an overview of comics as a mass-culture phenomenon (Chapter I),

passing through a description of American comics (Chapter II) and French comics (Chapter III) and ending with the analysis of three comic series: the Italian Dylan Dog *translated into American English, the American* Sandman *series by Neil Gaiman in its Italian translations and the French series* XIII *also translated into Italian (Chapters IV, V, VI).*

113. **Keywords: American comics; Franco-Belgian comics; Japanese comics; English/ Italian; French/Italian**

Rota, Valerio (2003) 'Il fumetto: traduzione e adattamento' [Comics translation and adaptation], *Testo a Fronte* 28: 155-172.

This article presents a general overview of comics in Italian translation, focusing in particular on comic books translated from English and French. The author describes the different production formats and cultural conventions associated with comics in different countries, with examples from American and Japanese comics, which are also by far the most translated comics in Italy. The main stages involved in the production of translated comics, which include but are not restricted to the translation of dialogues in balloons, is then explained. As concerns American superhero comics, titles and character names often allude to the Anglo-American literary canon, and references to Shakespeare or the Bible may go unnoticed either by the translator or the target reader. French comics, which usually require less graphical adaptations than American ones, find it nonetheless more difficult to enter the Italian market, probably because of a different target comics readership. Cultural conventions such as format and graphical presentation can only be adapted to a point, and translated comics are thus examples of 'foregneizing' rather than 'domesticating' translation.

114. **Keywords: Franco-Belgian comics; Word/image; Publication formats; French/ Italian**

Rota, Valerio (2004) 'The Translation's Visibility: David B.'s *L'Ascension du Haut Mal in Italy*', *Belphégor, 4(1)* (online) http://etc.dal.ca/belphegor/vol4_no1/articles/04_01_Rota_ davidb_en_cont.html

Translation is considered in its broader sense, which also includes the process of adaptation. While every kind of translation implies an adaptation and a "rewriting" of the work to be translated, this process is more evident in translated comics because their graphic peculiarity comes before their textual quality. Before being something to be read, a comic book is something to be seen. Each culture produces different kinds of comics: the size and format of publications, for historical and practical reasons, vary from nation to nation, accommodating to the tastes and expectations of the different reading public. In translated comics, the alterity of a foreign work becomes apparent because of the different styles and publication formats which characterize different goegraphic areas. The Italian publisher of David B.'s L'Ascension du Haut Mal *decided to shrink the original format in order to uniform it to the size of the other volumes published in the same Italian series, and to otherwise "domesticate" the French original, thus destroying the particularities of the original edition. Making the translation visible instead of "domesticating" the original to a local format is the best and simplest way to respect the original work.*

115. **Keywords: Japanese comics; Franco-Belgian comics; French/Italian; Publishing industry**

Rota, Valerio (2004) *La marca dello straniero. Fumetti tradotti e alterità [The Sign of the Foreign. Translated Comics and Otherness]*, Mottola (TA): Lilliput.

This slim volume contains three essays: an overview of literary translation and the book publishing industry in Italy; a discussion of the practices involved in the translation of comic books in comparison with literary, technical and audiovisual translation, focusing on comic books format (layout, colour, size, reading direction) and on the translation of

manga (Japanese comics) in Italy; and a short case study on two different Italian transla-
tions of L'Ascension du Haut Mal *by David B. The book contains a discussion of theoretical*
approaches to translation (Meschonnic, Venuti) and observations on professional and
practical aspects of translation, and provides a useful introduction to the translation of
comics in Italy within the context of audiovisual translation and the publishing industry.

116. **Keyword: Franco-Belgian comics; Translation of humour; French/German; Astérix**
     Rothe, Wolfgang (1974) 'Astérix and das Spiel mit der Sprache', *Die Neueren Sprachen* 73:
     241-261.

117. **Keywords: Children's literature; French/Polish**
     Skibińska, Elżbieta (2005) 'Niedoceniona wartość przymusu. O przekładzie pewnego
     komiksu dla dzieci' [The Underestimated Value of Compulsion: On the Translation of a
     Certain Comic for Children], in Urszula Kropiwiec, Maria Filipowicz-Rudek and Jadwiga
     Konieczna-Twardzikowa (eds) *Między oryginałem a przekładem XI – Między tekstem a
     obrazem: Przekład a telewizja, reklama, teatr, komiks, internet [Between the Original and
     Translation XI – Between the Text and the Image: Translation and Television, Advertising,
     Theatre, Film, Comics, and the Internet]*, Kraków: Księgarnia Akademicka, 91-104.
     *This article is an attempt to counter the low opinion in which children's books in general,
     and children's comics in particular, are still held in certain academic circles. Focussing on
     the challenges which such texts pose in terms of their translation, and drawing on Roman
     Lewicki's notion of the foreignness which is a characteristic of translation, the author pro-
     poses that this otherness may well be a distinct attraction in literature for children. This has
     interesting implications for the translator in terms of her / his role as cultural mediator in
     an age of globalization, with comics presenting an important case study in terms of their
     role in introducing children to reading practices at an early age. The challenge posed to the
     translator is great not only in intercultural terms, but also in terms of the spatial constrictions
     imposed by the genre. The author concludes with a detailed analysis of the Polish publica-
     tion* Już czytam, *which appeared in the mid-1990s and was a translation of the popular
     French comic* J'aime lire. *She focuses in particular on the cultural specificities attendant
     in translating cartoons for a younger readership unfamiliar with the culture of the source
     text.*

118. **Keywords: Spanish**
     Santoyo Mediavilla, Julio César (1987) *El delito de traducir: Teoría y crítica de la traduc-
     ción: antología* [The crime of translating: Theory and criticism of translation: Anthology],
     Barcelona: Universitat Autònoma de Barcelona.
     Contains a chapter on the translation of songs and comics.

119. **Keywords: American comics; English/Italian; Translation practice; Translator train-
     ing; Word/image**
     Scatasta, Gino (2002) 'La traduzione dei fumetti [Comics translation]', in Romana Zacchi
     and Massimiliano Morini (eds) *Manuale di traduzione dall'inglese*, Milano: Bruno Mon-
     dadori, 102-112.
     *This short essay, aimed at translation trainees, discusses the practice of comics translation
     starting from the author's own experience. Within a distinction between 'high-brow' and
     'low-brow' comics literature, the author argues that translations directed to the second and
     largest segment of readership are dominated by translation choices dictated by the market,
     which are generally target-user oriented. Translations of high-brow comics literature are
     instead more source-oriented. The author enumerates a number of practical details con-
     cerning the process of comics translation, and through the discussion of the translation into
     Italian of American super-hero comics, done by himself, illustrates recurring problems and
     standard solutions in the translation of this comics genre. Among the topics dealt with are*

the relationship between words and images from a translator's point of view and the role of the translated series editor.

120. **Keywords: Franco-Belgian comics; French/German; Translation of humour; Astérix**

Schmitt, Christian (1997) 'Form und rhetorische Figur als Übersetzungsproblem. Zur Wiedergabe von Wortspielen in Astérix Translaten' [Form and rhetoric figure as a problem of translation. On the equivalents of puns in the translations of Astérix], in Rudi Keller (ed.) *Linguistik und Literaturübersetzen*, Tübingen: Gunter Narr, 141-160.

121. **Keywords: Translation Studies**

Schmitt, Peter A. (1997) 'Comics und Cartoons: (k)ein Gegenstand der Übersetzungswissenschaft?' [Comics and Cartoons: A Topic Unsuited for Translation Studies?], in Horst W. Drescher (ed.) *Transfer. Übersetzen – Dolmetschen – Interkulturalität*, Frankfurt/Main etc.: Peter Lang, 619-662.

122. **Keywords: Translation Studies**

Schmitt, Peter A. (1998) 'Graphische Literatur, Comics' [Graphic literature, Comics], in Mary Snell-Hornby, Hans G. Hönig, Paul Kußmaul and Peter A. Schmitt (eds) *Handbuch Translation*, Tübingen: Stauffenburg, 199-269.

123. **Keywords: Franco-Belgian comics; America comics; Translation of humour; French/ German; Astérix**

Schnetzer, Michaela (2004) 'Problems in the Translation of Comics and Cartoons' (online) http://www-unix.oit.umass.edu/~michaela/Writing/comics%20translation.pdf *According to a survey of 107 publishers in 15 countries, the international market for comics is made up of 'exporters' (like the US, France, Belgium and, more recently, also Japan), which sell their comics to other countries, and 'importers' (like Scandinavia, Germany, Austria), which mainly purchase foreign-language comics. It is therefore no surprise that comics are an important segment of the translation industry and that, in German-speaking countries alone, comics translation amounts to some 40,000 pages per year. It is the goal of this paper to illustrate the various difficulties translators of comics and cartoons are faced with on a cultural, technical, and linguistic level, as well as to highlight some possible strategies and procedures for resolving such difficulties where possible. Emphasis is not placed on any specific language pairs, but examples draw mainly from comics in German, English, and French (both original versions and translations). A number of examples are taken from the French comic book series* Astérix *which has already been the subject of several studies in comics translation, first of all because the thirty-one albums in the series have been translated into 79 languages and 28 dialects (into Latin, among others!)* (Asterix around the World), *and secondly because the comics are extraordinarily rich in plays on words (Schwarz 1989:13), which constitute a very special problem in translation in general, and even more so in the translation of comics.*

124. **Keywords: Franco-Belgian comics; French/German; Astérix; Translation of humour**

Schwarz, Alexander (1989) *Comics übersetzen: besonders ins Deutsche und besonders in der Schweiz* [Translating comics: particularly into German and particularly in Switzerland]. Lausanne: CTL (Centre de traduction littéraire) de Lausanne, Université de Lausanne. (48 pp.)

125. **Keywords: Franco-Belgian comics; French/Spanish; Translation of interjections; Astérix; Tintin**

Sierra Soriano, Ascension (1999) 'L'interjection dans la BD: réflexions sur sa traduction' [Reflections on the Translation of the Interjection in Comic Books], *Meta* 44(4): 582-603.

In this paper the difficulties of translating interjections in comics are analysed. Interjections are classified, and the causes for translation difficulties are discussed. Some solutions are suggested in order to improve their translation.

126. **Keywords: Contrastive analysis**
Spillner, Bernd (1972) 'Kontrastive Analysen auf der Grundlage von Comic Strips' [Contrastive analysis on the basis of comic strips], in Gerhart Nickel (ed.) *Papers from the International Symposium on Applied Contrastive Linguistics (Stuttgart, October 11-13, 1971)*, Bielefeld: Cornelsen-Velkagen, 27-41.

127. **Keywords: Semiotics; Word/image; Translation of humour; Astérix**
Spillner, Bernd (1980) 'Semiotische Aspekte der Übersetzung von Comics-Texten' [Semiotic issues in the translation of Comics], in Wolfram Wilss (ed.), *Semiotik und Übersetzen*, Tübingen: Gunter Narr, 73-85.
The author interprets comics as complex semiotic texts and investigates the extent to which nonverbal elements are involved in the constitution of the sense of the whole text. The article analyses the quality and style in Astérix, limiting the scope of the analysis largely to plays on words and their relation to pictorial depiction. Two types of relation are possible, namely a terminological identity between the literal meaning of an idiom and the situation represented in the picture, or a contrast between the literal meaning of an idiom or metaphor and the images depicted, which reciprocally falsify themselves. Adopting a semiotic approach which correlates pictorial and linguistic information at a mutual analytical level, Spillner emphasized how pictorial manipulations are central to an integral account of the translation of comics.

128. **Keywords: Animated cartoons; English/Italian**
Tortoriello, Adriana (2006) 'Funny and Educational across Cultures: Subtitling *Winnie The Pooh* into Italian', *JoSTrans – The Journal of Specialised Translation* 06 (online) http://www.jostrans.org/issue06/art_tortoriello.php.
Subtitling a children's programme, especially a cartoon or animated programme, presents the subtitler with specific constraints and challenges. These are due, on a lexico-semantic and visual level, to the nature of the source language text, and on a pragmatic level, to that of the prospective audience. Through the analysis of some examples taken from the Italian subtitled version of the series The Book of Pooh, *this article seeks to consider in greater detail both the issues involved and the strategies the translator has put in place in order to deal with such a unique situation.*

129. **Keywords: Franco-Belgian comics; Translation of humour; French/Finnish**
Turkka, Pieta (1999) 'Le fils de monsieur Sansfrapper'? Systemaattinen luokittelu sanaleikkien kääntämisen lähtökohtana' [Le fils de monsieur Sansfrapper'? Systematic Classification as a Starting Point for Translating Word Play], in Rune Ingo, Oili Karihalme, Christer Laurén, Henrik Nikula and Jukka Tiusanen (eds) *VAKKI Symposium XIX (LSP and Translation Theory) 13-14 February 1999*, Vaasa: University of Vaasa, 354-363.
This article focuses on the issue of the translation of word play. The author suggests that the translation of word plays should be based, not only or not exclusively, on the meaning of the words containing the word play but also on the form and the central idea of the word play, e.g. pronunciation or polysemy. The aim of the paper therefore is not to present a general classification but to discuss examples of translation of word play based on a general classification. The article focuses on the translation of French comic books and intends to show that a systematic classification-based approach to word play may serve as a coherent and logical point of departure for translators.

130. **Keywords: French/English; Infinitives**
Turner, Nigel (2000) *Etude contrastive de l'infinitif en français et en anglais* [A con-

trastive analysis of the infinitive in French and in English], Ophrys: Gap, 272pp. *This book compares the English and French infinitives, first separately and then in a contrastive way. The corpus is drawn from literary texts, comics, press news and dialogues, together with their published translations.*

131. **Keywords: Translation of onomatopoeia; Translation quality evaluation**

Valero Garcés, Carmen (1995) 'Un subgénero literario en traducción: los cómics y tebeos' [A literary subgenre in translation: the comics], in Carmen Valero Garcés (ed.) *Apuntes sobre traducción literaria y análisis contrastivo de textos literarios traducidos,* Alcalá de Henares: Universidad de Alcalá de Henares, 93-106.

Comics can be considered a specific genre in which two different types of language are tied up: articulate language (i.e. words, sentences, etc.) and inarticulate language (i.e. representation of sounds and onomatopoeia), a specificity which imposes certain restrictions to the translator. This article proposes a model for the evaluation of the quality of translated comics, consisting in two phases: A first phase dealing with external factors and a second phase dealing with internal factors. External factors include: a) the historical, socio-cultural moment in which the original text is created; b) the type of reader addressed by it; c) the historical, socio-cultural moment in which the text is translated; d) the type of reader addressed by the target text; e) the possible influence of the initiator of the process of translation; f) the translator. Internal factors include: a) the treatment of colloquial language in the target text; b) technical limitations; c) the strategies used in the translation of inarticulate language.

132. **Keywords: American comics; English/Spanish; Translation of onomatopoeia**

Valero Garcés, Carmen (1995) 'Uso y traducción de formas inarticuladas y formas onomatopéyicas en comics y tebeos' [The use and translation of partially articulated forms and onomatopoeias in comics], in Carmen Valero Garcés (ed.) *Apuntes sobre traducción literaria y análisis contrastivo de textos literarios traducidos,* Alcalá de Henares: Universidad de Alcalá de Henares, 107-126.

The study of inarticulate and onomatopoeic forms has not traditionally received much attention, although certainly this field has sparked interest and curiosity among those with a particular sensitivity for problems of language. The main objective of this paper is to analyze how the translator treats and uses Spanish when translating onomatopoeia in comic books. On the basis of a contrastive analysis of Spanish and English onomatopoeia, the author discusses the strategies used by translators, paying particular attention to the influence of English on translated texts.

133. **Keywords: American comics; English/Spanish; Translation of onomatopoeia**

Valero-Garcés, Carmen (1996) 'Humor and Translation: American Comic Books in Spanish. A Case Study: R. Crumb', *Proceedings of the XVIII AEDEAN International Conference,* R. Sola et al. (eds), Alcalá de Henares: Servicio de Publicaciones de la Universidad, 351-359.

In comics, like in films and cartoons, 'image' and 'language' are tied up. 'Language' does not only refer to 'articulate' language (in balloons or outside them) but also to 'unarticulate' language, that is, representations of sounds (onomatopoeia) in the drawings. This paper analyses some of the problems found in translating onomatopoeia from the point of view of translation criticism. It discusses the Spanish translations of the underground comics by R. Crumb, focussing on the treatment of colloquial language and onomatopoeia.

134. **Keywords: Constrained translation; Translation of onomatopoeia; Translation of humour**

Valero Garcés, Carmen (1999) 'La traducción del cómic: retos, estrategias y resultados' [The translation of Comics: Challenges, Strategies and Results], *Babel a.f.i.a.l.* 8: 117-135.

Comics represent a type of literature which is often translated. However, the transfer from one language to another entails certain problems. The translation of comics belongs to a specific type of translation called 'constrained translation'. This type of text has two characteristics which differentiate it from the translation of a text where 'everything' we want to say is made explicit by means of words. Firstly, the message to be translated is not only based on written words. Secondly, the text may be subject to space constraints. These 'added' elements are not only part of the meaning but also impose certain conditions. Other aspects are problematic too and are discussed in this article, e.g. the translation of onomatopoeia or the representation of sounds which change from language to language, and the fact that in comic books the author plays with the language in order to entertain.

135. **Keywords: Constrained translation; Onomatopoeia; Translation of humour**
Valero Garcés, Carmen (2000) 'La traducción del cómic: retos, estrategias y resultados' [The translation of Comics: Challenges, Strategies and Results], *Trans: Revista de traductología* 4: 75-88.
A republication of Valero Garcés 1999.

136. **Keywords: Franco-Belgian comics; French/Spanish; Astérix**
Verrier, J. and X. Burrial (1991) 'Une lecture contrastive d'Astérix en français et en castillan' [A contrastive reading of Astérix in French and in Spanish], in Brigitte Lepinette, María Amparo Olivares Pardo and Amalia Emma Sopeña Balordi (eds), *Actas del primer coloquio internacional de traductología (2 – 4 mayo, 1989)*, Valencia: Universitat de València, 213-214.

137. **Keywords: Franco-Belgian comics; Constrained translation; Astérix**
Villena Alvarez, Ignacio (1999) *Problemática teórico-práctica de la traducción subordinada de cómics. Análisis de un caso práctico: las historietas de* Astérix *en francés y en español* [Theoretical and practical problems in the constrained translation of comics. Astérix in French and Spanish as a case in point], Doctoral Dissertation: Universidad de Málaga.
This work starts from a definition of subordinated translation and of its different instances. Subordinated translation is characterized from a general perspective and from a specific perspective, and is compared with other modalities of specialized translation. Then a corpus of Astérix stories is analyzed from a textual and factorial point of view, focussing on specific aspects which may pose translation problems, such as proper names, cultural references, etc. After the discussion, the author draws theoretical as well as practical (pedagogical) conclusions, and argues that there is a need to establish a special theory of subordinated translation.

138. **Keywords: Franco-Belgian comics; Translation of names; Astérix**
Villena Alvarez, Ignacio (1998) 'La traducción de los nombres propios en el cómic: Uderzo, croqué par ses amis' [The translation of names in comics: Uderzo, croqué par ses amis], in Félix Fernández, Leandro and Emilio Ortega Arjonilla (eds) *II Estudios sobre traducción e interpretación*, Málaga: Universidad de Málaga, 719-728.

139. **Keywords: Globalization; Hybridization; Animated cartoons**
Wang, Georgette and Emilie Yueh-yu Yeh (2005) 'Globalization and hybridization in cultural products. The cases of *Mulan* and *Mulan Crouching Tiger, Hidden Dragon*', *International Journal of Cultural Studies* 8(2): 175-193.
Hybridization has become part of an ongoing trend in cultural production, with both the globalization and localization of the culture industry. Hybridization, however, is not merely the mixing, blending and synthesizing of different elements that ultimately forms a culturally faceless whole. In the course of hybridization, cultures often generate new forms and make new connections with one another. This study looks at two globally popular films

that were adapted from Chinese works, Crouching Tiger, Hidden Dragon *and* Mulan, *as examples to illustrate the complexity involved in hybridization and the implications that it has for the debate on the globalization of culture. It was found that 'deculturalization', 'acculturalization' and 'reculturalization' can be used to characterize the hybridization of cultural products and that often the producer, with his/her background, aspirations and work style, has a key role to play in deciding how these features are organized and manifested.*

140. **Keywords: Franco-Belgian comics; French/German; Equivalence**

Würstle, Régine (1991) 'Äquivalenzprobleme bei der Übersetzung multimedialer Texte. Zur Übersetzung der Comics *Les Frustrés* von Claire Bretécher' [Problems of equivalence in the translation of multimedia texts. On the translation of the comics *Les Frustrés* by Claire Bretécher], in Christian Schmitt (ed.) *Neue Methoden der Sprachmittlung*, (Pro Lingua; 10), Wilhemsfeld: Verlag, S., 149-170.

Focusing on Les frustés *by Claire Brétecher, the author attempts to work out guidelines for measuring equivalence, based on the hierarchical demands of invariance. The author discusses linguistic-textual, pragmatic and cultural-semiotic criteria, and offers a bottom-up analysis involving considerations on the internal structure of the text in terms of semantic and syntax. She then moves on to consider pragmatic dimensions, which include the context of the situation of the transmitter, the receiver, the time and place of the original setting of the text, as well as its relationship to other texts within the source culture. The author argues that the purpose of translation is to portray the points of view and values of another culture. Therefore, cultural-specific elements should remain in their original form in the target language text.*

141. **Keywords: Gesture, symbol and image; Franco-Belgian comics; French/Spanish**

Yuste Frías, José (1998) 'El Pulgar Levantado: un buen ejemplo de la influencia del contexto cultural en la interpretación y traducción de un gesto simbólico' [The Upward Thumb: a good example of the influence of context in the interpretation and translation of a symbolic gesture], in F. Félix Fernández and E. Ortega Arjonilla (eds) *II Estudios sobre Traducción e Interpretación*, Málaga: Universidad de Málaga y Diputación Provincial de Málaga, vol. I, 411-418 (online) http://webs.uvigo.es/jyuste/ JoseYusteFrias1998c.pdf

In this paper the author analyses the reading and interpretation of a symbolic gesture (the upward thumb) that appears in the comic Astérix in Hispania *without any kind of verbal inscription, thus showing that symbols are not universal but should also be translated, mostly when they appear in images without text, as is so often the case with comics. The author clarifies that the gestural symbolism that accompanies the French interjection "Pouce!" Has nothing to do with the gestural symbolism of the all-American OK. The symbolic image studied in this paper is interpreted in this second sense by readers all around the world because, as José Yuste Frías points out, it is still a common place to think that images are not translated when translating comics.*

142. **Keywords: Sign, symbol and image; Franco-Belgian comics; French/Spanish; Translation of names; Astérix**

Yuste Frías, José (1998) 'Contenus de la traduction: signe et symbole' [Translation Contents: Sign and Symbol], in P. Orero [ed.] *III Congrés Internacional sobre Traducció*, Bellaterra (Barcelona): Servei de Publicacions de la Universitat Autònoma de Barcelona, 279-289 (online) http://webs.uvigo.es/jyuste/JoseYusteFrias1998a.pdf.

The author begins his paper drawing new theoretical, didactic and professional horizons in Translation Studies by singling out sign from symbol as Ferdinand de Saussure did. From that starting point the meaning of words in the language is explored in order to show that it is different from their sense in translation. This is illustrated with the translation of the proper names of the fortified camps appearing in one of the most translated series, Les aventures d'Astérix. *It is an invitation to every comics translation professional to always read, interpret and translate the symbolic structures of the imagery represented in the image together with the verbal dimension of the text.*

143. **Keywords: Word/image; Intersemiotic translation; Franco-Belgian comics; French/ Spanish**

Yuste Frías, José (2001) 'La traducción especializada de textos con imagen: el cómic' [Translating Texts with Images: the Case of the Comic Strip], in Departamento de Traducción e Interpretación (ed.) *'El traductor profesional ante el próximo milenio' II Jornadas sobre la formación y profesión del traductor e intérprete,* Villaviciosa de Odón (Madrid): Universidad Europea CEES, chap. IV. 4 [CD-ROM] (online) http://webs.uvigo.es/jyuste/ JoseYusteFrias%202001a/Portada.htm.

This paper constitutes a theoretical and practical study of the steps (analysis, reading and transfer of symbolic structures) involved in the translation of a text which is subordinate to an image, such as comic strips; its full colour iconic examples are available on-line. Accordingly, the translator faces the challenge of apprehending all the meaningful implications emerging from the simultaneous use of language and images in this text-type. This paper advocates the need to deal with the image as a key constitutive element of the 'text' being translated. It is often the case that the full understanding of what goes on in a given comic depends on the close reading of the drawing rather than the caption. This being so, the caption is said to be subordinate to and coordinated with the drawn picture, thus becoming a purely ornamental and aesthetic element, in comic strips, it is the drawn pictures themselves that speak to the reader; their lay-out, size, graphics, colours, signs, symbols and drawn gestures are all sense-making devices.

144. **Keywords: American comics; Word/image; Translation of humour; Constrained translation**

Zanettin, Federico (1998) 'Fumetti e traduzione multimediale' [Comics and multimedia translation], *inTRAlinea* 1 (online) http://www.intralinea.it/volumes/eng_open. php?id=P156.

Comics translation is seen as a type of medium-constrained translation, in which the translation of the written text is constrained by the visual text. This article considers exclusively the implications for translation of the interaction between the verbal and the visual code. The interpretation of idiomatic expressions and puns is often dependant of the interweaving of the two codes. Verbal expressions such as onomatopoeia, for instance, are often based on the communicative force of the graphic signs as well as on their being part of the visual text. After a short comparison of film and comics translation a number of examples are presented, in which translation choices with regards to the verbal narration are strongly constrained by the surrounding visual context. The author discusses elements of the 'grammar of comics' such as visual puns, visual metaphors and onomatopoetic expressions, and the implications they have on translation strategies.

145. **Keywords: Translation Studies; Semiotics; Word/image**

Zanettin, Federico (2004) 'Comics in Translation Studies. An Overview and Suggestions for Research', in *VII Seminário de Tradução Científica e Técnica em Língua Portuguesa Tradução e interculturalismo,* Lisboa: União Latina, 93-98.

Comics are a pervasive form of communication which happens to a large extent in translation, yet it has been a neglected area in Translation Studies research. This paper starts from a terminological discussion of comics and their semiotic status with regards to translation. It is argued that comics can be characterized as semiotic environments and that comics translation should be ultimately treated in terms of intercultural translation. An overview of the literature on comics translation and an exemplification of several approaches which may be fruitfully adopted in the analysis of this art form are provided.

146. **Keywords: Translation Studies; Word/image; Censorship**
Zanettin, Federico (2007) 'I fumetti in traduzione: approcci e propettive di ricerca' [Comics in translation. Research approaches and perspectives], in Vittoria Intonti, Graziella Todisco and Maristella Gatto (eds) *La traduzione. Lo stato dell'arte / Translation. The State of the Art*, Ravenna: Longo, 137-150.

It seems that most publications on comics within Translation Studies are written in languages other than English or, if in English, by scholars working in non-English speaking countries. This is perhaps due the fact that, on the one hand, comics are not generally held in high consideration in Anglophone cultures and, on the other, that English speaking countries have hardly a tradition of publishing comics in translation. This article first offers a general introduction to comics as an art form, and then provides an overview of different approaches to comics translation. The examples discussed focus on the interplay of visual and verbal elements and on the role of censorship in translated comics.

147. **Keywords: American cartoons; English/Arabic; Animated cartoons**
Zitawi, Jehan (2003) 'Cartoons and Censorship: Importing Children's Programmes to the Arab World', *The Linguist* 42(5): 140-142.

Children's programmes, animated films and cartoons constitute a major part of the audiovisual work available for children in the Arab world. The present study focuses on children's animated series dubbed from English into Arabic and shown on Arabic TV channels. The paper examines and compares the guidelines followed by Jordan national TV and a dual language children's channel based in the UAE; these guidelines serve to censor and filter dubbed children's animated series that include scenes which touch upon politics, religion or family ties. The study also presents various examples as evidence of the implementation of guidelines in various episodes taken from 15 dubbed animations which have been recently aired on Jordan national TV and the UAE based children's channel and are aimed at children between the ages of 4-12 years old.

148. **Keywords: American cartoons; English/Arabic; Film dubbing**
Zitawi, Jehan (2003) 'English-Arabic Dubbed Children's Cartoons: Strategies of Translating Idioms', *Across Languages and Cultures* 4(2): 237-251.

The present study focuses on children's cartoons dubbed from English into Arabic and shown on E-junior channels in Abu Dhabi and Dubai television. The paper examines the strategies adopted by Arab translators to render one of the most problematic areas in translation, that is idiomatic expressions, throughout the process of translating and dubbing children's cartoons. The analysis of the rendering of each idiomatic expression indicates that the following strategies are shown to be used in translating idioms for dubbing purposes: dynamic translation, naturalisation/localisation, addition, deletion and word-for-word translation.

149. **Keywords: American comics; English/Arabic; Politeness theory**
Zitawi, Jehan (2004) *The Translation of Disney Comics in the Arab World: A Pragmatic Perspective*, Doctoral Dissertation, University of Manchester.

This study attempts to examine the applicability of Brown and Levinson's politeness theory to a particularly challenging genre, namely Disney comics, and to extend the model beyond monolingual and monocultural contexts, to look at politeness strategies in translation between two very different cultures. The study thus sets out to test politeness theory to ascertain whether it can offer credible and coherent explanations of the potential for comics in translation to threaten the face(s) of Arab readers, and whether it can provide a robust framework for describing the pragmatic strategies employed by translators seeking to maintain the face(s) of Arab readers. The study argues that Brown and Levinson's politeness theory can be fruitfully applied to Disney comics translated from English into Arabic, provided it can be demonstrated that it is possible to identify a composite speaker and composite hearer in Disney comics, and Disney comics can be read as face threatening texts. The data used in this study consists of 278 Disney comics stories: 140 English stories and 138 Arabic stories translated and published by Dar Al-Hilal in Egypt, Al-Futtaim/ITP in Dubai, and Al-Qabas in Kuwait. The study also reveals a number of weaknesses inherent in Brown and Levinson's model and highlights the need to refine politeness theory in order to make it more applicable to the analysis of complex genres such as comics and complex types of face threat encoded in discourses which are normative in nature but which present themselves as benign.

Notes on Contributors

Raffaella Baccolini is Professor of English at the University of Bologna at Forlì. She is the author of *Tradition, Identity, Desire: Revisionist Strategies in H.D.'s Late Poetry*, and has published articles in English and Italian on women's writing, dystopia, sf, poetry and modernism. She has co-edited several volumes, including *Dark Horizons: Science Fiction and the Dystopian Imagination* and *Utopia Method Vision: The Use Value of Social Dreaming* (both with Tom Moylan) and *Le prospettive di genere: Discipine, soglie, confini*. She is currently working on history and memory in fiction and film.

Nadine Celotti is Professor of French Linguistics at the Advanced School of Modern Languages for Interpreters and Translators of the University of Trieste, Italy. She published several studies on translation issues regarding: comics, punctuation, translator training and specialized translation. Her research interests also cover French lexicology, French and Italian-French lexicography, discourse analysis.

Adele D'Arcagelo graduated in Modern Languages and Literatures at the University of Milan with a dissertation on Samuel Beckett as a poet and a self-translator. She holds an MA in Translation Studies from the University of Warwick, under the supervision of Susan Bassnett. She is a Lecturer at the University of Bologna, where she teaches translation from English into Italian at the School for Interpreters and Translators in Forlì. She has spoken at conferences and runs translation workshops and seminars in Italian universities. Her main research interests are literary and multimedia translation (film/theatre/comics). She has translated into Italian works by Samuel Beckett, Alan Bennett, Steven Berkoff and Liz Lochhead, among others.

Catherine Delesse is a Lecturer in English Linguistics at the Department of Languages, Université d'Artois (France). She wrote her PhD (1994) on 'Image, texte et métaopération' at the Université Paris III-Sorbonne Nouvelle, under the direction of Professor Henri Adamczewski. Her research interests cover linguistics, translation with a special focus on comics (*Tintin* and *Astérix* series), the relationship between image and text in comics, and contrastive linguistics. Her publications include 'Etude contrastive des marqueurs indéfinis anglais -body/-one et des particules indéterminées du russe -to/nibud' (2001); 'Ancrage du message linguistique et passage du/au sens dans la bande dessinée' (2006); and 'Les structures du type "X is said to/reported to V...: Discours rapporté ou modalité épistémique?' in *Discours rapporté(s) approche(s) linguistique et/ou traductologique* (2006), which she edited.

Elena Di Giovanni is Lecturer in translation at the Department of Linguistic and Literary Research of the University of Macerata. She taught for several years at the Advanced School of Modern Languages for Interpreters and Translators of the University of Bologna at Forlì. She holds a PhD in English Language and Translation on the representation of cultural otherness in Disney films. Her research areas include media translation (both dubbing and subtitling), translation for children and the role of language and translation in intercultural communication. She is currently engaged in research on the translation of animation for children as well as intercultural communication through the media. Her forthcoming publications include: Translation, Cultures and the Media, special issue of EJES (European Journal of English Studies), and 'The Idea of India: transrepresentations of the Indian culture in the Italian media' (Cambridge Scholars Press). She also works as a professional translator for the media and publishing industry.

Heike Jüngst holds a Dr. habil. degree on educational comics from the University of Leipzig, where she works as a junior researcher. She has taught ESP and translation at the universities of Germersheim, Mainz, Cambridge and Leipzig. Her current areas of research are translation of multimedial texts, subtitling, audiodescription and translation processes. She has published several articles on knowledge representation in comics, words and pictures in translation, and ESP teaching.

Valerio Rota holds a PhD in French Studies. His reserch interests include translation studies, comics and minor literary genres. He has written two essays on cultural trans-formations in translated comics, *Nuvole migranti - Viaggio nel fumetto tradotto* (Lilliput Editrice, 2001) and *La marca dello straniero* (Lilliput Editrice, 2004).

Carmen Valero Garcés holds a PhD in English Studies. She is a lecturer in English Linguistics and Translation, and Director of the Research and Training Programme on Public Service Interpreting and Translation (University of Alcalá, Madrid). Her research focuses mainly on translation studies, intercultural pragmatics and communication, and public service interpreting and translation. She is the editor, among other things, of *Interculturality, Translation, Humor, and Migration* (2003), *Traducción e Interpretación en los Servicios Públicos. Contextualización, Actualidad y Futuro* (2003); *Discursos (Dis)concordantes: Modos y Formas de Comunicación y Convivencia* (2003), *Formas de mediación intercultural e interpretación en los servicios públicos. Conceptos, datos, situaciones y práctica* (2005) as well as the author of several books and articles dealing with interpreting and translating in public services, cross-cultural communication, interpreting and translating, SLA and contrastive linguistics.

Federico Zanettin holds a PhD in Translation Studies (University of Bologna, 2001). He is Associate Professor of English Language and Translation at the University of Perugia. His research interests include corpus-based translation studies, comics translation and intercultural communication. He is co-editor of *Translation Studies Abstracts and the Bibliography of Translation Studies* and of the online Translation Studies journal *inTRAlinea*.

Jehan Zitawi is an Assistant Professor of Translation in the Department of English at Abu Dhabi University, United Arab Emirates. She is also the University Director of Accreditation and Acting Rector of University College. She received her BA in English Language and Literature in 1992, and her MA in Translation Studies in 1996 from Yarmouk University, Jordan. She received her doctorate in Translation Studies from the University of Manchester in 2004. She joined the Department of English at Abu Dhabi University in 2004. Her research areas of interest include translation of children's literature and comics, politeness theory, screen translation and legal translation. She has published in leading translation studies journals such as *Babel*, *META* and *Across Languages and Cultures*.

INDEX